D0781228

Applied Anthropology

WITHDRAWN

Applied Anthropology

Tools and Perspectives
for Contemporary Practice

Alexander M. Ervin

University of Saskatchewan

Allyn and Bacon

Boston ∎ London ∎ Toronto ∎ Sydney ∎ Tokyo ∎ Singapore

148881

Series Editor: Sarah L. Kelbaugh
Editor-in-Chief, Social Sciences: Karen Hanson
Series Editorial Assistant: Jennifer DiDomenico
Executive Marketing Manager: Lisa Kimball
Marketing Manager: Brooke Stoner
Production Editor: Christopher H. Rawlings
Editorial-Production Service: Omegatype Typography, Inc.
Composition and Prepress Buyer: Linda Cox
Manufacturing Buyer: Julie McNeill
Cover Administrator: Jennifer Hart
Electronic Composition: Omegatype Typography, Inc.

Copyright © 2000 by Allyn & Bacon
A Pearson Education Company
160 Gould Street
Needham Heights, MA 02494

Internet: www.abacon.com

All rights reserved. No part of the material protected by this copyright notice may be reproduced or utilized in any form or by any means, electronic or mechanical, including photocopying, recording, or by any information storage and retrieval system, without written permission from the copyright owner.

Between the time Website information is gathered and published, some sites may have closed. Also, the transcription of URLs can result in typographical errors. The publisher would appreciate notification where these occur so that they may be corrected in subsequent editions.

Many of the designations used by manufacturers and sellers to distinguish their products are claimed as trademarks. Where those designations appear in this book, and Allyn and Bacon was aware of a trademark claim, the designations have been printed in initial or all caps.

Library of Congress Cataloging-in-Publication Data

Ervin, Alexander M. (Alexander MacKay)
    Applied anthropology : tools and perspectives for contemporary
practice / Alexander M. Ervin.
      p. cm.
    Includes bibliographical references and index.
    ISBN 0-321-05690-6 (alk. paper)
    1. Applied anthropology. I. Title.
GN397.5.E78 2000   99-23012
301—dc21   CIP

Printed in the United States of America

10 9 8 7 6 5 4 3 2 1   04 03 02 00 99

Contents

Preface

Anthropology cannot be treated in a "cookbook," step-by-step fashion. It challenges people to exercise enormous flexibility, analytical capacity, and subtlety of thought, abilities that are especially important when sorting out the nuances of unfamiliar cultures. My challenge is to present the essentials for *actually doing* applied anthropology.

So, as I discuss the history and subject matter of applied anthropology, I emphasize methodologies in applied research. I could have stressed theory but much of the effective theory in anthropology is tied to specific areas, such as economics, poverty, ecology, health care, and conflict resolution. Then too, practitioners tell me that the greatest asset gained from university study has been their knowledge of methods. I want to give the reader a set of generalizable tools that can be used in various settings and domains. Students need to consider methods early in their training. This can be best accomplished through "hands-on" practicum assignments accompanying courses in applied anthropology.

Another asset for applied anthropologists is the ability to analyze, inform, and, one would hope, influence policy. Understanding formal decision-making and planning as sociocultural phenomena is heavily emphasized in the book. Policy analysis, by itself and in the contexts of need and impact assessments, program evaluation, and advocacy, is detailed.

I frequently make use of case studies. The case study approach is often the best way to teach anthropology. Because applied anthropology currently covers so many domains, varied case studies can familiarize students with the many options for practice. At the same time, each case illustrates such principles as bottom-up perspectives in program evaluation or the corroboration of qualitative and quantitative methods.

Although I generally treat the various content areas of practice indirectly through case studies and other examples, there is one exception. Anthropological practice in environmental issues is given a separate chapter. The challenge of the global environmental crisis has generated rapid advances in environmental anthropology. Current work by political ecologists should stimulate the interest of students and illustrate how exceptionally relevant anthropology can be.

Another decision needs explanation. Although the book covers most of the significant principles required for applied research, I mainly illustrate them with studies done in the United States and Canada. Why? First, I have a variety of applied experiences both in Canada and the United States, and I am much more familiar with the North American literature and policy contexts than international applications. Second, one of my major goals is to provide tangible and usable perspectives for the thousands of anthropology students who do not enter a Ph.D.-level program and will probably be working in domestic settings after graduation. Third, I wish to reverse the unfortunate image of anthropology as an exotic and arcane subject normally done in remote places. I hope to show its mainstream relevance. Anthropology is just as much an applied policy science as are sociology, political science, public health, business administration, educational foundations, and other subjects. When I was a student, the basic text in applied anthropology was Ward Goodenough's (1963) *Cooperation in Change,* which used international examples almost exclusively, yet his book was quite influential for domestic applied anthropology. Although I dare not consider this present book in the same league as Goodenough's classic, surely an alternate approach is possible—domestic examples can inform international applications. Of course, in spite of this North American emphasis, I do use some international examples.

Related to the North American perspective is a tendency to draw from my own experiences—social impact assessment in the Arctic, farming and rural communities on the prairies, refugee resettlement, needs assessments, urban social planning, participatory research, and advocacy—in some case studies and other illustrations. I do this not only because I think that the experience is informative but also because it is easier to write with confidence and accuracy about one's own work. I have also provided a very wide and representative range of both classic and recent works in applied anthropology.

I have had some important help and influences in writing this book. Ten years ago, while at the University of South Florida catching up on the advances of the applied anthropology, I benefited greatly from the hospitality and advice of the faculty. I am especially indebted to Al Wolfe, Jerry Smith, Michael Angrosino, and Gil Kushner. In fact, Gil Kushner provided the flash of "satori" for me that ultimately led to this book. In 1978, braving the chills of an Alberta February, he addressed the Canadian Anthropology Society's annual Congress, telling us of the remarkable innovations in training anthropology students for nonacademic practice in the United States.

Two mentors deserve mention. The late Jim Millar, my longtime departmental head, was a latecomer to academia. Having spent most of his life as a mining engineer, he was frequently uncomfortable and frustrated with academic passivity. He actively encouraged the development of a practical curriculum in our department, and, although he was an archaeologist, he saw the future of anthropology in its social, nonacademic applications. I am very grateful for his encouragement and friendship. One could not expect a better mentor and academic advisor than the late Demitri Shimkin at the University of Illinois. Demitri was above all an applied anthropologist and taught his students by example. When something needed to be done—from resolving a crisis in Holmes County to creating more socially relevant courses—he did it. This book benefits from my apprenticeship with Shimkin during the development of his pioneering course—American Communities and Their Problems. It is no accident that so many of Demitri's students are contributing to contemporary applied anthropology.

I also owe a collective debt to the founders, current members, executives, and staff of the Society for Applied Anthropology. This remarkably effective and welcoming organization has led the way in nurturing most of the anthropology that I discuss here, and much of the book's tone comes by way of osmosis from an ongoing relationship with the SfAA.

I would like to thank the five reviewers of my book proposal as well as those seven who reviewed the actual book, for their helpful commentary: Jean S. Forward, University of Massachusetts at Amherst; Winifred Mitchell, Minnesota State University—Mankato; J. Anthony Paredes, Florida State University; James M. Schaefer, Union College; Walter M. Vannette, Northern Arizona University; Alvin W. Wolfe, University of South Florida; and John Young, Oregon State University. I am indebted to the generosity of Nazeem Muhajarine, a colleague in the Department of Community Health and Epidemiology, who allowed me to follow his excellent outline for the design of questionnaires in Chapter 13. Five friends have been especially generous with their time and advice. Let me make the standard but absolutely necessary disclaimer that they cannot be faulted for any deficiencies in the final product. Gil Kushner, the "godfather" of applied training programs, provided me with many wise observations and cautions on the entire text. I have very much benefited from the highly-honed editorial and critical skills of Pat Higgins, my predecessor as editor of *Practicing Anthropology*. Rob Winthrop, an excellent example of a modern practitioner who combines "real world" savvy with scholarly erudition, commented on the earlier chapters. While criticizing my lapses of clarity, Niels Braroe, one of the best writers in anthropology, helped smooth the "bumps and ruts" of my writing in two drafts. Similarly, my very patient wife, Mary Ann Ervin, an excellent copyreader, provided another brain and set of eyeballs when mine had given out. She, too, corrected some errors as well as put up with an author's inevitable cranky moods. To her, Jennifer, Samantha, J. D., and Maggie, I dedicate this book.

CHAPTER

1

Orientations to an Anthropology of Policy and Practice

This book outlines the field of applied and practicing anthropology that directly serves the practical needs of communities and organizations in society. It reinforces the notion that anthropologists need not confine themselves to esoteric, antiquarian, and arcane topics, or minority groups in their practice. They can become engaged with the main issues—social well-being, health, environmental and economic crises—that affect us all. Anthropology contains a mother lode of resources to be reformulated and directed at practical issues.

Its strengths are a vast and deep knowledge base, holism, insights from qualitative methodologies, and, most of all, grounded connections to communities' realities, aspirations, and needs. Anthropology also inspires empathy, which is an essential quality in the search for solutions to human problems. Overall, the anthropological perspective provides a tool for exploring a human topic in considerable depth, from many angles, in comparison to other situations, and, most especially, from the point of view of the participants.

To achieve all of this, it is important to pay attention to policy analysis. It is crucial for anthropologists aspiring to improve institutions, communities, and peoples' lives to understand all the formal and informal ways that decisions are made. They need to know how they are made, on the basis of what kinds of information and values, through what kinds of culturally based filters, and through what kinds of power relationships of influence or authority. Meaningful analyses or recommendations for implementation arise from a good understanding of the complex total policy context. It is a mistake for the more academically inclined to study an issue—such as poverty and the family or violence—by itself, without placing the insights in the larger context of policy-making and its standard institutions. A sports analogy may be appropriate. Keeping one's eye on the ball is fundamental. For applied anthropology, maintaining one's attention on the context of policy is fundamental.

Before getting into the specifics of an applied anthropology of policy and practice, it is useful to explore how the field relates to the whole subject of anthropology.

Types of Anthropology

First of all, we are concerned with *sociocultural anthropology*—that discipline dealing with contemporary peoples and societies in comparative and holistic perspective. We are not discussing archaeology, linguistics, or physical anthropology, although those subdisciplines do have significant applied branches. There is an active forensics branch in physical anthropology, and linguistics has contributed much to language learning, speech therapy, and English-as-a-second-language training. Archaeologists have been very active in fields such as public archaeology and cultural resource management.

Sociocultural Anthropology

Academic Anthropology			**Applied Anthropology**	
o————————o—————————|o|————————o———————o				
Theoretical and Ethnographic Research	Studies of Social Issues	Policy Analysis	Academic Applied Research	Practicing Anthropology

But most of applied anthropology comes out of its sociocultural branch. Within sociocultural anthropology, we can see a continuum from basic or theoretical anthropology through social problems research, to policy analysis university-based applied anthropology, and finally to the practice of anthropology outside of academic settings. Boundaries along the points on the continuum are quite permeable. In my view, the work being done from policy analysis onward, including that done by applied and practicing anthropologists, is contained within a relatively distinct subdiscipline of applied anthropology. I will return to this controversial issue later.

Referring to the continuum and beginning with *basic and theoretical* anthropology, humanity's self-knowledge has been enriched by thousands of pieces of *ethnographic research* in an incredible variety of social settings primarily within the twentieth century. These have included studies of very different peoples such as hunters and gatherers, long-distance truckers, middle-class suburbanites, pastoral nomads, peasants, North American farmers, Washington bureaucrats, utopian communities, castes, urban welfare recipients, drug users, juvenile and motorcycle gangs, troupes of dramatic artists, fishermen, long-shoremen, horticulturalists, and countless other social groups. Those studies have been codified, analyzed, and cross-culturally compared to produce a rich set of generalizations about human beliefs, values, and institutions. Ethnography, cross-cultural comparisons, and generalizations have then provided the foundation for broad schools of thought about humanity and culture—theories and approaches such as structuralism, cultural materialism, postmodernism, interpretive anthropology, psychological anthropology, network theory, exchange theory, and so forth. Sometimes the theoretical foundations have generated the production of ethnography, although this dialectic of the inductive and deductive has probably been more skewed to the empirical or inductive in anthropology's case.

The collective works of thousands of ethnographers are, as a whole, a very impressive product. As Harris (1968), Voget (1975), and others have suggested, theories and styles of anthropology ultimately emerge from a societal context. These are framed by social needs but are often fashions or preoccupations of their times—unilineal evolutionism grew out of a nineteenth-century context of imperialism, cultural materialism out of a mid-twentieth-century technological American worldview, Structural Functionalism out of colonialist Britain, postmodernism and deconstructionism out of the alienation and protest of certain academic sectors, and so forth.

Although social and cultural theory is to some extent socially constructed, it still has its own particular logic and agenda as driven by university-based academics. Status, career advancements, and so forth are generated within the rather closed set of values and practices determined in the almost guild-like contexts of universities. The supposedly free exchange of ideas is valued yet monitored by peer review of books, journal articles, and academic grant proposals. The choice of particular topics—be they body decorations, oral literature, origin myths, anthropologies of the senses or emotions, comparisons of cognatic kinship systems, and so forth—is not generally determined or commissioned by problem-solving institutions or the appeals of the oppressed. Topics are selected by individuals in universities, approved by academic peers, supported by granting agencies and journals, and reinforced by professional academic societies such as the American Anthropological Association. Many good arguments can be brought forward in defence of such a system. Academia can establish rigorous professional standards. More important, goes the argument, those ideas most valuable for society will eventually be selected because of their intrinsic merit or "truthfulness," unsullied by vested interests or pressures from society. Clearly, though, generating knowledge directly useful to society is not the principal mandate of academic anthropology.

Nonetheless, academic anthropologists have chosen to explore *social issues* that are of much greater significance to members of society, the media, and, sometimes, policy makers. Such works often take the form of social criticism. They may also provide a sympathetic portrayal of some group or category that has been stigmatized by society. Some may even go so far as to accuse sectors of society of creating or exacerbating problems for others. Jules Henry's works, such as *Culture Against Man* (1965), were indictments of those institutions, practices, and values of American society that promote alienation and suffering of many individuals and families. Other researchers explored poverty in American urban life. For instance, Elliot Liebow's *Tally's Corner* (1967) showed how the alternative culture created by young, black males was a response to an essentially racist society that had no permanent place for them. Carol Stack's *All Our Kin* (1974) demonstrated how, in spite of the fact that American social assistance programs conspired against the stability of African American families, these families still showed remarkable resourcefulness and supportiveness through domestic networks of bilateral kin. Similarly, James Spradley's *You Owe Yourself a Drunk* (1970) accounted for the subcultures of tramps in the skid rows or tenderloins of American cities. In coping with the repression of law-enforcement agencies, they were caught in a revolving door of life sentences on "installment plans." A more recent and outstanding example of this approach is Phillipe Bourgois' *In Search of Respect: Selling Crack in El Barrio* (1996)—a political-economic and humanistic ethnography that provides a compelling understanding of American inner-city violence and drug dealing.

Such works show the promise of a knowledge base that can serve both applied and academic anthropologies. They show that anthropology has much to say about the issues of the day. Yet such works are not strictly applied, because the subjects are selected by the authors and supported through academic institutions. They rarely, if ever, lead to direct changes through policy-making institutions, but the findings and analysis are much more applicable than the more traditional forms of basic academic anthropology.

Next on our continuum is an activity that could be classified as *policy analysis*. This work is frequently done by people within academic institutions, but there is a direct analysis of values, and social structures in decision-making institutions meant to solve human and social problems. An important example of this kind of work is Gerald Britan's (1981) ethnography of an agency of the U.S. Department of Commerce and how decision-making is conducted in a policy context. Jack Weatherford, in *Tribes on the Hill* (1985), gives us a candid view of the values and processes of decision-making among members of that American policy-making institution, the U.S. Congress. These works are valuable for training applied or practicing anthropologists, but they are not examples of applied anthropology. These sorts of studies are attempts to do what Laura Nader (1972) called "studying up," to understand the values of the decision-making elites in society. Policy analysis most certainly has to be a part of applied or practicing anthropology. Unfortunately, as an adjunct of academic anthropology and as a crucial bridging link between application and theory, it is still too rare.

What then is *applied anthropology* for the purposes of this book? It is not passive research or mere social commentary. It is almost always commissioned by an organization outside of academia. The purpose may be to provide social and cultural background on the circumstances of particular peoples, but normally clients expect concrete recommendations for specific purposes; they want advice on the administration of particular policies and programs that usually involve some sort of human service or impact. For applied anthropologists, policy analysis and the understanding of the processes of decision-making with institutions are absolutely essential. Governments, nongovernment, nonprofit, and private profit-oriented groups as well as advocacy groups initiate the research, usually pay for it, and largely determine what the issue or problem is. The topic is not selected by the anthropologist, and this is the crucial distinction as compared to other types of research within anthropology. Furthermore, the work is meant to go beyond freelance commentary and contribute directly to decision-making. Usually, applied anthropology, as distinguished from practicing anthropology, is done by anthropologists working out of a university context on a part-time basis for an outside agency. More rarely, a university may commission a study of its needs or programs, or an anthropologist, acting as a private citizen, may choose a topic or an issue to apply his skills of anthropological research or advocacy. For instance, this author worked with a citizens' action group to successfully resist the establishment of a mega-casino in his city. The approach was that of documenting negative social impact.

Practicing anthropology is a label that has emerged since the 1970s. It refers to the work of anthropologically trained people who use their applied skills and knowledge, full-time, outside of academic settings, for practical purposes. Such people may do research of an applied nature such as needs assessments, program evaluations, and social impact assessments. But what sets them apart from applied anthropologists is that they can frequently design programs, policies, and services and sometimes directly implement and administer them.

Practicing anthropologists are engaged in action, administration, and implementation—not just critical reflection. They might do their work as independent consultants, or they might be employed full-time in consulting companies. Public service agencies such as policy and planning departments of federal, state, provincial, and municipal governments can be venues for them. Nonprofit private (or nongovernment organizations) that deliver human and social services, education, welfare, and health are settings in which large numbers of practicing anthropologists work. A growing number in the United States have found employment with profit-making corporations such as General Motors, Hallmark, Motorola, and Xerox, where they do research on personnel, production, and marketing matters. Other practicing anthropologists work for international and community development agencies such as the United States Agency for International Aid and Development (USAID) or through the World Bank, United Nations agencies, and international nongovernment organizations (NGOs) such as CARE, Oxfam, or the Red Cross. Needs assessments, evaluations, and impact studies are done for programs and services to benefit impoverished villagers in health, education, fisheries, agriculture, forestry, and other domains. In the international field, practicing anthropologists work with private corporations on issues such as the cultural sensitivity needed to do business in another culture or the creation of branch plants. Domestically and internationally, practicing anthropologists contribute to advocacy groups dealing with environmentalism, human rights, and consumer protection. Venues for the practice of anthropology are extremely varied. Just about any area with a human or social connection can benefit in some way from social science practice and quite frequently directly from anthropology.

Anthropologists practicing in nonacademic settings perform a multitude of roles. They can engage directly in community development work at a grassroots level, working with villagers in planning and setting up enterprises that benefit them. They can train or instruct people in such skills as cross-cultural sensitivity or research methods, mediate conflict, serve as expert witnesses in court cases, or engage in public advocacy for a cause. They might co-manage natural resources such as fish, wildlife, and forestry resources in a U.S. National Forest with federal, local, and tribal governments. Practicing anthropologists design and implement projects that optimize public use of national or state parks. They can do various types of research to provide the information necessary to establish land claims, conduct research into the cultural appropriateness of technology or human service programs, or analyze the basis of conflict or social problems.

The field of practicing anthropology may be viewed by some as amorphous, especially when compared to other practical professions such as nursing or social work. It does not yet have a precisely defined identity, and its boundaries are sometimes very hard to locate. People are frequently employed because they have generic skills from the social sciences or for technical writing, research, or some other valued area. That, incidentally or specifically, might include cross-cultural expertise—a more identifiable niche for anthropologists. Some of the roles that practicing anthropologists perform could be filled by people coming from sociology, psychology, nursing, education, public health, public administration, and a host of other disciplines. However, over time, anthropology graduates, showing initiative and enterprise, have made significant inroads into these fields and institutions and have demonstrated the utility of anthropological practice. Gradually and continuously, more nonanthropologists in policy-making institutions are becoming aware of anthropology and appreciative of the skills and insights of its practitioners.

Employment surveys suggest that a majority or at least a very significant minority of new Ph.D.-level anthropologists will enter into nonacademic practice. To these must be added the thousands more at the B.A. and M.A. levels who have always been graduating into such practice. Those at the master's level account for the majority of present practitioners, and we need to pay much more attention to their activities and identities as anthropologists (see Quirk and Jenakovich 1997). It is exceptionally important to nurture this profession alongside the more academically based applied anthropology, policy analysis, and the study of social issues. That has already begun through the establishment of several dozen master's-level practitioner training programs in the United States (see Kushner 1994).

How Does Applied Anthropology Relate to Anthropological Theory?

Natural sciences such as physics or chemistry develop basic research around important theoretical questions. The theories and findings then inform practice through the engineering branches of such disciplines. For the most part, the direction of theory to practice is one way. Other sciences such as medicine or psychiatry have a two-way or mutual reinforcement of theory and practice. In psychiatry, Freudian theory emerged and was elaborated through constant clinical interaction with patients, while new theory was tested by psychoanalysts. The relationship is similar to the constant interplay among clinical medicine, drug trials, surgical interventions, and theoretical formulation. Here, the relationships between theory and practice are reciprocal (see Hill and Baba 1997: 14–15).

What has been the situation regarding theory and practice in anthropology? Historically, there has been considerable variation. During the era of British Structural Functionalism, associated with A. R. Radcliffe-Brown, Bronislaw Malinowski, and E. E. Evans-Pritchard, a close relationship was largely conceived as one way in direction. Basic research and theoretical formulations (surrounding kinship, religion, and politics) were directed to understanding the social "anatomy" and "physiology" of tribal peoples then under the rule of the British Empire. Such information would supposedly inform enlightened colonial administration. However, as a legacy, there has been a stigmatized association with applied anthropology, theory, and colonialism. In Britain and many other First World or developed countries, there has been a distinct separation of academic theory from practice (see Shore and Wright 1997: 141).

In the United States, there was a close relationship between theory and practice in the 1930s and during World War II. As Baba (1994: 181) points out, Lloyd Warner's famous ethnographic study at the Western Electric Hawthorne Plant pointed to the significance of informal organization and made a significant breakthrough by explaining factors of productivity on the assembly line. That approach fueled a whole series of other studies in industrial and organizational anthropology as well as insights used in the more academic set of studies associated with "Yankee City." Similarly, during World War II, Ruth Benedict's configurationalist theory, focusing on consistent and patterned cultural values in each society, led to a workable explanation of Japanese values and behaviors that was used during the American occupation of Japan (Benedict 1946).

However, after the war, theory and practice diverged for complex reasons. A basic reason was concern among academics that anthropology should avoid major societal interventions for fear of unintentionally doing serious damage to people. This wariness was strongly influenced by the disillusionment of physicists who had participated in the construction of the atomic bomb. In addition, the vast majority of anthropologists were able to find employment in expanding academic institutions, where a premium was placed on basic and theoretical anthropology.

From the 1950s through mid-1970s, the major theories or approaches in anthropology—structuralism, neo-evolutionism, cultural materialism, political economy, interpretive anthropology—were nurtured in university settings. Middle-range theories such as substantive versus formalistic approaches in economics, cultural and human ecology, network theory in urban anthropology, componential analysis in kinship studies, acculturation approaches for the study of change, and many others were developed. Those of us who trained during this period were fed huge amounts of theory and debated the relative merits of competing theories. We were also exhorted by our thesis advisors to develop good theories for explaining our ethnographic research findings and to locate findings within theoretical debates. The standard aphorism of thesis advisors was that a good theory was the best methodological tool that an anthropologist could have.

From the early 1970s to the present, much of applied and practicing anthropology grew independently of theoretical or basic anthropology. Practicing anthropology had to respond to the needs of its clients, not intellectual curiosity. Grand or even medium-range theories play minimal roles in applied research, recommendations, or action plans. Most of the time intimate firsthand knowledge of peoples and communities and the discovery of culturally appropriate recommendations for ameliorating problems were the most important factors. Theoretical discussions are rarely part of an applied anthropologist's report to a client. Clients are not interested in them; they may even find abstraction tedious or incomprehensible. Representatives of client organizations or host communities are most interested in what they as policy makers and implementors specifically need to do given the restraints of their mandates and limited resources. At least on the surface, methods providing that kind of information count for much more than theory. These methods have included well-tested techniques of participant observation and grasps of the local language—a window to the local worldview.

In the meantime, much anthropological theory (especially the grand theories) developed from the 1950s through the 1970s did not lend itself to application. Because anthropological theory has been largely oriented to the production of knowledge—comparisons of and generalizations about humanity—it has drawn upon the labors of professors and graduate students for empirical insights. Unfortunately, it has not been inclined to draw upon the empirical knowledge gained by practitioners or applied anthropologists.

The result has been a relative impasse that has prevented a unified and free flow between academic, basic, and theoretical anthropology on one side and application or practice on the other. What the two sides do have in common are research methods, some important common perspectives (holism, etc.), and parallel domains of information—for example, family organization, community integration, and conflict. One side—the academic—is heavily oriented toward the theoretical; the other side—the practical—focuses on methodology and the useful information it produces.

What are the various ways to deal with this impasse? One that has been suggested is to simply view practicing anthropology as the fifth subdiscipline of anthropology (see Baba 1994; Chambers 1987; Fiske and Chambers 1995). This acknowledges that the needs, working conditions, ethical concerns, and the potentials for method and theoretical development have to be considered differently by practitioners. This recognition would give practitioners an equal place within anthropology and allow their highly dynamic field to take its shape as directed by those who know its best interests. It is not entirely clear whether the applied anthropologists in academia would be placed in such a fifth subdiscipline. Inclusion would be quite logical because university-based applied anthropology shares so many things with practice. However, remaining with academic sociocultural anthropology leaves open the question of responsibility for more desirable linkages between theory and practice.

At any rate, practice is rapidly becoming more respected and recognized within anthropology as a whole. In the early 1980s, the American Anthropological Association established the National Association for the Practice of Anthropology (NAPA) as a significant section of its organization. The older Society for Applied Anthropology established the journal *Practicing Anthropology* for that important constituency in 1978. Both organizations actively encourage the participation of practitioners at their annual conferences, foster the development of Local Practitioner Organizations (LPOs), and print special publications supporting practitioner needs. As Chambers points out

> . . . anthropology has a need for persons who are experts in translating and mediating the knowledge of our disciplines. The lack of development of a practitioner arm in anthropology does not ensure the purity of the anthropological enterprise so much as it guarantees that the knowledge of anthropology will be little used and that, when it is used it is likely to be misused. (Chambers 1987: 325)

Another suggested way of dealing with the impasse is to focus the development of theory within anthropology around issues of policy. Chambers cautiously discusses this model of applied anthropology as placing ". . . emphasis upon the potential of anthropological inquiry to contribute responsibly and in a broad perspective to the understanding of social issues" (1987: 319). Although he did not elaborate, it would provide the potential for a more abstract and potentially generalizable set of principles that could be applied to the many scenarios where constructive action is needed. Certainly, it would be highly desirable to have a few theories that might form the basis of plans to implement large- and small-scale changes. However, we are very far from constructing such theory. What can be achieved are sets of middle-range assumptions, principles, and prescriptions that could effectively inform us about significant areas of policy concern. These could include, for example, social welfare systems and aspects of health care such as substance abuse for which sustained research accumulates policy-relevant generalizations.

Shore and Wright (1997), in their review of British applied anthropology, make parallel suggestions for the development of applied anthropology as a policy science. They point out that policies are themselves inherently cultural phenomena—reflections or condensed symbols of the total society—as guides to conduct and practice. These insights allow them to conclude that

> A more coherent anthropology of policy and practice would therefore not only examine the epistemology or conceptual base upon which policy is formulated, but also its social impact, and, more importantly, its meaning for those individuals and communities that are at its receiving end. (1997: 144)

A more theoretically focused anthropology of policy would also direct us to "uncover the cultures of the policy professional, those in power, or those who attempt to impose their definitions of social situations and make them persist" (1997: 145). These would involve such matters as hidden hierarchies and agendas of government and industry dominating peoples' lives. Borrowing from Laura Nader (1980), Shore and Wright also recommend theoretical analyses of "vertical slices," linking issues, individuals, communities, institutions, corporations, and government—policy communities that go beyond a local or horizontal one. Single issues such as the welfare of children or the care of the aged or disabled could be followed up and down these vertical slices, and effective informed generalizations of a policy and theoretical nature could be formed.

These suggestions of theory, as focused on policy, do hold promise, but Chambers (1987: 320) provides an important caution. We must distinguish between policy analysis and the making of policy. The former can be done relatively easily by most anthropologists, because the capacity to critique or appraise policies already made is compatible with our research methods and perspectives. The real breakthrough comes with anthropological policy-making, where skills other than just scientific enquiry are required—skills of planning, management, and even lobbying.

Another approach that bridges the gap between theory and applied anthropology is the so-called *praxis* approach. Warry (1992: 155), one of its proponents, suggests that it "may serve to partially overcome the distinction between basic and applied research." He calls for applied anthropologists to engage in theoretical discussions in the context of actual practice with their research subjects, clients, and collaborators, who are not anthropologists, at the point of intervention—the community or the organization as it directly applies to the problem at hand. Theory is tested in the field through the practical information provided by the anthropologist but framed by theoretical assumptions. If theories or parts of them are not applicable, they are rejected or modified at the point of intervention. The successes or failures of actual practices would then inform further development of theory, which would be tested yet again in future contexts of practice. Although Warry does not make the comparison, it would bring us closer to the clinical model in medicine or psychiatry, in which theory and practice mutually reinforce each other and are held in mutual respect. The big difference is that the clients, community members, and stakeholders are major players in the construction of theory. That does not happen in medicine. Warry elaborates:

> A praxis approach in applied anthropology requires the development of methodology that is ethical and emancipatory—methods that engage research participants in action and theoretical discussion. A praxis anthropology requires analysis of the way in which value, perception, and belief mediate the translation of theory into strategic action. Praxis investigations would focus attention on cooperative activities that assist individuals to make decisions and assume responsibility for planned change, rather than conceding that task to the experts. (1992: 157)

He then goes on to describe a project in southern Ontario where he was involved with Native people in facilitating the transfer of responsibility for health care from the federal government to First Nations (the synonym for tribes in the Canadian context) governments. Pretransfer community health needs assessments were required, and they were to be done collaboratively with Native stakeholders. With Warry's facilitation, Native researchers conducted a survey of 235 randomly selected members of the general population. They conducted relatively open-ended interviews covering areas such as how people view the health of the individual and the community and attitudes about traditional medicine and contemporary health services. The opinions of another sixty Native leaders, health officials, and elders were carefully recorded. A great deal of attention was paid to consultation meetings with forty people who would be key actors in the ultimate transfer of services. Meetings, retreats, and workshops were frequently held in which theories and the "theories" behind methods (e.g., probability theory and the use of random selection in sampling) were examined. They discussed principles behind the identification of problems, the use of data, and how data enters into the analysis for practical planning. They painstakingly negotiated agreement on ethics, methods, and theories. Native perceptions of holistic health, well-being, and spirituality were all included in a unique and culturally satisfactory model for local health-care delivery. These developments were reinforced by the researchers' theoretical emphases that recognized the benefits of community health-care delivery (rather than a clinically based hospital). These were further supported by local models and desires for control that would de-emphasize the institutional approach (especially in mental health issues).

A negotiated reality about the meaning of health-care intervention emerged—one that was based on theoretical perceptions. In such contexts, and I think this is Warry's major point, theory directly serves society through its practice. So an applied anthropology need not be devoid of theory. The question is, what is to be most served by theory—the theory-building capacities of academic anthropology or the needs of people in society?

Like Warry, Merrill Singer (1994) proposes a community-centered praxis (CCP) in applied anthropology, one that is "nonimperialist" in that the issues, methods, and theories focus on the needs of communities rather than academic agendas. The approach has its roots in action or advocacy anthropology and in collaborative research or participatory action that

> . . . involves practical research that is carried out in and through indigenous community-*based* organizations (as contrasted with non-indigenous and externally controlled community-*placed* organizations) or other autochthonous movements of superordinated peoples. . . . (1994: 340)

He then goes on to describe his participation in an advocacy struggle that led to the establishment of a needle-exchange program for drug users in Hartford, Connecticut. The program was advocated by Hispanic and black organizations in the city to stem the spread of HIV/AIDS but opposed by the police as legitimizing criminal activity. Anthropological theoretical contributions centered on the significance of HIV/AIDS as being as much a socio-cultural phenomenon as it is a biomedical one.

Singer, like Warry, contends that here theory should primarily serve the community and society rather than academia. Such trends support what Ryan (1985) refers to as the "decolonization" of anthropology.

So in the end, we can ask ourselves the question again: In which direction should applied anthropology be going? Should it stress theory-building, linking theory to practice, and practice to theory? Should applied anthropologists emphasize methodology and policy analysis, even creating boundaries that distinguish themselves even more clearly from academics? Should there be a concerted effort to reinforce praxis and service to the community in a spirit of decolonialization? Alternatively, should efforts be made to unite anthropology in the common purpose of tying academic anthropology theory to practice—a major task?

In the current dynamic climate of anthropology, all of these things seem to be happening at the same time. Emphases depend on the values and visions of the particular anthropologists participating. The resulting variety is probably healthy because it gives us more options. Practice is now very well established, and students aspiring to practitioner roles will have plenty of examples to follow as well as a well-established body of knowledge, methods, and underlying theories. Furthermore, future generations of applied anthropologists will be better served by theories that more directly attend to their issues in practice, and, in turn, practice will inform theory.

One final note with regard to theory: given practical problems to solve, applied and practicing anthropologists have to be pragmatic. That requirement frequently forces them to draw upon theories from other social science disciplines—social psychology, community medicine, sociology, political science, human development and aging, agricultural economics, geography, public administration, marketing, and others. Often such alternative theory sources are directly informative about the problems at hand. Of course, practitioners can blend these sources with insights from anthropological theories or perspectives. Sometimes the logistics of the particular problem—for example, improving agricultural production—can lead to interdisciplinary cooperation with major input from anthropologists along with biologists, engineers, economists, and sociologists. In this case, a new theoretical synthesis—agrosystems research (see Shaner 1982)—has emerged, and it is not "owned" by any particular discipline. Such interdisciplinary synthesis should not be disparaged in an attempt to preserve anthropological purity. Indeed, most of our academic theories in anthropology were influenced by other intellectual trends—for example, the relationships of cultural evolution to biological evolution, culture and personality to psychology and psychiatry, postmodernist and interpretive anthropology to literary criticism and philosophy, and so forth. For practitioners it pays to be flexible in the choices of both method and theory and to have them pragmatically match the problem at hand.

Some Challenges

The realm of practice for anthropologists is incredibly wide, and is at least as wide as, if not wider than, the subject of anthropology itself. We do so many things that their variety does not make for immediate pigeonholing as to what precisely practicing anthropology is. Nor can we always easily articulate what is specifically anthropological about such practice. Many of the precise details of practice can vary, and they cannot be placed into neat classifications, in which precise and unique principles of the ethical practice can be detailed to match standard tasks and procedures. This may be less of a problem for other fields such as nursing, social work, medicine, law, and occupational therapy, where the tasks of service and the ethical requirements can be much more easily circumscribed. In other words, it would be a difficult task to write a composite job description for a practicing anthropologist, because so much variety and flexibility in tasks and roles exist.

How do anthropologists deal with these challenges? Although the field of anthropological practice may seem ambiguous or shapeless, that can be an advantage. Most of us who have been attracted to anthropology tend to be flexible, have a higher tolerance for ambiguity, and may be able to work more effectively on "boundary" or "peripheral" topics. Change has been rapid through rampant organizational restructuring and economic "globalization." Although specialized knowledge is still valuable, the capacities to uncover information at frontiers and find bridging solutions are becoming more necessary. Take health-care delivery as an example. Beyond hospital care, planners may now be required to look more at how local attitudes and resources (such as family support; friendship networks; voluntary organization; values; and means of sharing resources, shaping opinion, and communication) have an impact on local health. The objective might be to design a health-care system, making use of local strengths rather than simply applying a standardized delivery model. In instances like these, people with anthropological backgrounds have much to offer, because they are less committed to "worn tracks" or standard ways of doing things—they have the capacity to explore the unknown. Boundary areas are constantly expanding: having the imagination to fill them is the challenge for practicing anthropologists.

Another good way to face such challenges is to become more conversant with success stories in which applied anthropologists have made differences in problem-solving or policy contexts—focusing on the practical rather than the exotic or arcane (see Eddy and Partridge 1986; Wulff and Fiske 1987; van Willigen et al. 1989; Higgins and Parades 1999 for some very good examples). When we are exposed to stereotypical impressions of anthropology, we can counter or inform others with impressions of mainstream practicality. Also, becoming more conversant with this applied work helps us to more consistently develop our own pragmatic faith in the subject, which is a prerequisite for advocating our own skills and competency.

Students must broaden and intensify their skill bases by writing, communicating, researching, mediating, interpreting, analyzing, solving problems, and administrating. In the end, employers are more interested in the skills of the applicant than in a professional identity. But at that point, there is an opportunity to advocate the "value-added" benefits that can come out of anthropological backgrounds.

Student readers should realize that they will have many opportunities to make use of anthropological knowledge throughout their professional lives. Anthropology does not reside in a set of codified knowledge and principles strictly governed by an academic "priesthood." It is reinvented and practiced through the activities of thousands of anthropologists. Even though standards and disciplinary core principles are important, each person, to some extent, always creates his or her personal vision of what anthropology is and how it can be used. That vision may change several times over a lifetime, but a student should form the basis of that vision now. He or she can have a lifetime of continuing involvement in anthropology outside of the university, but that process has to begin with a plan followed by action.

Summary

The key emphasis of the book will be an exploration of a wide variety of nontraditional, nonacademic settings in North American communities and organizations, using applied tools and perspectives that focus on policy issues. The book will frequently use mainstream examples of anthropology's relevance. Orientation toward public service and problem-solving will be stressed through collaborative styles of application, including participatory action and advocacy research. Discussions of anthropology's place in well-established domains of policy practice, such as needs and social impact assessment as well as program evaluation, will be highlighted. In order to practice effectively, one must understand the basis of ethical research and practice. Beyond this, it is important to master applied methodological skills including rapid research. All in all, students are encouraged to develop a practical and personal vision of anthropology and their place in it as soon as possible. To continue this orientation to practicality and engagement, Chapter 2 will review the history of applied anthropology.

RECOMMENDED READINGS

Baba, Marietta L.
1994   The Fifth Subdiscipline: Anthropological Practice and the Future of Anthropology. *Human Organization,* Vol. 53(2): 174–186.

Chambers, Erve
1987   Applied Anthropology in the Post-Vietnam Era: Anticipations and Ironies. *Annual Review of Anthropology,* Vol. 66: 309–337.

Eddy, Elizabeth, and William L. Partridge (eds.)
1986   *Applied Anthropology in America.* Second Edition. New York: Columbia University Press.

Fiske, Shirley J., and Erve Chambers
1995   The Inventions of Practice. *Human Organization,* Vol. 55(1): 1–12.
1997   Status and Trends: Practice and Anthropology in the United States. In *The Global Practice of Anthropology.* Edited by Marietta Baba and Carole E. Hill. Pp. 283–311. Williamsburg, VA: College of William and Mary.

Higgins, Patricia J., and J. Anthony Parades (eds.)
1999   *Classics of Practicing Anthropology: 1978–1998.* Oklahoma City: Society for Applied Anthropology.

Hill, Carole E., and Marietta Baba
1997   The International Practice of Anthropology: An Overview. In *The Global Practice of Anthropology.* Edited by Marietta Baba and Carole E. Hill. Pp. 1–25. Williamsburg, VA: College of William and Mary.

Kushner, Gilbert
1994   Training Programs for the Practice of Applied Anthropology. *Human Organization,* Vol. 53: 186–192.

Quirk, Kathleen M., and Marsha Jenakovich (eds.)
1997   *Mastering Anthropology: Anthropologists Practicing with Masters' Degrees.* Special Issue, *Practicing Anthropology,* Vol. 19(2): 2–36.

Shore, Chris, and Susan Wright
1997   Colonial Gaze to Critique of Policy: British Anthropology in Policy and Practice. In *The Global Practice of Anthropology.* Edited by Marietta Baba and Carole E. Hill. Pp. 139–155. Williamsburg, VA: College of William and Mary.

Singer, Merrill
1994   Community-Centered Praxis: Toward an Alternative Non-Dominative Applied Anthropology. *Human Organization,* Vol. 53(4): 336–345.

van Willigen, John, Barbara Rylko-Bauer, and Ann McElroy (eds.)
1989   *Making Our Research Useful: Case Studies in the Utilization of Anthropological Knowledge.* Boulder, CO: Westview Press.

Warry, Wayne
1992   The Eleventh Thesis: Applied Anthropology as Praxis. *Human Organization,* Vol. 51(2):155–164.

Wulff, Robert M., and Shirley J. Fiske (eds.)
1987   *Anthropological Praxis: Translating Knowledge into Action.* Boulder, CO: Westview Press.

2 A Brief History of Applied Anthropology

Authors such as Harris (1968) and Voget (1975) provide rich histories of academic anthropology, but the neglect of similar accounts of anthropology's application is quite striking. This oversight contributes to a hazy impression of where applied anthropology really fits within the discipline. Some may see it as an appendix to academia or even as an enterprise born out of a shortage of university jobs. In contrast, I claim, as do some others (see van Willigen 1993), that application has been more at the forefront both in the earliest visions and through subsequent activities. Nonetheless, it is true that applied anthropology has waxed and waned in its 150 years of existence.

Nineteenth-Century Beginnings

Anthropology emerged by the middle of the 1800s through the efforts of amateurs, including British abolitionists who were concerned about the status of peoples native to the British colonies. They established the Ethnological Society of London in 1843 and then a factionalized offshoot, the Anthropological Society of London, in 1863. According to Reining, members of both groups advocated the application of anthropological knowledge to policy with the hope that it ". . . would aid in the emancipation of the human mind from preconceived notions" (Reining 1962: 595). However, this early rush toward applicable knowledge became mired down because of inflammatory controversies surrounding issues of race and poverty—crudely formed social Darwinism justifying social inequality dominated the Anthropological Society, and moderate liberalism motivated the Ethnological Society.

One response to the division was to firmly establish anthropology as a respectable academic science by withdrawing it from the more divisive issues of the day. This was accomplished in part through a re-amalgamation of the two societies into a forerunner of the Royal Anthropological Society of Great Britain and Ireland, shepherded by the famous biologist Sir Thomas Huxley. Legitimacy was further strengthened with the appointment of E. B. Tylor as an anthropologist at Oxford in 1883. But even Tylor saw anthropology as a reformer's science. One of his goals was to educate colonial officials about native customs. However, British anthropology turned to less practical topics until the mid-1920s. Yet Reining (1962) reminds us that anthropology's original vision was practical, intended to explore vital issues of human welfare such as poverty and conflict.

One of American anthropology's earliest forebears was Henry Schoolcraft. Schoolcraft was commissioned by Congress to report on the circumstances and prospects of Indian tribes in the United States. The results, contained in a six-volume report (Schoolcraft 1852–1857), gave background and direction to Indian policy (van Willigen 1993: 19). That expectation continued with Congress' 1879 establishment of the Bureau of American Ethnology attached to the Smithsonian Institution. The first director, Major John Wesley Powell, felt that inductive knowledge of tribal peoples was needed to ease their transition to the next stages of civilization and to rectify some problems that "civilized" people had created during contacts. But Congress expected usable information more quickly than it was received, even as researchers wanted longer periods to accumulate the information of their choice. Conflict over timing and content still plagues anthropologists and policy makers. After Powell removed himself from the controversy, the Bureau strayed from its original mandate to serve the more antiquarian curiosity of its staff (Hinsley 1979). However, one researcher, James Mooney (1896), can be cited for his remarkably advanced research on the Ghost Dance Religion. As a form of advocacy, he sympathetically portrayed the Ghost Dance, widespread among Western tribes, as a genuinely religious expression of coping with the severe dislocations produced by the U.S.-Indian wars and confinement to reservations.

In the nineteenth century, anthropology eventually became successful in gaining a foothold of respectability. Yet its professional numbers were minuscule, and the scope of its task enormous. The most important contributor to that venture was Franz Boas, who held the first North American appointment in anthropology at Clark University, later moving to Columbia. Boas did not consider himself an applied anthropologist, being primarily concerned with salvaging information about tribal cultures before they disappeared, but he did prepare the way for effective demonstrations of the uses of anthropology for policy. For instance, with scientific rigor and research, he attacked notions of racial determinism, claiming a more important role for culture and context. As a physical anthropologist, he submitted results from two massive studies to the United States Commissioner of Education. These works were a form of scientific advocacy, demonstrating that even physical growth and development of immigrants were strongly influenced by new social environments. Within a few generations immigrant physical characteristics approximated those of British North Americans. He provided factual arguments against the current policies to restrict immigration to British and Northwestern Europeans (Stocking 1979).

Applied Anthropology between the World Wars

By the mid-1920s, as the Boasian concern with documenting cultural history waned, anthropology turned to the study of contemporary societies. Part of this was due to the stimulus of British anthropologists Bronislaw Malinowski and Alfred Reginald Radcliffe-Brown. Both delivered their visions of anthropological enquiry during sojourns at American universities until the 1940s. Their versions of structural functionalism regarded present-day societies as organic entities that were maintained by interconnected institutions. To use an anatomical analogy, the main task for the anthropologist was to map the institutional "organs" of society and then to analyze their "bodily" functions in the style similar to that of physiology.

British anthropologists directed their research at tribal societies within the British Empire and the Dominions of New Zealand, South Africa, and Australia.

At the same time, the changes and disruptions on North American Indian reservations increasingly attracted the attention of American anthropologists. One breakthrough was Margaret Mead's (1932) study of the deteriorating conditions among the "Antlers," a pseudonym for a Plains tribe. A new strategy, the acculturation approach, gradually developed for the investigation of change among American Indians. It was an inductive perspective that incorporated some assumptions of the structural functionalist approach but also focused on changes in indigenous societies following sustained contact with European and American societies. In bare outline, the study begins by reconstructing a "baseline culture" and then describes significant events and strategies initiated by intruders (e.g., settlement, wars, trade). It details particular effects of cultural contact on areas such as language, socialization, subsistence, religion, values, authority, and land uses of the indigenous societies. Acculturation studies described reservation sociocultural systems as byproducts of these dynamics, outlining dimensions of both persistence and change. The study of acculturation was prominent in anthropology through the late 1960s and guided much of the work done by North Americanists (see Bee 1974; Redfield et al. 1936; Social Science Research Council 1954; Spicer 1961).

Both acculturation and functionalist approaches were associated with applied work that started in the 1930s and continued through the 1960s. In Britain, Malinowski encouraged the funding and training of anthropologists in applied research. In an article titled "Practical Anthropology," Malinowski (1929) laid out much of the agenda for that kind of work. He suggested that anthropologists provide information on land tenure, jurisprudence, health, demographics, and ongoing change. In far-flung and populous colonies with few British administrators available to govern them directly, it was thought best to leave intact as many indigenous customs that were broadly compatible with British policy as possible, allowing limited self-rule in tribal contexts. Any changes should be made as compatible with local customs as was feasible. Ethnographic information was valuable for such purposes. If, for instance, a new cash crop was introduced, cultivation should not seriously violate indigenous systems of land distribution because of the amount of internal conflict it might generate. Out of this era and extending well into the 1950s, a significant amount of data was generated, sometimes coming out of regional centers such as the Rhodes-Livingstone Institute (see Wilson 1940) in Central Africa. Evans-Pritchard's classic (1940) and influential study of the Nuer was done as background information for the Anglo-Egyptian administration of the Sudan. Some other highlights included Raymond Firth's (1936) analysis of overpopulation in Tikopia, Schapera's (1947) investigations of the effects of labor migration in Bechuanaland, and various studies by Lucy Mair (1957) in Africa.

In the United States anthropologists advised the Bureau of Indian Affairs (BIA) during the New Deal. Activated by the vision of John Collier, the new commissioner, the BIA undertook new policies for improvement. These were mandated by the Wheeler-Howard Act or Indian Reorganization Act of 1934. American Indian reservations had been devastated by disease, cultural disintegration, and demoralization. Indians had lost much land when the Allotment Act divided many reservations into 160-acre plots to be individually owned. The 1934 Act provided the means to recover land by drawing from the public domain and consolidating holdings under the control of elected tribal councils. The Act also made provisions for new forms of tribal government and promoted reforms in education and economic development. To get the information needed, Collier turned to the Bureau of American Ethnology, which started an Applied Anthropology Unit to study tribal social organization and to provide information about the needs for land acquisition. Some of the well-known anthropologists who served with that unit included Edward H. Spicer, Julian Steward, Morris Opler, Clyde Kluckhohn, Oscar Lewis, Gordon MacGregor, Laura Thompson, and Dorothea Leighton. Again, it was difficult to quickly provide the knowledge needed, and conflicts emerged between bureaucrats and anthropologists. Yet even after the unit disbanded, Collier continued to contract some policy research from anthropologists at the University of Chicago (McNickle 1979).

One project reveals the dilemmas for anthropologists working with New Deal Indian policy. It involved problems of overgrazing and soil erosion on the Navaho reservation (Kimball 1979). A joint program for tackling the problem engaged the BIA and the Soil Conservation Service, which sought to restrict livestock ownership by Navaho. The bureaucrats' approach was heavy-handed, paternalistic, and bitterly resisted by the Navaho. Anthropologists John Provinse and Sol Kimball were brought in to ease conflict and foster cooperation between the bureaucrats and Indians. Among their useful findings was a corporate grouping of linked families that they called the "land-use community." They recommended that officials cooperate with those units rather than impose arbitrary restrictions upon individual stockholders. The anthropologists developed a working arrangement with one such group, but the plan was abruptly scuttled by bureaucrats who resented threats to their prerogative for centralized planning. Unfortunately, many contemporary applied anthropologists can recount similar frustrations today.

According to Julian Steward (1969), a disillusioned participant, Collier's New Deal policies were based on a misplaced paternalism and a romantic image of American Indians. Steward maintains that much of the relatively uniform policy was unrealistic and unfair because there was diversity of opinion among Indians with, for example, factions on reservations representing "traditionalist" versus "progressive" interests. Sometimes the provisions of government were incompatible with the desires of particular groups as Clemmer (1969, 1974) documents in his portrayal of the imposition of a united reservation system upon the Hopi, who saw their separate communities as sovereign.

It is tempting to harshly criticize this era of applied anthropology, most especially with regard to Britain, and perceive anthropology as a handmaiden of imperialism (Gjessing 1968; Willis 1974). However, the actions might be better evaluated according to the standards and values of the times. In the case of Britain, the concept of indirect rule, maintaining the essence of tribal customs and institutions whenever possible, was morally defensible to most anthropologists faced with colonial realities. For instance, Firth (1981) denies that Malinowski was the archlackey of colonialism as some have portrayed him. He was capable of severely criticizing colonial practices that damaged tribal peoples. It should also be remembered that he did help educate Jomo Kenyatta, the first president of Kenya, who was most certainly an anti-imperialist. Still, as Asad (1973) suggests, it is important to objectively review anthropology's role in the colonial encounter, especially in the context of unbalanced power relationships.

Anthropologists who participated in New Deal BIA policies wished to mitigate its more heavy-handed approaches. Also, to maintain a sense of perspective, consider some of the alternative assimilationist policies that preceded and followed the New Deal. The Dawes

Act led to the selling of previously Indian-owned lands, and the Termination Acts of the 1950s led to the elimination of several complete reservations. New Deal Indian policy definitely shored up land rights for many and provided consistent, albeit sometimes flawed, tribal government.

Also as part of the New Deal, anthropological studies were done by the Bureau of Agricultural Economics, an agency of the U.S. Department of Agriculture. The Bureau was set up to examine the problems of rural poverty and the relationship of farming to community viability. A set of ethnographies with a common research design (see Olen and Loomis 1941; Kollmorgen 1942; Macleish and Young 1942; Moe and Taylor 1942; Bell 1942; Wynne 1943) examined dairy, wheat, corn, and cotton farmers in the Midwest, New England, the Southwest, and the South. They all took into account factors of ethnicity (e.g., Amish and Mexican Americans), scale and mechanization of farm operations, class, values, local conflicts, and community cohesion. Also among the Bureau's reports was Walter Goldschmidt's (1947) study, which showed the huge discrepancies in the implementation of federal irrigation policy in California. Small producers, the intended beneficiaries of irrigation, produced more per acre, yet large corporate farms gained much more from public irrigation while proportionately producing less. Another study by Horace Miner (1949) demonstrated how certain federal farm policies (e.g., payments for not growing surplus crops) were counterproductive to local value systems. Unfortunately, the Bureau of Agricultural Economics was eventually terminated for political reasons.

One other advanced branch of applied anthropology, that of business and industrial anthropology, originated during the 1930s. W. Lloyd Warner, newly appointed to the Harvard School of Human Relations, was interested in extending the ethnographic approach to complex societies. An opportunity arose with a study, overseen by psychologist Elton Mayo, of industrial productivity and worker morale at the massive Hawthorne Electric Company plant in Chicago. Separate work groups were ethnographically observed and their members interviewed as if they were participants in small-scale societies. This research demonstrated that there were many more motivators of workers' behavior than just wages. Workers could no longer be seen as analogous to functioning parts of a machine. Worker morale and productivity needed to be perceived as more organic, based on shared values and interactions within small groups. Furthermore, with regard to the more contemporary anthropological study of business, industry, and organizations, the importance of effective informal organization was clearly recognized in any successes. Warner and some colleagues went on to do anthropological research on complex American communities—through the Yankee City series (Warner 1941–1947). Associates such as Burleigh Gardner (1945), F. L. W. Richardson (1955), and William Whyte (1948) used anthropological principles in various industrial and commercial ventures. For more information on this era, see Baba (1986), Richardson (1979), and Schwartzman (1993).

World War II and Its Aftermath

In 1941, an exceptionally significant event in the development of applied anthropology occurred, the founding of the Society for Applied Anthropology (SfAA). This was the first professional association devoted to the application of anthropology. Various anthropologists and sympathetic colleagues in a few other cognate disciplines, such as rural sociology and social psychology, gathered at Harvard and Washington for two spring meetings to form a professional association with the primary objective of ". . . scientific investigation of the principles controlling the relations of human beings to one another . . . and the wide application of these principles to practical problems." At the second meeting, papers on colonial or Indian administration, social welfare, mental health, national morale, diet, and industry were delivered. The participants included Margaret Mead, Gregory Bateson, William F. Whyte, George P. Murdock, Ruth Underhill, Ruth Benedict, and fifty others. The following year an influential journal, *Applied Anthropology* (later *Human Organization*), began publication. In 1949, the Society produced its code of ethics, an essential guide for applied anthropologists. Current and future practitioners of applied anthropology owe a tremendous debt to the founders of the SfAA. Without its influence, applied anthropology would not be as coherent and effective as it is today.

American anthropologists made significant contributions to the war effort. Margaret Mead (1979) tells how anthropologists and other social scientists met with high-level administration officials in 1940 to discuss ways to maintain national morale should the United States declare war. After Pearl Harbor, Mead was placed in charge of the Committee on Food Habits attached to the National Research Council. Her group (including Lloyd Warner and Ruth Benedict) advised on programs for emergency feeding and rationing and measured public opinion about aid to allies. Mead also studied the social impact of having over a million U.S. servicemen stationed in Britain, focusing on the clash of values between American soldiers and British civilians and military and making recommendations for the improvement of relations (Mead 1944).

Another group, prominently involving British anthropologist Gregory Bateson, established areal institutes at universities across the country—focusing on regions such as the Far East, Oceania, the Middle East, Latin America, Africa, and the Soviet Union. The idea was to teach foreign-service officers, the military, and others the region's history, language, culture, society, and politics relevant to national defense and U.S. participation in global affairs. Most immediate were preparations for military intelligence and language study, especially for the Pacific theater.

Bateson, in 1943, was employed by the Office of Strategic Services along with Rhoda Métraux, Geoffrey Gorer, Clyde Kluckhohn, and Ruth Benedict. Here, "enemy" societies were studied at a distance through interviews, written materials, and films. Important work was done on the Japanese by Ruth Benedict and her associates. Their insight made it possible to understand the culturally based behavior of the Japanese during the U.S. liberation of Pacific islands. It also helped prepare for the postwar occupation of Japan and influenced the decision not to depose Emperor Hirohito (see Benedict 1946; Mead 1979; Mead and Métraux 1953; Yans-McLaughlin 1980).

Through the Smithsonian Institution and the Social Science Research Council, anthropologists established databases relevant to small-scale societies that the Allies were encountering in their war efforts. Some anthropologists used their anthropological knowledge while serving in the military. For instance, Demitri Shimkin, as an officer in the U.S. Army Intelligence Corps, advised and helped maintain a liaison with Russians in Siberia, especially in transferring military supplies there. Appropriately, Northern Eurasia and its peoples were among Shimkin's many academic specialties.

Exceptionally painful for social scientists and many people in the United States was the wartime relocation of 110,000 Japanese Americans from California to the American Southwest. Also present in Canada, this discrimination did not extend to citizens descended from other "enemy" nationalities. It was generated by misguided motives of some overly influential generals and commercial interests on the West Coast. To administer this regrettable policy, the War Relocation Authority (WRA) was established. According to Spicer (1979), the agency did not have a concentration-camp mentality but, instead, tried to make the best of a very bad policy and intended to relocate and integrate Japanese Americans back into society as soon as possible. Relocation camps were viewed only as temporary way stations, to be dismantled quickly when feasible. Yet some (Willis 1974) harshly criticize anthropological participation in this program as collusion with imperialism.

One of the camps was established under the joint authority of the WRA and the BIA on an Indian reservation at Poston on the Colorado River. John Collier arranged to have an applied social science unit established there under the direction of psychiatrist/anthropologist Alexander Leighton and anthropologists Edward H. Spicer and Elizabeth Colson. Just as the unit was being established, major conflicts occurred among the residents and also between the residents and the bureaucrats. Leighton and colleagues were put to the test in resolving these issues. Later Leighton (1945), in his *Governing of Men,* wrote of the insights gained under a theoretical framework explicating social stress.

The use of applied social scientists, including thirteen other anthropologists, such as Margaret Lantis and Weston Labarre, increased with the establishment of the Bureau of Sociological Research and the Community Analysis Section, which were carefully integrated into the total program. Both units reported to John Provinse, an anthropologist operating at the highest levels of the WRA. The units formulated and monitored policies and acted as cross-cultural interpreters (for more information, see Spicer 1952, 1979; Leighton 1945).

One immediate aftermath of World War II was the use of anthropological expertise in the administration of the Trust Territory of Micronesia, including the islands of Truk, Yap, Palau, Ponape, and the Marshalls. The work had begun during the war when anthropologists George P. Murdock and Felix Keesing provided background and intelligence materials to the U.S. Navy for the eventual liberation of the islands from the Japanese. Right after the war, an extensive program of anthropological background research began. In 1951 the Navy turned the Trust Territory over to the Department of the Interior. In both administrations, several dozen anthropologists served as researchers and district anthropologists, providing in-depth studies of problems associated with relocation, devastated economies, communication, housing, and other topics. They supervised particular tasks, such as arranging for wages and royalties from development to go to clans instead of individuals. Some prominent anthropologists who served in these applied roles included Ward Goodenough, Homer Barnett, David Schneider, Philip Drucker, Douglas Oliver, and Thomas Gladwin (for more details, see Barnett 1956; Fischer 1979).

Academic Applied Anthropology and Consulting for Development, 1950–1970

After the war, anthropologists returned to universities. Because of the tremendous expansion in higher education that continued through the 1960s, anthropologists had many opportunities for career advancement, and research grants for scholarly studies were readily accessible. There was also growing disillusionment about associating with policy makers and the possible corrupted use of scientific information. Two things contributed to this 1950s pessimism—the dropping of atomic bombs on Japan and Joseph McCarthy's attacks on left-leaning intellectuals, scholars, and artists (Yans-McLaughlin 1980).

Academic anthropology flourished. More domains of study, such as economic, political, medical, and urban anthropology; enculturation; and education, were either initiated or became more sophisticated. Important new methodological contributions, such as network and componential analyses, were developed, and the collection of sophisticated ethnographic information greatly expanded.

Applied anthropology did not disappear during this era. Working out of university settings, an effective minority of anthropologists did applied anthropology largely on a part-time, consulting, and public-service basis. Work continued with Native North Americans. Anthropologists served as expert witnesses on behalf of tribes making land claims before the U.S. Indian Land Claims Commission (see Lurie 1955) and spoke in defense of religious freedoms as associated with the Native American Church or Peyote Cult (see Stewart 1983).

It was on behalf of American Indians that *Action Anthropology* was devised by Sol Tax. In 1948 Tax had begun a field school for six University of Chicago graduate students at the Fox or Mesquawkie Indian reservation in Iowa. He saw the Fox informants as *coinvestigators* and the investigators as *students* of the Fox. The approach was to engage the Fox themselves in the fieldwork, to establish with them the directions in which their society was going, what their principal needs were, and then attach value and priority to them. Together, they were to engage in action after determining desired courses of action. The beliefs and opinions of the Fox always had precedence over any suggestions by outside investigators. Projects included a craft industry centered around the designs of a talented artist and a program for Fox students to attend college (see Tax 1958; Gearing 1960; Peattie 1960; Piddington 1960).

Another historically significant project, with a different approach, was the Vicos Project directed by Allan Holmberg. Holmberg (1958) refers to his method as the "Research and Development" approach to change. Definitely a form of interventionist strategy, it is based on the assumptions that progress can be made toward the realization of human dignity and that people can use scientific knowledge to further social goals. Here, power and knowledge gained from research were used by social scientists to improve the lives of a dominated and impoverished people. Power was to be gradually shared until the scientists could completely devolve it to community members. In the case of Vicos, community-based research was used to identify desired changes; the results of the changes were monitored for further refinement or use elsewhere.

This experiment is not likely to be repeated today. Through funds from the Cornell University Board of Governors, Holmberg purchased a lease on a 40,000-acre Peruvian hacienda that included almost 2,000 Quechua serfs whose ancestors had been bonded to the land for about 400 years. Previously, serfs had to provide weekly labor to the patron. The medieval-like serfdom had left Vicos residents with the lowest economic, health, and political status in Peru. The Vicos experiment, 1952–1957, was supported by Peruvian anthropologists and the Peruvian Indianist Institute. In the end, the people of Vicos were allowed to buy out their own lease, thus achieving autonomy from the hacienda system. Along the way, much was accomplished. Scientists and villagers collaborated to establish a local authority system and gained collective ownership of the manor land. Profits were used for the public good. Schooling increased significantly; economic production by individual families went up four or five times, and a new clinic improved health. The Vicos Project remains a unique and fascinating project in applied anthropology. Yet it raises questions about ethics and styles of intervention still discussed in classrooms. Was it too paternalistic? Was it proper for anthropologists to conduct experiments of any kind?

Development, both for impoverished American communities and through U.S.-sponsored international aid programs, was a major focus for some university-based anthropologists. Cornell University's anthropology program, under the direction of Alexander Leighton, Morris Opler, John Adair, and Allan Holmberg, along with Edward H. Spicer and colleagues at the University of Arizona, were leaders in these areas. One especially important contribution was Spicer's (1952) edited collection, *Human Problems in Technological Change,* which systematically explored the unintended consequences of community modernization and technological intervention in India, Australia, Micronesia, Alaska, and the American Southwest. A related approach was taken by George Foster at Berkeley (1962, 1969), who outlined the significant dimensions of social and cultural change; cultural, psychological, and social barriers to planned change; and possible stimulants for positive change. Foster consulted with United Nations and U.S. aid agencies for several decades especially on the interplay between Western medical systems and indigenous health beliefs and practices (see Foster and Anderson 1978). Other landmarks were Margaret Mead's *Cultural Patterns and Technological Change* (1955), and *New Lives for Old* (1956), Charles J. Erasmus' (1961) critique of U.S. aid programs, and Edward Hall's (1959) advice on the subtleties of cross-cultural encounters.

Of all of the anthropological overviews of development, the most influential may have been Ward Goodenough's (1963) *Cooperation in Change,* which charts the fundamental factors of culture, society, values, beliefs, identity, and the principal dimensions of change that may face development agents. Its anthropological expertise is blended with a psychological and cognitive approach focusing on factors such as identity that helps agents of change anticipate obstacles as well as recognize opportunities for initiating change. Goodenough underscores the necessity to understand wants and needs as perceived by the local people. Using Anthony F. C. Wallace's (1956) concept of revitalization movements, he suggests that development works best, if at all, when its agents conform to strongly felt local needs that are ideologically or even religiously driven by the desire for improvement.

Applied Anthropology in Canada

Canadian applied anthropology developed much later because, until the 1960s, there were few anthropologists in a vast country. It was sustained only by the ethnographic and archaeological activities of the National Museum in Ottawa, two widely separated small departments of anthropology (Toronto and British Columbia), and a handful of social anthropologists scattered within sociology departments.

The first notable applied work in Canada was done by Harry Hawthorn of the University of British Columbia. In 1947, he arranged a conference of British Columbian Indian chiefs to discuss issues of Indian welfare and how anthropologists could contribute. This effort continued during the 1950s through government-commissioned studies of the conditions of British Columbian Indians, the feasibility of extending federal Social Security benefits to Indians (Hawthorn et al. 1958), and a special study of the social conditions of the conflict between a culturally distinct religious sect, the Doukabhours, and mainstream rural residents of interior British Columbia (Hawthorn 1955).

Another 1950s hallmark of Canadian applied anthropology was the establishment of the longitudinal Stirling County Study of community mental health in southern Nova Scotia. This interdisciplinary applied research program was developed by Alexander and Dorothea Leighton (Leighton 1959). Although American, the Leightons maintained very close collaborative links with Canadian researchers. Some significant leaders in Canadian anthropology, including Marc-Adélard Tremblay (see Hughes et al. 1960), got their starts through this project. Tremblay (1990) went on to found the modern Quebec version of social anthropology and participated in many other applied projects.

One of these projects was done jointly with Harry Hawthorn in the 1960s. In 1961 the Canadian Indian Act was revised to discontinue earlier repressions such as outlawing the Potlatch and Sun Dance. Indians were granted citizenship and more opportunities to participate in the larger society. Following this legislation, Hawthorn and Tremblay (Hawthorn et al. 1967) along with fifty other researchers conducted a countrywide survey examining social, political, economic, and cultural conditions with recommendations to the federal government. During the same period, a series of applied anthropological studies was done in Canada's Arctic and Subarctic territories to advise the government on aspects of development (see, for instance, Vallee 1962; van Stone 1963).

Most significant, though, was the remarkable growth of anthropology in Canada during the 1960s. Where there had been only two departments at the beginning of the decade, there were twenty-six as well as thirteen augmented departments of sociology and anthropology by the end of the 1960s with corresponding increases in the number of anthropologists and their work. Through the 1970s and 1980s, the domains of application rapidly expanded in areas such as indigenous self-determination and land uses (see Freeman 1976; Salisbury 1986), multiculturalism, immigration, and refugee resettlement (Buchignani 1982; Gilad 1990), agriculture (Ervin 1985; Hedley 1976), mining (Rouse 1993) and fishing (Anderson 1978; Davis 1989), medical anthropology (O'Neil et al. 1993), and other topics. In the 1990s, applied anthropology in Canada was proportionately on a rough par with the United States. Its relative strengths today are the development of anthropological advocacy and participatory-action research. Its weaknesses are gaps in the development of specific application-oriented training programs and a relative lack of interest in fostering the practicing domain (see Ervin 1997a for more details).

The Emergence of the "New Applied Anthropology" of Policy and Practice: 1970 to the Present

Michael Angrosino (1976) refers to the "New Applied Anthropology," an anthropology that focuses on policy and practice. This multifaceted approach emerged during the early 1970s, became crystallized in the 1980s, and is currently receiving even more attention.

Its foundations were laid in the 1960s, which saw a rising public consciousness of social issues. This was an era of anti-imperialistic struggles, manifested in the emergence of nationalism, the establishment of new African States, the Cold War, and the outbreak of nationalistic wars like Vietnam. Domestically, it was expressed through movements focusing on civil rights, feminism, gay rights, environmentalism, and Native self-determination as well as a growing awareness of the negative consequences of development, consumerism, enforced dependencies, and ravages of the environment. The 1960s were years of significant social criticism as well as confidence in the possibilities for humane and effective public policy.

This resulted in an unparalleled period of growth and activity for the social sciences. In both Canada and the United States, increases in university enrollments were phenomenal. Anthropology, one of the smallest of disciplines, benefited from a great hiring boom in universities. Many students entered graduate school, and many new M.A. and Ph.D. programs were established. Anthropologists did an enormous amount of productive research in this era. Growing numbers of students and faculty brought strongly felt pressures for relevance and attention to social responsibilities.

It was becoming clear that anthropologists could no longer study or conceptualize isolated communities with undisturbed traditional cultures and social structures. Nor could social scientists comfortably expect to attach themselves to the status quo. Some called for social science models that explained or critiqued social inequalities, social conflict, revolution, illness, and urban migration and emphasized commitment and advocacy for the oppressed (see Berreman 1968; Gjessing 1968; Gough 1968; Hymes 1974). The actual results of this foment fell short of the original hopes and, sometimes, radical visions, although there was doubtless some shifting of consciousness toward the aspirations of the oppressed and colonialized.

During that time, many anthropologists got drawn into applied activities on a part-time basis, sometimes being called upon for advice by government or international aid agencies. This situation arose largely because of the cultural and linguistic knowledge that anthropologists had about specific groups affected by policy proposals that included the building of dams, extensions of health care or education, attempts to introduce market crops, proposals for relocation, campaigns to get local people to participate in literacy and disease control campaigns, and many other projects. More significantly, anthropologists frequently became involved in working for groups affected by proposed development. This was so especially in North America as such groups became more organized in attempts at resistance or self-determination. The involvement might be motivated by humanitarian concerns or by a recognition that they owed their burgeoning academic careers to the cooperation of the peoples they studied. Many anthropologists adopted a style of application combining expertise with advocacy and learned to take more subordinate or background roles as the indigenous leaders of such movements found their own voices in policy arenas. Among anthropologists, the importance of self-determination and consultation was more firmly established.

Urban problems surrounding poverty and racism became a research and applied topic for anthropologists (see Valentine 1968). In addition, many members of minorities were now becoming social scientists and working with formal organizations devoted to helping impoverished minority peoples. In a few large departments, such as those at Cornell, Chicago, U.C.L.A., Arizona, Columbia, McGill, Illinois, Pennsylvania, Berkeley, and North Carolina, some distinguished faculty continued to provide role models of application.

Then another factor entered into the picture. Large numbers of people were graduating with Ph.D.'s and M.A.'s in anthropology, but the available academic positions had been filled as of the early 1970s. Often by choice as well as necessity, many graduates sought other jobs, and this crisis of hiring led to a surge of creativity among anthropologists in opening new niches of practice. Many entered government; others began working for international development agencies, private companies, and nonprofit human service agencies; still others went into business for themselves as consultants. Some were hired by universities but in settings in which their knowledge was used for practical tasks or training. Schools of medicine, architecture, social work, nursing, and public health provided some new jobs. Some anthropologists saw the practical value of second graduate degrees, often a master's in public health or urban planning. Many of these pioneers upgraded their skills on the job, developing competence in their domains of practice but also in quantitative methodologies and interdisciplinary fields like program evaluation and social impact assessment.

At the same time, the social and policy sciences or professions were undergoing a convergence that would make anthropological approaches less marginal. Here was the arena for the discussions of organizational and corporate cultures that were common in the early to mid-1980s (see Peters and Waterman 1982). It was recognized that an organization's effectiveness depended on the nature of its collective values, which were not necessarily products of rational, technocratic, or standard ways of organizing businesses or institutions. Although anthropologists may justly criticize these excursions into "corporate culture" as superficial poaching into anthropological domains, nonetheless, they may have helped to bring about a wider understanding of the value of anthropological-like investigations.

Also crucial to a new applied anthropology of policy and practice was the establishment of specialized training programs for work in nonacademic and nontraditional anthropology. Anthropology programs tended to beget other academic anthropologists. The pioneers in practicing niches reported that they had to learn many things through an enormous amount of on-the-job training. They also had to shed many academic habits. As a result some people started to consider other forms of explicitly practical training. One of the first of these was established in the late 1960s—a program in applied anthropology at the University of Kentucky. Then in an attempt to more directly prepare anthropologists for service for society, the first training program for nonacademic practitioners was established at the University of South Florida in Tampa in 1974. Conceived and implemented by Gilbert Kushner and his colleagues, most prominently Alvin Wolfe, Robert Wulff, and Erve Chambers, that program at first emphasized the specialty tracks of urban and medical anthropology as well as cultural resource management or public archaeology. Students learned the core literature of issues and theory for each of their practical tracks as well as applied methods from anthropology and interdisciplinary contexts. Students also took courses from relevant cognate areas such as urban planning or public health. Capping the training was an internship program in which the students worked on a problem defined and completed in collaboration with an institution or agency. The product was both an agency report and an M.A. thesis. Later the South Florida department instituted a Ph.D. program in applied anthropology along the same lines. By now about thirty departments in the United States have similar programs, for the most part, at the M.A. level (for more information on training programs see Kushner 1994; Kushner and Wolfe 1993; Trotter 1988; Wolfe et al. 1981; see also the web site for the Applied Anthropology Computer Network, ANTHAP, at http://www.acs.oakland.edu/~dow/anthap.htm).

During the 1980s, textbooks by Chambers (1985) and van Willigen (1986) effectively charted the new field of policy and practice for the first time. The Society for Applied Anthropology supplemented *Human Organization* by sponsoring a second journal, *Practicing*

Anthropology (also innovated at the University of South Florida), that was devoted to the experiences of applied anthropologists outside of academic settings. In the early 1980s, the American Anthropological Association developed a new unit, the National Association for the Practice of Anthropology, for similar purposes.

Summary

For students of applied anthropology, this history is important for several reasons. For one, some of the approaches of earlier applied anthropologists are still strikingly insightful (see Goodenough 1963, for example). Although additional positive lessons can be learned from these examples, aspiring applied anthropologists need to be alerted to the pitfalls and occasional excesses of the past, especially those associated with paternalism and colonialism. Those warnings are appropriate in a subject that requires scrupulous attention to matters of social responsibility. A history of application is also significant, because the reader gains insight about the shifts in topical interests and the steady opening of new domains for practice—ranging from colonialized tribal societies to complex organizations in modern societies.

The rest of the book examines the essential ingredients of the new applied anthropology of policy and practice. As Chambers (1987) reminds us, it still can be conceived as a work in progress.

RECOMMENDED READINGS

Chambers, Erve
1987   Applied Anthropology in the Post-Vietnam Era: Anticipations and Ironies. *Annual Review of Anthropology,* Vol. 66: 309–337.

Clifton, James A. (ed.)
1970   *Readings in the Uses of the Sciences of Man.* New York: Houghton Mifflin.

Ervin, Alexander M.
1997   Anthropological Practice in Anglophone Canada: Multiculturalism, Indigenous Rights and Mainstream Policy Potentials. In *The Global Practice of Anthropology.* Edited by Marietta Baba and Carole E. Hill. Pp. 47–81. Williamsburg, VA: College of William and Mary.

Goldschmidt, Walter (ed.)
1979   *The Uses of Anthropology.* Washington, DC: Special Publication No. 11 of the American Anthropological Association.

Partridge, William L., and Elizabeth M. Eddy
1986   The Development of Applied Anthropology in America. In *Applied Anthropology in America.* Second Edition. Edited by Elizabeth M. Eddy and William L. Partridge. Pp. 3–56. New York: Columbia University Press.

van Willigen, John
1991   *Anthropology in Use: A Sourcebook on Anthropological Practice.* Boulder, CO: Westview.
1993   The Development of Applied Anthropology. In *Applied Anthropology: An Introduction.* Pp. 17–41. Westport, CT: Bergin and Garvey.

CHAPTER

3 Ethics in Applied Research and Practice

The practice of anthropology requires scrupulous attention to ethics. Much is at stake—the research, recommendations, advocacy, and policy implementations directly affect real people. So it is essential that applied anthropologists be aware of all the fine points of acceptable behavior for their work. In framing a discussion for anthropologists, I focus on some very specific and widely held principles of ethics within formal codes. I will also outline some special problems and guidelines that have been identified as particular to practice in nonacademic settings. It is useful to begin by considering the potential publics or interests to which anthropologists have obligations. These publics come into varying degrees of prominence as anthropologists have to make decisions of an ethical nature.

The Host Community

Many assume that the most crucial party is the *host community* or *society*. Certain groups or categories of people are the intended beneficiaries of new policies or existing services. The applied anthropologist has to develop some type of liaison with those groups. The "host" might be a small-scale community in the classical sense—people who live in an identifiable location, are relatively homogeneous, and have a sense of solidarity.

Yet even small-scale communities or societies will have some degree of heterogeneity. There will always be differences in power relations and expectations for policies. For instance, during the mid-1970s in Subarctic Canada, communities were researched and public hearings were held about the desirability of building oil and gas pipelines. There were some marked divisions based on ethnicity, socioeconomic status, occupation, and other variables. These all influenced opinions on the prospect of pipelines being built near their communities. Some, mainly white businessmen and Métis (mixed white and Native), supported the notion because it would bring jobs and profits. Dene (northern Native people) opposed the proposals because pipelines would interfere with trapping and traditional land rights that had yet to be legally clarified.

When it comes to large-scale, urban communities, there are obviously even more publics with divergent interests. For instance, impoverished Native migrants to cities may have some features in common with recently arrived immigrants or refugees living in the same poor neighborhoods. Ostensibly they have similar needs for social services or health facilities, but usually there are also some important cultural differences. Anglo policy makers may make erroneous assumptions because notions of "multiculturalism" or shared "cultures" of poverty imply that they can design umbrella programs that aim to cover the needs of many minority and marginalized peoples at the same time. Yet attempts to implement a homogeneous policy could lead to more damage than benefits. Practicing anthropologists have to be mindful of such potential mistakes.

Other challenges may face practitioners when the people in question do not actually form a community at all. Chronically ill children at risk of death, single parents, or battered women are not actual subcommunities. Organized communities have more effective ways of responding to what they consider inappropriate behavior by researchers or practicing anthropologists. Isolated individuals represented in categories do not. So anthropologists should view them *as if* they were communities, to exercise a set of checks and balances on their own behavior.

Most anthropologists would agree that the host community (and by implication its individual members) should come first in any ethical considerations. Sorting out this responsibility is complex but essential.

The Client

The next major interest to consider is the *client*, the person, agency, or organization that has commissioned and is paying for the work. It is very convenient and much simpler if the client is also the host community. Then, at least at the beginning and perhaps at some later stages of the work, anthropologists can hope that they are doing "good works"—providing insight, testimony, and recommendations that the host community can use to its advantage. But, as already suggested, the "host" community may be highly fragmented and factionalized. What is more, elected officials of the community or the boards of a self-help organization might not always represent the best interests of their constituents.

More frequently the client is a third party providing services to a host community population. A familiar scenario is that of a government agency seeking information through research. Or the client may be a nongovernment organization such as a charitable foundation or a nonprofit social or health service agency such as a family service bureau. It could be a union seeking to expand its membership and anticipate the needs of some yet-to-be-organized category of workers. Corporations may wish to have marketing research done, set up a branch plant in some new region, or improve productivity among their workers.

There is always a possibility that the relationships between the supposed beneficiaries and the client are not very good. In fact, there may be a history of perceived abuses or misunderstandings. Although the proposed research may be earnestly intended to improve a bad situation, it may sometimes be better that the practitioner/researcher *does not* participate in the project because he lacks the means to bring about a solution or an understanding. Often though, the situation is not that extreme and there may be an equally good reason to get involved. The practitioner might have the mediation skills needed or be able to develop an effective research design to the satisfaction and benefit of all parties.

The practitioner must realize that he will have a contractual relationship with the client. That contract may even legally supersede any strongly felt obligations to the researched host community. Conflicts between the anthropologists' responsibilities to hosts and clients may be the most common ethical dilemma in applied anthropology. For that reason, an effective, ethically informed contract is crucial to whatever unfolds during the rest of the work. Anthropologists have a strong obligation to inform the clients about essential ingredients of anthropological ethics, such as informed consent and confidentiality, the nature of anthropological research, and changing ethical climates.

The client is not always a homogeneous unit either. There may be differing points of view among individuals or subagencies of the same institution. More delicacy and care is required when a number of clients are in partnership for the same research. This can happen, say, when a state or federal government may be engaged in partnership with a nongovernment organization, a tribal government, and a specific community in an applied project for which the anthropologist is hired.

The Profession of Anthropology

The third general party toward which the applied anthropologist should feel some responsibility is the *discipline and profession of anthropology*. This responsibility is complex and layered. First, there is the subject of anthropology itself—its reputable name should be upheld. More controversially for applied anthropology, there is an expectation that all findings should ultimately be shared through books, articles, and conference publications, but that may breach obligations to host communities or clients who consider themselves owners of confidential information. The applied anthropologist, with the permission of his or her hosts/clients, might instead publish articles that describe methodology and sketch very broad dimensions of the domain under question but leave many important and interesting details out of the equation. Many of the most important and significant applied studies may never reach a general anthropological audience. There is another aspect to this—the applied or practicing anthropologist may be too busy doing the actual work to find the time to publish it. Lamentably, the most significant proportion of the applied anthropological literature may remain buried in technical or classified reports.

We also have responsibilities to each other as colleagues. Applied and practicing anthropology tends to be collaborative, rarely employing the solitary approach of academic ethnographic fieldwork. Practicing anthropologists share research tasks with each other as well as practitioners from other fields; they jointly analyze and write up the data and frequently have partnerships within consulting firms. These responsibilities also extend to other colleagues who may not be anthropologists. These could be consultants from other applied social, health, and educational sciences, as well as members of the more technical professions such as engineering, biology, and agronomy. Then there are the research assistants who may be undergraduate or graduate students of anthropology. Practitioners have obligations to act responsibly to them—effectively mentoring them, protecting them from dangers and health hazards, not exploiting them in their work, giving them proper credit, and seeing that they are properly remunerated.

Finally, there are situations in which research colleagues are members of the host community or client organization. This generates a whole new set of responsibilities, including proper training, proper credit, and protection of such colleagues from potential negative repercussions from their community or organization. When the anthropologist is in charge, he or she is obliged to ensure ethical practice among such local colleagues with respect to their own community.

The General Public

Another highly significant party is the *public*. It should be kept informed of strategic and useful information about important issues. A host of opportunities and obligations come to mind, attached to issues like poverty, race and ethnic relations, the negative dimensions of development, and historical injustices. The anthropologist may write op-ed pieces, allow him- or herself to be interviewed by the media, appear at public hearings, give talks, and volunteer time to citizens' groups. Advocacy is a part of this expectation. Surprisingly, this general expectation is still underdeveloped in anthropology. Perhaps this comes from the academic antipathy for "popularizing."

Professional Codes of Ethics for Research and Practice

To give substance to this discussion of ethical principles I will draw from three ethical codes established by professional associations. They have been formulated by the Society for Applied Anthropology (1983), the National Association for the Practice of Anthropology (1988), and the Society of Applied Anthropology in Canada (1983). There is a certain amount of overlap among them, which means that there has been consistency of experience and opinion from several generations of anthropologists. They can be seen as governed by notions of fairness and the need to protect vulnerable people.

Informed Consent

Informed consent is probably the most significant, although sometimes the most controversial, dimension of ethical expectations for both academic and applied work (see Fluehr-Lobban 1994, 1996; Herrera 1996; Wax 1995, 1996). When research is being done, the subjects should be fully aware of it; anthropological work should not be clandestine. Permission to proceed must be sought. What topics are they planning to investigate? Who will receive the results? All of the major questions that will be asked should be revealed at the beginning. The explicit purposes of the research should be disclosed in any applied project. Finally, the people involved should know all of the potential benefits and risks of participation.

On some occasions, the process of permission seeking is straightforward. When dealing with Indian reservations or small Arctic villages, informed consent must be received through tribal or village councils. Research within formal organizations such as corporations, unions, government agencies, or nonprofit organizations requires formal permission through official channels. Within an organization, the enquiry may pertain to clients, employees, or all conceivable participants, including management, board, and other decision makers. Such communities or organizations tend to carefully scrutinize the risks and benefits of participation. Gatekeepers in formal organizations can be suspicious of outsiders' intentions, especially those framed through research designs. They want to know the full details and the consequences of their participation. They tend to be more inclined to refuse permission than to consent, taking the approach "that it is better to be safe than sorry." They may act this way because they cannot truly assess the long-term consequences on their funding and reputation if they participate.

The "Clinical" Model of Informed Consent

Beyond community or organizational research, certain aspects of informed consent from individuals have proven problematic for anthropologists in recent years. Universities, research foundations, governments, and other sponsors of research have required that social scientists, including anthropologists, provide assurance of the ethical foundations of their research. But in designing these safeguards, the standards have most frequently been derived from those of clinical and experimental sciences. In such controlled settings, researchers might, for instance, seek volunteers to test new drugs and therapeutic procedures or to participate in experiments that might attempt to measure their resistance or reactions to pain; their attitudes toward sensitive subjects such as sexuality, drug use, or self-esteem; or their mental or physical performance.

Such research may reveal knowledge construed as valuable for humanity as a whole. In the case of drug trials or of new psychological therapies, there might be some direct benefits to subjects. Yet there may also be huge possibilities for abuse or damage. What would be the effect of exposing people (especially children) to pictures of acts of sexuality or of mutilated bodies? What unknown side effects might be the result of participating in trials for a new drug? How might the participants feel about participating in drug trials if they learn that there is a 50 percent chance that they might be taking placebos? What are the effects on the dignity and feelings of the self-worth of individuals who are being manipulated for research purposes? Surely, volunteers have a right to know everything that is going on: what is to be asked of them and what is going to be done to them. They need to know, in as much detail as possible, about the known risks and benefits of participation. The researcher also has to clearly explain unexpected risks to the participants, so that they know they are taking chances.

To satisfy an ethics review committee, there are two particular requirements. One is a succinct document that, in laymen's language, explains the research purposes, methods, and design; details what exactly is expected of the participants; and clearly notes risks and benefits. The second document is a very short form letter with blank spaces for names and dates to be signed by the participants in the experiment, indicating that they are aware of what is going to happen to them and that they have been made aware of the risks and benefits of participation. It should contain wording to the effect that the subject is willing to allow the information to be used, analyzed, and written about in books, reports, articles, and conference presentations. This is a legal contract between the researcher and the research participant or subject. If there is a breach of this agreement, the researcher and the sponsoring institute can be sued.

This procedure is necessary for the protection of all concerned in risky experimental and clinical research. Furthermore, the balance of power is not equal between the experimenter/clinician and the research participant in those situations. The former has completely defined and controlled the whole setting and activities, which are not natural ones that the participants would normally engage in or feel comfortable doing. The rest of what transpires is by definition "controlled." The only real power that the subject or respondent has is to quit.

We may ask if these circumstances apply to the anthropologist and his or her informants in the field. There are differences between these clinical contracts and ethnographic work. In ethnography the settings are natural—communities, neighborhoods—and the anthropologists are strangers or outsiders. *They* have to make adjustments, often as barely tolerated intruders, sometimes as welcome guests. If the anthropologist is mistrusted or viewed as a source of irritation, he or she may be asked to leave. Or peoples' body language or other evidence of their disdain may make the anthropologist so uncomfortable she will leave as soon as she can.

There are subtle complexities to fitting into the community. Many anthropologists may become persistent and "thick-skinned," and, exercising perseverance, they may remain in spite of discomfort. There is also the possibility, although much rarer these days, that the members of the community will tolerate and comply with the anthropologist's research out of a generalized fear, because the anthropologist is seen as a representative or agent of a more powerful and potentially threatening cosmopolitan society. Much more positively and more frequently, the anthropologist is welcomed as an equal co-investigator/consultant in a village or community that is researching its own conditions for practical reasons, especially when the project has been designed with maximum consultation. But what all of this tells us is that anthropologists rarely have any power over their subjects in the sense that clinicians do.

Other problems have to do with the open-ended nature of most anthropological research. Ethnography is highly inductive and not very sequential or linear, and there are constant shifts in research topics. Anthropologists often have to drop an activity or a methodological approach when a new unexpected lead or event occurs. They often find that their initial set of research topics, let alone all the specific questions to be asked of people, is meaningless and has to be reformulated. Even when they have a good idea of what the general research or policy questions are, it is most often not until they have been on the site for a while that they can ascertain what is important to the topics. If they have initially gone through the standardized exercise of informed consent, it could turn out to be a form of inadvertent deception, because the whole research design has to change. Anthropologists need the latitude to readjust their vision of what they are doing.

Also, consider how the anthropologist typically gains information during fieldwork. Although formal interviews, questionnaires, and systematic observations of specified events are possible, most of the work consists of unexpected and seemingly random encounters, observations, and conversations. The researcher observes a social encounter here, attends a ceremony there, and has frequent casual conversations, in which a normal range of pleasantries and small talk is embedded. Within these situations, the ethnographer extracts a sprinkling of observations and opinions pertaining to the main research questions. How can the anthropologist administer informed consent within the ebb and flow of such encounters?

There is another subtle dimension to this, especially when anthropologists are working in cross-cultural settings where there is already some degree of tension. Approaching a potential informant with a long list of risks and benefits as well as a legal release consent form is like "Mirandaizing" the person. I take the analogy from the *Miranda* decision of the U.S. Supreme Court, which was meant to protect recently arrested people from being manipulated into making statements that could be construed as confessions without the presence of a lawyer and full knowledge of their legal rights. Consider the typical cop show on TV; it frequently shows the detectives arresting a suspect, handcuffing him, and reading him his rights, "You have a right to remain silent. . . . Anything you say may be used against you in a court of law. . . ." Forewarned, the prisoner usually remains silent for his own good. Presenting the documents pertaining to informed consent to potential participants in our type of research can result in the same kind of response of "better safe than sorry." Approaching someone in the field with these documents is a very awkward social encounter. It creates enormous problems for the anthropologist.

However, we still need to consider this dilemma from the point of view of our potential collaborators and informants. Here, I give several examples from my own fieldwork in Alaska and Northern Canada.

Years ago when I did my first fieldwork, I was one evening the guest of an Inuit couple. Unexpectedly, they got into an argument over some very personal matters. Yet within their angry dialogue were some very interesting opinions and facts directly relevant to my research. All of a sudden there was a lull, and both of them turned to me. The wife said, "Sandy, you are not going to write notes on this, are you?" They knew I was doing research but had let their guard down and were treating me like a trusted friend. I did not write field notes on this encounter because they explicitly asked me not to, but I would certainly otherwise have done so.

Another much more serious example occurred when I was doing field research on the process of Native urbanization in Fairbanks, Alaska. A Native friend, in a state of distress, told me a tale of transgression that had led the members of his community to ostracize him for the rest of his life. It was a fascinating tale of the still-existing operation of traditional Alaskan Native justice systems, but I did not record this conversation because of the vulnerable position it put both of us in.

A chilling reality for anthropologists in the United States is that, like journalists, anthropologists can have their notes and testimony subpoenaed by a court of law, even across borders. About five years ago, a Canadian anthropologist was doing research, using a life-history approach, about a religion that was rapidly growing among black inmates in both Canadian and American prisons. She had gained the trust and informed consent of prisoners in a northern state. In a fishing expedition, state prosecutors looking for evidence about some unsolved crimes had requested the extradition of her field notes and potentially the anthropologist herself to testify. As far as I know, she and her lawyers had successfully resisted the extradition, but this was a close call—one that could affect us all.

From these anecdotes, it should be clear that informed consent is no simple, straightforward matter. How do we accomplish this, given all the problems that I have indicated as emerging from the clinical/experimental approach taken by ethical review committees? My basic answer is that, for the time being, we should learn to live with the sometimes draconian regulations of ethical review boards because we have no choice. These requirements are often legal ones, and they do ultimately protect both the anthropologist and the research subjects. They force us to carefully scrutinize the consequences of our proposed research. They compel us to be proactive and anticipate possibilities, and that, in itself, is good.

Furthermore, these days anthropologists are making more direct use of questionnaires, relatively structured questioning in key-informant interviews, and group-interviewing techniques. It is easier to anticipate how such methodologies will be conducted and what the risks and benefits will be. In applied or practicing situations, it is rare for people to go into a fieldwork situation simply to do open-ended participant observation. Applied anthropologists, especially when they are operating with specific policy objectives, need to know what they are looking for. In most cases, they also have to have a relatively thorough understanding of the society and phenomena in question. Accordingly, it should be possible to anticipate many more eventualities in research design than was once the case.

At the same time, as he or she complies with standards based on clinical research, each anthropologist should try to educate ethical review committees about the special circumstances facing anthropologists in field research to persuade them to consider more flexible but effective ways of dealing with informed consent in real-world settings. In the meantime, we should continue to search for alternative models to provide complete assurance of meaningful informed consent. Most of our other ethical expectations hinge on this very real issue.

Confidentiality and Personal Rights to Privacy

The researcher or practitioner should ensure that the actual names of the participants or informants will not be used in any reports or publications. When informants' comments or behaviors are described in reports, they should be disguised so that the identities of individuals cannot be guessed. Potential informants should not feel the need to give in to overly persistent researchers. The usual approach also requires that anthropologists not divulge information about them and their opinions to other members of their own community, officials, or those who might have commissioned the study. Informants are frequently given pseudonyms in reports or monographs. Sometimes, to illustrate circumstances and opinions, composite semifictional informants or participants may be created using real situations to illustrate appropriate points. This is unusual in social science in general but considered perfectly acceptable in anthropology if used sparingly and carefully.

It is a frequent practice not to directly identify the community or organization in which the research is located. Again the standard approach is to use a pseudonym to protect the community from any negative consequences. This device is never completely foolproof because many people, especially policy makers, who are interested in the local issues might be able to identify the community anyway from clues in the report or simply because they knew that the research was being done there. There is also a drawback to this practice. When the community's name has been disguised, the knowledge contained in the report cannot be used by other researchers as part of an accumulating body of data about that community or region. It may be a crucial impediment in the growth of an effective policy science if that information about ongoing events and long-term trends is valuable.

Yet what is most important in maintaining confidentiality is the protection of individuals and potentially vulnerable subgroups. The most serious ethical difficulties and potential negative consequences could come from the breaches of the twin concerns of confidentiality and informed consent.

Dissemination of Knowledge

In the academic world, anthropologists have an ethical obligation to make their knowledge widely known. In many instances in the applied realm, the knowledge is potentially significant for policy that could have positive or negative consequences for many people. It is assumed that there should be no secrecy. It is also assumed that the community or segment of society that was researched should have full access to any reports written about it. The report should be framed in accessible language. In the North American context, that usually means standard grade ten English, but it might also require that a report or a significant abstract of it be written in the local language. Several colleagues have done applied research in the Northwest Territories of Canada, which have a very strict ordinance governing research done in communities with large proportions of speakers of Native languages. Researchers are required to have reports, or substantial summaries, translated into Inuktituk or Dene languages. They are also expected to return to the community and attend a town meeting at which findings and recommendations are discussed before they are sent on to the next level of decision-making.

Although most anthropologists would agree that the public "has a right to know" and that there are many benefits to promoting the practical aspects of anthropology, there are several significant exceptions to this rule, some of which are legal requirements. In Chapter 10, we will describe John Peterson Jr.'s (1974) work for the Choctaw Tribal Council. He was not allowed to share his research findings with the public nor even with the discipline of anthropology. Yet most of us can understand that this was essential for his ongoing relations with the Choctaw and, by extension, for anthropology's reputation with Native or Indian communities in North America. Frequently, Native people have felt exploited by research that brings them no benefits or that does not accurately reflect their realities. They may feel publication to be an unwelcome exposure of themselves or an invasion of their privacy.

There are other issues in disseminating applied work. One is that, although research materials should be part of longstanding attempts to resolve particular policy problems—settling land or resource disputes, lobbying for a more effective health care or educational delivery system, and so forth—the data may be tentative or have to remain classified until the issue is settled. Applied work may also be highly sensitive and subject to misinterpretation. For instance, information related to poverty or the family has sometimes been used in inappropriate and ideological ways to suggest associations about drug use or crime that cannot really be proved. In the past, such ideologies have sometimes promoted a "blame the victim" set of explanations.

Serious ethical problems are raised when anthropologists collect ethnographic knowledge about people for clandestine or intelligence purposes. During the 1960s, there was frequent discussion among anthropologists about the large-scale studies commissioned by various branches of the Pentagon on tribal and peasant peoples in Latin America, Southeast Asia, and Africa. These reports remain classified. Ethnographers, because of their particular visions of social responsibilities (and perhaps patriotism), may have felt that they were doing the right thing in doing this work. Others might think differently about the lack of informed consent in them.

A relatively minor breach of ethics can be attributed to this secret research: the researchers failed to contribute to our basic ethnographic knowledge of peoples and culture areas, a basic mandate of anthropology. The information could have stimulated the cumulative advancement of anthropological theory surrounding particular issues. Still, the most serious problem here was that the peoples themselves had no opportunity to assess how they were portrayed. Were there inaccuracies or superficialities leading to inappropriate policies? Was the information placed in the hands of foreign governments that might have had hostile or oppressive intentions toward minority groups?

Related to the presumed desirability of publishing materials in academic or policy journals to benefit the discipline of anthropology, another factor arises. Beyond any restrictions placed by employers, most practicing anthropologists simply do not have the time to publish because they are too busy doing research, consulting and advising, writing new proposals and technical reports, supervising others' work, and managing and planning work that can be used for policy purposes. There is no particular advantage, beyond personal satisfaction, for practicing anthropologists to submit their work to academic journals. Unlike academically based anthropologists, publication does not contribute to gaining tenure, promotion, or merit increments. For academics, these are very meaningful incentives, but for practitioners, the time spent on such articles may actually be costly because of the heavy and constant workload expected by clients or employers or the burdens of consulting work.

Special Concerns and Dilemmas for Practicing Anthropologists

Clearly, the realities of nonacademic practice place very different requirements and pressures upon practitioners. Yet until recently, the significant codes of ethics in the discipline were designed by those with a tenured base of employment in universities and with attitudes shaped by academic agendas even if they have had applied experience. In a volume (Fluehr-Lobban 1991) on ethics in anthropology, Barbara Frankel and M. G. Trend (1991), in an aptly titled article "Principles, Pressures and Paychecks . . . ," explore some of these unresolved issues.

They point out four major differences between pressures placed on practitioners and those placed on academics. The first relates to security. Academic anthropologists usually experience enormous insecurity at the very beginning of their careers. They have to do fieldwork, write their dissertations, and then write articles and books to satisfy stringent peer reviews. After undergoing all of this anxiety

> . . . (if they have published, not perished) they win a lifetime of saying and doing pretty much as they please. It is a career line that trades a life of voluntary poverty for the joys of intellectual freedom and job security. (Frankel and Trend, 185)

For practitioners, job security depends upon pleasing a current employer. The saying "you're only as good as your last project" creates a pressure to produce quickly and to please bosses or clients. Considerable vulnerability is present, because, for instance, many government contractors have built clauses into their contracts whereby the projects can be suddenly terminated merely by giving notice.

The second pressure on practitioners is the realization that knowledge is seen as a means to an end, or a commodity, rather than an important end in itself. Therefore, practical research tends to be directed toward the client's short-term perspective of what he needs to know, not problems or issues that the anthropologists might see as important to investigate from a larger perspective.

Other more serious threats to intellectual integrity are dangers "that short-run goals and a need to maximize profit, minimize costs, or to produce a research product that will satisfy the client" will result in research that could be superficial or even erroneous (Frankel and Trend, 186). This can be even more unsettling when decisions have been made to go ahead with dubious programs and policies, and there are subtle pressures to conform findings to preconceived biases. It creates enormous pressure on practitioners when they are expected to be loyal to the employer and his standards rather than to the standards of truth and scientific integrity as defined by the academic discipline in which the practitioners trained.

A third area relates to sources of self-esteem. Academics receive their rewards and accolades because of products that indicate their skills and successes to other academics and students. They accomplish this through conference papers, lectures, books, and articles. They are rewarded through status, tenure, promotion, and merit increments. The opposite can occur—they might not receive any of these rewards and not have a good reputation. But as Frankel and Trend (187) remind us, after tenure, most of these pressures would be psychological rather than direct threats to security.

The nonacademic practitioners have such pressures in reverse. "Publish or perish" does not hold for them. In fact they may be sanctioned by employers if they publish materials owned by the client. Practitioners have to find substitutes. These may include getting bonuses for acquiring large contracts, hiring more staff, obtaining higher ranks in their organizations, gaining access to power and insider knowledge, and feeling "pride in exhibiting competence in solving a problem for whomever wants it solved and will pay someone to solve it" (Frankel and Trend, 187). There is a danger of taking on research problems for the personal challenge of using one's abilities to solve a problem even when the whole enterprise might be ethically suspect.

The final pressure noted by Frankel and Trend relates to the frequent possibility of losing control over one's work and what is done with it. A report can be written and recommendations made, but there may be no control over what the sponsoring agency or employer does with the work. It may be quite perilous to criticize those in power—what a tenured academic, at least in theory, has a right to do. The loss of control could also come about because the employee has to turn to another project and cannot continue to monitor the results of recommendations from the first project.

The authors leave us with many more questions than answers, but the gist of their article is that we have to rethink, and with a charitable attitude, the ethical requirements and pressures placed on nonacademic practitioners. Our formal ethical codes are sometimes inappropriate to the realities of practice. Yet the nagging question remains—should there be a segregation of academic from practicing anthropologists with each group going its own ethical way?

In the same book, Gilbert, Tashima, and Fishman (1991) further address the concerns of practitioners as opposed to academics. They report on a set of guidelines for ethical practice produced by the National Association for the Practice of Anthropology (1988). The guidelines deal with several issues and place a very large emphasis on accountability.

One issue relates to a recognition that the work of practicing anthropologists can have immediate impact on those with whom anthropologists work or collaborate. There are always pressures for ethnographers in fieldwork situations to consult with people about how they will be represented in final reports. The practitioners have a double burden because they know that the findings could well have direct impacts on people's lives. They are then obligated to assess, as comprehensively as possible, the potential impacts of this research on the group or several groups to be affected. The issue of differential power cannot be ignored. Anthropologists are obliged to discuss this with the affected populations and must do so *before* a contract is signed or a job accepted.

Another issue pertains to the fact that practicing anthropologists are frequently in contact with communities, policy makers, agencies, businesses, and other formal bodies. This sort of visibility carries the responsibility of representing the discipline of anthropology to a larger world. Practitioners cannot escape this obligation and therefore have to be professionally competent in all their activities. The practicing anthropologist cannot escape to the relative shelter of the university. He or she has to meet and satisfy, or be confronted by, the various stakeholders and parties that may have very different expectations of performance or results. Such obligations require the practitioner to be forthright about skills, methods, recommendations, and ethical issues.

Summary: Collaboration and Collegiality in Ethical Consultation

Thinking, debating, and writing about professional ethics is an absorbing and vital exercise for anthropology, but it is also a perilous topic. It seems that for any principle, we can also find legitimate caveats, exceptions, or contexts in which situational ethics, based on general guidelines, are more appropriate. Furthermore, new ethical dilemmas are always arising. Senior professors or veterans of many years of practice will continue to face hard decisions throughout their careers. Another pitfall is that, by writing or talking about ethics, we can sound sanctimonious or preachy. Some may be quick to condemn the decisions of others, but sometimes that is based more on particular visions of social responsibilities, resulting in a more ideologically based disapproval than a question of pure professional ethics. For instance, some anthropologists may feel that it is inappropriate to work for business and that we should only work for the oppressed. But that decision is not a matter of professional ethics.

The work of practicing anthropologists can be very complicated. They have to answer to a number of bosses and publics beyond what abstract codes can anticipate. Yet the ethical practice of nonacademic practitioners is, in many respects, effective, because such practitioners have to survive on their reputations. If they were engaged in unethical or dubious practice, they could not do it for very long. Their bad reputations would catch up with them relatively quickly.

So out of these muddles and conflicts, how should we approach ethics for practice? To begin with, a student should become familiar with all of the ethical codes that have been formulated and read the core literature that relates to ethics, both academic and applied. A very significant way of transmitting ethical perspectives has been through the swapping of "war stories." For almost a decade, the National Association for the Practice of Anthropology, through the efforts of Neil Tashima and Cathleen Crain, has been providing an ethical forum and workshop at the annual meetings of the American Anthropological Association. There, practitioners discuss ethical dilemmas of their practice and invite the audience members to make suggestions about how they might resolve them. What is interesting is that there are often several solutions for the same problem.

A number of practitioner cases were discussed at the 1996 meetings. One practitioner may have "jumped the gun" in revealing details of research findings before the actual owners of the information had given their permission. In another case, a lucrative bidding contract was offered, but there was inadequate time to prepare an effective proposal and provide for appropriate informed consent. Finally, a government department that legally owned the data had asked researchers to provide complete transcripts of focus groups that had already been conducted with a promise of confidentiality. At the meeting session, practitioners told the audience how they had resolved them. Practitioners may actually make use of the suggestions provided by the audience.

This positive approach leads to the most effective pursuit of good ethical practice. Joan Cassell (1980) in an article titled "Ethical Principles for Conducting Fieldwork," recommends that anthropologists regularly consult peers and colleagues to review research designs before commencing work. After the project is finished, the same process should be repeated, ideally with the same colleagues looking at the ethics associated with the analysis stages. That could be extended to consideration of how reports are to be written or the ways information is disseminated to the public, clients, and professional communities. The reality is that all of us, no matter what our stage of professional development and experience, can use this kind of help. There are just too many ethical difficulties that can unexpectedly arise for even veterans to feel overconfident about their ethical practice.

The best venue for such mutual counseling on ethics might be through a local practitioners' organization (LPO). LPOs can provide peer group support. Discussions about ethics might be among the best reasons to form an LPO. It is probably best for practitioners to provide support and advice for each other rather than to rely on the standards and advice of academic anthropologists, because there can be such a difference in working conditions. If there are not enough local colleagues to form such organizations, with the aid of networks such as ANTHAP (http://www.acs.oakland.edu/~dow/anthap.htm) and others on the Internet, people can get advice and debriefing without face-to-face encounters. Such consultations should be done in a context of collegiality and consist of helpful advice, not involve sanctimonious accusative roles.

RECOMMENDED READINGS

Berreman, Gerald D.
1968   Is Anthropology Alive? Social Responsibility in Social Anthropology. *Current Anthropology,* Vol. 9: 391–397.

Cassell, Joan
1980   Ethical Principles for Conducting Fieldwork. *American Anthropologist,* Vol. 82: 29–42.

Fluehr-Lobban, Carolyn
1994   Informed Consent in Anthropological Research: We Are not Exempt. *Human Organization,* Vol. 53: 1–11.
1996   Reply to Wax and Herrera. *Human Organization,* Vol. 55: 240–241.

Fluehr-Lobban, Carolyn (ed.)
1991   *Ethics and the Profession of Anthropology: Dialogue for a New Era.* Philadelphia: University of Pennsylvania Press.

Frankel, Barbara, and M. G. Trend
1991   Principles, Pressures, and Paychecks: The Anthropologist as Employee. In *Ethics and the Profession of Anthropology: Dialogue for a New Era.* Edited by Carolyn Fluehr-Lobban. Pp. 175–198. Philadelphia: University of Pennsylvania Press.

Gilbert, M. Jean, Nathaniel Tashima, and Claudia Fishman
1991   Ethics and Practicing Anthropologists' Dialogue with the Larger World: Considerations in the Formulation of Ethical Guidelines for Practicing Anthropologists. In *Ethics and the Profession of Anthropology: Dialogue for a New Era.* Edited by Carolyn Fluehr-Lobban. Pp. 198–211. Philadelphia: University of Pennsylvania Press.

Gjessing, Gutorm
1968   The Social Responsibility of the Social Scientist. *Current Anthropology,* Vol. 9: 397–403.

Gough, Kathleen
1968   New Proposals for Anthropologists. *Current Anthropology,* Vol. 9: 403–407.

Herrera, C. D.
1996   Informed Consent and Ethical Exemptions. *Human Organization,* Vol. 55: 235–238.

Jacobs, Sue-Ellen, and Joan Cassell (eds.)
1987   *Handbook of Ethical Issues in Anthropology.* Washington, DC: American Anthropological Association.

Wax, Murray L.
1995   Informed Consent in Applied Research: A Commentary. *Human Organization,* Vol. 54: 330–331.
1996   Reply to Herrera. *Human Organization,* Vol. 55: 238–240.

Weaver, Thomas (ed.)
1973   *To See Ourselves: Anthropology and Modern Social Issues.* Glenview, IL: Scott, Foresman.

4

What Is Policy and How Does It Relate to Anthropology?

The Many Meanings and Contexts of Policy

An understanding of policy and its analysis is essential for the application of anthropology. In fact, most of the topics contained in this book are really subtopics of policy analysis, and most examples describe or critique the development of actual policies. Anthropology can be quite effective for policy analysis because issues and topics within the domain of policy are almost as all-encompassing as those in culture and society.

Policy is a complex, dynamic, and somewhat amorphous subject constantly shifting in content and emphasis. Members of the public (and even some experts in the field) frequently associate policy with government—lawmaking, bureaucracy, and other legal or administrative actions. Here policy is perceived as formal and limited in scope, the work of professional or elected policy makers who are specialists in generating laws, plans, and programs. They have the authority, personnel, financial resources, and the organizational means to implement them. This type of policy reaches into the economy, social welfare, external relations, communications, transportation, energy, and the environment.

Policy has these connotations, but it also involves much more. Policy suggests plans, principles, guidelines, directives, intentions, and an anticipation of future actions and results or the avoidance of undesirable circumstances. Significantly, policy assumes that thoughtfully directed social action can lead to desirable outcomes. Policy implies foresight and planning; policies provide blueprints for actions.

Policy formulation and implementation are complex social processes that extend beyond visible legislative and bureaucratic spheres. There is much below the surface, and only the tip can be observed in any legislative or bureaucratic activity. Policies always emerge out of a much wider and deeper context of social action and cultural expectation. For example, we could ask what brought a particular issue to the fore, to make it of public concern, and then ask how it is approached with laws, planning, and funding. Following implementation, what are the day-to-day consequences of new policies on sectors of the society? Do they improve lives? Are there unintended consequences? Who are the publics involved in any policy issue, and do their interests compete? What are their possible points of agreement and alliance? Who controls the power in such situations and what is the power-holder's agenda? How is the issue socially constructed and then acted upon before it is legitimized and becomes policy—what are the advocacy or lobbying processes? What are the explicit, formal, and institutional dimensions of policy? For anthropologists, what are the informal, less visible dimensions of policy-making? Also—and very significant for anthropologists—how do values and cultural ideologies exhibit themselves in the policy process?

On one level, policy is associated with formal institutions and organizations. In contemporary nation-states, especially industrialized First World countries, such formal institutions and organizations predominate and are made manifest through bureaucracy. Cultural assumptions of rationality, efficiency, and the need for explicit planning pervade such institutions. Since World War II and especially in the emerging "Information Age" of the 1980s and 1990s, there has been even more emphasis on policy as a continuous process. The various levels of policy formulation and planning are carried out within special units that gather and process information for those making the policies. Change is a preoccupation of policy-making. Sometimes the act of changing policy is seen as a rapid "catchup" to circumstances that have left an organization ill-prepared or unresponsive. Other times the intention is "proactive," to anticipate future events and adequately prepare for and even influence such changes. There are expectations that an institution's policies will be adapted or maybe even completely rewritten. This could be to meet changes in fiscal realities, changing social expectations, or the coming to power of elected officials with a whole new set of expectations of how society should work and a new mandate to change the directions of policy.

Policy is similarly pervasive within private-sector organizations such as corporations. Executives have board and planning meetings, where they formulate long- and short-range plans. They decide on new products, services, and markets that they should target, restructuring strategies that they might take, and so on. Policy also concerns nongovernment, charitable organizations dealing with social and health-related functions. Internationally oriented NGOs such as the Red Cross or Oxfam build policies as do environmental groups like the Sierra Club and the World Wildlife Federation. In any North American city, hundreds of small-scale organizations deal with immigrant resettlement, services to the disabled, poverty reduction, improving the well-being of children, and countless other things. Beyond these more formal organizations, people may mobilize themselves at a grassroots level for advocacy, lobbying, or self-help. Some of these groups are rudimentary in organization; others are highly developed, but all have to be concerned about policy at some level or another.

Policy-making organizations invariably show concerns beyond their internal matters. For example, such organizations have to deal with external relations among groups like or unlike themselves. Policies of advocacy groups are shaped in the ways that they are allied and opposed to each other, and then they influence planning by government agencies. The policy directions of society as a whole (or certain institutional sectors like health care or education) will be shaped by the interaction of organizations in an atmosphere of both competition and cooperation. Policies will be shaped by the rational attempt to formulate them in the style of procedural "blueprints," but they will often actually be shaped by failures, incomplete formulations, or most frequently, brokered compromises. Beyond such interactions among organizations, policies are often influenced by many outside factors. Population changes, shortages of resources, threats of disease, and other disruptions or social forces can rapidly redirect policy.

What does this cursory overview tell us? It suggests that policy is almost as broad a study as that of contemporary society itself. Policy studies cannot then be seen as limited to the well-established policy sciences such as political studies or economics. Anthropology and sociology are as relevant as these other subjects and are not simply auxiliaries.

Policy-making and implementation are not just political and social processes; they are also cultural. Once again, the anthropological connection should be quite clear. The rules, intentions, and aims of policy are always ideological; they are more systematic formulations of the way people assume that society works or should work and how consistent action within institutions will maintain or bring about desirable situations. Through their cultural assumptions, people seek desirable outcomes in their interactions with each other, their environment, and their technology. People are guided in these formulations by their culture, and policy statements are themselves cultural products.

What lines within anthropology might distinguish policy from nonpolicy research? Among the societies that anthropologists have studied, there is certainly variation as to the presence or absence of policy-making activities. Many nonstate societies, at the village, band, or other social level, operate with long-established traditional consensuses. Decisions are revealed within frameworks of consistent belief and action, and there may not be frequent or prolonged public discussions about future expectations or desired changes. In contrast, industrialized, highly urbanized societies with many formal organizations and dominated by ideologies that stress future orientations, planning, bureaucracy, rationality, and efficiency will all be preoccupied by policy. There is a wide range of possibilities in between these polar types.

But with such dichotomizing, we may be guilty of facile stereotyping if we said that "traditional" societies lacked institutions of policy and planning. It may be more appropriate to see procedures for the equivalent of policy planning as embedded in other institutions and assumptions rather than explicit within bureaucracies. When such peoples make long-term decisions—to participate in land reform, to move the site of a village, to enter into an alliance with other villages, to accept a missionary into their presence, and so forth—the cultural equivalents of policy planning and dialogue surely come into play. These actions might be consensus building, interfamily discussions, open village debates, and even the use of rituals of divination and other ceremonial mechanisms. Such societies might not have formal planning and policy institutions, but, ironically, they may have the capacities for making better policies because they are closer to the roots of the issue and the possibilities of consensus. Some sort of group decision-making (or policy) is always present. What we have learned from traditional societies about the nonformalized and holistic dimensions of decision-making can be transferred to the study of policy-making in the more bureaucratic institutions of contemporary society. Here, informal practices and unstated but understood assumptions may be just as significant in policy development as are formal bureaucratic mechanisms. Thus, we may say that policy-making is present in all societies and human institutions at all times. When a husband and wife get together to negotiate ways of raising their children, they are setting family policy. However, to be fair to the difficult enterprise that we are trying to deal with here, I think that we should realize that certain societies and institutions pay more direct attention to policy-making than other types do.

Policy as a Process

Borrowing from the political scientist Charles Jones (1977), it is useful to consider policy as a process rather than as a set institution or finished product. Broadly, Jones suggests that policy is "behavioral consistency and repetitiveness associated with efforts in and through government to resolve problems" (1977: 5). Policy is very dynamic at any time. When we look at what seems to be policy, we actually see a stage or phase in a sequence of events contributing to consistency and repetitiveness of action. Policy is in the process of emerging over a long time rather than a sudden, finished product. Jones (1977: 10) suggests a set of stages for tracing the development of policy in government settings.

Let us make a quick gloss of them. First of all, there has to be a perception that there is some social problem to solve. Whatever the issue, it has to be defined and assessed, and attention has to be paid to it for it to enter into the policy arena. Anthropologists study how issues percolate out of society through the media, special interest groups, advocacy, and citizen concern to become matters of formal public concern. Applied anthropologists can directly contribute to the stages of problem perception and definition through involvement in research and advocacy. Next is a stage, aggregation, that involves the identification of those portions of the public who are concerned about the issue and who go about finding each other and then organize to influence the issue. Representation follows—involving the ways that the organization and issues reach the attention of legislators.

At the stage of action in government, first a broad formulation of policies attending to problems is developed. Examples are formulations developed to address the need for affordable housing, regional economic development, disease prevention, and many other topics through processes of debate and research. Then specific programs are ultimately designed and formally funded. Depending on the level of government and the domain in question, anthropologists may also be involved during this stage. Next, more specifically formulated policies and programs are enacted for actual social settings. These might include the details of bringing about improved low-rental housing programs in particular communities, retraining programs in others, and countless other examples. Anthropologists might sometimes be involved in the direct delivery of services or in the actual implementation and administration of programs (say, as civil servants), but this is less frequent than the other stages of policy. The next stage is more consistent with applied and practicing anthropology's traditional skills of evaluating or appraising the effectiveness of programs or assessing needs. Findings from anthropology can be very useful in the resolution or reformulation of programs.

Such a policy process, as hastily sketched, can be exceptionally complex and at any stage could involve many thousands of people, depending on the scope of the issues under consideration. Jones' formulation is intended for the study of public policy, but the reader can intuit how similar schemes related to process could be constructed for private and nonprofit sectors.

The Significance of Anthropology for Policy

The first thing to consider is that anything marked for policy planning always has a significant human component. The ingredients of issues in fisheries, forestry, technology, medicine, and so forth are always cultural. For instance, saving fish stocks is not simply a biological issue, because even the definition of what is considered a fish is a cultural process. Also, humans can be categorized into very many different publics based on differing interests. These many interests are dictated by differences in social structure, values, goals, and perceptions of the future. Among other things, multiculturalism is a fact of life for just about every country in the world. Even if a country seems more or less ethnically homogeneous, a kind of de facto multiculturalism will be present with differences of region, socioeconomic status, gender, occupation, and other important variables.

Any policy planning needs an accounting of such factors. It is important to disaggregate the public into as many subpublics as are relevant to the issue, to try to determine what their needs are in reference to the issue in question, to map out potential conflicts, and to assess the reactions of different publics to proposals. One of the roles for anthropologists would be to assist in the making of more specific policies and programs that are compatible with the varieties of publics. On the other hand, governments live in times of scarce resources, so it is very difficult to fund policies and programs that are tailored to all of the minute publics that we could identify. So, there is a prevailing pressure to come up with public policy solutions that can cover the needs of as many of the publics as possible. Even beyond that task, there is currently more pressure to find ways to combine policies that are relevant to several areas of human activity all at once. Health promotion and illness prevention might be linked to economic development, job creation, pollution control, and dimensions related to the environment. So seeking out the linkages among those various institutional domains can be a key role for anthropologists.

A significant activity for anthropologists is finding what is common among many publics relevant to any policy question. A "textbook" example (see Scaglion 1987) relates to the exceptionally pluralistic setting of Papua New Guinea. In that emerging nation, there are at least 750 languages spoken and about a thousand different customary legal systems among 3,500,000 people. In the midst of such diversity, consider the frustrations of trying to design a noncolonialistic and widely compatible legal system. Richard Scaglion, an anthropologist in charge of a research team working for the National Law Reform Commission, examined diverse tribal conflict resolution systems to identify the most common themes of solving conflicts so that they might be used in developing an effective common code of criminal justice for the entire country. A database was established dealing with issues like customary compensation, polygamy, domestic violence, and so forth. Some practices were drafted into law, such as the recognition of certain types of compensation in wealth and services for claims of death, injury, and personal damage (Scaglion: 103). Thus a knowledge base generated by an anthropologist was directly useful in the design of national laws and policies.

Domains of Policy Activities within Anthropology

Enumerating some of the broad areas in which anthropologists have contributed or have the potential to contribute more in policy and practice should orient the reader to the practical potential of the subject. Scanning the bibliography at the end of the book will provide the reader with references covering most of these and other topics.

Socioeconomic Issues

Sustainable and culturally appropriate economic development, both domestic and international, has long been an applied area for anthropologists. Anthropologists' contributions can take many forms, one being impact assessments of mega-projects that were originally intended to create profits and improve economic infrastructures for depressed regions. The anthropology of development, or the critique of modernization efforts, has been a significant part of anthropological policy analysis. Similarly, there has also been an anthropology of work and the workplace that examines such occupational subgroupings as long-distance truckers, miners, longshoreman, "pink-collar" workers, and many other examples. The anthropology of work will probably generate more anthropological interest in the future because of the extensive transformations in the economy and in the expectations surrounding labor. For instance, how does the workplace respond to family needs when there are so many pressures on working parents for more productivity in an atmosphere of job insecurity? A growing anthropology of business is related to both development and work. What are the regional and cross-border implications of the North American Free Trade Agreement? What are the implications of international migratory labor on the laborers and their families who are not provided services of social assistance, education, and health during seasonal movements?

The Environment and Resource-Based Industries

Anthropology has helped to make farmers' desires relevant to the marketing strategies of governments in Third World regions. Also, anthropologists are assessing the roles and needs of women, who are at the very forefront of agricultural production in many Third World cases. Anthropologists, for example, investigate the effects of the reduction of fish stocks off the Grand Banks of Newfoundland, the moratorium on fishing, and the impacts on communities, fishermen, and their families. Anthropologists have examined attempts to use aquaculture systems as substitutes for offshore fishing. Anthropologists provide research and advocacy on behalf of Northern Indians and Inuit who have been harmed by fur boycotts implemented by European governments that, in turn, have been under the pressure from environmental lobbyists. Disaster and risk assessment is another dimension of environmental policy research. Anthropologists have been studying and providing recommendations relevant to natural and man-made disasters such as oil spills, hurricanes, or famines. Environmental risk assessment is a relatively new but important field for environmental anthropology. It calculates and accounts for cultural perceptions of the risks associated with, for example, nuclear reactors, nuclear waste and chemical dumps, and other hazards in local communities. Anthropology's involvement in social impact assessment of development projects such as dams, highways, and petroleum projects has been well established for the past thirty years.

Technological Innovation

Related to economy and the environment are the many dimensions of technological innovation and the impacts of their introduction. An extensive literature discusses policy implications of the introduction of very diverse items like steel axes, snowmobiles, and massive hydroelectric and irrigation projects. Current anthropological concerns are the profound effects of computers, the Internet, fax machines, and so forth on the workplace and society as a whole. In business and industrial anthropology, anthropologists study the effects of automation and other production strategies on the workforce.

Health

Medical anthropology has undergone enormous expansion over the last thirty years and has made many contributions to policy. In Canada, for instance, the federal government has been transferring control of health services for Native people from the Department of Health and Welfare directly to First Nations governments. The transitions have required policy studies that carefully monitored local needs in prevention and care and recommended how best to make use of local resources and to design more effective delivery systems. In general, health care systems have been forced to curtail expenses and to put more emphasis on preventive approaches. Anthropologists engaged in health promotions research seek linkages in the community, society, and culture that can be seen as synergistically related to peoples' health. Appropriate cultural ways to ensure peoples' well-being through health education and local collaborations are sought. For example, anthropology can evaluate health needs or the effectiveness of early diagnostic programs for prostate or breast cancer in ways that are culturally appropriate. Anthropologists do many other types of health-related research, such as looking for linkages related to beliefs, behaviors, and specific health problems such as drug and alcohol abuse and rehabilitation, specific diseases and disabilities, and the care of the elderly. The policy implications of medical anthropology are enormous.

Education

The anthropology of education has been significant for curriculum design and the evaluation of programs, especially in the United States. As anthropologists have frequently demonstrated, much of socialization or education occurs outside of the class. Enculturation is a comprehensive sociocultural phenomenon, and there are ethnically preferred and traditional ways for training the young that have to be considered in order for formal education to be effective and complementary to local styles. Furthermore, it is advisable to have children's education rooted in contexts that will enhance their pride and identity. Given the significant pluralism that we find in countries like the United States and Canada, this calls for attention to the needs or possibilities of designing cultural variations on curriculum. Then, in turn, these experiments have to be evaluated. Ethnographic evaluation in classroom settings has become a major field within educational anthropology.

Social Policy

Social policy, including issues of welfare, unemployment, poverty, and housing, has been a key part of anthropology, especially as associated with race relations. Anthropologists, in addition to examining the underlying social and cultural dimensions associated with poverty for many different urban populations, have evaluated programs to alleviate unemployment and poverty. There are studies about single motherhood, the family, the status of children, and so forth. Related to poverty has been the anthropological study of urban planning as in the design of urban low-rental housing projects, which run the risk of being social and cultural disasters when improperly planned. Anthropologists have been looking at other dimensions associated with social policy such as divorce, domestic abuse, the welfare of children, and many factors related to gender.

A significant subdomain of social policy concerns immigration and refugee relocation. Millions of people are being displaced by wars, political events, natural disasters, economic upheavals, and combinations of these variables. International efforts at relief and refugee resettlement have motivated anthropological evaluation and policy consultation because of the multitude of cross-cultural differences and conflicts involved. Continuing to maintain the United Nations Convention on Refugees requires that countries annually provide sanctuary for hundreds of thousands of refugees in First World countries like the United States, Canada, Australia, and Germany as well as millions in states bordering on the disruption. Anthropologists and other social scientists have been monitoring and advising governments and nongovernmental organizations on the details of such resettlement into host communities. Similar policy research surrounds voluntary migration or regular immigration. Issues associated with multiculturalism as a continuing byproduct of immigration are yet another aspect of policy anthropology.

Indigenous Peoples

Our earliest (and sometimes most controversial) policy contributions have related to the administration of Aboriginal, Native, or tribal peoples in such diverse places as Australia, the United States, Canada, New Zealand, India, the Pacific Trust Islands, Africa, Papua New Guinea, Brazil, and other countries. Anthropology's contributions here have been well established, and in most cases anthropological involvement has been benign and supportive of the aspirations and needs of tribal peoples. Today anthropologists are active in supporting indigenous self-government.

Emerging Fields

Anthropologists have also been involved in public policy research in cultural preservation, recreation, and the role of national parks and public-owned lands. The establishment of parks may come in conflict with local or traditional usages whether or not they are aboriginal. Proposals for the use of public lands in the American Southwest have conflicted with American Indian perceptions of their sacred or "holy" lands. Land use planning and tourist development in national, provincial, and state parks may involve needs assessments related to potential recreational use as in finding ways of stimulating local economic development through tapping tourist resources while not disturbing the local environment or disturbing local cultural authenticity.

Anthropology has also had policy-relevant roles in communications and transportation. During the 1970s, anthropologists examined the consequences of the twenty-four-hour extension of satellite communications (including TV) on isolated communities in Alaska and the Canadian Arctic. How were local Native people affected by almost completely one-way intrusions of foreign culture into their lives? Were there ways that local communities could have their own input into these powerful communication media for the purpose of enhancing their own culture? Transportation has been a growing domain for public policy studies with, for instance, research into the subcultures of long-distance truckers and the ways that they cope with government regulations and perceptions of occupational safety.

This section outlined in very broad brush strokes some areas in which anthropologists have participated in policy. It is incomplete. New areas are constantly being generated, and anthropology will always have important things to reveal about human activity. That will also apply to the actual process of making policy itself. The anthropology of bureaucracy and of the nature of organizations is itself part of policy analysis. Also, the categorization of policy areas here is somewhat static and does not effectively characterize the many over-laps and elaborations. Furthermore, most of the policy topics raised in this overview relate to public policy domains covered by the activities of national, state, provincial, and municipal governments. Much more could have been written here about anthropological roles in the private sectors of policy, business, and industrial anthropology; international non-government organizations such as the Red Cross or Oxfam; and the role of anthropology in policy as pertaining to community-based nonprofit agencies engaged in human services. It should be clear that anthropology is definitely a policy science contributing to a multitude of domains.

Some Roles Taken by Anthropologists in Policy Analysis and Practice

The range of roles taken by anthropologists in policy is broad. At one end of a continuum, there is the more academic style of policy analysis. This can be exemplified by the work of the late Sally Weaver (1981). Her book *Making Canadian Indian Policy: The Hidden Agenda* analyzes policy planning directed toward Canada's Aboriginal people during the late 1960s and early 1970s. She explored the underlying cultural assumptions that upper-middle-class, senior civil servants had about policy. Their naive, well-intended assumptions were that assimilation and the transfer of services and jurisdictions to the provinces would better serve the well-being of Native people than continuing federal reservation-based Indian policies. Such policies were proposed in spite of the already well-documented disaster of federal termination policies in the United States when treaty rights were similarly overturned. Other uncommissioned academic policy analyses have provided critiques of existing policies while advocating reforms. For example, Charles Valentine's work, *Culture and Poverty* (1968), reviewed the various theories from anthropology and sociology that attempted to link poverty in the United States to subcultural differences of behavior and attitude or show how poverty itself generally perpetuated a unique culture. Out of all of this, he developed a set of policy recommendations informed by anthropological theory (e.g., revitalization movements, political economy) that would provide a national policy agenda for ameliorating poverty in the United States.

In other cases, anthropologists have been directly commissioned to do more focused policy and applied research through direct employment, contracts, and participation in commissions. That work might involve supervision and research in a major task force that is investigating an issue like immigrant health, Native self-government, or public health. Anthropologists might be hired as consultants to evaluate programs designed to meet a social group's needs; they might serve as expert witnesses in court inquiries that are meant to legitimize or guide the formulation of new policies or directions. They might be hired to assist in the design and implementation of new programs relevant to community and economic development in the Third World or aboriginal communities in North America. And they can work as full-time researchers and administrators with government agencies designed to deliver services in health, education, or welfare.

Practicing anthropologists may do policy work through consulting and contracts, often through companies that they own. A good example is the work of Robert Winthrop who manages Cultural Solutions in Ashland, Oregon. Winthrop offers general applied research and other policy-relevant services, such as cultural conflict resolution, cultural preservation, and cultural aspects of community and organizational development. In one such study, Winthrop acted as a coordinator of a contract provided by the U.S. Forest Service, and he, in turn, subcontracted it to the Karuk tribe. Although Winthrop provided technical support, the completed report provided a policy statement on how the tribe preferred to manage resources in the Klamath National Forest according to its own values and traditions. Another project assessed the impact of a 170-mile pipeline construction on Indian land, including negotiating acceptable compensation strategies. Other projects focused on Euro-American jurisdictions. One helped an Oregon city review its management effectiveness and improve city planning. Winthrop (personal communication) stresses that practitioners doing these kinds of policy work need to phrase findings in language that is understandable to the noninitiated and to have good analytical skills permitting them to understand the larger picture in such rapidly changing scenarios. They also must know how to truly work collaboratively (especially when the clients are Indian tribes) and be able to effectively manage client relations.

A significant but rarer policy role is filled by managerial anthropologists. Such anthropologists directly administer government programs or manage private corporations, overseeing the implementation and evaluations of decisions developed through policy. They rarely do policy research themselves. As Martin Topper (1995) points out, most policy is formulated at higher levels by politicians and some senior-level bureaucrats. Some anthropologists have served as managerial types at this level, filling out the details of policies or suggesting new ones. When any research is needed, it is usually contracted to others. Managerial anthropologists then use that work to formulate new policies or improve old ones. In effect, they act as brokers between the consultants who did the original policy research and the higher-level policy makers.

Beyond that, as in the U.S. federal government, there are offices or agencies that oversee implementation in regions or communities. Here policy is carried out. Again, managerial anthropologists might operate at these levels, evaluating and using research contracted to other anthropologists. The object of that research is not to change policy (which was formulated at a higher level) but to improve its implementation by solving more narrowly defined local problems. Managerial anthropologists retain the anthropological capacity to do the "quick study" (although not of a research nature). They can rapidly assess the crucial working contexts of policy and incorporate anthropological knowledge and skills for the multidisciplinary decision-making normally done by teams by understanding and operating through the organization's culture of formal and informal rules. Topper briefly mentions his own roles as a managerial anthropologist with the Indian Health Service and the Environmental Protection Agency.

A managerial anthropologist who operated at the highest levels of policy-making was Philleo Nash, who served as President Truman's White House advisor on race relations in the 1940s. There, he dealt with such issues as racial tensions, civil rights, statehood for Hawaii and Alaska, and more self-determination for Puerto Rico and the Virgin Islands. After his White House service, he successfully ran for Lieutenant Governor of Wisconsin, serving from 1959 to 1961. As policy, his election platform included opposition to the termination of reservation status for Menominee Indians (Nash 1989). Later he was appointed Commissioner of Indian Affairs and served from 1961 to 1966 along with Associate Commissioner James Officer, another high-level managerial anthropologist. In comparison to previous Commissioners, Nash was very successful in gaining Congressional appropriations for the Bureau, working smoothly with line staff, maintaining good relations with tribal leaders, and defending the interests of Native Americans (Officer 1989). Besides his personal qualities and dedication to public service, his anthropological perspectives were a major part of Nash's success in policy-making and administration.

Some Anthropological Stages of Policy Engagement

Wulff and Fiske (1987b: 4–9) provide us with a useful framework for policy work. Stage one involves defining the problem or information production. Anthropologists provide detailed discussion of a particular problem or issue, help to define it more carefully, and look for underlying causes and interrelationships. The second stage involves choosing an alternative or policy formulation, looking at different ways that a problem might be resolved or ameliorated. The feasibility of proposed choices may be further tested through research looking at values, costs, benefits, and other criteria. The third stage is more focused and involves deciding what to do and how to do it: it involves planning and implementing interventions. Many more specifics, resources, and human effort go into actual action and the operations of specific programs and services. The final stage involves assessing what happened, or evaluation. Here again, the research skills of anthropologists can be quite valuable.

Summary

Policy contains a variety of dimensions and opportunities for anthropological analysis and practice. Sometimes it is useful to separate policy analysis from policy practice. The former is passive, analytical, and even academic. It may go no further than a general policy critique. The latter involves action and the use of specific knowledge for dealing with human problems through laws, programs, and services. It may directly involve planning, delivery, management, administration, negotiation, mediation, collaboration, and consultation. Nonetheless, what strengths anthropologists take into such practice rest ultimately on their capacities to do policy analysis. Those strengths will be discussed in the next chapter.

RECOMMENDED READINGS

Goldschmidt, Walter (ed.)
1979   *The Uses of Anthropology.* Washington, DC: American Anthropological Association.
1986   *Anthropology and Public Policy; A Dialogue.* Washington, DC: American Anthropological Association.

Hinshaw, Robert E.
1980   Anthropology, Administration and Public Policy. *Annual Review of Anthropology,* Vol. 9: 497–522.

Jones, Charles O.
1977   *An Introduction to the Study of Public Policy.* Second Edition. North Scituate, MA: Duxbury Press.

Maday, Bela C. (ed.)
1975   *Anthropology and Society.* Washington, DC: The Anthropological Society of Washington.

Sanday, Peggy Reeves (ed.)
1976   *Anthropology and the Public Interest: Fieldwork and Theory.* New York: Academic Press.

CHAPTER

5 Strengths, Weaknesses, and Future Directions in Policy Analysis and Practice

We begin this chapter with a case study. The purpose is to show that anthropologists must become actively engaged directly at the points of decision-making, intervention, or implementation. They must use the interpersonal skills of forming networks of alliance and exercising persuasion and reciprocity, which go beyond any analytical capacities that they may have as anthropologists. After completing this case study, we then outline the specific assets anthropologists bring to policy analysis and practice. We also look at areas in which improvement is needed.

Case Study of Policy Research and Action: The *Comadrona* Project

This case study shows that policy-oriented anthropological insights are more usefully communicated at the places in which policy is made rather than through academic outlets. Also, such insights need to be grounded in the contexts of actual community relations, human needs, and program realities rather than in abstract generalizations.

The setting is Hartford, Connecticut, where two anthropologists, Pertti Pelto and Jean Schensul (1986), were involved with the recently formed Hispanic Health Council, which had received a federal grant to develop a demonstration project to improve health behavior and health outcomes for Puerto Rican women. The most significant health issues were a very high rate of teenage pregnancy and high infant mortality as well as the poor health of young children.

As a way to deal with these health problems, an approach labeled *Comadrona* was developed. A *comadrona* is the traditional birth attendant in Puerto Rico. A number of principles compatible with local needs but consistent with other anthropological experiences were used to shape policy for the project.

The first of these was an emphasis on ethnic pride and identity; the staff were largely Puerto Rican, and all the training materials were culturally appropriate. Second, there was an emphasis on cultural brokerage. Go-betweens—Puerto Ricans themselves—provided health education and advocacy for Puerto Rican women and assisted in interactions with the health providers, many of whom were not Puerto Rican. Third, the project made great use of both existing and newly created support networks in the ethnic community in neighborhoods, schools, volunteer groups, and organizations. Women who could make use of the projects' resources and information were identified and then encouraged through these networks. The fourth approach involved the development of a database that emphasized factors and statistics related to pregnancy and prenatal and postnatal care with the view of developing, monitoring, and advocating the goals of the project.

After the second year of the project, this database had shown increased numbers of women using the health care system by the first trimesters of their pregnancies. Continuities in care were maintained; there was compliance with medication. Most important, the number of babies with low birth weights decreased and rates of breast-feeding increased as did the use of family planning. So the four goals of the project were designed with the needs of the local clients in mind, but they were also consistent with other types of anthropological inquiry done elsewhere: the projects all demonstrated the value of ethnic identity and community networks of support.

During the course of the project, program staff developed alliances with other people involved in health care work in Hartford. In the process, they had communicated to them the principles and emerging results of the project. A network of supportive alliance was created that would be useful later.

However, a series of dramatic events changed some policy directions in the city during the second year. A local health systems agency released a report showing that Hartford had the fourth-highest infant mortality rate in the United States, and this rate was highest in the city's Hispanic population and next largest in the African American community. The report also discussed the high rates of teenage pregnancy as well as the alarmingly low rates of average birth weights.

This report was released before the successes of the *Comadrona* project were widely known. Suddenly a large amount of media coverage was devoted to this apparent crisis of the health care system. As a result, city and state health departments as well as two private donor foundations responded to media and public concerns. In conjunction with the state and municipal health officials, they hired two consultants to do a study and develop a policy and specific programs for dealing with the problems. The recommended solution to the problem was a citywide plan, characterized by top-down planning and the coordination of services rather than one that worked closely with ethnic communities. All existing programs were to be amalgamated under the direction of the two consultants who had done the research and planning. The key ingredients to programming would be home visits and direct health education. However, none of the approaches would be ethnically specific, and none of them would use the existing networks of community support. To those already familiar with the problems, the solutions required inappropriate centralization. The newer policies were designed in a top-down fashion by a few people within the health care system.

The African American and Hispanic organizations that already had programs underway opposed these solutions. In order to counter the new proposal, the *Comadrona* staff used anthropological research to show the ever-growing success of their programming. The *Comadrona* staff and researchers were able to call upon the support of their allies for decentralization and ethnically specific programs. *Comadrona* and its allies prevailed. A compromise plan widened the range of stakeholders to include the preexisting community groups such as *Comadrona.* They all became eligible for funding from the foundations. Although the plan explored rational and common solutions to the citywide problems of teenage pregnancies and the health problems of young women and their children, the approach emphasized localized control.

Pelto and Schensul (1986) suggest that the policy successes in this particular case were assisted by their good use of ethnographic data and sound anthropological principles, but more important was the direct use of networks of support and alliance that had been created and reinforced through other activities such as membership on health committees. Information does not speak for itself; its advocates must be cultivated. The major lesson here is that anthropologists involved in policy research and action must be involved directly in their communities and must be aware of the important networks and individuals in decision-making. They must be actively engaged and not assume that anthropological information will speak for itself. Engagement and understanding of the fields of action are far more important.

Anthropological Assets for Policy Analysis and Practice

Yet anthropology has numerous strengths that make it useful for policy participation; in effect, the subject is preadapted to be a policy science. A number of authors (Geilhufe 1979; Cochrane 1980; Pelto and Schensul 1986; Weaver 1985a, 1985b) have analyzed anthropology's participation in policy. Drawing on this body of work, a list of assets for anthropology as policy science includes (1) the systems-functional-holistic approach, (2) the emic approach and value analysis, (3) the cross-cultural comparative approach, (4) cultural interpretation, (5) the ethnographic approach, (6) interdisciplinary capabilities, (7) capacities to frame policy information descriptively or theoretically, and (8) a focus on the community.

The Systems-Functional-Holistic Approach

As Weaver (1985b: 200) suggests, the systems-functional-holistic approach gives us the potential of seeing the larger picture. It provides the perspective to show how institutions or policies fit or are in disharmony with the community, region, and nation. Policies are seen in their connections within society as a whole, other policies, the environment, and so forth. Metaphorically, anthropology encourages a wide lateral or web-like vision that can lead us to unexpected linkages or discoveries. Changes in health care policy may be tied to family well-being and connected to subsistence, consumption, and the economy. The perspective is effective for anticipating potential consequences of particular actions. Apparently innocent decisions of policy might have costly, unexpected, negative consequences. Geilhufe (1979: 578) points out that anthropologists are especially useful in foreign aid and international development programs in which specific policies are brought into unfamiliar settings. Anthropologists may be able to anticipate unintended and harmful consequences of good intentions. Mapping out as many of the linkages as possible encourages analysts to come up with policies or decisions that simultaneously benefit several institutions or subgroupings.

The Emic Approach and Value Analysis

The emic approach, looking at things from the point of view of insiders or through the values of participants, has been recognized as a strength by both Weaver (1985b: 200) and Geilhufe (1979: 577). Anthropologists, with their grasp of context and the views of the intended recipients, may be of help. People who are "targets" of social policy are able to express their own needs or objections to proposals. They are quite capable of making their own suggestions for improvements in their lives. However, policy makers still pay attention to "expert" opinion. The anthropologist discussing a people's customary style of socialization may help to corroborate appeals for an educational system that makes use of elders and places more emphasis on learning by direct example rather than instruction. Anthropologists can verify policy needs meaningful to populations misunderstood by dominant elites. Similarly, anthropologists can show the constraints and opportunities for solutions because they have a better understanding of the attitudes and values of intended recipients.

Anthropologists can also point out that policies established by politicians and bureaucratic experts are not simply objective, rational, effective, and efficient solutions to human problems. The policies themselves may represent the cultural bias of the policy makers—not necessarily the solutions best fitted to the needs of the intended beneficiaries. They may be programs and policies that the powerful feel most comfortable with because of *their* values. When plans do not work, policy makers tend not to blame themselves for making poor policies. Instead they may blame the recipients of noncompliance. Analysis of the cultural biases of policy makers (usually upper-middle-class professionals) can be a useful contribution by the anthropologist. However, such critiques are not helpful when they are delivered in harsh, self-righteous, and frequently one-sided manners, which may offend rather than edify. It is a very delicate area of communication in which many of us need to do some work.

Yet as Geilhufe (1979: 577) points out, there are potential broker or communicator roles for the anthropologist in showing how value biases may have colored planning or how those of the intended population were overlooked. This may be very difficult because the values of the decision makers may be closely linked to their professional identities blinding them to their bias. Yet the question usually boils down to whether the policy is compatible with the values of the intended beneficiaries.

Among the policy makers, there are usually competing points of view on what are the most desirable ways of solving human problems. These may range over the political spectrum—social democrat, liberal, conservative, neoconservative, Marxist, and so forth. A liberal might expect that if more jobs are made available with preferential hiring, then employment will improve for minorities and crime rates will go down. A conservative might assume that public safety will increase if harsher sentences serve as deterrents for crime. Pelto and Schensul (1986: 507) liken these theories of action to folk theories, parallel to folk theories of medicine. People operate by them and have great faith in them, but there are no ultimate proofs, and their assumptions are rarely examined scientifically.

In policy analysis, anthropologists have much to contribute since they are specialists in making explicit the worldviews or ideologies of different peoples and organizations. Anthropologists can explicate the differing views of the stakeholders or players in alliance or opposition to each other. Penny van Esterik demonstrates that in her (1989) analysis of a protracted advocacy struggle against the Nestlé Corporation, which was promoting the use of inappropriate and health-threatening bottles and formulas for infants in the Third World. Van Esterik showed that there were four quite distinct ideologies even among allied women's groups (e.g., radical feminists versus more conservative LaLeche advocates).

Anthropologists can help their clients understand the beliefs and values of opponents, allies, and decision makers in trying to develop a plan of action that will favor the points that they are advocating. Anthropologists can explicitly reveal more of the motivating forces behind the other parties' interests. Sometimes anthropologists might be able to serve as mediators—helping to shape effective policy from shared assumptions among the varied interests. That capacity to analyze underlying assumptions is a very powerful asset in policy analysis and formulation.

The Cross-Cultural Comparative Approach

Cross-cultural comparison is an exceptionally valuable approach for policy analysis and the policy process, but it is still underexploited. Our scholarly literature, as Weaver (1985b: 200) points out, contains thousands of case studies in which there are many implicit, but often hidden, variations in the ways people solve problems. This database includes an enormous amount of raw material for innovation in policy-making, but most of it has not been brought to the forefront and made explicit.

For instance, there are cases on resolution or mediation that could be used in human justice systems directly or by modification. Many are probably much more humane and rehabilitative than the punitive approaches taken in complex state societies in the developed world. In Canadian Native communities, healing and sentencing circles that emphasize restitution and community service as well as bringing offenders in deeper contact with Native spirituality and cultural traditions might be more conducive to the public safety of the community than incarcerating young people in prison for long periods of time. Parallel policies with the appropriate cultural fit could be entertained.

There should also be more attention to cross-cultural comparison with regard to actual attempts at policy solutions. For instance, in the domain of indigenous rights or self-determination, there is much to be learned by comparing existing systems among indigenous peoples in Australia, New Zealand, Canada, and the United States. Elements of solutions could be found through inquiries into these; mistakes can also be avoided. Overall, they might be applied to new attempts to develop or improve self-determination.

Cultural Interpretation

Anthropologists have the potential to act as cultural interpreters (Weaver 1985b: 200)—roles that may be valuable in negotiating conflict or developing culturally appropriate solutions. It is basic to the profession to attempt to understand the "other," and anthropologists are experienced in explaining other points of view and communicating them in print and lectures. So, at least intellectually, it prepares us for the role of brokers seeking out areas of agreement among policy goals and cultural values. There is a great potential, built into anthropology, for mediation (see Chambers 1985: 26–33).

The Ethnographic Approach

In-depth contextual information is always useful for policy formulation, especially when the decision makers have little knowledge of the people or community in question. A long-time familiarity with a region or culture is often the first asset that allows the anthropologist to be drawn into policy consultation. Weaver does point out, though, that anthropologists may be called into relatively unfamiliar settings, and this places pressures on them to come up with quick answers. In turn, this places a premium on rapid assessment procedures and the capacity to work in teams. However, ethnography will always be a special strength of applied anthropology for service within the policy sciences.

Furthermore, Pelto and Schensul (1986) suggest that anthropologists can and should draw attention to the significant actors and foci of power in any policy domain such as health or education. Through such ethnographic mapping and network analysis, they can identify opposing and potentially allied forces to their clients' positions. It is always important to understand who are the significant gatekeepers—people with authority, influence, or capacities to shape opinion or make things happen—and to consult with them before making any attempt to implement programs.

Interdisciplinary Capabilities

Nancy Geilhufe (1979) identifies another anthropological strength—its eclectic and interdisciplinary nature. Anthropology itself is a multidisciplinary subject, peerless in its potentials to draw knowledge from its biological, social, and linguistic subdisciplines as well as the arts and humanities. The capacity to bring together information through such diversity is unparalleled for both academic and practical purposes. Also, anthropology has developed many interdisciplinary connections to cognate subjects, many of which are also policy sciences. Anthropologists have a ready capacity to draw from the methods, theories, and bodies of data of these other subjects and synthesize them through anthropological perspectives. Anthropologists are intellectually prepared to work in interdisciplinary teams, a growing norm in policy research.

Capacities to Frame Policy Information Descriptively or Theoretically

Ultimately, policy analysis requires advocacy or persuasion through oral discussion and other ways of negotiation (Pelto and Schensul 1986: 509–511). Anthropologists present their arguments for particular approaches to problem-solving through descriptive materials, theoretical presentations, or a combination of the two. Descriptive materials are essentially ethnographic and show the underlying circumstances, values, and beliefs of a particular people in areas like health behavior or socialization. Because of ethnographic description, the policy makers might then be convinced that a recommended set of procedures for extending health care or improving schooling should take into account the realities and aspirations of local people, or they may become aware of severe constraints that will cause the original formulations to fail. Similarly, theoretical discussions could draw from comparative and general research on the same topics. Of course, theoretical framing has to be understandable to lay persons. If done effectively, presentations with ethnographic or theoretical content may convince people to follow particular policy solutions they might not have considered.

A Focus on the Community

The final asset is the anthropological capacity to conceptualize, map, and portray the community. Policies formulated at higher levels such as states, regions, provinces, or nations ultimately have to be implemented at particular contact points. Those contact points are where actual people live and where policies are delivered through programs and services. Most frequently we are talking about communities. Even when they are working in complex settings like cities in developed countries, anthropologists can map the social and power structures as well as the other ingredients of any communities where they do research or practice. They come to know how things are done locally and who are the key actors or stakeholders. Network theories and other similar approaches can be valuable here.

Anthropology has a lot to draw upon in making contributions to effective and human policy. Our biggest contribution may be making policy makers aware of the fact, that, as much as they may desire it, uniform policy designs usually cannot meet the needs of the public. The reality is that there are many publics with different social, economic, regional, ethnic, and cultural realities. Policies must be tailor made to meet such realities, otherwise they will lead to more grief, conflict, and expense.

Some Weaknesses and Some Needs for Improvement

Anthropology does have its problems. The most serious problem is that much of the anthropological literature is neither accessible nor useful to the public or policy makers. Anthropologists' writings have been either filled with details or overburdened with theory and jargon. There may be few direct recommendations or even explicit recognition or understandings of the problems that need to be solved.

Another problem is a lack of sustained attention to issues and problems once they have been identified. For instance, anthropologists used to have plenty to say about cultural change as related to development. But this has been largely shed for newer fashions in anthropology. Alternatively, anthropologists have somewhat thin knowledge bases about particular topics. For instance, conflict resolution is a highly important contemporary domain, but only a few anthropologists have attached themselves to it (see Magistro 1996). Overall, we are spread widely and thinly, with rapid turnovers in policy-oriented knowledge bases.

Even when they have the expertise, many anthropologists are not good communicators beyond their narrow circles of colleagues. Anthropologists have not been effective advocates for their own accomplishments. More important, they still have much to do to become effective advocates for the peoples and causes that they might espouse. During several public crises of the 1990s involving Aboriginal peoples in Canada (including the armed standoff by Mohawk at Oka, Quebec, and the protracted coverage of the social breakdown of Davis Inlet in Labrador), anthropologists (with some notable exceptions) had surprisingly little to say to the media. In the United States, there were similar omissions during the Termination policies of the Eisenhower administration and the armed struggle between the U.S. government and the American Indian Movement in South Dakota during the 1970s. After over a hundred years of North American anthropology devoted to Aboriginal issues, where were the relevant commentators from anthropology?

Related to this has been a hesitation in making the value judgments that are unavoidable in policy pursuits. Collectively, anthropologists still exhibit timidity in the expression or critique of values. There can be a number of reasons for such tentativeness. Many see social issues as exceedingly complex and are worried that they might be missing some important ingredients in any analysis; therefore, their conclusions might prove to be faulty or costly. Another very important inhibition relates to the fact that many people are loath to speak on behalf of other peoples such as ethnic minorities, feeling that they might be appropriating their "voices" and, therefore, speaking out of turn. But, as a result, anthropological commentaries often seem anemic to policy makers and the peoples whose causes they should be advocating. Policy makers and the public might feel that they are not getting any sense of direction from anthropological fence-sitting, that they are getting an overload of background material but no valuable advice.

Ethnography, our greatest methodological strength, can also be our greatest weakness. Many studies, in their holistic complexity, have taken too long to complete, and this has alienated many of those who contract research. Anthropologists must recognize that there are significant deadlines in decision-making cycles.

Conclusions about problems and solutions may be divorced from the actual contexts in which they have to be ultimately administered. Many academic anthropologists working with North American Native peoples, on or off reservations, do not know very much about the Bureau of Indian Affairs or the Department of Indian and Northern Affairs in Canada and their many subbranches (including those devoted to policy), let alone the highly significant institutions that are emerging within Native governments themselves. We still need to ethnographically understand the institutional contexts in which the problems might be solved. And that requires an understanding of power relations. This is so even when (or perhaps especially when) those institutions might contain large parts of the problems themselves.

Weaver (1985b) along with Spicer (1976) encourages more anthropologists to take on roles as administrators, thus expanding our insiders' knowledge. We should learn more about policy science and continue to "study up" by examining the cultures of policy makers. To expand our capacities, we should be sending copies of our policy-relevant reports to policy makers and to journals devoted to policy.

Cochrane (1980) raises the important point that policy studies are "liminal" in several ways. They are neither wholly scientific nor are they wholly pragmatic, neither purely academic nor purely bureaucratic. Their aim is to establish goals and the means of achieving them. Science can inform such a process, but much more than skill in science is needed. In fact, Cochrane suggests that the more scientific the advice is, the less likely that it is sufficiently comprehensive. Any assets of scientific discovery must be supplemented by judgment, experience, and effective knowledge of the policy contexts under question. Ultimately, what is most important in judging the value of a policy analysis is whether its advice actually works.

Then, more specifically, Cochrane suggests that anthropologists must try to assess future events. We often avoid this, begging off because we are fearful of making the wrong predictions and possibly contributing to harmful policy. We are also reticent because we do not have full confidence in our theories of society and change. Cochrane warns us that policy makers become exasperated with people who will not try to assess future events and the consequences of policy. He claims that policy makers do not really mind that much if social scientists are wrong in their predictions from time to time.

Policy engagement always requires professionalism by the researchers at all stages of the process. Reports should be clear and timely, giving reliable information when it is needed most. There should be adequate treatment of all topics commissioned, and the implications of any policies and programs should be wide-ranging enough to cover any consequences of action. In making recommendations, alternatives for action and policy development should be presented. Above all, they should meet the capabilities, goals, and resources of the organizations in question; they should have a reasonable chance of success. If new goals or radically different approaches are suggested, then they should be fleshed out with some very particular details of how to actually reapportion strategies, resources, and personnel. In other words, such suggestions should be grounded, helpful, realistic, informed, and not based on naiveté. Beyond any advocacy and directions given in the report, the policy scientist has to advocate for the findings and recommendations. Crisp, clear, and well-illustrated oral presentations are crucial. Frequent short reports with effective executive summaries are important. The anthropologist or policy scientist should be prepared to make use of even more direct approaches. Conversations and formal meetings with the important decision makers and stakeholders are essential. In some situations, the policy scientist should know how to interact with the media to advocate the findings.

In order to be relevant, anthropologists should be prepared to do the equivalent of several ethnographies at once—of the agency and larger society as well as the affected population. For instance, in the refugee relocation field in which I have done some work, there would be the traditional type of ethnography in which one would come to learn of a particular ethnic subsociety in a host community—say, Salvadorians, Chileans, Vietnamese, or Kampucheans. A problem-oriented ethnography is generally required, focusing on health needs, family socialization and its conflicts with host community schooling, employment discrimination, un- and underemployment, and so forth. Any of these studies could then be broadly located within the policy domains of immigration and multiculturalism.

Another set of institutions is highly relevant to the research—that of the bureaucracies and agencies responsible for implementing policies for resettlement and social integration. These organizations then might have to be examined ethnographically (perhaps in very rapid fashion) and their linkages identified. Here, too, would be a need for an understanding of roles, networks of relationships, hierarchies of relationships, formal and informal decision making apparatuses, the constraints and opportunities for initiating new policies, and standardized ways of dealing with ethnic organizations and their conflicts. An awareness of the cultural dimensions of the bureaucracies would be essential for preparing analyses and usable reports. Among other things, it would be desirable to know the parameters of responsibilities and the typical ways of communicating within the agencies. Then there would be specialized bureaucratic language and unconscious assumptions associated with such institutions. Bureaucrats would speak of budget years, refer to particular programs, and use obscure acronyms. Consider some of the terms in one area in which I have worked—CEIC (Canada Employment and Immigration Commission), ISAP (Immigrant Settlement and Adaptation Program), AAP (Adjustment Assistance Program), Sec State (Secretary of State, a federal department responsible for citizenship and language programs), host group program, SLTP (Second Language Training Program), JFC (job-finding clubs), and so on—a veritable "alphabet soup" of acronyms and operating concepts. Such a terminology would be specific to the domain in question and would be part of a culturally specific discourse needed to understand action and policy. It is just as significant as the cultural code of a remote New Guinea village.

Summary

It should be very clear by now that anthropology is a policy science. It contains much within its traditions of method, theory, and knowledge that can be useful for analysis, advocacy, formulation, implementation, administration, evaluation, and direct participation in policy. Policy-making is a societal process, and it is associated with values, ideology, and beliefs, in other words, culture. Anthropologists have many functions in policy fields, especially demonstrating the cultural appropriateness or inappropriateness of policies as designed for particular peoples and working at the community, organizational, or subsocietal levels. Yet anthropologists still need to pay much more attention to how they frame their policy-relevant contributions.

The next five chapters describe more fully developed domains of policy analysis and participation in which applied and practicing anthropologists have been making significant contributions. These areas are needs assessment, program evaluation and social impact assessment, environmental anthropology, and advocacy.

RECOMMENDED READINGS

Bernard, H. Russell
1974   Scientists and Policy Makers: An Ethnography of Communication. *Human Organization,* Vol. 33(3): 261–276.

Chambers, Erve
1977   Policy Research at the Local Level. *Human Organization,* Vol. 36: 418–421.
1985   *Applied Anthropology: A Practical Guide.* Englewood Cliffs, NJ: Prentice Hall.

Cochrane, Glynne
1980   Policy Studies and Anthropology. *Current Anthropology,* Vol. 21(4): 445–459.

Geilhufe, Nancy L.
1979   Anthropology and Policy Analysis. *Current Anthropology,* Vol. 20(3): 577–579.

Pelto, Pertti J., and Jean J. Schensul
1986   Toward a Framework for Policy Research in Anthropology. Edited by Elizabeth Eddy and William L. Partridge. *Applied Anthropology in America.* Second Edition. New York: Columbia University Press. pp. 505–528.

Weaver, Thomas
1985a   Anthropology as a Policy Science: Part I, A Critique. *Human Organization,* Vol. 44(2): 97–106.
1985b   Anthropology as a Policy Science: Part II, Development and Training. *Human Organization,* Vol. 44(3): 197–206.

CHAPTER

6

Needs Assessment

Of all of the stages in the policy process, needs assessment may be the most compatible with anthropology because of its natural historical approach. Ethnographers go to actual social situations and describe the details and structures of peoples' lives in context. Next to the peoples themselves, few can be as potentially familiar with their needs and definitions of needs as anthropologists. A good proportion of the anthropological literature has described politically subordinated and impoverished peoples. Motivated by empathy, anthropologists often advocate for such peoples' needs whether or not they were commissioned to do so. Ethnographers are usually aware of conditions that hinder community well-being, such as inadequate land bases, discrepancies in health care and education, and barriers to self-determination. So anthropology serves needs assessment because it generates knowledge of context, thus shaping understanding of what is needed in the first place.

Yet, needs assessment is not merely a description of a situation and its difficulties. Something more formal is meant by the term. To separate it from program evaluation (with which it is sometimes combined), I define needs assessment as a process of identifying and seeking solutions to the problems of particular peoples or institutions, regardless of whether programs or solutions have already been designed to ameliorate them. It has become a major part of policy planning, and policy formulators frequently review needs, but remember that there can be major discrepancies in the way different groups define needs. Needs are very much related to values. So, in the determination of values pertaining to needs, anthropological perspectives can be quite useful.

There is a somewhat understandable tendency for policy makers to seek uniform solutions for as many people as possible, but that is often how problems are exacerbated. Anthropologists can play a valuable role in disentangling needs by pointing out special or unique circumstances for particular groups. Coming from another direction, we can also see how needs or needs areas might be broadly similar among separate groups, but workable policy solutions should differ. Consider an epidemiological survey of a population that reveals chronic health problems to be more or less evenly distributed among various sectors of the elderly in a community. Standardized services might then be designed to meet the needs of the elderly and their caregivers. But we might discover that one ethnic group is more affluent than others, has retained well-developed extended family systems, and has wider community linkages such as religious and ethnic organizations. All of these assets support their family caregivers to a greater extent. Other ethnic groups may be much more impoverished, powerless, and socially fragmented. Without adequate resources, they have not been able to maintain effective community and extended family supports. Yet another category might consist largely of single elderly males living in impoverished conditions in single-room-occupancy hotels in a city's tenderloin. These elderly males live in virtual social isolation, and charitable responses to them have been minimal and very impersonal. These different situations call for different solutions in the design of social, health, and community services even though the health needs of these elderly people may be the same. Basically, here is where the ethnographic approach is important for showing variations in actual circumstances relevant to real people. Some solutions would call for more direct services to the more vulnerable (such as more direct home-care visits), and others would call for a variety of services, including reinforcements of existing support networks (e.g., counseling or financial supplements to family caregivers and improvements to a local seniors' center).

What Do We Mean by Needs?

There can be so many competing views of what constitutes a real need as distinguished from a want or an item on a "wish list." Accordingly, it is useful to clarify what is meant by social needs and to examine their varieties. Even beyond the practice of needs assessment, that inquiry is useful because so much of human service programming is ultimately formulated with some notion of need in mind. For such clarification, an article by Jonathan Bradshaw (1972) is useful.

Bradshaw identifies four types of needs—normative, felt, expressed, and comparative. *Normative needs* are determined by the experts or administrators in charge of services. These are standards and have been established as desirable or ideal from studies or long-term experiences with services. Sometimes they are presumed to be directly measurable as exemplified by clinical norms established in the health field. For example, desirable or normal blood pressure ranges or weight ranges have been established. Nutritionists might determine that each person requires 1,800 calories per day and so many grams of protein. Experts in social policy devise poverty lines based on income and living spaces, measured in square feet, for families of certain sizes. Once clinical or normative standards are established, then needs are determined by examining discrepancies from those norms.

Felt needs are elicited when people are asked what they actually want. Felt needs may be difficult to establish because of the possibility that people will inflate vague desires into more compelling needs. On the other hand, felt needs may be hard to elicit because people may be reluctant to bring certain types of needs to their consciousness. For example, "traditional" middle-aged wives suffering from spousal abuse may admit to the need for shelters or counseling only when pressed. Barriers such as the value of subservience to husbands in some culturally based authority systems may preclude their readily complaining about abuse.

Expressed needs are felt needs that become demands or petitions for action. People may lobby, write, or demonstrate for a particular need. Several years ago in my city, Saskatoon, Native students protested against a massive reduction in their federal living and tuition allowances while they were attending the university. They were expressing their needs directly. Needs will also be expressed if there are long waiting lists or heavy uses of existing programs. Because of the backlog of clients, the family service bureaus in Saskatoon have a minimum waiting period of at least three months before family counseling can be provided for those having difficulties in their marriages. Similarly, our local immigrant settlement agency has had very long waiting lists for employment training programs. Many immigrants have a great deal of difficulty getting jobs, partly because of the obvious fact that they do not have North American job experiences. They also have certain difficulties in knowing what to expect on the job and with résumé writing and other job-orientation problems. These expressed needs are demonstrated by participating in or applying for job-training programs.

The fourth type of need is *comparative need.* Suppose that a standard set of needs has been identified for particular categories of people, but services have been supplied to only some of them. The neglected groups would be perceived as in comparative need.

A good example comes from Florida. Support groups had been established at hospitals for the family caregivers (usually middle-aged or elderly women) of Alzheimer's disease patients. The latter required enormous amounts of attention from their caregivers, who live very exhausted, harried lives and often have many other responsibilities. Support groups seemed quite useful for providing advice and comfort. However, only white middle-class people showed up at the support groups. Neil Henderson, an anthropologist working out of the Suncoast Gerontology Center, led a team that extended support groups to black and Hispanic people in Tampa and Jacksonville. Demographic and health data suggested that prevalency rates for Alzheimer's disease were equal in all segments of the population. It was assumed that minority populations would have comparative needs for support groups. The pilot studies, while confirming this, also demonstrated that a number of needs were culturally specific. With Hispanics, for instance, the support group itself operated as a "fictive" family. Hispanic families have a need for solidarity and privacy, especially regarding afflictions perceived as mental illness. Since senile dementia was a major symptom of Alzheimer's disease patients, shame had inhibited discussing the problem outside the family. But in the context of support groups, nonrelated people interacted in a familial way, giving assistance and emotional support beyond the discussion groups (Henderson et al. 1993; Henderson 1997).

Bradshaw reveals complications in the ways that types of needs can be interpreted or linked. When overlaps occur and all four types of needs are present, there may be no problem in establishing policies or programs, provided there is enough money available. For instance, consider the case of home-care visits and Meals on Wheels services for the relatively immobile but still largely independent elderly. There is widespread agreement in the community and supportive research among health care professionals (normative) that such services are effective in maintaining peoples' health and independence. The elderly and concerned relatives in the community readily agree that such services would be welcome in their area. A local organization of senior citizens already has expressed the need to their local health board and to their politicians. It is clear that there is a comparative need, because other nearby towns or counties have such services.

But other scenarios are not so clear cut. A need might be formulated by experts and generally felt by potential clients but not actually demanded or expressed by them in any meaningful way. An example is the need for sex education or family-planning services among unmarried teenage girls. The young women themselves might agree that such programs would be useful but have not yet expressed that view through any tangible behavior.

If services were supplied, the felt needs might then be expressed through use of them, but, on the other hand, the services might be underutilized or ignored. Sometimes needs can be identified by experts and supplied but not be felt or expressed, as in the familiar case of postnatal public health visits to examine mothers and their babies after release from the hospital. A need may be identified by research, felt, and expressed but not yet supplied. An example is counseling and support services for single fathers, who typically constitute about 10 percent of the single-parent population. Most services have been modeled on the needs of the single mother. Still another possibility are needs that are not appreciated or supplied by experts but strongly felt and expressed by people. Several years ago, I helped a blind and visually impaired group make their own informational needs assessment. One of the needs they identified was access to information on alternative holistic health services. This need, which was not recognized or met by health-care agencies, was still felt by members of this group.

Purposes and Expectations of Needs Assessments

What are the purposes of needs assessments? Jack McKillip (1987, 1998) suggests that needs analyses are done on the assumption that specific actions can be taken within the agencies' mandates. For instance, in an assessment of seniors for a mental health clinic, it would not be appropriate to concentrate on housing needs if the agency's mandate cannot attend to that. However, there may be a significant set of needs and issues associated with the use of alcohol and alcoholism. That second set of topics may be more appropriate to the agency's mandate and should, therefore, be examined thoroughly.

Some anthropologists run the danger of being naive about the policy contexts of their research. They may be tempted to examine subjects that stimulate their particular academic interests or sympathy. In the case of the elderly and the mental health clinic, there would be nothing wrong with noting the relevance of housing and linking it to the enhancement of mental health, but, pragmatically, it is more important to recognize and concentrate on the concerns mandated to the agency.

When needs are identified, it is also important to assess them in terms of their possible variable content. In a research project for an immigrant service agency, immigrant clients revealed that they had a strongly felt and expressed need for intensive, skill-based, employment-training programs that would help orient them to the expectations in job settings (Ervin 1994a). They hoped that such classes would also train them in the uses of modern technology, such as computers, fax machines, and the Internet. They thought it quite urgent that programs be developed to assist them in getting job recertification, high school equivalency diplomas, and university entrance. In their experience, employment programs were very rudimentary and were only suitable for low-level entry jobs that often lead to no significant advancement. Many immigrants never actually found work because of the very high unemployment rates during the recessions of the 1980s and the fact that it was virtually impossible to get jobs without North American job experience. Jobs were very important for immigrants as a measure of their self-worth and were necessary to increase their standard of living, support their families, and gain the required financial resources to begin official procedures that would allow them to be reunited with family members still in the home country.

The significant point here is that a need should not just be stated: it should be revealed in its fullest context with its important corollaries and derivative needs.

Most organizations commissioning needs assessments expect guidance in establishing priorities. Simply listing needs and describing them are not enough. They must be ranked to generate actions following recommendations. There are various methods of establishing relative priority, such as Delphi and nominal groups, that will be discussed later in this chapter and elsewhere in the book.

It is also essential to keep in fairly constant communication with the agency that has commissioned the researcher and with the people for whom any recommendations are intended—the decision makers and any other relevant audiences. As McKillip (1987: 9) phrases it, the process is interactive. Feedback should be frequent until effective conclusions, priorities, and solutions are crystallized.

Needs assessments can be required for a number of purposes. They can be used in preparing for grant applications and other funding requests. They are used for budgeting, setting priorities, and developing programs. They might be commissioned to raise public awareness about undesirable situations or to clarify views of particular client groups. They might also be the fulfillment of a political promise. Of course, policy makers may follow through on a mandate just to make it look as if they are doing something about perceived problems or because complaints have been raised. For all these reasons, the researcher must understand the purposes of the research and understand consequences of findings.

Models or Types of Needs Assessments

McKillip (1987: 18–43) suggests three types of needs assessment that can be initiated by agencies—the discrepancy, marketing, and decision-making models. In the *discrepancy model,* an expert group has determined particular goals and has developed ways of measuring performance. If there is a discrepancy in the achievement of these goals, then a need for improvement exists. For instance, a school district uses standardized scores for mathematics or tests of English comprehension that measure "normal" ranges of competency. However, several categories of students continue to fail achievement tests. The discrepancy approach suggests that the school board should develop remedial programs to improve the skills of these students.

The second type—the *marketing model*—is agency centered and not always completely service oriented. Take the situation of an agency that has been designed to meet a number of needs, but its clientele has been steadily shrinking, and it is in danger of losing its funding from government or charitable agencies. In order to discover how to best serve its clients' needs, it conducts a needs assessment, searching out felt and expressed needs. It can then redesign or initiate policies and programs to best suit these needs and use the findings to seek funding for its own survival.

The agency might be sincerely involved in a marketing campaign to improve its services and perform legitimate public service. Several years ago in Saskatoon, a venerable service agency found that its services were drastically underused through no particular fault of its own. Since the nineteenth century, this charitable organization had initiated home visits to look after the health needs of very poor and chronically ill elderly people. But over the decades, various government agencies had taken over practically all of the functions that it had pioneered, and the organization was in danger of going out of operation. This NGO was considering commissioning a needs assessment to seek out new services and new clients, ones that would still resemble their original mandate. They centered the assessment on the needs for home-based respite services for families and caregivers of the mentally ill, autistic children, and other disabled relatives. Any services developed would be truly beneficial to the community—not just simply survival mechanisms for the agency.

The third approach—the *decision-making model*—is a preferable and more developed model but is still agency based. Its underlying assumption is a rational one: it assumes that a focus on the actual needs and values of current and potential clients will lead to better services by an organization. In such a decision-making approach, there is a very careful selection of indicators and sources of data to assess what needs there are. All sorts of needs could be considered—including normative, felt, expressed, and comparative ones. Needs would be carefully sifted from wants, and significant priorities would be established. Policy recommendations would be developed to specifically consider plans of action, budgets, and program development. Each scenario would consider resources already available and what supplements would be needed. The associated pros and cons of possible actions would be listed. Such a strategy would indicate which existing services or approaches are currently underused and which might need to be shut down in order to use the personnel, time, and resources to establish new directions and programs to meet needs and newly discovered priorities. Such a model would have to take into account the values and expectations of both the clients or beneficiaries and the staff. Yet this is still, ultimately, an organization-centered needs assessment.

Let me raise a fourth approach not discussed by McKillip—the *participatory-action model,* which may or may not be institutionally focused. This model is discussed in much greater detail in another chapter of this book, but I will review its essence here. The approach is bottom-up in focus. A group of people (clients, potential clients, members of self-help groups) research, assess, and prioritize their own needs on the basis of group discussions or social science techniques that they have mastered. They may or may not have a social scientist working with them as a coequal or advisor. The important feature is that the participants have ownership and control over the research questions, the data, and the research process. They also decide courses of action to be taken. This approach counters the imbalance created by bureaucracies and other dominant power structures and allows people to empower themselves.

The blind and visually impaired advocacy and self-help group that I worked with was trying to articulate their informational needs. The members were dissatisfied with the role taken by a larger national organization that serviced the visually impaired and felt that this organization had monopolized the role of "speaking" for the visually impaired and acting as an intermediary with the larger, "sighted" society. The group wanted to break the stifling relationship with the paternalistic organization and articulate its own needs directly to the larger society. It also wanted to express these needs as rights, but first it had to develop an inventory of policy priorities. I advised group members on some research strategies and worked with them in the collection of data. They acted independently of major organizations and were not clients (see Chapter 15 for more details).

Methods and Sources of Data for Needs Assessments

Next to be considered are the methods, sources of data, and the actual logistics of needs assessments. There are many sources of data and methods for ascertaining needs. Some of them are discussed at greater length in other chapters, but a review of them here is in order to establish the possible logistics for research design. They are:

1. **Rates under Treatment (or Rates of Utilization).** This quantitative approach totals the number of people using existing programs and makes breakdowns by age, sex, socioeconomic status, ethnicity, and so forth. Presumably those programs that fill existing needs show high use and long waiting lists, yet such assumptions could be rather crude for several reasons. Sometimes, large numbers of users indicate only that a service is available, possibly for free. A service might be a way for people to socialize. Similarly, agencies might encourage people to use their services and programs to provide the justification for keeping them going. Yet, if a program or service is not being used, that does not necessarily mean that there is no underlying need. For example, services for the mentally ill tend to be very much underutilized because the services carry a social stigma.

2. **Social, Socioeconomic, and Health Indicators.** Demographic and statistical data can monitor significant changes that mirror needs in the society and community. If the number of non-English-speaking immigrants increases dramatically, that might suggest a need for extensive English-as-a-Second-Language instruction. If the number of teenage pregnancies in a region have increased dramatically recently, this might suggest the need for increased services in counseling or sex education for teenagers and teenage mothers, in particular.

3. **Test Scores.** If a capacity is measurable (e.g., mathematical, geographical, or historical knowledge), then scores on tests given in the schools might indicate discrepancies in performance that suggest the need for remedial programming. For that purpose, samples of work (e.g., art and essays) might also serve as indications of need fulfillment or discrepancy.

4. **Documents.** All sorts of sources might be considered here—public archives, briefs, records (such as journals), reports, the print media, and other written documents that are important to society. Generally, these would be supplementary or supportive of other approaches or sources of data and might show how the perception of certain needs has entered into the public discourse. A classic anthropological example is the archival material that demonstrates widespread historical land use and occupancy, thus justifying land compensation for contemporary Native peoples.

5. **Survey Questionnaires.** Questionnaires to confirm or rank needs would normally be constructed after establishing the possible extent of needs. The types of surveys that can be used include telephone, mailed, or direct questioning and vary from highly structured to open ended in format.

6. **Key-Informant Interviews.** Interviews can be considered at two levels. First, recognized community leaders or people who, by nature of their work, are fairly knowledgeable about local conditions can be consulted. Then there are those people who represent many walks of life or the subjects of the category under review. Under

normal circumstances they are not viewed (nor do they view themselves) as experts, but, in fact, they are experts because of their direct and authentic experience of the issues (e.g., drug addiction, spousal abuse, trapping life styles) and so should be interviewed.

7. **Group-Interviewing Techniques (Focus, Nominal, and Delphi Groups).** Relatively unstructured focus groups can generate new and contextualized information on needs, issues, and solutions. Participants in small groups of seven to twelve people can be drawn from all sectors of the community, or they might all be experts (again perhaps by direct experience) on the needs in question. The nominal-group approach is much more structured and requires that people express their lists of needs in a round-robin fashion and then prioritize exercises on secret ballots. Delphi groups are "nominal groups" at a distance—the participants do not get together but communicate anonymously and prioritize needs through the mail, with the results being collated by a research team (see Chapter 12).

8. **Community Forums or Hearings and Briefs.** Meetings can involve large numbers of people at hearings sponsored by the organization seeking information on needs. Being open ended, they allow members of the affected community or population to voice their perceptions or concerns. Unexpected perceptions, facts, and opinions about the issues are often revealed. Official positions of community organizations can be presented, and individuals can voice their own concerns. Those not able to attend might provide briefs. Forums can also serve as a means of introducing the intentions of the research or investigation. Because of the public response, they can also allow for more revelation of the political context of the issues.

9. **Observations and Participant Observations.** It would seem quite useful for investigators to actually observe the circumstances of the community and its important subsectors to understand its context and to become intimate with actual or observed needs. Even more effective is the time-honored anthropological approach in which the investigator becomes deeply immersed in local day-to-day affairs. Through long-time familiarity, the investigator observes behavior and comes to understand the categories and nuances of the native point of view. It is an invaluable way to get beyond normative expectations.

Developing the Right Strategies for Needs Assessments

There is a wealth of approaches, methods, and sources of data available for needs assessments. How does an assessor choose the ingredients of an effective applied research design? Steadham (1980) provides us with a few good suggestions: time and money are the key considerations.

The worst scenario—a deadline of two or three weeks and the expectation of a report within another two weeks—severely limits research tools. If the assessment is to be focused on the needs of a particular agency or institution, there can be a manageable number of key informant interviews, a focus group or two, and a rapid examination of the existing records and documents.

The other related factor is the money available for the research. Some techniques can be extremely time consuming and costly. Key informant interviews, although very revealing, take up hours of collecting and transcribing. Ultimately, they only cover a small part of the community or group under scrutiny. Survey questionnaires, although sources of valid information and covering representative samples of the community, can soak up large amounts of money very rapidly. Constructing sample frames, designing questions, pretesting them, and training interviewers are all very costly. Other costs are the wages and time of interviewers as they go door to door to do the actual interviewing. If mailed interviews are used, then the costs of postage for the interviews and reminder letters should be taken into account. Expenses have to be anticipated, including the copying of archival or other documents.

Another consideration is whether the agency or jurisdiction commissioning the needs assessment is committed to immediate policy and programming changes or to a broad and long-range view of circumstances. Sometimes research may be done only to appear to be doing something or to allow people to ventilate frustrations with no real intention of changing anything. The aim is merely to gain more time or to forestall further pressure from the community. If they participate at all, researchers should be very careful in not selecting research methods, such as community forums and focus groups, that might unrealistically raise expectation levels.

Great care must be taken in choosing research methods that respect confidentiality. We have to consider the degree of sensitivity needed on certain topics (e.g., mental illness, drug abuse) and that stigmatized people might be easily identified within small communities. Again, focus groups and community forums may risk sensitive or inflammatory opinions coming to public view. As the colloquial expression goes, public forums may "raise more heat than light"; they could actually stir up conflict in the community rather than resolve it. Confidentiality needs to be considered in the writing of reports in institutions if a needs assessment could reveal opinions or community secrets to others in a small community or agency. Sometimes, however, it may be important to reveal the opinions and comments of participants in the project when they lend authenticity, poignancy, or immediacy, and, sometimes, the participants expect to issue their views as a form of authorship.

Another consideration is a calculation of how much feedback is advisable during the research project. It may be timely to use focus groups and community hearings to test preliminary findings and recommendations to assess validity as well as to gauge commitment to any proposed changes. This is also done to promote a sense of ownership among participants and helps to ensure that something actually will be done. Attempt to define the extent to which staff or policy makers should influence the needs assessment. If this is an agency or government-driven exercise (which it usually is), are we most interested in the felt and expressed needs of a certain group, such as single mothers on welfare or street adolescents? If there is a mandate to rectify policies and services from their point of view, we may wish to exclude staff at social service agencies because their normative views may be too deeply entrenched. On the other hand, if the project seeks some accommodation among normative, expressed, and felt needs, it may be a very good idea to include experts and staff.

Another set of considerations might relate to cultural distance and the degree of difficulty that outside agencies may have encountered with local people in the past. Clients may have developed a fair amount of suspicion and cynicism about any actions by external agents. With Native American groups, for instance, it might be much wiser to approach the whole realm of needs slowly and through ethnographic approaches. More directed approaches like questionnaires, key-informant interviews, and focus groups may not be culturally acceptable until toward the end of the project when trust has been established and there is need for direct verification. In situations like these, it is probably advisable to encourage more participation in defining the problem so that the people concerned will feel more committed.

Within reason, use as many techniques and sources as is feasible or manageable to allow corroboration or cross-checking of information on needs, thus lending more validity to the findings. For instance, indicator data may point to high pregnancy rates for single teenage females living in poverty in areas with high crime rates. Key-informant interviews with community leaders, as well as focus groups with teenage mothers themselves, corroborate the vulnerability of these women. This would suggest remedial actions with regard to safety, counseling, and poverty reduction. It is a good idea to consider using at least three or four procedures when time and money permit.

A final part of assessment is allocating time not only for obtaining information but also for advocating research findings. There is a need to educate or persuade people about the significance of the findings and to work on constructing solutions. Above all, scheduling is critical. Figure out how long it will take to do each task, when each should be completed, and when to move on to the next, keeping in mind the necessity of providing margins or lead time because the unexpected almost always happens.

Case Study: The Saskatoon Needs Assessment Project

Background and Purposes

The following case illustrates how choices are actually made in research design. In the winter of 1990, I was asked by the executive director of my local United Way to do a community needs assessment for the whole city (Ervin et al. 1991a, 1991b; Ervin 1997b). Funding priorities among its twenty-eight agencies had not changed for thirty years, and its allocations committee wished to have new information about the community. In addition, an evaluation by the national office of the United Way had recommended that the organization become more directly acquainted with local needs and services in health and social sectors to coordinate long-range planning among its agencies. So a needs assessment was approved by the board, and $14,000 ($20,000 Canadian) was allocated for it. It was to be completed in six months—in time for the annual fall funding allocations. Officials hoped that the study would provide some simple formula for helping them to make their hard financial decisions, but they also wanted a general study of community conditions that could be used by other government and nongovernment agencies. For nongovernment charitable organizations, pressures were becoming overwhelming. Because of government cutbacks in direct services and funding to human service agencies, more and more was expected of the nonprofit sector. The United Way had to sort out these difficulties in its planning.

Designing the Research and Engaging Stakeholders

I had about three weeks to complete a research design before putting three students to work during the summer to collect data, leaving enough time to get the report written by mid-fall. The task was to examine the social circumstances surrounding human service delivery needs for a city of 200,000, set priorities, and make recommendations within six months—a tall order.

Research design and strategy meetings were held with the research assistants, a committee of stakeholders from the United Way, and a few member agencies. We cleared our ideas with them, including a plan to have a series of consultative meetings with the larger number of stakeholders who would be affected by any recommendations. We also consulted with the twenty-eight executive directors of United Way agencies at meetings and individually and with the full board of the United Way. Altogether, almost thirty meetings were held in less than a month to set the directions for this large, cumbersome project.

Early on, we saw serious apprehensions developing among the agencies. Some assumed that our project was meant to cut off funding or to interfere with their autonomy by forcing them to take up services that they had not chosen. Reassurance took up a lot of time, energy, and patience. Anybody doing this sort of research should be prepared to be put on the "hot seat" and realize that his or her own good and honest intentions are not always sufficient in dealing with the human relationships aspects of any applied research.

Preliminary tasks were decided upon and accomplished during the first month. The students started to collect and annotate all of the significant technical reports published about community social issues over the past twenty years. Then we started to gather all of the available demographic, social, socioeconomic, and health statistics relevant to the city over the past twenty years from standard sources such as Statistics Canada, Saskatchewan Health, and the City Planning Department. Statistics were collated, revised, placed in tables and graphs, and interpreted. We decided to collect social indicators that would point out broadly measurable trends in the community and to suggest needs that were very general in scope. We used one measurement of rate of utilization—the exponential rise in the use of food-bank services within one decade. This underscored a frequently mentioned need to attend to the dilemmas of hunger.

Among United Way board members there was an expectation that we needed to conduct a broadly based questionnaire survey of a random sample of the city's population to discover the community's needs. It was assumed that the survey would be a good marketing tool. If we could discover what the general population saw as the most important needs, fund-raising strategies would be developed to encourage citizens to be more generous. However, the notion of a broadly based questionnaire was soon rejected. Our very limited budget would have been swallowed up by direct, phone, or mail interviewing, not to mention any pretesting costs. It would also have been difficult to get access to data for a sampling frame. Telephone numbers were obtainable, but the telephone company had strict regulations and time-consuming clearance procedures. Yet the biggest argument against a survey came from the executive directors of the hard-pressed member agencies of the United Way. They felt that the public was not well informed about the range of pressing social issues and would only respond with ideas that had been generated by media coverage. They would probably overlook long-term, not very visible, or unappealing social issues such as those associated with mental illness, chronic illness, and disabilities, including epilepsy, arthritis, and visual impairment. Although the public would identify some significant issues, perhaps domestic abuse, child welfare, or the conditions of urban Native people, it is unlikely that they would have mentioned the other issues that cause distress and continuing difficulty to people. So a general survey of the community was rejected. There might have been grounds to include one had the budget been bigger and had there been more time. Certainly, there should be more knowledge of local public opinion for the marketing in charitable fund-raising.

Through a directory of community services, we classified human services into seventeen sectors, which included employment, housing, poverty, disability and chronic illness, mental health, immigrant issues, women, Native issues, youth, the elderly, continuing education, prevention and recreation, substance abuse, human justice services, and so forth. These sectors were divided into groupings of three or four, and responsibility for each was assigned to one of the three student assistants and myself. For example, I had the sectors of immigrant and refugee resettlement, chronic illness and disability, mental health, and general health.

Each of us was responsible for finding out as much as possible about the contexts and needs of assigned sectors through key-informant interviews, technical reports, and, wherever possible, focus groups. Altogether, 135 key-informant interviews and six focus groups were completed over the next four months.

Another mainstay of the data-collecting process was the use of a three-staged Delphi questionnaire (see Chapter 12). We asked the twenty-eight executive directors (or their delegates) one basic question—what are the pressing needs in the human service delivery area, irrespective of who is charged with dealing with them? The response to the question and the subsequent two stages of prioritizing and establishing supportive comments took slightly more than ninety days. It included sixteen substages and required a great deal of care in scheduling. This time-consuming method began at the start of the project. Nonetheless, the information from the Delphi questionnaire was extremely useful in establishing a framework for priorities of needs, and the primary focus of the needs assessment was to review priorities at the United Way and its member agencies.

The final step was a set of community forums in which oral briefs were presented. These forums were held in the fall after the other procedures had been completed. These direct and open public consultations were to allow for more publicity about the project and United Way operations during the annual fall fund-raising campaign. By having board members, who were mostly businesspeople, attend these hearings, the board could gain more familiarity with social issues relevant to the city. Timing was also strategic because mid-fall is when nongovernmental charitable human service organizations tend to be best prepared for any concerted action after their summer recesses. These forums would allow organizations to present issues and needs in their own manner, according to their own agenda. An added purpose of the hearings was to allow all possible points of view to come forward.

Thus the needs assessment relied on six methods or sources of data. The most important were the 135 key-informant interviews, the Delphi questionnaire, the collection of social indicators, and the community forums and briefs. Focus groups and the materials found in previous studies were secondary influences. We used a relatively large number of approaches because of the great complexity of the study. During the first month of organizational meetings, we had to be very diligent about the planning, timing, and coordination of all the details. We drew up a large (four feet long) organizational chart that, in the vertical column, listed all the main tasks. Then, on the horizontal axis, all the starting dates through the four months of student research time were indicated. Using colored markers, the required dates of completion were indicated at the appropriate coincidence of the two axes. The actual date of completion was indicated with another marker.

Results

The most difficult part of the analysis was to establish needs that were general to the city as a whole. As a first step, I took all of the social indicators that we had been able to collect and interpreted some of the trends for the city. These included demographic, social, socioeconomic, and health-related trends. Saskatoon's population had gone through a very large growth period in the late 1970s and into the 1980s but was now leveling off, but the proportions of seniors, non-European immigrants, and Native peoples had increased significantly. The numbers of single-parent households had also been steadily growing, and traditional nuclear families were declining in proportion as was the average size of families. The numbers of unemployed and social assistance recipients had increased dramatically. For a while, the city had one of the highest rates of unemployment in Canada, and the median income was the lowest of western Canadian cities. The proportions of working poor were growing at a greater rate than in other western Canadian cities. Rates of use of the city's food bank had grown exponentially. Many of these downward trends were tied to several severe recessions that had affected Saskatchewan during the 1980s, at a time when government and non-government funding for services had been greatly slashed. Also, it was discovered that approximately 10 percent of the population was disabled at various levels of impairment. As a broad guess I suggested that approximately 50,000 people or 25 percent of the population was potentially in need of the sort of services that were provided by United Way or parallel agencies.

When the indicators had provided the context, we moved on to a description of priority needs of the community as a whole. For that purpose, we used the Delphi questionnaire results as a framework. These results were corroborated and often supplemented from key-informant interviews, focus groups, and community forum briefs. For instance, in the Delphi questionnaire it was surprising that the need for more counseling, services, and shelters for women and children suffering from abuse ranked rather low even though the significant majority of the respondents were women. Yet, this need was raised in practically every key-informant interview and was poignantly emphasized over and over at the community forums. So, we added this to the list of core needs relevant to the community as a whole. Similarly, although a concern for dealing with Native urban problems was highly ranked in the Delphi, we added a corollary to it. We suggested that there was a need for a separate but parallel set of services for Native people, because this concept was raised by Native key informants themselves. At this time, very few Native people used the generic services that were available to everybody. Most observers conceded that agencies had yet to develop cross-cultural sensitivity. Aboriginal or Native quests for greater self-determination and control over institutions that govern their lives had to be taken into account.

These examples demonstrate that there are no precise ways to prioritize needs and judgment calls, and a wider sense of the politics involved is thus sometimes required. A few of the communitywide needs included the need to eliminate hunger and, therefore, to provide food banks and, more specifically, to address the overall problem of child hunger; the need to put more emphasis on preventative services, especially as related to programs for youth and children; and the need to address some of the generic problems in the access of transportation for disadvantaged people in the city. Beyond some of these basic needs, we added a category of "meta-needs," which pertained to issues that went beyond the specifics of material needs and were largely related to factors of organization. We felt that there was a need for a social planning council to facilitate coordination of programs and services during very tough financial times. Major improvements were needed to access information at several levels—for individuals, agencies, and the community as a whole. There was a need to extend and coordinate volunteer programming and to foster self-help advocacy groups.

The study also contained a set of recommendations specifically for the United Way that had arisen during our many key-informant interviews. This set included notions of helping nonmember agencies through small start-up grants, sponsoring skill-enhancing conferences for groups such as self-help groups, and making the board membership of the United Way more representative of the community instead of being dominated by the business sector. Some suggested that the United Way should become a more active advocate for disadvantaged groups in the city rather than limiting itself to fund-raising.

Beyond the chapters relating to the city as a whole, we produced another seventeen chapters discussing 235 needs associated with each of the specialized human service areas. Priority, context, and interrelationships were amplified.

Summary

This case study also illustrates the sorts of considerations to take into account when sorting out logistics in a research design dictated both by constraints and opportunities of time, money, and goals for the research. Every needs assessment will differ in size, priorities, and challenges. Assessments may tend to focus on unmet needs or deal with more specific sectors or groupings in the community (e.g., battered children, immigrants, the disabled), but logistics and research design will have to be sorted out from variables like the ones we had to consider.

The case study also documents anthropology's potential for conducting mainstream community policy analysis and formulation. Although the notions surrounding community are much more complex these days, anthropologists are still the specialists in this domain. A very flexible but primarily qualitative set of methodologies was required to retrieve a wide range of pertinent information in the seventeen complicated but ultimately interconnected areas of human service. We needed to identify insiders' perspectives and the significant issues in each area. We also had to find out what was common to them all and establish the level of priority for each need. For instance, one widely held priority centered on prevention or proactivity within most areas (hunger, disability, substance abuse). Women's issues were related to disabilities and chronic illness because women so frequently fulfill unpaid and arduous roles as volunteer and family caregivers. Employment training was considered highly essential for Native people, immigrants, women, the disabled, the poor, and so forth. Anthropological sensitivity was able to reinforce the need for a largely separate but parallel service for urban Native people because they tended to vastly underutilize existing human service facilities.

Anthropologists are especially well attuned and preadapted to conduct formal needs assessments because of their focus on cultural and social awareness. After all, they have been doing these assessments implicitly for decades as ethnographers.

RECOMMENDED READINGS

Bradshaw, Jonathan
1972   The Concept of Social Need. *New Society,* Vol. 30: 640–643.

Guyette, Susan
1996   *Planning for Balanced Development: A Guide for Native American and Rural Communities.* Santa Fe, NM: Clearlight Publications.

McKillip, Jack
1998   Needs Analysis: Forces and Techniques. In *Handbook of Applied Research Methods.* Edited by Leonard Bickman and Debra J. Rog. Pp. 261–285. Thousand Oaks, CA: Sage.
1987   *Needs Analysis: Tools for the Human Services and Education.* Newbury Park, CA: Sage.

Neuber, Keith A.
1980   *Needs Assessment: A Model for Community Planning.* Beverly Hills, CA: Sage.

Steadham, Stephen
1980   Learning to Select a Needs Assessment Strategy. *Training and Development Journal,* Vol. 34(1): 56–62.

Witkin, R. B.
1994   Needs Assessment Since 1981: The State of the Practice. *Evaluation Practice,* Vol. 15: 17–27.

CHAPTER

7

Program Evaluation

Accountability is a major issue in policy because most programs and services will come under some form of scrutiny. In contrast to outlining needs, making critical judgments about and comparisons of people's performances does not come easily for many anthropologists. This may be the result of the anthropological tradition of cultural relativism that has tended to view nonjudgmentally most forms of organization, behavior, and performance (see Camino 1997: 50). Practitioners must overcome that reticence while still respecting and comprehending the opinions and sensitivities of the participants.

This chapter outlines the broad features of evaluation—methods, models, logistics, and problem areas and provides some anthropological case studies. Before doing these things, it is a good idea to examine how evaluation fits into the larger picture of policy-making and why it has become so important in recent years.

Program Evaluation in the Policy Cycle

Where do programs and services come from? In the most "rational" type of scenario, they could come directly out of "scientifically" identified needs, yet their identification should involve at least an equal measure of grassroots participation. Programs and services should be designed to meet real needs and bring about meaningful improvements in peoples' lives.

In the real world, most programs and services do not develop out of original, well-focused needs assessments. Instead, they are usually products of political or administrative hunches based on presumed ongoing familiarities with the issues. They could also be partly the byproducts of lobbying by groups in society concerned or affected by the issue. Frequently, programs are simply the result of some ongoing momentum. Once a set of policies and programs has been established, there is a tendency to continue to expand and elaborate them. As we all know (or at least suspect), staff in bureaucracies often unconsciously do this to perpetuate their own organizational agendas, to ensure their survival, particularly if they are competing with other agencies and departments. A broad set of stated goals and justifications suggests that they are actually meeting societal needs, yet skepticism, encouraged by persistent complaints from "beneficiaries," for example, Native Americans, welfare recipients, and fishermen, might make us wonder.

The main motivation for program evaluation comes from funders, who want programs and policies to be made accountable—to produce identifiable benefits that justify the money spent on them. This seems to be the case with most American legislation from the early 1970s onwards, and presumably that also applies to many state, municipal, and county jurisdictions. In Canada, evaluations of programs and policies have come later but are rapidly catching up; now most organizations have built-in mandates for review. There are also many pilot projects being developed (e.g., to reduce drug abuse or to educate the public on the dangers of HIV/AIDS), and those projects must be evaluated before they are expanded. Financial crises supposedly justifying downsizing and restructuring put more emphasis on program evaluation.

There are similar expectations in the private sphere. Profit-oriented companies are often more decisive about eliminating or radically revising those programs that are found to be ineffective. Nonprofit nongovernment organizations also have growing expectations and pressures to engage in evaluation. The Red Cross, for example, might want to evaluate the effectiveness of their blood-donor or disaster-relief efforts. More localized and less well-funded organizations, relying on foundations and government funding on a contractual basis, are frequently expected to undergo external evaluations. The timing for evaluations is normally explicitly written into their contracts.

These trends have generated a whole new professional niche of program evaluation with its own accumulated literature and standards of practice. In the United States, many evaluators have found employment with independent research firms that are contracted as third-party evaluators for public programs and services. In Canada, program evaluators are more visibly attached to policy research and planning units within provincial health or social services departments and federal departments such as Indian Affairs and Northern Development. Even then, care is usually taken that an impartial third party does the work. For instance, in Saskatchewan, a provincially funded applied research unit, the Health Research and Utilization Commission, with a separate board monitors health treatment and prevention programs and has anthropologists on its staff. In Canada there has also been a steadily growing trend towards the privatization of some applied research, so consulting opportunities for program evaluators have started to increase in private firms.

Self-evaluation is another form of accountability that is gaining acceptance. Staff and perhaps board members (sometimes with client representatives) are expected to critically review their own programs and services and measure rates of progress as related to their mission statements, goals, and objectives. Such reviews of program and policy success may lead to revisions in long-range planning and changes in mission statements. New goals and ventures are established and old ones dropped. However, these self-studies can be intimidating and stressful, especially when the projects are dealing with highly charged issues like substance or domestic abuse. A facilitator, specializing in applied social research or program evaluation, might be called in to lead the staff through the evaluation process. Such a facilitator does not evaluate but rather guides the participants through standard review procedures. These exercises can be used as training sessions as well, sometimes on the assumption that the organization will conduct the next self-study on its own.

Training in the social sciences is a suitable foundation for program evaluation. Some evaluators specialize in particular topical areas such as health, education, or agronomy. Others can range across several domains. As would be expected, the earliest and most numerous professional opportunities were in the more quantitatively oriented policy sciences—epidemiology, sociology, social psychology, economics, and business or public administration.

But over time, an anthropological or, at least, qualitative dimension of evaluation became more important. One of the obvious reasons is that the many evaluations are directed toward "nonstandard" minority groupings or others that do not fit normative expectations. In fact, dealing with ethnic minorities has been the usual reason to call in an anthropologist, but, over time, we have discovered other "nonstandard" populations within the presumed majority. In addition, through ethnography, anthropologists can provide special insights about mainstream institutions.

Regarding program evaluation, a number of fundamentals need to be kept in mind. The first is that evaluations tend to be program or organization specific, so it is essential to understand their detailed purposes, often stated as goals and objectives. Most frequently the goals are what is evaluated, i.e., evaluators ask how effectively a program or organization is meeting its goals and objectives. As we shall discuss later, evaluations can be divided into three types—outcome, process, and systems evaluations—of increasing complexity. Outcome evaluations simply measure results (focusing on ends); process evaluations focus on the capacities of a program to deliver services (looking at means more than ends); systems evaluations look at how programs or organizations operate within larger contexts such as communities or natural environments.

Before elaborating on these types, we will examine some methodological and logistic considerations for evaluations.

Methodological Considerations: An Emphasis on Measurement in Quantitative Approaches

The types of data and research methods for program evaluation and needs assessment are much alike. Statistics on trends or changes as well as rates of utilization are essential to measure progress. In the health field, changes in mortality, morbidity, and other factors that reflect improved health can be important indicators of the effectiveness of particular programs. In the *Comadrona* project described in Chapter 4, successes were measured by lower rates of infant mortality and increased weights of babies during their first year. As an index of evaluation, rates of utilization demonstrated that the strategies (ethnic pride, ethnically specific staff, support groups and natural networks of communication in the community) were leading to success as shown by the significant increase in clinic use by pregnant Puerto Rican women.

Several years ago, when I was involved in refugee resettlement, I became aware of a program evaluation that had been done primarily on the basis of statistical comparisons and that initiated a new set of programs. During the Vietnamese "Boat People" crisis of 1979–1980, about 60,000 refugees were accepted into Canada. Half were relocated through private sponsorship. Churches, synagogues, service clubs, and other groups of citizens guaranteed $5,000 in support of each newcomer and provided housing, clothing, and household gear plus other services. Government-sponsored refugees' expenses were paid through a federal program for the first year. Assistance with language and employment readiness was collectively provided by local nongovernmental immigrant resettlement organizations. A project comparing the two programs—government and private sponsorship—showed that privately sponsored refugees entered into the workforce an average of three weeks earlier than the refugees sponsored by government. To the government, this meant that the immigrants would no longer be financially dependent on social assistance. They could now pay back their airfare, and they could become taxpayers in their new country. An average of three weeks per person multiplied by average wages and numbers of employed immigrants was a sizeable savings. Moreover, refugees could now start to save money to sponsor their own relatives still in the home country or languishing in United Nations relief camps in Third World countries.

All of this evidence focused on the three-week advantage of private sponsorship: it was suggested that private sponsorship involving community-based personal links provided more intimacy in daily contact, introduction to preexisting community-based support systems, and access to information that led more directly to getting jobs quickly.

Some of us expressed skepticism when the evidence was presented. What was the quality of the jobs? How long did the refugees keep them? What was the average pay? Were they on their way to reestablishing their professional or trade certifications? Were these privately sponsored people being adequately trained in English and other areas of adaptation and integration?

Yet the upshot of the evaluation and policy debate was that the federal government funded the Host Group Program as a subsidiary to its overall strategy of sponsorship. The Host Group was intended to be similar to the private sponsoring group but without any of the financial obligations of private sponsorship. Each host group had to consist of at least three adults, who were given support by a coordinator and training in cross-cultural sensitivity. It was assumed that this program would give government-sponsored refugees some of the more directly supportive links to the community as private sponsorship did. A new program was designed on the basis of an evaluation that emphasized quantitative measurement of outcomes (i.e., speed of employment and saving of government money). This example also shows how evaluations fit into the policy cycle: one evaluation leads to a new program or the refinement of an old one.

Quantitative evaluation often leads researchers to use formal questionnaires to measure satisfaction and provide suggestions for changes in programs or services. Likert-scaled questions (see Chapter 13), ranging from "extremely satisfied" to "extremely dissatisfied," are often very useful ways to assess how current and previous clients feel about the program as a whole, the efforts of staff, the specifics, and the results of the program.

In educational evaluation, standardized "before and after" skill tests measure capacities in mathematics and literacy. The effectiveness of life skills, pre-employment training, or other courses designed to improve the capacities of the disadvantaged might be evaluated by tests that can measure increased self-esteem. Various approaches to improving worker morale at a factory might ultimately be intended to improve overall productivity, which could be measured by increased profits and increases in the number of units manufactured (e.g., light bulbs, yards of electric wiring, etc., in the case of the classic Hawthorne Electric Company study—see Schwartzman 1993).

Qualitative Approaches

Key-informant interviews provide qualitative information about the staff and intended beneficiaries' views of a program. In focus groups, staff, clients, and managers come together to share information and opinions on the effectiveness of services. More formal group approaches, such as nominal and Delphi panels (see Chapters 6 and 12) can identify obstacles, opportunities, successes, and perhaps, needed changes in mission statements, long-range goals, and short-term objectives. Continuing focus groups consisting of stakeholder representatives might supply important feedback to an ongoing research project so that the collaborative use of the results and recommendations is more likely.

The use of public (or sometimes confidential) records is essential for almost any program evaluation. We always need a history of how the program and policy under question was conceived in the first place. Memos, letters, position papers, previous studies such as needs assessments, staff records, meeting reports, minutes, and financial statements should be sorted through. These can be supplemented with oral histories of the evolution of programs. Any kind of measurement or assessment would have to keep the original goals and objectives in mind. Sometimes the goals are not explicit or change over time, so the researchers may have to do a lot of digging on their own, sorting through documents and informant statements to identify the purposes and criteria for evaluation of the program.

Another less common technique is the use of public forums and written briefs to outline the views of a group. This technique would be appropriate if the program was making major impacts upon the community or if community cooperation was essential to the success of the program. These programs could include health promotion strategies to improve nutrition, deal with infant hunger, eliminate diseases, replenish soil, and other programs.

From our perspective as anthropologists, the most significant qualitative methodology is that of participant observation or ethnography. Being around the actual daily operations of a program throughout its seasonal cycle is extremely revealing. Most methodologies rely on peoples' selective memories, but being there and being able to describe what actually transpired is indispensable. It also aids the discovery of unexpected dimensions that may contribute to success or failure—things that were not anticipated during the formulation period. For instance, people may be attracted to services because they are physically accessible, perhaps because the facilities are near downtown bus services, rather than because of the program's content. Furthermore, services may be socially accessible because of the informal, friendly, respectful, and interested helping styles of the staff. Alternatively, the nonuse of services might be caused by physical or social inaccessibility when, otherwise, the program is sound.

Most observation in program evaluation is less direct because applied social scientists rarely can be staff members or recipients of a service. Occasionally such opportunities arise. Michael Quinn Patton (1980: 140–141) speaks of his experiences as a student and an evaluator of a wilderness training program designed to give adults more confidence and survival skills in the outdoors.

Just as is true in the conduct of a needs assessment, decisions have to be made about the choice of methods and sources and data to make evaluations. Budget, time, staff, and purposes of the evaluation are all important along with considerations of privacy and the degree to which the public needs to be consulted. It makes sense to combine several methods, using some mixture of quantitative and qualitative approaches. As usual, the more approaches that point to the same conclusions, the better. By using different methods, you can also draw attention to particular things that need to be improved. On the other hand, if different approaches show contradictory conclusions, we need to explore some things more deeply. It is possible for a program to have measurable successes in predicated outcomes and yet leave the clients very dissatisfied with their experience. The reverse is also possible.

The Growth of Qualitative Methodologies

Earlier emphases on quantitative measurement were probably influenced by the bureaucratic mind set that held that programs and services can be accountable through rational standards of efficiency. In the end, such an approach does not work because of the complex and organic nature of any human activity. Moreover, the exclusive use of quantitative measures, which appear more "scientific," may actually distort underlying realities. Alternatively, qualitative and quantitative investigations could actually reflect two separated realities, and the discordance needs to be explained for an effective evaluation.

Michael Quinn Patton (1980: 23–30), a sociologist and long-time expert, has advocated the use of qualitative methodologies in program evaluation. He cites the case of a new accountability system introduced by the Kalamazoo, Michigan, School Board in the early 1970s. It employed standardized ratings systems—achievement tests of students in the fall and spring, statements of performance objectives, teacher peer ratings, student and parent ratings of teachers, principal ratings of teachers, and teacher self-ratings. The system received national attention and was viewed as a potential model for other jurisdictions. The school board initially viewed any resistance to it as a method of avoiding accountability.

Commissioned by a teacher's union, a questionnaire survey was administered to the teachers to obtain their perspectives on the experience. Ninety percent of the respondents disagreed with the Kalamazoo School Board's contention that the "accountability system is designed to personalize and individualize education." They felt that the system definitely did not help teachers to become more effective nor did it improve educational planning and performance. The school board objected that the questionnaire results were biased and that the teachers were never really interested in compliance.

Yet the questionnaire contained two revealing open-ended questions about the accountability system. Seventy percent of the respondents emphatically responded to these questions, and the responses were included, verbatim, in the report.

Two sample responses follow:

> I don't feel that fear is necessary in an accountability situation. The person at the head of a school system has to be human, not just a machine. You just don't treat people as if they were machines. . . . I'm not saying that accountability is not good. I am saying the one we have is *lousy.*

> The system is creating an atmosphere of fear and intimidation . . . people are tense, hostile and losing their humanity. . . . Gone is the good will and team spirit of administration and staff. . . . One can work in these conditions but why if it is to "shape up" a few poor teachers. Instead it is having disastrous results on the whole faculty community.

So much heated controversy was generated that the superintendent of the schools resigned. The succeeding superintendent developed a new set of relationships with the teachers and a mutually acceptable accountability system, so that there was more general satisfaction a year later.

What brought about the change? Although the Kalamazoo School Board might reject standardized close-ended questions as biased, it could not ignore the passionate urgency in the words of the teachers themselves. There was fear, anguish, and genuine concern among teachers dedicated to their profession. Obviously, something was very wrong about the situation, and something had to be done before it got worse.

Such is the power of qualitatively derived data; as Patton puts it,

> Direct quotations are a source of raw data in qualitative measurement, revealing respondents' level of emotion, the way in which they have organized their world, their thoughts about what is happening, their experiences, and their basic perceptions. The task for the qualitative methodologists is to provide a framework within which people can respond in a way that represents accurately and thoroughly their points of view about the world, or that part of the world about which they are talking—for example, their experience with a particular program being evaluated (1980: 28).

Policy makers can make decisions supported by compelling qualitative techniques that represent the realities and the authentic perceptions of the staff, clients, and participants. A busy administrator may be overwhelmed by charts, statistics, and complicated survey analyses in a report, and the qualitative information may frequently speak more directly to the truth of the program or service being evaluated. At their worst, such quantitative methodologies limit the exercise of evaluation to preconceived categories established by the biases of research scientists or to categories and concepts that reflect cultural criteria of the administrators, funders, or other policy makers.

The applied policy sciences and traditionally quantitative disciplines, such as social psychology and epidemiology and community health, are discovering the merits, sometimes with all of the passion of the recently converted, of qualitative analysis, including participatory research.

Approaches to Program Evaluation

Outcome Evaluations

Traditionally, the approach most favored by program evaluators, funders, and policy makers focused on outcomes (Chambers 1985: 162; Weiss 1972: 34–42). This model deals precisely with the measurable benefits of a program that has been designed to bring about some favored outcome. On this basis, programs are considered successes, failures, or in need of revision.

As a hypothetical example (based on a real program design in Vancouver), consider an eight-week course designed to find recently arrived immigrants employment in the "hospitality industry" (i.e., hotels and restaurants). It is very difficult, with minimal English skills and no North American job experience, for people from the Third World to get jobs in the United States or Canada. Without jobs, they will remain on social assistance for an indefinite period. The solution is a training program that assists people into jobs as chambermaids, janitors, busboys, and kitchen help in the local large hotels. The pilot program consists of ten men and ten women students, all of whom have completed a twenty-five week course in English-as-a-Second Language. Three instructors are hired—one to teach and manage the program, one to teach and counsel, and one to organize and oversee a short internship program. Three weeks of instruction cover résumé writing, employee–employer relations, labor relations law, advice on getting along with hotel customers and fellow employees, instruction on standards of cleanliness, and discussion of cultural orientations in the workplace. The next four weeks are spent in a specific restaurant or hotel that has been prearranged by the third instructor, in which they will be paid minimum wages. Students then return for one more week of discussions of their job experiences. It is hoped 90 percent of the students will be employed by hotels and restaurants in the city and that by the end of six months at least 70 percent will have kept their jobs.

The evaluation is straightforward. Were the specific objectives of the program achieved or did they fall short? In evaluating the outcomes, the analysis does not deal with wider questions or detailed nuances. For example, although it provides short-term jobs and reduces welfare roles, does such a program place the immigrants in a job "ghetto"? In other words, might it be better to prepare immigrants for long-range possibilities of employment that extend beyond the low-level entry jobs? Could they be recertified into their previous professions or trained for new ones? However, when such an outcome evaluation is done, the researchers focus on the actual outcomes measured against the goals and objectives set.

Process Evaluations

The *process* approach (Chambers 1985: 163; Patton 1980: 60–64) to program evaluation is another option. Rather than measuring outcomes in specific programs, process evaluations look at overall progress through the steps or means to the desired ends. In reality, this is more appropriate for human service delivery, because desired outcomes do not occur over short periods, and measurement of success tends to be elusive.

To maintain some continuity with the previous example, consider the circumstances of involuntary immigrants or refugees to the United States or Canada. Two overall goals could be identified. One is integration—inclusion in the wider society through jobs, knowledge, use of mainstream institutions, and the same rights as members of the larger society. This could be measured by such markers as taking out citizenship or getting a satisfactory job. Yet, in reality, the process of integration never ends just there. The other broad goal is adaptation—to cope or adapt to the circumstances in the host country. Ingredients of adaptation could include language acquisition and competency in other aspects of communication, knowledge of host society customs, the capacity to develop new social support systems involving members of the host community as well as the person's own ethnic group, and many other modes of psychosocial coping. To some extent, success would have to be self-reported—that is, the individual achieves integration or adaptation, case by case. For any specific individual, life courses would have their "ups and downs"—sometimes they would be doing poorly, other times well. Also, one individual might be more preoccupied with one mode of adaptation and integration task than another. The tasks, such as getting jobs, being reunited with one's family, or dealing with past stress, would all vary in their intensity or poignancy from person to person. Similarly, immigrants would differ according to class and ethnic origins. The task of measuring success in a multitude of separate and overlapping circumstances in an immigrant population is infinitely complex and cannot be easily measured by a fixed set of outcome criteria.

In response to diffuse needs, nonprofit organizations have emerged to serve refugee and immigrant peoples. Any attempt at assessing their performance would require a process style of evaluation. These evaluations would center on the capacities of the staff and individual programs to serve their clients ongoing and changing needs. Questions could be asked about accessibility—are the services available at convenient times, and is physical space (i.e., classrooms, etc.) effective and comfortable? Equally important, are the services accessible, emotionally and socially? Is the staff open, friendly, and concerned about the clients? Are the staff members cross-culturally sensitive? Are there enough supplementary services, such as translation assistance or day-care facilities for women who would otherwise have to stay at home? Do the services of the organization create dependency among its clientele, or do they provide tools so that clients can achieve success outside the agency?

In a process evaluation, very little measurement of direct outcomes is done. In fact, many long-term benefits of the program might not be obvious right away; immigrants may use and improve upon their language skills or employment readiness as the years go by. A certain amount of success could be indicated by the fact that the immigrants no longer make use of the agency's services.

Anthropological work in program evaluation often calls for emphases on process rather than precisely measurable outcomes such as simple successes or failure. Clearly too, most evaluation in human service domains calls for process approaches, because of the complexity of the issues and because outcomes do not appear linearly. Of course, it is important for anthropologists to measure outcomes wherever possible because of the need for effectiveness and accountability.

Systems Evaluations

A third type, the *systems* approach (Chambers 1985: 163, 164), would seem to be even more compatible with the expectations of anthropologists. Systems modeling seeks cause-and-effect relationships of an organization's activities within a larger framework of the community and sometimes the natural environment. All of the components and contexts seen as related to the programs and services would be "mapped." This calls for the holistic, lateral, or web-like thinking that has been the hallmark of most good anthropological analysis. In scrutinizing operations of an immigrant settlement agency in the promotion of adaptation and integration, we could look at its effectiveness in the larger contexts of the host community. It would need a wide view to mark the boundaries of the system. Anthropologists are notably better than others at doing that. Not everything would be relevant in the identification of the system, and, of course, some things would have higher priority than others. What are the relationships of the agency to other groups that deal with immigrants and refugees— federal, municipal, county, state, or provincial agencies offering health, education, or social services? Are other groups responsible for parallel services such as English-language or employment-readiness training? How well coordinated are the efforts? Is there redundancy? In the interaction of the agencies and organizations involved, has there been smooth coordination, or have conflict, jealousy, and "turf wars" emerged? Has the organization made an impact on the community? Are members of the community aware of the role of the settlement agency? Do they appreciate its efforts? Has the organization been able to draw upon a significant number of volunteers to assist in the integration of newcomers to their city? Has the agency been able to convey some general understanding of the immigrant experience to the larger community? How effective has it been in orienting its own staff and volunteers in cross-cultural sensitivity in order to better serve its clients? How effective has it been in establishing contacts and working relationships with companies providing employment in the city? A similar set of relationships could also be examined with regard to landlords, neighborhood relationships, and housing, which would be another dimension of the agency's mandate to assist in integration of immigrants and refugees. With a systems analysis, many of the procedures of process modeling could be incorporated. Some types of outcome modeling could also be included when effective measurement is possible. One measure could be the proportion of refugees who have chosen to remain in their initial host community as opposed to those who seek secondary migration to larger centers where jobs are available and there are larger enclaves of their particular ethnic groups.

For applied anthropology that deals in program evaluation, I think that most of the best work is within the realm of systems analyses, for which we may be ideally equipped. Consider some of these topics—the establishment of health promotion projects to increase awareness of sexually transmitted diseases in residents of an Indian reservation, the establishment of a soil regeneration program to improve long-term agricultural productivity and conservation purposes; the establishment of an oral traditions heritage program for the young in a district of Appalachia. All of these programs, like most dealt with by anthropologists, would have to consider interconnected systems of influence beyond the bare essentials of the programs. Obviously, general considerations of the community's values would have to be considered. For instance, years ago Horace Miner (1949) showed us how incongruous a U.S. federal program that paid farmers not to grow corn was! The intention was to clear existing surpluses and to keep prices up. Miner explained that it did not work because it contradicted the underlying purpose of all farmers, which is to nurture the maximum growth of plants and animals. Any systems analysis of a program's compatibility would have to identify key stakeholders and gatekeepers in the community whose cooperation is essential for success. A systems analysis would consider how a program affected other areas of community and regional life. For instance, a hiring program to involve Native youth in the construction of a northern pipeline might actually have negative consequences. Young people would be attracted to high-paying jobs that are not permanent and, as a result, would not continue with their education.

Ideally, the anthropological investigator should be involved as soon as possible in any program evaluation so that ongoing feedback can be established to recommend improvements as the program proceeds. This is especially important if the project or service is a pilot program, which may later be extended in other contexts. It is very important to provide as much detail as possible to understand how the program unfolds and the dynamics of cause and effect. Given the background of the discipline, anthropologists should be able to provide the rich details needed in such circumstances. Anthropologists have much to offer, especially in those areas calling for process or systems analysis. Still, we will have to remind ourselves that such evaluations are program specific, and we must pay close attention to the discrete details of goals and objectives and operations of the program itself as well as to the policy formulations that established it in the first place.

Some General Considerations

For those about to be evaluated, the prospect can be very threatening. It may conjure up images of time-motion experts measuring productivity with stopwatches or other forms of intrusion (see Levis-Pilz 1997). But today, many people have become used to long-range planning and a policy cycle involving periodic evaluations. In a spirit of professionalism, many staff members may look forward to them as ways of reviewing past accomplishments, considering new challenges, finding ways to make improvements, and discovering means to better serve their clients. Just as experienced applied anthropologists can detect negative reception of their work, they also can sense a favorable atmosphere. In either case, it is obviously essential to do some preliminary investigation into the nature of the organization, the expectations of the staff, and the likelihood of the organization actually making use of the findings.

How an evaluation is constructed can influence utilization. There are always considerations of how much to involve staff and other significant stakeholders right from the beginning. As Patton (1982: 58) points out, different approaches are taken. One can be a type parallel to that taken by an accountant, an independent and potentially aggressive evaluator can carefully scrutinize a program, focusing on its accountability and searching for possible inappropriate behaviors or operations. An "aloof and value-free" scientist can attempt to gain impeccable data about program personnel and their activities as if seeking truth in a laboratory research project. But as a result

> Program staff typically have an aversion to being treated as outlaws or research subjects. They have become sophisticated in ways of sabotaging evaluations. (Patton 1982: 59)

Most stakeholders are quite happy to ignore the findings of evaluators (ignoring bad-tasting medicine is the analogy used by Patton). They are often avoided even when they are perceived as good for the organization, simply because the participants feel no stake in or identification with them. Persuasion or force may be needed for compliance.

Although proponents can justify these approaches, most anthropologists would feel uncomfortable with them. Patton advocates consultation and consensus building. The greatest advantage of the collaborative approach is that it really fosters utilization, enhancing the possibility that the research findings will actually be used. It ensures a greater degree of accessibility for the findings by clients. As a way of increasing the likelihood of utilization, stakeholders should be involved as early as feasible in the whole process. Personal engagement in the earliest stages involves

> . . . goals clarification, issues identification, ways of operationalizing outcomes, matching research design to program design, determining sampling strategies, organizing data collection, interpreting results and drawing conclusions. These processes take stakeholders through a gradual awakening to program complexities and realities, an awakening that contains understandings and insights that will find their way into program developments over time. . . . *The stakeholder assumption, then, includes the expectation that stakeholders need to expend time and effort to figure out what is worth doing in an evaluation; they need help in focusing on worthwhile questions; and they need to experience the full evaluation*

process, which is really a learning experience, is to realize its potential multilayered effects. (Patton 1982: 62)

Accordingly, the first step calls for the formation of a stakeholders' committee representing the various constituencies having power, authority, and influence or likely to be most affected by any changes. Members should believe that the evaluation is worth doing and be willing to commit the necessary time. Patton suggests a minimum number of three and a maximum of ten people. An environment of openness should allay fears and suspicions. Members can sensitize one another to different possibilities and competing values. As a result, the views of all parties could be broadened. New ideas can emerge out of the group dynamic, and, most important, a sense of shared investment can develop. Members of the stakeholder task group, besides setting the agenda with the evaluator, might also provide some new information crucial to the evaluation. They should also be engaged in some of the data analysis. The stakeholders must specify the kinds of information that they are more likely to find informative and actually use.

Are there occasions when an evaluation should not be attempted? It is a warning signal when the sponsor of an evaluation seems to be strongly set on proving or disproving something. There may be pressure to make a weak program look better on the surface and cover up its failures by selecting subjective and basically laudatory comments by certain participants. On the other hand, biased decision makers might try to use an evaluation as an excuse to eliminate a program regardless of its merit. Evaluations can also be a way of delaying appropriate actions that have already been planned. In such cases, stakeholders say that they are waiting for the evaluation results. Policy makers can also commission an evaluation as a way of appearing to do something and being accountable to society. In the end, little attention is paid to the results (Rutman 1980: 33, 34).

In spite of these cautions, we will now turn to a few case studies showing how the anthropological difference was important in program evaluation.

Case Study: An Anthropological Evaluation of an American Government Agency

Over the past two decades, applied anthropologists have been pushing their research interests and application into more mainstream domains. One especially interesting example of this is Gerald Britan's (1981) ethnographic evaluation of an agency in the U.S. Department of Commerce. Organizational systems and behavior have been more the domain of sociologists and social psychologists, but Britan's work shows the unique possibilities for anthropology.

Britan was asked by the National Academy of Sciences to evaluate the effectiveness and performance of a newly created agency—the Experimental Technology Incentive Program (ETIP). That agency was developed to meet a perceived crisis in American industry— that it was falling behind its international competitors. The problem was diagnosed as a decline in incentive to innovate. The purpose of ETIP was to stimulate innovation through cooperative programs with American companies as well as in indirect ways with other federal departments and agencies.

During the two years (1975–77) that Britan was there, anywhere between fourteen to thirty-two projects were in progress. Some of these projects studied the basis of industrial innovation. Others promoted research and development among private companies, sometimes in partnership with ETIP. One example was a joint effort with a company, a university, and ETIP, that worked on ways to eliminate flammability in some fabrics. Another project was undertaken with the Small Business Administration to reduce red tape and provide loans to companies working on new designs. Yet another dimension of the agency's activities was to encourage other agencies to purchase innovatively from the private sector, thus stimulating further innovation.

The rationale behind ETIP's strategy was that the federal government was by far the largest purchaser of manufactured items. Until then the fundamental approach in any competitive bidding had been to specify some minimal design standards and then award the contract to the lowest bidder who met the standards. As an experiment, ETIP tried to get some agencies to seek higher standards rather than just meet minimal ones (for example, the Department of Veterans Affairs and the Federal Supply Service's purchases of water heaters, air conditioners, stoves, and lawn mowers).

However, the new agency failed to gain a foothold in the public service and was terminated after only a few years. Using the ethnographic approach, Britan was able to show reasons for its failure. Significant problems lay within the cultural and social organization of the federal bureaucracy, which was much more informal or unstated than normal within a bureaucracy. For one thing, ETIP had its own particular mandate and agenda, but so did all the other agencies with which it had tried to collaborate. Officials in other agencies were more intent on developing their own initiatives than on following any of the ones developed by ETIP. ETIP had a particular budget that was meant to facilitate its interagency projects, and portions of that budget would be transferred to other departments to facilitate the projects promoted by ETIP. Yet, after two years, ETIP found itself in a very strange and unenviable position (for a government agency) of having a $2,000,000 surplus left at the end of the budget year. In government (at least during that era), a surplus was a sign that something was wrong with an agency that could not spend its allocations. All of the other agencies and departments that ETIP attempted to work with were scrambling, but with better success, to spend all of their budgets first. Directors of other agencies had little sympathy with the idea of trying to help ETIP by complying with its proposals.

Another area of difficulty was staffing. ETIP was a new agency and its staff was made up of civil servants taken away from other departments or agencies. Many viewed working for ETIP as a short stay before moving on to positions more to their liking. As a result, the agency quickly gained a reputation for employment transience. To overcome this, a person from outside the public service was hired as a director. That new director hired some temporary staff from universities who also saw their employment as transient, and, because of their different work styles and ways of making decisions, came into frequent conflict with the public servants.

Because there were very high rates of turnover, there was neither time nor inclination to develop organizational stability and loyalty. Nor did anybody develop a plan of action to secure the agency's survival. There were some successes in the procurement areas, but the agency was disbanded.

Britan shows us the value of the ethnographic approach. He demonstrates the benefit of long-term familiarity with the daily conduct of programs. He was able to describe an institutional context that had to be understood before making any sense of specific formal programs and measurable outcomes. His work underscores the importance of context and process, relatively long-term ethnography, and the significance of informal organization.

Case Study: Mexican American Strawberry Co-Op in California

As with most of the areas that we have been considering in this book, the issues of consultation and insiders' perspectives are crucial. Anthropological contributions can serve as alternative viewpoints rather than always relying on the overly detached external and top-down biases of traditional policy makers and evaluators.

Miriam Wells (1981) provides a case study that illustrates such benefits. Her research examined a strawberry cooperative with 52 members and 88 hectares. The program had emerged in 1973 to improve the lives of impoverished Mexican American farm workers and their families by promoting farm ownership and more direct participation in the economy. Fifty such co-op farms had been established, but by the end of the 1970s only fifteen remained. At the beginning, they had been given federal loans as part of the larger American "War on Poverty." The fifteen remaining farms continued to be supported by a combination of public and private loans and grants from private foundations.

Initially, emphasis was placed on very broad social and economic goals, but as time went on there was a shift to more purely economic criteria. From time to time, the co-op underwent program evaluations sponsored by the funding agencies. According to these outcome evaluations, the farm had not performed well, especially in comparison with privately owned farms. Wells gives an example of one of these evaluations focusing on production as outcome. In 1979 the co-op produced 32,383 kilograms per hectare as opposed to the state average of 44,928 kilograms; the co-op's gross was $23,079.92 per hectare compared to the state average of $35,468.98. As a measure of the poorer quality of the co-op produce, the proportion of crops allocated to fresh versus freezer sales was 43/57 as compared to the state average of 69/31. Furthermore, the evaluators expressed concerns over very high turnovers in co-op membership, which were seen as a reflection of organizational instability and internal factionalism. The external evaluators also complained that the co-op members did not pay enough attention to the advice of hired consultants and university agronomists and spent far too much of their time on activities that were not part of their production activities. Apparently members felt that consultants threatened their control over their own enterprise.

The external funders—including state and federal agencies as well as the bank and foundation financiers of the co-op—were becoming skeptical about the long-term viability of the co-op. They felt that the co-op was not showing sufficient self-reliance and profitability to compete and survive in the private sector.

Yet, after an alternative open-ended program evaluation of the perspectives of the participants, Wells concluded that the farm actually performed quite well. Not only did members express satisfaction, the project was meeting many of its original goals. Wells interviewed thirty-one of the fifty-two members, asking them to elaborate on why they joined the co-op and why they stayed. Responses compared their current situations to their previous circumstances as farm laborers or sharecroppers.

There were clear economic gains. Previous average salaries of farm workers and foremen ranged from $6,299 to $9,500, but during the 1970s, average payments were $6,400 in 1973 (the start-up year), $23,000 in 1976, $16,000 in 1977, and $15,000 in 1979, with the market accounting for yearly fluctuations. Clearly there had been significant gains. Workers had been able to buy new or secondhand automobiles since the time of the start-up; 45 percent had bought or were in the process of buying homes, and 42 percent had started savings accounts. Previously, 63 percent had depended on welfare and food stamps, but now none did.

An important aspect of economic well-being was raised by many participants. They saw participation in the co-op as an important means to a better future. In part, this helped to explain the high turnover rates that external evaluators had complained about. Some of the negative indicators of performance were, in fact, actually positive; two former members had been able to buy their own farms and twelve others had started another co-op. Such success would not have been possible without their co-op experience, in which they had gained savings, experience in production and management, and had established essential relationships with bankers and farm advisors. Wells points out that current members were also making these contacts as well as building skills of production, planning, and business management. There were marked benefits in income for everyone, but the co-op was the starting point of important economic mobility.

They also valued the very tangible changes in their work situation that enabled them to control the whole work process and set policies. They valued ownership of land through the co-op, the participation itself, and the promise of future possibilities for themselves. This value was rooted in Mexican ideals of agrarian reform that had parallels with the "American dream" associated with the family farm. Such participation gave them access to social status in the surrounding rural community. They also escaped the oppressive middleman. Their new style of work gave them a sense of security and reduced conflict, because they now maintained nonhierarchical and cooperative relations in their operations. They could also make their own organizational decisions about directing their common funds into such areas as emergency loans, the sponsorship of social gatherings, and a proposed day-care center. Small things counted—like determining the pace of their tasks and the quantity and quality of their production. They daily enjoyed the cooperative atmosphere while working with each other.

Participants saw many social advantages to their new circumstances. Migratory labor had been very detrimental to their family life. Children who were separated from their parents for long periods could drift into the temptations of delinquency, and schooling was frequently disrupted. In the co-op, there was much more stability. Children and youth could be gradually brought into the operations while continuing their schooling nearby. It was especially important for the male co-op members to know that their wives and daughters could now work in the fields without being subjected to harassing sexual advances by strangers. Instead, an atmosphere of respect and family honor was encouraged. Prospects for the children had increased enormously—almost all were going to school. Parents now had aspirations that they would have never dared have before—that their children go to college.

Socially, they also valued their interaction with each other as partners, ending the previous isolation and competition that they had experienced as migratory farm laborers. Membership in the co-op gave them a way to gain some desired services such as child care, health insurance, and a credit union—although they were still in the planning stages for the credit union. Farmers experienced a rise in their self-esteem and also felt that their status had risen in the community. They were taxpayers and no longer had to rely on social assistance. They stayed in the area, becoming registered voters and familiar with the local state representative. They also maintained contact with other political actors and bureaucrats. Some had traveled to state and national capitals to lobby for their interests; some participated in a state task force on the problems of small farmers and cooperatives, and they had representation on the State Strawberry Advisory Board that regulated their industry.

Wells concluded that the participation in the co-op had significantly improved lives. What is most important, the co-op had accomplished many of the original policy goals. It had become an important means for Mexican Americans to participate in the larger society, and through its mainstream institutions, it had improved their capacities for civic participation. Co-op participation had allowed them to realize important values of family solidarity and mutual support among friends and relatives while maintaining respect for the individual.

Wells' ethnographic approaches to program evaluation devote attention to the expectations and evaluation criteria of the participants. She also directs us to the wider and longer-term social goals of any program. Many of those may be still in process and, therefore, not subject to quantitative measurements of performance or outcome. In the case of the strawberry co-op, social and political goals had been an explicit part of the original formulation but, ironically, had been lost sight of, and the more recent evaluations had emphasized narrower goals of economic performance that were secondary in the original formulation.

Case Study: Helping to Enhance Self-Evaluations

Merry Wood (1996) was hired by the Greater Vancouver Mental Health Service Society, an organization of 400 staff members in nine mental health teams serving the cities of Vancouver and Richmond, British Columbia. This organization delivered direct front-line services in the areas of adult, family, children's, and geriatric rehabilitation and in housing. Wood's duties were long-range planning, needs assessment, program evaluation, and planning and management—tasks that called for frequent liaison with each staff team.

Her main assignment was to develop a handbook for self-evaluation to be used for improvement of their agency programs. There were ever-increasing pressures for effectiveness and accountability due to the restructuring of public health services, beginning with the drastic reductions in transfer payments from the federal government. Each municipality had to carefully scrutinize local health services for effectiveness and redundancies. That led to the restructuring of health boards into larger "rationalized" regional entities. Within them, there are now yearly requirements for evaluating the effectiveness of all their services. Program evaluations are also needed for periodic accreditation of medical and mental health services.

The model that she built was a simple four-part policy cycle that consisted of assessment, planning, implementation, and evaluation—and back to assessment again. Many people from the various disciplines represented in the agency, such as social work, psychology, nursing, or sociology, identified with the significance of each of these stages, and some saw them as analogous to the procedures they followed in helping individual clients through counseling and services. Her collaboration produced a short manual that could be used by each subunit to review its policies and programs with the fundamental view of improving services.

The approach consists of ten steps. Beginning with *assessment,* it involves examining or drafting a *mission statement*—a succinct summary of what the program is all about. That statement includes the identification of *desired ends* and an accounting of the *population* to be served and the specification of *approaches* that need to be taken to get the desired results.

The second step, also part of assessment, includes setting the *goals* and aspirations needed to fulfill the mission. To develop goals, participants need to identify the component parts of the desired end results, areas that need to be covered if they are going to accomplish their mission.

Step three involves setting specific *objectives* for any particular year. Using a mnemonic device, she suggests that objectives should be SMART—specific, measurable, achievable, realistic, and time limited.

Overall planning for any year might involve establishing new programs or changing an old one; the stage is also known as establishing program or *process* objectives. These could include increasing the staff, shortening the waiting lists for clients, and other actions. If the program is already well established, primary *outcome* objectives should be set. Outcome objectives describe benefits that can come to the clients as a result of their participating in the program.

The fourth step is the establishment of *indicators of success,* measurements showing the extent to which the objectives are being achieved. Wood suggests that

> . . . if your objective is to have each client make progress on a personal goal within one year of admission to the program, then one indicator of success is the percentage of clients who feel that they have made progress on one or more goals after one year. (1996: 20)

The fifth step involves the choice of *measurement tools* by which participants document and track each indicator of success. Using the example in step four, a measurement tool could be a set of questions given to clients at the beginning and end of the program. It would include queries about the setting, the specific services, and the assessment of personal goals accomplished for that year.

Step six consists of *data analysis* or aggregating all of the information collected over the year into digestible forms. Step seven is a series of meetings focused on *data interpretation.* That always involves the staff even if an outside person was involved in the initial analysis.

From that, step eight—*problem identification*–follows. There may be discoveries that one or more of the objectives were not being satisfactorily met. Discussions should then lead backwards, looking for any root causes. Step nine involves identifying factors that have been involved in the less-than-satisfactory results and considering how they might be addressed.

The final tenth step involves *revision,* and this brings the participants back into the assessment and planning stages of the annual cycle. Again this leads to possible revisions of mission, goals, objectives, indicators, and measurement tools.

Wood found that the best approach to encouraging self-study in program evaluation was to avoid constructing a long step-by-step manual and to keep the text (only eight pages) to a minimum. With each group, it was also highly important to be involved in a direct and personal way. In such instances, the anthropologist works best as a facilitator. In identifying the anthropological contribution to this kind of work, she puts it this way:

> For me, the greatest pleasure and satisfaction in my job comes from the act of facilitation. Facilitating a group of staff, whether around evaluation or something else, is like pulling the collective conscious and unconsciousness out of a small society. If I elicit a program's mission, goals and objectives, I hear about a world view. If I lead the interpretation of evaluative data, I hear about the difference between "real" and "ideal." And because I work in groups, not individual interviews, it is the staff who try to piece their individual perspectives together. I just stand at the white board and write and erase and rewrite until they agree: yes, this is what we are about. (1996: 19)

Other Examples of Anthropological Program Evaluations

Erve Chambers (1977b) writes of his experiences working for a consulting company evaluating an innovative program developed through the U.S. Department of Housing and Urban Development. The program in question was designed to give financial assistance to low-income families to allow them more freedom of choice in rental housing. It was also meant to induce builders to provide better facilities because they would have to meet federal inspection standards. Giving low-income or welfare people choice through income supplements was meant to allow the recipients to bypass public housing and to eventually eliminate some expensive mortgage assistance plans that compelled the federal government to finance new construction of or rehabilitation of public housing. Chambers worked in a field setting in Boston, one of eight sites where ethnographers were located, and evaluated the effects upon the families in terms of their empowerment and the effects on their costs of living.

Richard Salisbury (1986), in his discussions of the anthropological research on impacts of the massive James Bay Hydro Electric Project on the Cree in Northern Quebec, writes of program evaluations by various co-workers who evaluated the programs established through the James Bay Agreement. One of these was a guaranteed annual income program, in lieu of welfare, that unexpectedly encouraged an increase in commercial trapping among men. That way of life and economic pursuit had been on a steady decline, but the guaranteed annual income program, rather than accelerating further declines in trapping, encouraged it because the men now could upgrade their equipment and engage in a culturally valued activity. Another study done on behalf of the Department of Indian Affairs evaluated the consequences of a new political and administrative structure that regionalized Cree government with respect to health, education, economic development, social services, and other functions. Salisbury and his colleagues discovered that, although there were benefits, the growing bureaucratization of Cree society had created more conflicts among senior Cree bureaucrats and villagers as well as among Cree and Euro-Canadians in their separate bureaucracies. Eventually Salisbury's advice was taken by all parties in efforts to eliminate some of those tensions.

Yet another very large domain in which evaluators have made considerable use of anthropological techniques is educational ethnography. There, the performances, successes, and failures relating to both innovations and the operations of on-going school curricula are investigated at classroom settings by educational anthropologists and others skilled in ethnography (see Fetterman 1984, 1986).

Strategic planning as a related field that Dennis Wiedman (1998) sees as compatible for anthropologists because of their capacities to see the larger picture, collaborate effectively within organizations, work from the participants' points of view, and potentially mediate internal conflicts. Strategic planning is directly related to evaluation, because it requires an examination of goals, objectives, strengths, weaknesses, external obstacles, and performance. Yet it goes beyond these dimensions, leading to action plans that follow reviews of values, visions, and mission statements. It includes exercises leading to specific objectives, prioritization, budgeting, and implementation, all followed by periodic assessments and evaluations. Anthropologists can play many roles—trainers, facilitators, recorders, and evaluators—in strategic planning, which is becoming a major part of the policy cycle in most large organizations. For instance, Wiedman (1992), working out of the provost's office at Florida International University, used strategic planning to guide a rapidly changing university to fulfill its evolving mandate for over 30,000 students.

Summary

With a wide variety of methodological tools, models, and the professional expectations of the field, anthropologists can be major contributors to program evaluation. They are well equipped for establishing context, finding significant dimensions of process within wider systems. Ethnography is useful for discovering the underlying organizational or community cultures in which most other variables in programs are lodged. Nonetheless, anthropologists need to pay more attention to measurement or its qualitative equivalent and be more prepared to be critical in their evaluations. Also, aspiring evaluators need more tools and perspectives than can be discussed in this chapter, so considerable reading, practicum experience, and courses are recommended.

RECOMMENDED READINGS

Camino, Linda A.
1997   What Can Anthropologists Offer Ethnographic Evaluation? In *Practicing Anthropology in a Post-modern World: Lessons and Insights from Federal Contract Research*, NAPA Bulletin no. 17. Edited by Michael C. Reed. Pp. 41–57. Washington, DC: National Association for the Practice of Anthropology.

Chelimsky, Eleanor, and William R. Sadish (eds.)
1997   *Evaluation for the 21st. Century, A Handbook.* Thousand Oaks, CA: Sage.

Fetterman, David (ed.)
1984   *Ethnography in Educational Evaluation.* Beverly Hills, CA: Sage.
1986   *Educational Evaluation.* Beverly Hills, CA: Sage.

Fink, Arlene, and Jacqueline Kosecoff
1978   *An Evaluation Primer.* Beverly Hills, CA: Sage.

Patton, Michael Q.
1980   *Qualitative Evaluation Techniques.* Beverly Hills, CA: Sage.
1982   *Practical Evaluation.* Beverly Hills, CA: Sage.
1990   *Qualitative Evaluation and Research Methods.* Newbury Park, CA: Sage.

Reed, Michael C. (ed.)
1997   *Practicing Anthropology in a Postmodern World: Lessons and Insights from Federal Contract Research,* NAPA Bulletin no. 17. Washington, DC: National Association for the Practice of Anthropology.

CHAPTER

8

Social Impact Assessment

Of all of the sectors of policy research, social impact assessment (SIA) requires the greatest range of information. It is usually the most challenging sector because it demands prediction of future events based on understanding complicated current and future social processes and can make considerable use of anthropological knowledge. Yet rarely does the anthropologist work alone in this field—research teams are almost always multidisciplinary.

Social impact assessment can cover many different types of projects. For example, the impacts of large hydroelectric and irrigation developments that dam and divert waters have frequently been examined by anthropologists. Channel diversions, oil drilling, refineries, pipelines, highways, pulp mills, chemical and nuclear waste disposal facilities, and the construction of company or government towns are other types of proposals that have called for SIA.

Such projects can cost hundreds of millions, even billions, of dollars. When they are proposed, they are expected to eventually generate significant benefits. Much is at stake and usually many interests are involved, including some in the profit-making sector and those of politicians who can increase tax revenues or create jobs.

Such projects are usually proposed within an ideology of "development." By transforming natural, renewable, and nonrenewable resources into products that humans can use directly or in manufacturing, the actions are viewed as benefiting the economy and society as a whole. A nation's or region's wealth increases, providing jobs, consumer power, and income to individuals, thus increasing prosperity. This, in turn, improves other aspects of an economic infrastructure because of many spinoffs of service in transportation, communication, and retail activities.

Since the 1960s, there have been countervailing concerns about the environmental impacts of development and fears that the ultimate costs and damage to the environment may be greater than any short-term economic benefits. Spurred on by environmental lobbying, federal, state, and provincial laws now require the assessment of nonmonetary costs of damage to the environment. Another concern has been that there could be serious negative social and socioeconomic tremors from rapid development. Anthropologists, as well as other concerned observers, have demonstrated that, in many cases, so-called "development" has been a formula for social disaster (see Bodley 1998). Instead of prospering and benefiting from "modernizing," many people became its victims. The freedom, self-reliance, and core meaning to life that came from subsistence through local agriculture or hunting and gathering can all be destroyed. People then become subject to the vagaries of the market for their livelihood. Those who are unable to maintain adequate full-time employment become more impoverished and subject to the control of outsiders. There may be declines in health and nutrition. Families and communities may suffer more intragroup violence, and drug and alcohol abuse may result, along with the loss of traditional conflict controls. Relocations or intrusions upon the landscape violate people's identities and important spiritual connections. Adding to social disasters, the impact upon the physical environment frequently reduces such people's well-being through habitat destructions, pollution, overpopulation, soil degradation, and loss of traditional food sources.

Recognizing such possibilities, environmental laws often require that social impacts be measured as well as environmental and economic ones. Accordingly, anthropologists are frequently hired by government monitoring agencies or third-party consulting firms to anticipate impacts on communities close to the proposed developments. Our colleagues in public archaeology have developed parallel niches in archaeology and cultural resource management as they assess the impact of construction on local heritage in prehistoric and historic villages, forts, gravesites, and battlefields.

A comprehensive impact study usually contains component projects, including those of economists, human geographers, town planners, sociologists, public health officials, wildlife biologists, soil scientists, engineers, and others as well as anthropologists and archaeologists. Systems analysts, working through government agencies or consulting firms, usually develop the final syntheses and interpretations of the component studies. Final decisions as to whether to proceed and at what level of development are made by senior government officials.

This chapter will outline the major stages of SIA, issues of public consultation versus technical expertise, and the role of ethnography and cultural ecology in impact studies. I will begin with a case study that illustrates some very wide-ranging, deep, and largely negative impacts of relocation on Northern Canadian Inuit and Dene peoples and the often unanticipated and severely disruptive dimensions of planned change. Avoiding or minimizing such damage is the main reason for SIA.

Case Study: The Construction of a "Science" Town in the Canadian Arctic

Background: Impetus for Development

The Mackenzie Delta is a zone of several thousand square miles in the western Arctic near the Alaska and Yukon borders. Its principal river, the Mackenzie, enters the Arctic Ocean at the Beaufort Sea (Ervin 1968, 1969). Traditionally, Dene, Inuit, and Métis peoples had lived largely off the land and engaged in a dual economy based on traditional subsistence as well as cash and credit from fur trapping.

After World War II, the Canadian government began to pay much more attention to its northern territories. The discovery of important oil and gas and mineral reserves made the area potentially attractive for economic development. Also, pressure was put on the Canadian government to fulfill humanitarian responsibilities of health, education, and social well-being for indigenous peoples. Policy makers felt that it was important to prepare northern

Native people for modernity through schooling and more exposure to wage-labor opportunities. Yet planning for northern development was centralized with top-down decision-making, making it a form of internal colonialism.

During the 1950s, a major stage in regional development was the construction of a large-scale "science town" that was to bring to the Arctic the material standards of living of southern Canada. It was to provide a centralized commercial and service center with a large hospital and a residential school to serve Native people over a vast region. The hospital was to contain all the facilities of an urban hospital, thus eliminating the necessity for medical evacuations to southern Canada. Government facilities for the region were to be expanded and centralized. Oil companies, commercial airlines, hotels, restaurants, stores, and construction companies were encouraged to establish there. The town was to be linked to southern Canada and the rest of the world through modern transportation and communication.

The whole plan was formulated by bureaucrats in Ottawa, and the site was chosen on engineering rather than social criteria and without consulting local residents. Then for several years Native northerners and transient workers from the south constructed the new town of Inuvik. By the late 1950s and early 1960s, the construction was more or less complete, and many people abandoned their trap lines and moved there.

Impacts

The impact upon the people of the Mackenzie Delta was profound. The vast majority of them lived permanently in settlements. Of the approximately 5,000 people (including Euro-Canadians) living in the region by the mid-1960s, only about 150 lived off the land. Although there were four other villages, the region was dominated by the brand-new town of Inuvik, which contained over half of the region's population.

Over half of the population of Inuvik consisted of what locals called "southerners," transient workers from southern Canada. A large proportion of them were white-collar workers or professionals associated with the new infrastructure of modernization such as doctors, nurses, teachers, social workers, police, administrators and bureaucrats of various sorts, and military personnel.

Federal facilities, institutions, and buildings dominated the town. Inuvik also had a much larger commercial district than other settlements. The Hudson's Bay Company combined the functions of supermarket and department store. Hotels, restaurants, laundries, a movie theater, and a radio station were built.

All of the transplanted facilities and institutions as well as the homes of the newcomers were located in the "serviced" part of town, built at great public expense to meet the high standards of living. Compensated for high costs of living, the newcomers received generous northern "isolation allowances" and subsidized housing in the form of modern furnished apartments or bungalows. The vast majority of southerners were transient—intending to stay only for a few years and return home after their teaching or nursing contracts were over. Many came directly from Ottawa, the federal capital, were transferred north for bureaucratic reasons, and looked upon their Inuvik sojourn as a rung on the ladder of career advancement. Although transient, the southerners and their institutions came to dominate and define the overall culture of Inuvik.

Native people became marginalized in their homeland. Because the main construction phases were now completed, only about one quarter of Inuit, Dene, and Métis household heads held permanent jobs in the late 1960s. The vast majority of skilled blue-collar jobs, such as electricians, plumbers, mechanics, and carpenters, were held by southerners, who had the necessary union and craftsmen credentials. Women fared slightly better, because there were not as many southerner competitors for such positions as laundresses, waitresses, teachers, nurse's aides, and cleaning ladies.

This grim economic situation took a heavy toll on family structures. Although three quarters of the families were two-parent households, 25 percent were mother-headed households, sometimes with three generations supported through jobs, social assistance, and the federal Children's Allowance Program. Such a structure had been virtually unheard of in the fur-trapping or Aboriginal eras. Also new were households of young, single women and their children, who, in the past, would have been incorporated and supported within extended households. Male-headed households tended to be quite large, frequently containing ten or more people in very crowded conditions, often permanently on social assistance. A great deal of stress was placed on the men because of their low incomes, the high costs of Arctic town life, their large families, and pressures from extended kin to share meager resources.

All but two of the northerner households resided in the "unserviced" end of town, which lacked modern water, heating, and sewage facilities. Water was picked up by buckets, and sewage was disposed at stations scattered throughout this district. The most common type of house was a temporary construction shack of 512 square feet. When the construction phase was over, it was discovered that there had been a miscalculation, and only permanent public servants, or those able to pay the exorbitant rent, were able to receive serviced housing. Underemployed northerners of Métis, Dene, and Inuit ancestry as well as a few white former trappers and their families had to live in the impoverished and overcrowded unserviced zone.

Economically and socially, the southern Canadian style of life almost completely overwhelmed Native northerners, placing them in disadvantaged positions. Politically, administrators of the federal public service controlled the settlement and its hinterland. At that time, Inuvik had a colonial style of government with an elected "advisory" council, similar to a municipal council but without the power to initiate by-laws.

Southern bureaucrats and their families in the serviced end of town rarely interacted with Native northerners. Instead, tension and muted hostilities emerged between the two groups. As a reflection of this distance, the approximately 1,500 southern transients had formed forty-eight clubs and organizations to organize their leisure and voluntary activities during the very long winters. Only one had emerged among Native northerners, a fledgling social and recreational club.

Schooling presented severe challenges for northerner children and youth. The curriculum was designed on a format suitable for urban North America. Although schooling was compulsory until the age of sixteen, there were many failures and the dropout rates were very high. The alienation of youth was further expressed by the increasing numbers of petty crimes and assaults, crimes that had not existed in nontown settings.

Psychological alienation was associated with circumstances that set some people apart from others, giving them a marginalized status. Young, unmarried Native women, especially those who had children through liaisons with white transients, were stigmatized and separated from their extended families and the general community. Northerners who had spent long periods in residential high schools and gained more skills for town living were considered "too white" in their values and behavior. People from the bush or smaller settlements, who from time to time tried to make commitments to the town, were sometimes viewed as freeloaders if they outstayed their welcome without making contributions. Others who had chosen a middle-class nuclear-family life-style were considered snobs and not really "Native" anymore. Conflicts were emerging between men and women because women had more possibilities for a steady income. Men's employment and capacities to support their families were jeopardized by the new economy.

Conflicts and stress became magnified. Traditionally, male household heads were independent, self-reliant trappers who took pride in their hard work and the support that they provided their families. Now few meaningful jobs were available to them, and they were directly under the control of outside southern transients. They could not return to their trap lines because they had abandoned their equipment, and any new ventures would be very expensive and open to failure in an uncertain fur market. Furthermore, their wives and children wanted to stay in the town. Finally, Native northerners had never lived so close together and in such large numbers. This alone led to much more conflict and tension, reinforcing the frustrations from all of the other problems.

Associated with these stresses were high rates of alcohol consumption. Inuvik had the highest rates of alcohol consumption in the whole country as measured through liquor store purchases and sales through the bars. Over 90 percent of arrests for offenses such as petty theft, assault, and wife-battering were associated with alcohol consumption. Now, many Natives felt a deep sense of stress, anxiety, anger, and frustration with their present predicament.

What went so wrong? There had been a pervasive faith in the positive effects of modernization and economic development, but this mega-project, the building of a new town and the relocation of a whole community, was done primarily for engineering and economic reasons rather than being based on carefully thought-out human needs or consequences. There was virtually no consultation with the people to be most affected, and the decision makers were distant, both geographically and culturally. Decisions were based on the convenience of those who were going to administer the new services. New infrastructure and services were intended to benefit the oil and gas industry, which has still not made a significant contribution to the regional economy. Economic planning was to allow Native northerners to abandon a trapping life-style and enter into a supposedly more secure and prosperous wage labor. Yet nobody actually made sure that there would be an adequate number of jobs available for these people. Nobody sorted out the complex interrelationships among variables of family structure, cultural values, economics, education, the introduction of large numbers of outsiders, and other dimensions upon the populations indigenous to the area. No one attempted to consult and plan the transitions using the local people's ideas. For instance, the site chosen was in an area largely devoid of fish and game. Many of these former trappers in Inuvik suggested that their adjustment to this new life would have been much more effective if they had been able to still hunt, fish, and do some trapping from Inuvik. If they could not get wage labor, and most of them could not, then they had to get social assistance, which eroded both their self-esteem and their ability to support their families.

The findings of this project, along with other studies done in Alaska and northern Canada, cast doubt on the benefits of grand-scale development projects for northern Natives. More local consultations were developed for any new policy initiatives, and more and more local autonomy has been provided to communities and the territories as a whole since the time of these negative impacts. Yet much of the damage had already been done, and northern peoples are still trying to adjust to the problems generated by this period of modernization. Lessons like these these can be learned from many places in the world.

Next we turn to some of the more formal and standard aspects of social impact assessments.

The Stages of Social Impact Assessment

Because of the complexity of social impact assessment and because the anthropologist is normally a member of a large multidisciplinary team, it is a good idea to get an overall perspective on all the phases of SIA. According to Wolf (1983), there are ten stages. As a broad illustration we could begin with proposals to build pipelines from the Arctic to the United States and southern Canada during the late 1960s and early 1970s that became reality with the building of the Trans-Alaska Pipeline system (a proposal to build such a line through the Mackenzie Valley in Arctic Canada was deferred).

The first stages in planning are *problem identification* and *scoping*. In the 1970s the problem was identified as a shortage of oil and gas resources for increasing needs in heating, transportation, and industrial development. Public demands for energy are almost insatiable, and sources nearer larger population centers have been dwindling. To meet a crisis in energy costs, national policy makers might examine several solutions—alternative energy sources, conservation, and finding ways to reduce demand. One favored approach has been to increase domestic petroleum production through increased exploration and the tapping of resources in more distant hinterlands—such as the Beaufort Sea in Alaska and Arctic Canada.

National and even international energy policy proposal approaches would then be formulated to develop these resources. The formulation of such policies would involve politicians, government agencies, and private interests, such as petroleum companies, pipeline consortiums, trucking and shipping companies, and others.

In the scenario, there is a broad plan to start drilling and transporting known resources of oil and gas by linking them with existing pipelines in southern areas or bringing them down by ships to port facilities in Washington. It is here that the broad *scoping* aspects of SIA would anticipate all of the likely regions, peoples, and interests that could be affected by such projects. What states, provinces, and territories will gain some benefits or suffer some disruption? Where will the pipeline pass through in these jurisdictions? What communities would be most affected by the pipeline? Perhaps it will be near particular towns and villages, running along a particular river valley, or near an existing highway that makes it easier for the logistics of construction or provides a shorter distance from source to destination. What other communities and regions might be secondarily affected? There could be communities that, because of their sizes and existing facilities, will become takeoff points for mobilizing labor and supplying equipment yet are not directly on the pipeline route.

Scoping involves a preliminary identification of the publics or social groups that could be affected by the project. In turn, scoping will lead to *profiling,* which will describe the existing circumstances of peoples most affected and try to project the impacts on them regarding costs and benefits. Presumably, consumers in the "Lower 48" of the United States or in the southern regions of the Canadian provinces would benefit by having greater supplies of oil and gas, perhaps eventually at lower costs. Communities manufacturing the pipes and providing the equipment would also benefit as will companies doing the major work. Certain categories of workers and unions representing truckers and pipefitters would also benefit because of the high-wage employment opportunities for their members.

When looking at the communities most directly affected, we could anticipate some mixtures of costs and benefits. During a boom period, local merchants and contractors might benefit enormously from the outside money being spent in the area. Many local workers could benefit through high wages during the construction period, and the pipeline might generate some significant long-term jobs. However, others might bear enormous costs due to the losses or disruptions of their livelihoods or because of the destructions of traditional habitats for hunting, fishing, and trapping. The cost of material goods might become highly inflated, because of scarcities and high demand, and that would negatively affect less-affluent residents. And what will happen to the local people when the boom period is over? In most of these cases, as in the earlier Inuvik example, they could end up with far fewer benefits and with severe long-range costs.

The stages of problem identification and scoping would also include methods for the identification of factors, ingredients, and populations in the natural, nonhuman world such as animal and plant species, soils, water sources, habitats, ecosystems, and many other aspects. Ultimately, these dimensions could be united with social factors through very complex systems modeling. In scoping, as many factors as possible must be considered, and some general directions of the costs and benefits should be anticipated. But the research design resulting from these identifications should be open ended enough so that the unanticipated can be discovered.

The next stage is the *formulation of alternatives.* This could include scenarios from one extreme—not proceeding with the project at all—to the other—maximizing the project regarding money, labor, complexity, and scale of the technology involved. The development of alternative scenarios would involve considerations of the sources of funding—private, or public, or mixtures of both, degrees of involvement of labor forces from outside the area, and the involvement of large numbers of local people in the labor force. The formulation of alternatives would consider and specify as many of the technical details as could be anticipated.

Profiling is the stage that is most crucial for estimating social costs. Anthropologists, human geographers, or sociologists would be most involved at this point. For our northern pipeline, the populations and communities might include a string of existing settlements along the proposed route that might serve as staging points for the construction. Those communities would contain different subpopulations, ethnic and socioeconomic groups, classes, and occupations and be linked to people living in local rural areas. It is in these situations that anthropologists can be most useful because they can outline the important variables and institutions relevant to any subpopulations. As a matter of fact, the ingredients that are usually profiled are very similar to those considered in traditional holistic ethnographies—the main strength of anthropology.

In a cultural ecological framework, subsistence factors are probably the most significant. How do the people gain their livelihood from the land and waters in the region? What are some of the other key dimensions of the social economy, such as wage labor, employment, and underemployment? Demographics is always important. How does the population break down in regard to age, sex, ethnicity, and significant categories such as levels of education? Health can be highly significant and would include factors of morbidity, mortality, and all of the characteristics of particular health problems. Health factors would also be likely to include an inventory of the local health resources and their use.

A description of community organization is essential. This would include a sketch of all the significant social groupings and discussions of how local leadership is determined, how decisions are made, the degree of conflict present, how it is resolved, and an inventory of all significant community facilities and organizations. Descriptions of local family structures, kinship, inheritance rules, land tenure systems, and resource allocations would all be included. Collecting information about socialization and education in formal and traditional senses might be important because, for instance, educational levels might prove significant for any possible future employment or training of local workers. Religion and spirituality should not be excluded. For instance, local people might regard certain features in the landscape as sacred. There might be serious conflicts if these features were disturbed during construction.

Finally, significant values, as expressed culturally and as related to the development issues, should be taken into account. Such ethnographic profiling would not be just a static characterization or listing of traits but would be a dynamic, holistic, and meaningful connection of the ingredients. It would attempt to show existing strengths and weaknesses of the local region or community. Ideally, it would demonstrate informal and not-so-obvious dimensions of the local culture, which might include, for example, the normative powers of gossip, social solidarity, and homogeneity in maintaining social cohesion and minimizing antisocial behavior. Profiling might look at the degree to which people in the local area are already used to contacts with outsiders or at how often they had gone beyond the region and into more cosmopolitan areas seeking wage labor in the past. It might attempt to assess the degree to which locals actively seek change, perhaps to better their material conditions. Alternatively, it might note that people had developed a mistrust of outsiders and outside development because of previous fiascoes or exploitations. As much as possible, all of these data should be placed in a deeper time context. Trends might be outlined through time in a series of studies of important issues such as changes in family structure and socioeconomic strategies.

An anthropologically trained observer might collect all of this information, but a division of labor is more likely among a team of social scientists including economists, geographers, and sociologists who collect more quantitative data while the anthropologists provide context and cultural background. To some extent, that might depend on the complexity of the region or its communities. It also might be a function of whether there is pressure to collect the information rapidly. Methodologies and sources of data could include censuses, archives, public documents, questionnaires, focus groups, and key-informant interviews, but many people, including geographers and sociologists, have told me that the best and most effective methods of profiling the significant features are ethnographic. This is because all the important categories of impact cannot be anticipated until the local people are involved and investigated in their own context. One of the overall goals of profiling is to try to measure the current status of all the significant categories in anticipation of the next stage.

For an anthropologist, the next stage could present the greatest challenge. It is that of *projection.* Predictions can draw upon substantive research on similar topics in other communities. The social scientist would usually make use of the findings of general social science as well as literature specific to the area and the topics examined. Certain theoretical orientations from sociocultural change studies in anthropology could be of some guidance. These include cultural ecology, cultural change theories, political economy, and much of the important literature and controversies associated with development and modernization.

For example, the projections might identify trends toward modernization or increasing reliance on wage labor or transfer payments. Trends might also include the abandonment of traditional economies, or, alternatively, their current robustness, especially as associated with the local people's sense of their own identity in connection with their spiritual linkages to the land. Overall, a set of informed predictions is expected.

At any rate such projections would blend into the next stage, that of *assessment.* We return to each of the alternative scenarios for development, looking at each and then assessing its likely impact on the communities. Suppose, for example, that the various pipeline alternatives would or would not involve bringing in a certain number of outside workers. We could then ask what would be the effects of bringing in 10,000 unattached male workers into an isolated northern region upon family life, community cohesion, and conflict resolution. We could compare that to using local labor and having any outsiders located at a fly-in construction camp. Essential variables like this would be considered in conjunction with each other while looking for systematic connections and presenting alternative scenarios. These modelings are usually done through sophisticated computer and systems analysis and rarely by the anthropologist.

The projections are then written up in digestible forms for the significant policy makers and for the people to be affected. Complex quantitative analyses are packaged into readable qualitative forms. Then *evaluation* occurs. Once the significant publics are identified, we can speculate on costs and benefits for each one according to the alternative scenarios. These publics should be consulted directly, possibly through public hearings and forums. After these evaluations and consultations, we choose the most desirable scenario. However, it may be discovered that the costs are more than anticipated and the disadvantages too extreme for local peoples and the environment. So then the whole development plan is scrapped permanently or postponed until such costs and disadvantages can be overcome.

That actually happens from time to time. For instance, during the 1960s the proposed Ramparts Dam Project in Alaska, involving the U.S. Army Corps of Engineers, was canceled because of the enormous damage expected to important wildlife habitats, especially to duck-breeding grounds. It also would have disrupted the local Dene people by the proposed relocation of their communities. Similarly, in the mid-1970s, the Mackenzie Valley Pipeline proposal was indefinitely shelved because of the projected large-scale disruptions of Native people living along its projected pathway.

Let us assume that there are enough compelling reasons for going ahead with one of the projected versions. Costs and benefits have been recognized and documented through the projections and evaluations. This leads to the stage of *mitigation,* requiring calculation of compensations to those peoples who will be most seriously and negatively affected by the project. Most of them usually live in the vicinity of the construction sites. Perhaps these people will receive a major cash settlement to be distributed on a per-capita basis, or a development fund could be established to assist future generations. People may be relocated to a more favorable or equivalent setting. A new town might be built for them. A significant proportion of the jobs created, both during and after the construction period, might be guaranteed for them. If they currently do not have the skills to perform these jobs, then specialized training programs might be developed for them. The people themselves may have desired changes in their communities before the proposal was considered. They may have wished for better housing or improved health or educational facilities. These may be provided to them, through mitigation, as a way of improving their standard of living and as compensation, or mitigation, for likely damages. It is in the process of mitigation that anthropologists may play helpful roles. They can verify and detail the claims of traditional users of the environment; they may help to document current needs and aspirations; they may document how the project may disrupt peoples' lives.

The final two stages of the process of social impact assessment are *management* and *monitoring*. Management is usually performed by the government of the jurisdiction most affected by the project, perhaps in partnership with the companies engaged in the development along with representatives of local communities. It focuses on the goals and regulations established by the previous stages, including the actual construction. Usually a great deal of scrutiny is required to see that the social, human, and environmental considerations are nurtured rather than just the technological and economically oriented ones. Monitoring involves careful examination of the actual outcomes of the project according to the criteria originally established. This is essential for any considerations of possible expansions of the project. This has been the case in northern Quebec, where a number of anthropologists from McGill and McMaster Universities have been studying the consequences of the first phase of the massive James Bay Hydro Agreement that affected the Cree and Inuit in northern Quebec (Salisbury 1986).

Ethnography and the Ecological Perspective in Social Impact Assessment

Public consultations through community meetings, briefs, and hearings are important as sources of information. Focus groups, key-informant interviews, questionnaires, archival research, and the use of public documents along with a standard reliance on quantifiable measures, such as social and economic indicators, are all important and can be used by the applied anthropologist. But ethnography is of primary importance with its emphasis on participant observation.

Roy Roper (1983) illustrates the usefulness of this approach through a case study. Furthermore, he adds another dimension, cultural ecology, one of anthropology's more powerful theoretical orientations. The case study illustrating his point is related to farming in eastern Illinois. Roper describes impacts of a proposed large-scale water reservoir that would greatly expand possibilities for irrigation. But, in the process, many farmers would have been displaced, and their communities would be affected in other ways. Through participant observation, he became immersed in the local context, and, through his cultural ecological perspective, he became familiar with important local behaviors and attitudes that related to the use and meanings of land. He provided details on households and domestic arrangements that were crucial to land use.

To begin with, he observed that all farm units are not at an advanced stage of development. Within individual lifetimes, different farmers would be at different stages of a developmental cycle. Young farmers are at the most difficult stage—they are encumbered by large land debts and the need for capital equipment such as tractors and combines. Older farmers may be much better off, having paid for their land and increased the scales of their operations and resulting profits. Farmers approaching retirement are facing the task of gradually disentangling themselves from their operations, selling or renting land to others, and perhaps setting up their sons or other heirs in farming.

The original plan called for the displaced farmers to be relocated in other regions. There they would receive cash settlements to purchase new land based on the values of their previous properties. Roper concluded that if the plan proceeded this way, farmers would not be equitably mitigated. Those nearing retirement might find such buyouts adequate and very timely for their needs. Others in more advanced stages of their operations would likely make effective adaptations to farming in the new area. But the most disadvantaged would be the younger farmers, whose assets would be few in terms of land and machinery and whose debts would be very high. If they were moved to a different area, they would not have the advantages of the support of extended kin or other well-established networks of neighbors and friends. Those willing to give them a "break," such as bachelor farmers and those disentangling from their operations, would not be there to provide assistance in rental agreements or through the gradual sale of necessary land to them.

In any process of mitigation, there should be different considerations for each type of farmer, according to their developmental stage, family type, and farm operation. In discussing these realities, Roper refers to the *fallacy of aggregation,* whereby impacts and needs of a minority group or category are submerged within larger or more "average" categories or circumstances. Aggregation is usually brought about by the more standard econometric approach—statistically it would total assets in land machinery and other holdings and come up with some per-capita figure that then could be applied in a compensation formula for all those having to be displaced.

So, anthropologists can be extremely effective in presenting valuable insights, through empirical participant observation when demonstrating the ranges of variation within seemingly homogeneous groupings (such as Illinois farmers) as well as when different ethnic or cultural groupings are involved.

Roper demonstrates the value of the cultural-ecological approach in SIA. The ecological approach can place human behavior in its local context, describing land and water resources. Land is frequently at the center of proposed development. Land can be viewed ethnographically in social and cultural context and from many angles. Land is a source for extracting resources for cash, for subsistence, and for exchange with others. Land can be seen as a context for an occupation. It can be seen as a medium of exchange for power or status. Anthropologists could show the meanings and values attached to land and demonstrate how land interrelates to events and contexts like birth, succession, migration, retirement, and within local seasonal cycles. Categorically and processually, land can account for the social units, and the ranges of variation that are found in connection with other factors and characteristic decisions that are generally associated with each type. Among the processual dimensions are the development of units through time and the types of decisions that each type of farmer has to make according to household or operational needs.

Beyond these cultural ecological factors, he suggests that ethnographic analysis is a very effective way for presenting the relevant information because of its qualitative dimensions. It puts a human face on any decisions that must be made because it describes real people living actual lives. The alternative types of data presentation, involving statistics, graphs, and tables, do not have the same sensitivity in showing the plight of real human beings who are faced with change. As Roper (1983: 104) says, ethnography can "be equated with empathy." At the same time, while speaking a simple, accurate, and empathetically human language, ethnography can become continuously more refined and capable of describing process, domestic cycles, and internal variations.

Challenges and Controversies

Anthropologists face challenges and controversies in the social impact assessment field, and they have to be prepared for them. In many cases, social impact assessment is not a neutral process. The monitoring or administration of studies may be done by government agencies, supposedly acting as guardians of the public interest. It might even be done through the financing and administration of the mining, petroleum, pulp, and paper companies, which made the proposal in the first place. In both situations there may be very strong expectations and subtle pressures on contract researchers to make them discover good reasons why the project should go ahead and why any social costs should be minimized. The company wants the profits, the government wants to take credit for job creation as well as benefit from the increase in tax revenues, and there may be various pressures on the government through unions, construction companies, or other lobbying to proceed with development.

By training and general inclination, anthropologists may be genuinely concerned about the impact on the local communities, especially when they see much greater local costs as likely impacts. Yet ironically, the local people might resent the anthropologist's presence, perhaps intuitively anticipating the coaptation of his or her findings in favor of the development proposal better than he or she does. The locals may be annoyed because the anthropologist seems to legitimize a process merely by participating in it. Moreover, the community itself may be divided into several factions, for and against the development. The anthropologist is faced with the dilemma of deciding which side to promote and how to convey the subtleties of the differing points of view.

Other difficulties may result from working within a multidisciplinary team. A lone anthropologist may be an added-on, subordinate member of a group oriented toward "hard" numerical data that supposedly will precisely "measure" costs and benefits in dollar terms. Anthropologists may be frustrated because they cannot persuade the other members of the team that qualitative methods are necessary to get the local points of view about dimensions of life that are important to them and have impact on them. They may object that there is not enough attention given to meaningful public consultation or that the proposals offered for mitigation are completely naive and inappropriate to the people affected. Given their understandings of qualitative methodologies and ethnography, anthropologists may be dissatisfied with the time allocated for completing the baseline or profiling studies regarding the current conditions about the people. An important part of the seasonal cycle may be neglected if the findings have to be completed by a certain date.

In most cases, solutions or comfortable compromises can resolve many of these difficulties. Much of the answer is as simple as clarifying appropriate contracts and understandings at the very beginning. Certain conditions would have to be met—that there be full consultation and partnerships in research with the communities in question; that some coresearchers and assistants have to be hired from the community; that minority opinions be fully aired; and that all reports be fully vetted and discussed through public meetings and forums. Anthropologists should make arrangements with employers for a set of preliminary discussions with the community under consideration before going any further with an SIA. In some cases, it could even be arranged for the community to receive subcontract funding and hire some people for their own social impact assessment. The anthropologist could make sure that the importance of his or her place on the research team is fully understood and that his or her report be allowed to stand on its own.

Anthropologists also have the option of working "outside of the system," of doing a formal social impact assessment as an advocate for the local or "native" cause. Anthropologists, in consultation with other opponents of the development, could also rally the press toward understanding the inequities or damages involved in the proposed development.

Finally, it should be pointed out that, even though it is always prudent to anticipate the worst, social impact assessments are frequently benign. There are situations with ample time for consultation; the positions of the anthropologists are secure and uncompromised, and the processes of assessment and mitigation are conscientious and fair. In some significant cases, proposals have been abandoned and governments have learned from the accumulated wisdom of environmental and social impact studies.

Summary

Anthropologists engaged in social impact assessment as a potential career track are beginning to find policy makers and fellow investigators from other disciplines fairly open and understanding of anthropology's value for the field. Anthropologists have repeatedly proved the merit of ethnography in developing effective sociocultural baselines for profiling institutions, behavior, and beliefs that need to be projected in terms of probable impacts from proposed developments. For that purpose, theoretical and conceptual frameworks derived from cultural and human ecologies and the anthropological study of change—through acculturation, studies of technological innovation and social effects, and modernization and development—have all given useful insights for predictions and formulations run through systems analysis. Of all the subfields within applied anthropology, SIA has probably gained the most from academic theory and previous ethnographic studies. Also, in an unusual circumstance of actual practice, applied impact studies, in turn, have great potential to contribute to further theoretical insights.

RECOMMENDED READINGS

Bee, Robert L.
1974   *Patterns and Processes: An Introduction to Anthropological Strategies for the Study of Sociocultural Change.* New York: The Free Press.

Bodley, John H.
1998   *Victims of Progress.* Fourth Edition. Mountain View, CA: Mayfield.
1995   *Anthropology and Contemporary Human Problems.* Third Edition. Mountain View, CA: Mayfield.

Bowles, Roy T.
1981   *Social Impact Assessment in Small Communities: An Integrated View of Selected Literature.* Scarborough, Ontario: Butterworths.

Derman, William, and Scott Whiteford (eds.)
1985   *Social Impact Analysis and Development Planning in the Third World.* Boulder, CO: Westview.

Dixon, Mim
1978   *What Happened to Fairbanks? The Effects of the Trans-Alaska Oil Pipeline on the Community of Fairbanks, Alaska.* Boulder, CO: Westview.

Erickson, Paul A.
1994   The Social Environment. In *A Practical Guide to Environmental Impact.* Pp. 147–201. San Diego: Academic Press.

Finsterbusch, Kurt, L. G. Llewellen, and C. P. Wolf (eds.)
1983   *Social Impact Assessment Methods.* Beverly Hills, CA: Sage.

Jacobs, Sue-Ellen
1977   *Social Impact Assessment: Experiences in Evaluation Research.* Mississippi State University Occasional Papers in Anthropology.

Lane, Theodore
1987   *Developing America's Northern Frontier.* Lanham, MD: University Press of America.

Preister, Kevin
1987   Issue Centered Social Impact Assessment. In *Anthropological Praxis; Translating Knowledge into Action.* Edited by Robert M. Wulff and Shirley J. Fiske. Pp. 39–56. Boulder, CO: Westview Press.

Tester, Frank J., and W. Mykes (eds.)
1981   *Social Impact Assessment: Theory Method and Practice.* Calgary, Alberta: Detselig Enterprises.

CHAPTER

9 Some Recent Trends in the Application of Environmental Anthropology

Recent trends in environmental anthropology, outgrowths of the social and environmental impact studies outlined in the last chapter, make further use of anthropological strengths. In this chapter, I will discuss disaster and involuntary migration research, environmental risk assessment, and the use of political ecology in human rights advocacy.

Disasters and Involuntary Migration

An especially good reason for anthropological attention to the increasing severity and frequency of natural and technological disasters is that

> Disasters occur at the interface of society, technology, and environment and are fundamentally the outcomes of these features. In very graphic ways, disasters signal the failure of a society to adapt successfully to certain features of its natural and socially constructed environment in a sustained fashion. (Oliver-Smith 1996: 303)

Much of the research has taken place in non-Euro-American settings, in the Third World, and has dealt with such catastrophes as earthquakes, famines, floods, and chemical leaks. But some North American disasters have also been examined, including the *Exxon Valdez* oil spill in Alaska, hurricanes in the American southeast, and earthquakes in Alaska and California (see Bolton et al. 1993).

As with disaster research in other disciplines, anthropological contributions always have had applied implications. Research has been done on warning systems to prepare local populations for hazards (e.g., housing safety for hurricanes and earthquakes), aspects of mitigation, effective organization of emergency food and shelter, and postdisaster reconstruction. Disaster responses are similar in many ways to involuntary migration (see Hansen and Oliver-Smith 1982) caused by development projects (e.g., the constructions of dams), wars and revolutions, and resettlement as a result of prolonged droughts and famines. Researchers have examined the impacts of these disasters on individuals, families, and their communities and explored institutional responses to ease resettlement, effective short-term coping, and long-term adaptation.

The study of disaster and involuntary migration contains a very wide variety of inter-related topics. How do peoples culturally perceive disasters and hazards? To what extent do their moral and ethical beliefs enter explanations and responses? To what extent does a relo-cation cause the breakdown of a community, which is frequently tied to a traditional "ground" or location by historical and spiritual connections? What do disasters tell us about existing social and power relations in a society? What is the relationship between victims and national and international organizations charged with relief and reconstruction? Do people become helpless victims, or can they undertake their own quests for empowerment and self-determination?

Environmental Risk Assessment

Related to disasters, practicing anthropologists Amy Wolfe (1988) and Edward Liebow (Liebow and Wolfe 1993) write of the relationship of anthropology to the assessment of envi-ronmental risk. This is an area of inquiry previously dominated by epidemiologists, statisti-cians, and engineers. Those scientists conceived of natural and physical risks in terms of the probability of risk and the magnitudes of possible physical and health impacts. Yet beyond health or monetary costs, there are other meanings to risk: ". . . changes in lifestyle, violation of cherished values, unacceptable distribution of costs and benefits, or lack of trust in opera-tors and regulators" (Wolfe 1988: 4). Furthermore, there are unique variations to each risk situation. Assessment has to be done not only according to the technical but also to the socio-cultural contexts. In situating facilities that contain potential harm (e.g., radioactivity or chemical wastes), social, cultural, and political information is needed as much as technical information. Among the scientists collaborating in this field, anthropologists are at the non-probabilistic and nonstatistical end of the spectrum. What is considered to be risk by local people may be considered a separate matter and be of equal or greater concern than any tech-nical, expert, and statistical calculations of probable effects.

There is often a chasm of risk perception between the "experts" and those who would be most affected by a disaster. For instance, the nuclear power industry and its technological proponents see few problems with nuclear power; they claim that risks from mines, power plants, and storage facilities can be more or less precisely determined and contained with sci-entific accuracy. Yet laypersons frequently oppose such facilities on the grounds that they are unsafe. Faced with public resistance, the experts in the field have divided risks into those that are "real" and those that are "perceived." The latter, by implication, are fictitious or unin-formed. However, from an anthropological perspective, that dichotomy, which often domi-nates the policy agenda, is both misleading and counterproductive. People may have genuine concerns that are based on their knowledge of disasters elsewhere or their mistrust formed by previous bad experiences with the involved agencies. They may object to a process of decision-making that relegates them to bit players in their own communities. Furthermore, they may see the dangers of having these facilities forced upon them. Decisions to situate a potentially dangerous facility there could stir up deep social divisions within a community that could last much longer than its construction. One of the perceived risks might be a threat to valued lifestyles or spiritual connections to a cherished landscape. Besides, communities might have justifiable skepticism about the technical claims of experts, and those fears, in themselves, may create risks. These and other legitimate risks need to be empirically uncovered in each community.

Case Study: Anthropology and Ground-Water Contamination

The possible contamination of underground water from landfills, storage tanks, industrial waste, agricultural runoffs, and other sources is of growing concern to many North American communities. Janet Fitchen (1988) participated in a multidisciplinary research project that examined a dozen communities, primarily in New York State, in which private and public water supply wells had to be closed because of contamination. Her task was to study the institutional and public responses to the crises, and her cultural analysis proved to be quite insightful.

Clean-up, mitigation for damage, establishment of monitoring procedures, and the resolution of such problems can take as long as ten years. State and federal agencies of environmental protection, state health and conservation departments, and municipal agencies can exacerbate the delays and, therefore, heighten public frustration and anger. To add to the discord, the institutions responsible for clean-up frequently quarrel with each other. So although at one level clean-up is a technological problem, its institutional and social ramifications can be quite profound.

Fitchen's research was meant to improve institutional responses to groundwater crises, but she suggests that her conclusions may be useful for other contamination problems. Anthropological approaches led her to look at community responses through a cultural framework, but she also considered the ideologies of the technical specialists who dealt with ground-water problems. Initially, she found that attempts to explain findings and recommendations to the technicians and managers revealed a cultural problem. Sanitation and water engineers, as well as others involved in environmental protection enterprise, are essentially problem or task oriented—they have a worldview that emphasizes action and instrumentality. Their concerns are with precise definitions of any problem and the collection of specific information that will directly lead to solutions. They look for technical fixes and consider the "people factor" a source of irritation and irrationality.

Her breakthrough with the technicians came when she was able to explain public behavior that had caused the experts anxiety and frustration in their attempts to do what they thought were their jobs. Although they still would have preferred to ignore the human factor, contamination experts had been taking quite personally any caustic criticism of them at public forums. By outlining some implicit dimensions of American culture, she was able to explain public motivations. One of these concepts was individualism, manifested in a mistrust of public officials by laypersons who seek more active roles for themselves in monitoring efforts. Especially significant were the hostile reactions that frequently mystify experts when they answer questions about health risks. The experts tend to respond in scientific language, referring to large aggregated populations and to mathematical probabilities of contamination. The angry response from the public is shaped by individual desires to get direct answers: "Should *I* drink the water? *Yes* or *no*?"

Privacy was another cultural concern. Fitchen found that testers of water quality should avoid the back yards of people and concentrate on front yards, which are considered more in the public domain. Breaching these and other informal rules might unnecessarily stimulate "raw nerves" or sensitive areas of resentment.

An understanding of context is highly important for these workers. They cannot assume that every community is the same and rely on assumptions derived from the last community treated. Each community's sense of uniqueness is a source of pride and should be respected. Related to context are local attitudes toward sources of contamination. Contamination from nature is generally more acceptable than that from an industrial plant, although the natural source (e.g., radon in basements) may be more dangerous. Moreover, if the company is viewed as an asset to the community, its contamination is considered less serious than if there had been conflicts over its activity in the past. In the latter case, citizens are more likely to be adversarial.

Finally, Fitchen recommends that each problem be viewed within a processual and interactive framework. Risk assessments and clean-ups are not one-way processes—they are interactive. The public has a major role even if it has not been formally assigned. Instruction on how to deal with the problems and compliance is more effectively delivered by discussions with relatives and friends than by formal notices from health departments. Furthermore, peoples' compliance and perceptions of the problem can change favorably if the technicians become attuned to local perceptions and needs. A bad situation could be transformed into a more cooperative one.

Case Study: Nuclear Wastes and Risk Assessment

In 1982 the U.S. government established the Nuclear Waste Policy Act, under which highly radioactive byproducts from over 100 nuclear power plants would be stored in two deep underground facilities (Liebow 1988). In addition to dangers in transporting the byproducts to the sites, there was also a severe risk of local contamination because the fuel would remain radioactive for another 10,000 years. One site was to be established in the West, where there are fewer people but more land; the other was to be in the East, where there were far more nuclear plants but much larger populations and little land that is isolated from population centers. After initial screening, the Department of Energy (DOE), in 1986, chose three relatively remote sites in the West for further impact assessment. These were Deaf County, Texas, Yucca Mountain, Nevada, and Hanford, Washington. For apparently political reasons, the DOE also announced that the choice of an eastern site would be postponed indefinitely, with the western choice to be the single national site for nuclear waste disposal at this time.

The Hanford, Washington, site was considered because, for forty years, it had contained a military nuclear waste facility, and there was presumed to be a more favorable local attitude toward a nuclear waste facility. Among those who might be affected were three tribes, the Yakima, Umatilla, and Nez Perce. All three tribes had reservations close to Hanford, and the lands that they ceded still had ancient spiritual meanings. These tribes remembered negative experiences from the early 1940s, when Indian people were forced to relocate to make room for the Manhattan Project.

Anthropologist Edward Liebow was assigned impact and risk assessment research with these tribes. He outlined some important differences in the definition of nuclear risks.

On one side, there is a complex, hierarchical organization—the U.S. Department of Energy—with thousands of employees. Individual choices and perceptions tend to be directed toward organizational stability and individual careerism "rather than the creative search for solutions to unprecedented problems" (Liebow 1988: 11). Accordingly, it is difficult to incorporate the unexpected within the organization. Procedures and the criteria for identifying risks have already been established, and any new warnings raised by community workers in the field are not welcomed. From the cultural perspective of the DOE, there are two kinds of risk—"real" and "perceived." Perceived risks are seen as not being "real." The "real" risks are based on scientific standards rather than perceptions of people in affected communities. So the fundamental answer to the nuclear waste problem from the DOE's perspective is to

> Put the waste deep underground, where it will be isolated and therefore rendered harmless. Put it in the West, where people are more sparsely settled, and where we have already committed certain areas to a radioactive future through our bomb-making and testing activities. (Liebow 1988: 11)

Yet, from the perspective of the ten millennia in which the highly dangerous wastes will be present, Liebow reminds us that the certainty or objectivity of the DOE experts evaporates. Liebow summarizes the Indians' objections.

> To place this material in the earth is to violate the source of our world's animating forces. It is from this place that we derive our sense of identity; if something goes wrong, you can leave and still have your identity, but we cannot. (1988: 11)

Additional Indian concerns surrounded sovereignty and self-government, resource management, and the social and economic well-being of their communities besides the highly significant factors of spirituality and identity.

> The tribes have been concerned about the repository's development potentially disturbing important cultural resources and religious freedoms, both of which are afforded legal protections. Tribal sovereignty and the tribal right to self-government are also protected by law, as is the tribe's right to manage natural resources within their own jurisdictions. Changes in economic activity and an influx of repository workers from outside the region have also been of some concern to the tribe. (1988: 12)

Most tellingly, the historical experiences of these Native groups with U.S. government institutions—including annexations of their territories and relocations—have probably intensified their sense of potential threat. Furthermore, as in many non-Indian communities, there is understandable skepticism about the capacities of the DOE to properly manage any such site for such a very long time.

Following the impact studies and comparisons of the three potential sites, Yucca Mountain in Nevada was chosen as the repository. There was also a positive byproduct of the Hanford study. Liebow and his colleagues were able to arrange a revisit to the previously restricted Manhattan Project site by some tribal members. A testing facility that had been built into the side of a very prominent spiritual landmark was removed, and the desecration is being environmentally and spiritually repaired under tribal supervision.

Liebow provides a few more general observations that are useful in environmental risk assessment. Misunderstandings can occur when people use the same term (e.g., risk) to mean different things. Members of the public may frequently judge their assessment of risk based on the credibility of the agencies that are responsible for managing facilities. Differences in risk judgments come from differences in knowledge bases and in definition of facts but also from values. Risk assessment experts judge the opinions of the lay public as "inexpert," but that does not make the public's opinions wrong or in need of change. Public opinion needs to be taken into account in risk management planning. Studies of risk assessment should research in detail the populations to be affected, not just the factors defined by laboratory science. This needs to be done for any site selections, for management of risks, and for any needed mitigation.

Political Ecology, the Environment, and Human Rights Advocacy

The older approaches in environmental anthropology—cultural ecology and human ecology as associated with people like Julian Steward (1955) or Roy Rappaport (1968)—were valuable for showing the relationships of human communities to their environments. Those links were culturally mediated mechanisms (technology, ritual, etc.) that channeled forms of energy to humans and their activities. However, most of this work was flawed by its tendency to see communities such as hunters and gatherers, horticulturalists, and pastoralists as isolated and within somewhat artificially bounded ecosystems. These approaches were not very well designed for dealing with complex societies. Conceptually, they did not prepare us for studying the penetration by external economies; the exploitation and disruptions of ecosystems, and, most crucially, the ways that such threats contributed to a growing and very complex environmental crisis.

As a response to that challenge, Greenberg and Park (1994) describe the emergence of a much wider and, potentially, more integrated perspective—that of political ecology. Here, research in anthropology, biology, and other social and historical disciplines is melded with the much-older field of political economy. Political economy studies the organization of work, factors of production, inequality, class and ethnic conflict, values, historical transformations, economic exchange, and many other subjects. Recently, it has examined the relationships among societies and regions of the world with the penetration of mercantilism and, later, capitalism into less-developed hinterlands. A major advance in the political economy approach in anthropology came with the publication of Eric Wolf's (1982) *Europe and the People without History*. That work linked the subject material of anthropology—peoples, their communities, and nations—into a single, worldwide social and economic system. Still, a major deficiency of the political economy approach has been its neglect of biological and ecological phenomena that have become globally interconnected through the various environmental crises (e.g., deforestation, overfishing, and industrial pollution). This emerging field of political ecology attempts to bridge all of these important linkages, placing an emphasis on political, social, and economic impacts on the environment and local people.

An excellent example of such explication is found in the work of Barbara Johnston (1994) and her colleagues in *Who Pays the Price? The Sociocultural Context of Environmental Crisis*. In 1990, the Sierra Club had challenged a United Nations human rights commission to consider the relationship of human rights abuse to such problems as government-sanctioned environmental degradation and the deteriorating health and welfare of minority communities. Subsequently, a U.N. report recommended more detailed examinations of human rights abuse and the environment as they apply to four areas—natural habitats, natural resources, human settlements, and human health. Taking up the challenge, the Society for Applied Anthropology (SfAA) organized a study headed by Johnston at the Center for Political Ecology at Santa Cruz. She and her colleagues emphasized the problems of groups and communities, rather than individuals, and challenged the sovereign power of the state in environmental activities to influence the United Nations in its design of a new charter of environmental rights.

Setting the stage for that theme, Clay (1994) writes of the relationships of states to nations. Today there are over 190 states in the world but over 6,000 nations. Nations, or ethnic groups, have distinct languages, cultures, histories, territories, have existed for centuries (even millennia), and had their own systems of government and laws before the imposition of state sovereignty. Most of these preexisting nations retain distinct identities in primacy over those attached to their states. Very few genuinely homogeneous "nation states" actually exist, because the dominant national groups in pluralistic states attempt to assimilate and override the rights of minority nations. In many cases, state violations of these nations' rights were first steps toward environmental degradation. Numbering at least 600,000,000 people, or 10 percent to 15 percent of the world's population, these nations have legitimate claims to about 30 percent of the earth's surface and resources as well as rights to local autonomy. Laws in most states have conspired to deny these nations their rights to autonomy and to their resources. The nation's people may be allowed to own land but not the subsoil resources; they may own the land but not the trees, thus allowing for large-scale commercial clearcutting of tropical forests; they may be allowed to own the land but not the waters contained. Furthermore, nonindigenous colonists are frequently encouraged to take over large amounts of indigenous nations' territories without any compensations. Following these intrusions, large amounts of land are redirected to such environmentally inappropriate enterprises as intensive farming, ranching, lumbering, mining, and commercial fishing. Meanwhile, people in the indigenous nations are hampered in their ability to exercise their own conservation practices, which have previously successfully preserved the resources. Currently, approximately 100 wars rage between nations and states over such resources and rights. Many people are displaced, maimed, and killed, and large amounts of natural resources are destroyed in the process. Over half of the crushing debt of Third World countries is the result of conducting these wars, thus perpetuating the cycle by not attending to rights of peoples for clean water, adequate food, and shelter. These issues are quite complex, but they frame a global crisis, destroying fragile ecosystems.

Barbara Johnston (1994: 1–17, 217–237) provides us with further overviews of human rights abuse through environmental degradation and underscores the fact that many of these subordinated nations, along with other marginalized populations, suffer the most. The prosperity and relative ease of life of the North American middle class comes at the price of others' pain. Using her own Californian context, she points out that the oil and electricity use in that state contributes to cancer, respiratory diseases, and malnutrition among poor African Americans living near refineries and power stations. This is also true for indigenous peoples in Ecuador, where large amounts of petroleum toxic waste products are dumped into rivers while the refined products make their way to the United States. The massive amounts of water redirected to maintain the Californian life-style damage aquifers, create salinization problems, and affect distant hinterlands and peoples in many other ways, such as by reducing salmon runs and water flows in parts of the American West where Native Americans live. Intensive corporate agriculture that uses large amounts of chemicals frequently leads to the poisoning of farm workers (usually minorities) and immediate health damages such as rashes, chemical burns, vomiting, and the longer-term effects of cancer, sterility, stillbirth, and other grief. Furthermore, even when relatively effective domestic environmental regulations exist, First World residents' produce is produced cheaply through the unregulated use of chemicals in developing countries, where 90 percent of the pesticide deaths occur. So Johnston underscores the fact that,

> . . . if the price of our consuming culture is environmental degradation and the deterioration of human health, the benefits, as well as the burdens, are not shared equitably. My ability to survive and thrive depends upon the restriction of other peoples' rights to a healthy life. (1994: 5)

Johnston then enumerates those rights:

> The right to health, a decent existence, work, and occupational safety and health; the right to an adequate standard of living, freedom from hunger, an adequate and wholesome diet, and decent housing; the right to education, culture, equality, and nondiscrimination, dignity, and harmonious development of the personality; the right to security of persons and of the family; the right to peace; and the right to development are all rights established by existing United Nations covenants. (1994: 7)

Although humans have always had to adapt to environmental stress, in modern times, stress is mainly the result of human actions.

> These include growing deserts, decreasing forests, declining fisheries, poisoned food, water and air, and climatic extremes and weather events which continue to intensify—floods, hurricanes, and droughts. (1994: 8)

These crises are rarely contained within limited areas, and many of the people most affected are denied the information they need to anticipate and cope with the problems. Human and environmental rights have always been treated separately—human rights have been framed morally and environmental issues economically. Abuses of human rights are rampant through attempts to gain control of the land, labor, resources, and waters of peripheral peoples, often living in what are defined as marginal zones. All of this is aided by a cultural and political discourse that defines them as backwards, primitive, ignorant, and lazy while development is being promoted. There is selective victimization, wherein the power-less suffer, because their rights are seen as expendable in the cause of national security, energy, and consumption needs. For most of us, prosperous or not, the centralization of authority and capital diminishes the power and integrity of communities. A result of that is to contribute "further to the distance between decision and consequence" (1994: 234), fostering the illusion among the North American middle class that prosperity is free for the taking. But because humans do not live apart from nature, and nobody is ultimately immune from the global environmental crisis, the voices of citizens and responsible researchers, coming from community knowledge, need to be heard in environmental policy debates.

Case Study: Uranium Mining on American Indian Reservations

It is interesting to note that, although much of American history has been devoted to displacing and dislocating Indians onto peripheral lands, these lands still contain 50 percent of low-sulphur coal, 25 percent of domestic oil, and 60 percent of uranium reserves in the United States. In spite of that potential wealth, Indians still experience the lowest income, diet, and health standards among Americans (Johnston and Dawson 1994). They have suffered disproportionately, especially in the Southwest, with regard to losses of water through deforestation and loss of land for weapons testing, waste disposal, and mining. Although they had regained some autonomy through the Indian Reorganization Acts of the 1930s, major damage was done before the various federal and state laws relating to clean air and water and waste disposal went into effect (Johnston and Dawson 1994: 142, 143).

Some of the most serious damage is related to uranium mining, which disproportionately affects the Navaho in the Four Corners region of the Southwest, also home to Utes, Hopi, Zuni, Laguna, and Acoma. Private corporations were given leases negotiated by the Bureau of Indian Affairs and ratified by some tribal councils. Some Navaho were involved in independent mining operations. An estimated 3,000 Navaho miners worked at approximately 1,200 mines from the 1950s through the 1970s although the boom subsided by the end of the 1950s when the U.S. government had gained most of what it needed for weaponry.

The uranium was all owned by the Atomic Energy Commission (AEC), which was not then responsible for maintaining health and safety relations. It was difficult to monitor and regulate working conditions because they were under the jurisdictions of the states, and there were few qualified inspectors. Nonetheless, inspections in the 1950s found main ventilator fans not working and radiation at 100 times the permissible levels at one prominent facility at Shiprock, New Mexico. Information, as reconstructed, gives us a picture of extremely inadequate working conditions. Navaho miners worked in very dusty and poorly ventilated mine shafts, eating their lunches there, drinking contaminated water, and returning home at night to their families wearing dusty, radioactive clothing. Most serious of all, they were not told of any health hazards, nor were they advised of any precautions that they should take.

The impacts on the Navaho have been extreme and continuous. For instance, seventy acres of tailings with 80 percent of their radioactivity intact were left on the surface, less than sixty feet from a river near the Shiprock operations and less than one mile from heavy settlement. Of the 150 Navaho miners who worked at the Shiprock facility, thirty-eight had died of radioactive-induced cancer by 1980, and another ninety-five had contracted serious respiratory diseases and cancers. In 1979, a mill tailing dam broke in Churchrock, New Mexico, and released more than 100,000,000 gallons of severely contaminated water that affected about 1,700 people and their livestock. They were told that they could continue to eat their livestock but were not allowed to export their mutton to the rest of the United States or to Europe, a clear double standard. It is noteworthy that although 60 percent of the American deposits lie within reservations, 100 percent of the mines and the vast majority of waste products are concentrated there. All of this reflects a national policy that subjects a group of marginalized citizens to the most extreme risks associated with nuclear power (Johnston and Dawson 1994: 142–155).

It has been difficult to gain compensation because latency periods before illness appears might be twenty-five or thirty years. In compensation cases, rules require that it be clearly established that the damage is actually work related, and claims normally had to be made within one year of cause. None of the workers had been informed of their rights nor warned of the dangers of radiation, a situation complicated by the fact that they spoke largely Navaho. Miners diagnosed by the U.S. Public Health Service with radiation-related afflictions were not told about it when they were released from employment. Families lived and played near the tailings; livestock grazed there; and people got their water nearby. Services, advocacy, and referral were only minimally provided by social or legal services. This was made all the more difficult because of language and cultural barriers as well as physical distance for the Navaho when trying to deal with bureaucracy. Overall, the U.S. government failed to meet its obligations to these miners and their families, especially given the trustee relationship that the government has with Native Americans. Although there has been some minimal and retroactive compensation for miners and their widows through the 1990 Radiation Exposure Compensation Act, it does not cover miners' families or offspring who had health problems as a result of living in uranium-contaminated settings.

It has been especially stressful for the Navaho because their belief system sees health within an exceptionally wide and holistic and spiritual framework rather than as a series of individual ailments. These radiation problems, then, were seen as part of major calamities. Furthermore, their strong sense of place did not easily allow relocation as a potential solution to contamination (Dawson 1992).

Summary

Clearly then, anthropologists have much to offer environmental policy. Acting as consultants and expert community researchers, they can engage in classical social impact assessments of development proposals. They might also fine tune their assessment expertise into more specialized realms of hazard risk or disaster research. As the last example demonstrated, a form of "whistle blowing" or advocacy regarding health and environmental injustices is also useful when it is well informed and pointed in its explication of damage. Results may not be immediate, but they can contribute to longer-term possibilities for mitigation and avoidance of such mistakes or injustices in the future. Other roles are possible. Collaboration in the preservation and compilation of local environmental knowledge can be useful for cultural heritage and educational purposes as well as providing information valuable (e.g., the healing powers of traditional medicines) for the wider society. Anthropologists might have roles in assisting in the design of environmental co-management projects involving forests, fisheries, and mammals when jurisdictions overlap among federal, state, or provincial and First Nations or tribal governments. Negotiated agreements may emerge out of the anthropologists' capacities to find common ground and possible flexibility for new options. An example of that, on a large scale, was Milton Freeman's collaborative research (1976) on behalf of the Canadian government and a number of Inuit groups to determine Aboriginal knowledge of the environment and their practices of conservation. Other types of work might include anthropologists' collaboration with environmental lobby groups, such as the World Wildlife Federation and the Sierra Club, in researching policies that take into account the needs of human groups such as the hunting rights of Alaskan Natives in newly created National Parks and Wildlife Preserves or ways of promoting sustainable energy through alternatives like wind power.

RECOMMENDED READINGS

Acury, Thomas H., and Barbara Rose Johnston (eds.)
1995   Anthropological Contributions to Environmental Education. Special Issue of *Practicing Anthropology,* Vol. 17(4): 3–36.

Donahue, John M., and Barbara Rose Johnston (eds.)
1998   *Water, Culture and Power: Local Struggles in a Global Context.* Washington, DC: Island Press.

Hansen, Art, and Anthony Oliver-Smith (eds.)
1982   *Involuntary Migration and Resettlement: The Problems and Responses of Dislocated Peoples.* Boulder, CO: Westview.

Johnston, Barbara Rose (ed.)
1994   *Who Pays the Price? The Sociocultural Context of Environmental Crisis.* Washington, DC: Island Press.
1997   *Life and Death Matters: Human Rights and the Environment at the End of the Millennium.* Walnut Creek, CA: Altamira.

Kormondy, Edward J., and Daniel E. Brown
1998   *Fundamentals of Human Ecology.* Upper Saddle River, NJ: Prentice Hall.

Liebow, Edward B., and Amy K. Wolfe (eds.)
1993   *Communities at Risk: Communication and Choice of Environmental Hazards.* Special Issue of *The Environmental Professional,* Vol. 15(3): 237–316.

Moran, Emilio F.
1982   *Human Adaptability: An Introduction to Ecological Anthropology.* Boulder, CO: Westview.

Moran, Emilio F. (ed.)
1990   *The Ecosystem Approach in Anthropology: From Concept to Practice.* Ann Arbor: The University of Michigan Press.

Oliver-Smith, Anthony
1996   Anthropological Research on Hazards and Disasters. *Annual Review of Anthropology,* Vol. 25: 308–328.

Wolfe, Amy K.
1988   Anthropology in Environmental Risk Studies. *Practicing Anthropology,* Vol. 10: 3–4.

CHAPTER
10   Advocacy Anthropology

A majority of anthropologists would like to see their discipline benefit the best interests of humanity as a whole. Although intended as scientific inquiry, much of the ethnographic literature elicits sympathetic understandings of the people portrayed. As Penny Van Esterik (1985) sees it, the collective works of anthropology have been part of a lowercase letter "a" advocacy.

Yet in her classification, uppercase or capital "A" advocacy is more active and involves formal and explicit actions of advocacy. One version is legal advocacy, in which anthropologists are commissioned or volunteer to support the case of clients through research or expert testimony in court. Clients may be seeking redress for damages related to lost livelihoods and traditional lands. There is a long history of land claims advocacy in the United States, where anthropologists provided research and court appearances before the Indian Claims Commission (Lurie 1955). In Canada anthropologists do research, testify, and appear before courts and government commissions on behalf of First Nations (tribal) governments. Another form of capital "A" advocacy involves participation in sustained lobbying activities that attempt to influence public opinion and changes in policy. The attempts of Barbara Johnston and her colleagues to guide the United Nations toward a charter of environmental human rights are an example of that. Advocacy is also a big part of Action Anthropology, where anthropologists directly and collaboratively contribute their research efforts to community groups (Schensul 1974).

In their review of advocacy, Stephen and Jean Schensul (1978: 122) point out that most scientific and professional practice has served the interests of the sociopolitically dominant groups. Anthropological advocates work to strengthen the representation of marginal groups and to help laypersons overcome barriers to more meaningful participation in society. Furthermore, an "underlying feature of these advocacy activities is oriented toward building innovation and change on the culture resources and felt needs that exist in the community" (Schensul and Schensul 1978: 55). So, advocacy ultimately covers much of the scope of contemporary applied anthropology, especially in its relationship to policy.

"The Truth, yet Not Necessarily the Whole Truth"

An exploration of the relationship of the two fields is contained in *Anthropology and Advocacy* edited by Robert Paine (1985). Although anthropologists have frequently spoken on behalf of different people, he points out that there has been little professional training for that role. Advocacy largely deals in information and involves delivering messages—making the vague more explicit, interpreting what has not been properly understood, and providing new information.

Paine asks for a definition of advocational truth. He concludes that there are as many truths as there are audiences. Presumably, he means that facts and observations correspond to the position that the advocate supports and that they need to be tailored for particular groups of people. So Paine points out that the advocate normally "should speak the truth, yet not necessarily the whole truth." In other words, advocates generally withhold information that does not support their clients' causes.

Paine explores some ethical dilemmas that anthropological advocates need to address. What happens when an anthropologist is unable to accept the clients' views of the facts or if the client group's position is personally repugnant? Paine does not suggest solutions to these dilemmas, but we are challenged to think about what our own solutions might be. Often the answer is straightforward: one just does not participate. For most anthropologists, taking up a position or being employed by a government to oppose an indigenous group's land claim position should be easy to turn down. (However, anthropologists have, in a very few cases, actually taken positions opposing Aboriginal land claims.) Most anthropologists would also refuse to support the cause of a major corporation that has used unethical advertising procedures that targeted impoverished and otherwise vulnerable consumers.

But other situations are not so straightforward. Let me provide a personal example. Six or seven years ago, I was approached by a lawyer to do research on behalf of six Alberta Indian bands. They were preparing a legal challenge to the Canadian government's decision to re-enfranchise Native women who had lost official Indian status and treaty rights because they had married non-Natives. I turned down a lucrative offer to engage in advocacy research. The lawyer responded, "How could you, of all people, an anthropologist, not want to protect the rights of a people to determine who their own members are?"

He did have a point, but I replied that this challenge was unjust because, in most cases, the women had married non-Natives on the basis of their personal preference not because they rejected their own culture. If the women divorced, which often happened, they became single mothers living in poverty. They were denied benefits that they had previously been entitled to by virtue of their Indian status. Then, to add to the injustice, this disenfranchisement was passed on to their children, who did not benefit from the funding for health, welfare, and education that would have been theirs by virtue of band membership. In sharp contrast, Indian men who married non-Native women did not lose their status or rights. If they divorced, their non-Native wives did not lose the status and privileges that they had gained through the marriage. All of this seemed unfair to me, and, because I saw the new legislation as an appropriate redress of the former injustice, I did not want to work against it. To do so would be against the best interests of the women and children being denied services.

Another anthropologist took the case. He felt comfortable with the required position of advocacy; he saw another advocacy truth in this situation—the principle that social groupings such as Native or Indian reservations should have the right to determine who their own members are. Their notions of membership, based upon their own rationale, should be rooted not only in law but in traditional criteria. Furthermore, there were difficulties in complying with the new law. With a fixed amount of financial resources, band governments would have to look after the needs of women and children who would be coming back to overcrowded reserves. The case entails the issues of sovereignty and self-determination because band and tribal organizations in Canada have been engaged in a prolonged struggle to gain First Nations' status within the Canadian constitution. Surely, one could argue that to deny them determination of their own membership would make a mockery of any notion of self-determination.

I once raised this case in my applied anthropology class. One student was an Indian woman married to a former chief, and she herself had served as a band councilor. She was adamantly opposed to my position and did not have much sympathy for those women who had lost their status. She saw them as people who had rejected their heritage. Another student in the class made a compromise suggestion that an anthropologist could be an effective revealer and arbitrator of the truth. She suggested that, when hired, anthropologists should not support a position but instead should use their objective or scientific abilities to reveal all of the facts to the judges. I replied that that solution would not work, that anthropologists would have to pick a position and consistently follow through on it. In addition, they would morally and legally be required to support the position of the band, because they were hired by the band in the first place. The Indian woman agreed with me on that point.

Beyond sticking to a position, the anthropologist should provide the very best possible evidence to support it throughout all stages of the advocacy. It would be highly counterproductive to raise and document the opposing point of view unless the anthropologist intended to refute that view by even better anthropological evidence.

Paine asks another question: How can we prevent our advocacy from encouraging a situation of dependency among members or even leaders of the client group? There is such a risk when the anthropologist becomes a principal spokesperson for very impoverished, culturally distinct but marginalized groups. Such people would be unfamiliar with sources of power and leverages of influence among the media, bureaucrats, and politicians. Consider isolated tribal groups in Amazonia under the threat of environmental degradation through development. The anthropologist/advocate may take an important direct role in articulating the message to appropriate audiences. She or he may do most of the behind-the-scenes-work, making the important introductions, drafting statements and speeches, making suggestions about the appropriate logistics for influencing the decision makers or the public. She or he may even organize fund-raising to maintain the cause. Sometimes the advocacy cause persists for many years without complete or satisfactory resolution—as many as twenty-five to thirty years could be required in some land disputes. In situations like this, the client group could conceivably depend upon the services of anthropologist/advocates for many years. Fortunately, such a situation is less likely these days, as members of groups insist on taking a public role in their own causes, and anthropologists and others act as auxiliary consultants.

There is another pitfall. How does the anthropologist/advocate discourage the overly optimistic view that the results will be successful or act to bolster crushed hopes? Advocates working on behalf of some isolated or marginal group may appear to have knowledge or connections, because of their origins, education, class, or ethnicity, that they may not actually possess. On the surface, the anthropologist, often a young, white person of middle-class background, might seem to have more "metropolitan" connections to sources of power and influence than the group he or she is working for. The anthropologist's involvement may only be the very first step in a long process, one that perhaps will lead to failure. Anthropologist/advocates must be very careful and make this limitation clear to those for whom they advocate.

Advocates should be clear as to what and whom they are supporting. Any society or community is divided or factionalized at some level. Not everybody would agree to the advocacy position even if, on the surface, it seems to be a just cause. Anthropologist/advocates will have to learn to navigate through such complexities and conflict to make the crucial decision whether to become involved in the first place. Somewhat different problems arise when anthropologists advocate for people who do not form an actual group, but are, instead, a category that shares some attributes. Examples might include homeless people, children, rape victims, single fathers, and so forth. Even here, it is important for anthropologists not to speak out of turn and hastily appropriate the legitimate voice of those who are being unjustly treated.

In spite of these difficulties, Paine deems it important that more anthropologists feel the "call" to advocacy. Anthropology may actually need an advocacy arm in order to maintain itself in a rapidly changing world that may not have much need for its more academic skills. Paine suggests that we study major societal issues in order to have our findings and perspectives taken seriously. Clearly, anthropologists need to advocate much more effectively for their own worth as social commentators.

To sharpen our advocacy skills, Paine suggests a number of points that need attention. When we are engaged in advocacy, we should try to make the foundations of our methodologies and findings clear to the principal stakeholders, the public, and other researchers. This means demonstrating that our findings are based on respectable standards of truth, not just sentiment and wishful thinking, and that these encompass representativeness, sampling, validity, reliability, and effective ways of summarizing the views of other peoples. Anthropologists as advocates need to establish their credentials. According to Paine, anthropologists might have to develop some narrower foci to their expertise. Instead of looking at a single culture in all of its aspects, anthropologists might specialize in one problem area or one aspect of culture in all of its contexts. Specializations have not been uncommon in anthropology, with people choosing certain topics such as poverty, child well-being, gender disparities, risk assessment, and occupational safety and viewing these topics in cross-cultural contexts.

The Case against Anthropological Advocacy

Some are very skeptical about anthropological advocacy. They doubt that the practitioners of a science devoted to describing and analyzing all of the behaviors and ideologies of humanity can choose one cause and advocate it to the exclusion of others. Anthropologists need to remain objective. They need to keep a distance, avoid partisanship, and try to tell all sides of issues. Insofar as they would engage in the application of anthropology, their duties would be to provide fair and comprehensive analyses of the issues. Ultimately, the key ingredients for policy would emerge from nonpartisan information.

A strong representation of the academic part of this position has been taken by Hastrup and Elass (1990). They contend that anthropology and advocacy are incompatible, even though some anthropologists have a moral conviction to engage in advocacy. Obstacles for a legitimate anthropological advocacy are present because "anthropology seeks to comprehend the context of local interests, while advocacy implies the pursuit of one interest." To do advocacy, one must step outside the profession. These opponents of advocacy maintain that "no cause can be legitimized in anthropological terms."

To illustrate their views, Hastrup and Elass refer to their own 1988 fieldwork among the Arhuacos of Colombia. A proposal was being developed for an intensive horticultural program that was intended as launching the revitalization of their traditional culture and, in turn, providing a more autonomous status for Arhuacos within Colombia. The authors were asked by one group in the community to help assist with the proposal. They declined for a number of reasons, some of which were personal. They suspected that they had been asked mainly because the Arhuacos wanted someone else to do the paperwork and to avoid the frustrations of dealing with the Bureau of Indigenous Affairs. They also pointed to conflicts within the region. In their view, the intruding non-indigenous *colonos* who might be displaced were exploited marginal peasants trying to survive in a competitive world, and advocacy on behalf of the Arhuacos would show favoritism. Furthermore, the indigenous people themselves were divided between modernists and traditionalists. Not all of the population supported the proposal, although the degree of internal opposition was unclear.

The authors felt that their participation would entail a patronizing role, reinforcing "postcolonial" and "romantic" stereotypes. Their attitude is summarized by their imaginary response to the Arhuacos.

> When some of the Arhuacos asked us to plead their particular cause to government and funding agencies, they immediately had our sympathy as well as our professional interest. They still have it; but before we can go on we must talk with them about the complexity of the social reality. They are not unaware of the conflicting interests, of course, but it appears that in their relation to the outside world (including ourselves) they still want to present themselves as a united community and therefore tend to be silent on issues of local conflict. We cannot take this self-presentation at face value; it masks a divided truth. Ultimately, our uncovering this "truth" may enable the Arhuacos to speak more convincingly for themselves. (1990: 307)

Beyond the specifics of their own study, Hastrup and Elass cite a literature that is critical of advocacy, arguing that advocacy discourse is overemotional, oversimplified, overdramatic, and not equivalent to "the sound anthropological principle of suspended judgment until the complex patterns have been uncovered" (1990: 306). They also suggest that "we should never forget that a commitment to improving the world is no substitute for understanding it" (1990: 306). Overall, the article asserts the superiority of pure academic research over applied work and most certainly of pure academic research over advocacy. For the most part, commentators also seem to be broadly supportive of the authors' positions. Per Mathiesen (1990: 208) refers to a statement allegedly made by Frederick Barth, the distinguished Norwegian anthropologist. Barth's completely unsupported but fine-sounding aphorism states "that the significant difference between basic anthropological research and applied research is that basic research is the more applicable."

Response to the Criticism: The Pro-Advocacy and Anthropology Case

Hastrup and Elass have done anthropology a service by stating their case openly. Anthropology sometimes seems an undisciplined "discipline" because there are no clear-cut subject boundaries. Debate is essential if its practitioners (academic or otherwise) are to discover their own bearings and senses of social responsibility. Hastrup and Elass have outlined a strong case against anthropological advocacy that warns us of pitfalls and difficulties that need attention. It also forces partisans of advocacy to make their case.

To begin with, we might ask who actually is in breach of responsibility, the imaginary anthropological advocates for the Arhuaco cause or those who declined participation. One thing that has always been notable about anthropology is that it cannot be a purely "ivory tower" subject; it operates with real people in real communities. Furthermore, those communities always contain internal contradictions and confrontations as well as conflicts with other sectors of society, including those that have power over them. Anthropologists cannot avoid these differences. At the same time, they cannot merely insert themselves into other people's communities and expect their hosts to be willing bit players in their research. They should not be objectified—like rocks or plants—for the purposes of natural historical inquiry. Also, such outside researchers are advancing their own careers and fulfilling the agendas of university-based scholarship according to the latest scientific, literary, and philosophical fashions that obsess anthropology at any given time. Anthropology, although possibly itself in the long run a valuable institution that promotes varieties of human adaptation, is like any other science in that the truths of the day are always tentative. Therefore, they are subject to revisions with later advances in theory or method. Accordingly, it seems somewhat counterproductive and even pretentious to value the academic agenda above that of the felt needs of the people involved. We should, with an appropriate blend of humility and confidence, apply our research skills to people's needs. There is no particular reason why people such as the Arhuacos have any obligation to engage in our scientific and academic ventures. The engagement in research compels some form of reciprocity.

Although Hastrup and Elass declined the invitation to engage in advocacy, we do not know that they have had any previous experience in applied anthropology, policy analysis, or advocacy. In general, their knowledge of applied anthropology is superficial, merely a few references to Malinowski. How do we know that their possible engagement in advocacy would have been misguided? It might actually have done a lot of good. Participation may have led to the kind of benefits sought by the Arhuacos. By engaging themselves, the anthropologists might have shown the Arhuacos that the anthropologists can be trusted and are committed to their well-being. The Arhuacos might have then reciprocated and provided those social scientists with deeper and more complete information that would have benefited their more purely academic studies, thus enhancing the scientific dimensions of their academic anthropology. As it stands, we do not have any convincing empirical evidence of damage that might have been done if the anthropological advocacy had been conducted.

Hastrup and Elass contend that advocacy is hasty, oversimplified, and overdramatic, but there is nothing that compels advocacy to be that way. Advocacy can be dispassionate, empirical, substantiated, careful in the way that it is framed, and based on very substantial information and research. Moreover, much of what sometimes passes for academic anthropology often actually consists of advocacy. Countless times I have heard presentations at academic conferences or read articles or books that are essentially one-sided. They describe minorities, ethnic groups, and others as disadvantaged, exploited, or damaged by powerful elites, missionaries, and commercial interests. What is more, it is quite appropriate to describe power imbalances and generate information about the oppressed. Yet I have noticed that the majority of these academic works are most often still reserved for the safe and generally placid atmosphere of academic conferences rather than exposed to the comments of the media and public forums. Little of the valid data and field observation makes its way to a large audience or even into academic journals. Is this because we have repressive standards of peer refereeing that remove most advocacy components of any arguments? Or is it because anthropologists grow timid and remove the flavor of social criticism before submitting their works to peer review? Do they fear the thrust and parry of public debate?

Much that has passed for objective anthropology, in fact, is presented in overly careful abstractions that describe institutions (e.g., kinship, religious ceremonies) as if no people were present. Because they are abstractions, these writings do not give much evidence of real-life experiences of living people. As an example, early ethnographers, such as Robert Lowie (1935), provided us with careful descriptions of a reported way of life that disappeared a long time ago among the Crow. At the same time, Crow communities were suffering the devastation of disease and the breakup of their land holdings through the Dawes or Allotment Act. Although such ethnography is valuable, it still might have been far better if he and the other Boasians had described real conditions and advocated for the real needs of American Indians.

Certainly people who find themselves being researched are rarely content with academic studies of their communities. They want information that can improve their lives rather than furthering someone's career in the social sciences. So it could be argued that anthropologists should collect data that could ultimately serve advocacy purposes. Most of the time academic anthropology is not of much use to many people. Except for a few scholars who might be interested in the esoterica of such topics as the genres of comparative oral literatures, deconstructing gender, and the countless other things that academic anthropologists have chosen to investigate, there is a small audience for their writing. Most of the time, such information is arcane, obscure, and too poorly framed for any use in advocacy, let alone policy analysis. Although much of it may be excellent scholarship, these publications are largely gathering dust in libraries. There is absolutely no evidence that its collection was any more proficient or scientific than the information collected for applied and advocacy studies.

In sum, anthropology cannot avoid advocacy if it wishes to engage in contemporary practice. There is a great need for anthropological advocacy, and those whom we study are unlikely to tolerate our presence if we satisfy our academic curiosity without giving them something in exchange. Furthermore, applied anthropology must, at the minimum, frequently advocate its findings to influence policy (Ervin 1991).

Research and Technical Writing: An Advocacy Role for Practicing Anthropologists

Anthropologists may work for minority-group organizations or tribal governments to negotiate property or resource disputes, promote sovereignty, develop social, health, or educational programming, and, above all, seek funding for programming from governments. They must make their cases through research and position papers. The up-front lobbying or public advocacy is usually done by elected authorities (presidents, chiefs, and councilors), but much of the background work for this type of advocacy is done by hired consultants and staff.

John Peterson Jr. (1974) describes some attributes and conditions for a supporting advocacy role. Anthropologists do most of their work behind the scenes here, providing research and other technical support for existing causes or proposals. As an analogy, he compares trial lawyers and brief lawyers in Great Britain. Brief lawyers never go before the courts, but they frame and fill in the most proficient arguments and details for their clients. Similarly, advocate anthropologists provide their clients with a number of alternate approaches and the details to be used in arguments.

Advocate anthropologists present one side of a case, the side of their clients. Information is only for client purposes; no record is allowed to be kept. All work is completely confidential. In Peterson's case, he was asked by the tribal chairman of the Choctaw Tribe in Mississippi to prepare a certain document, given access to certain information and sources, and then expected to prepare a case behind closed doors. Drafts of the document were destroyed, and he was forbidden to use any of the information for other purposes, such as books or academic articles. In effect, he became a full-time technical writer for the tribe and supervised the writing of other technical reports to support the client's causes or proposals.

Peterson illustrates the differences between a full-time advocate and an academic anthropologist. The first is a different *orientation to the self.* Advocates must be comfortable in subordinate positions and satisfied to remain in the background. Advocates must not assume to know more than their clients and must not expect to get credit. Second, the *orientation to a reference group* must be different. The advocate does not work in the field of anthropology as a scientific discipline. His client is not in the least bit interested in the advancement of method, theory, and knowledge in anthropology. The consultant or technician serves the interests of the client group—that is, his reference group. Advanced anthropological theory, method, and knowledge should only be of interest in the sense that advocates are expected to draw upon those skills in the service of clients. As advocates, they have no obligation to anthropology. A potential conflict exists, because scientific ethics require open access to data. However, in this subordinate role, all data must be kept confidential, and the advocate must accept all terms dictated by the client.

A third difference can be found in *measures of success.* Only the standards of the clients are valid. In Peterson's work, measurement of his success was a tribal triumph, in which his efforts as an anthropologist were totally unrecognized. The role of spokesperson in such advocacy must be relinquished by anthropologists and other similar outsiders.

Compared to the academic anthropologists, the advocate has different *standards of performance.* Like measurements of success, standards should only be considered in terms of the priorities and goals of the client reference group. In academic anthropology, sets of standards are relevant to scholarly excellence and revolve around method, theory, sources of data, quantities and qualities of data, validity, reliability, and writing style. In academia these standards are paramount and are validated by peer review and other techniques of quality control. A proposal is not accepted, a grant not given, or a paper or book not allowed to come into print until it has met the highest standards. But such delays or quality controls may not be feasible in settings of advocacy. It is a matter of doing the best possible with whatever resources a person has available.

As a corollary, there is generally a difference in *time orientations*. The researcher-advocate must get his or her work done within certain deadlines. A proposal, position paper, or a response to an offer is worthless if it is too late. Elegance and theoretical sophistication cannot be motivating factors in these settings. Instead, timeliness, clarity, and impact of argument, along with reasonable supporting statements, are far more important.

Other skills and aptitudes are useful for the anthropologist/advocate. Some of them may overlap with academic anthropology. Skills at *cross-cultural communication* do have some parallels with academic anthropology but with a slightly different flavor. Rarely, in these contexts, can advocates speak for themselves or from their own perspectives. They must speak from the point of view of the client group. This might be done when significant representatives of the client group are present as well as important decision makers representing agencies of the dominant society. Here, the advocate may be expected to make a presentation, often of a technical nature, that explains the point of view of his client group in terms relevant to the dominant group. This may be done to obtain funds and other resources. Presumably, advocate anthropologists often share certain characteristics of the members of the dominant society's policy-making institutions. They may come from similar ethnic and class backgrounds; therefore, the translations may be more effective. But such advocates must be careful that they remain true to their clients' original assumptions and goals and that they maintain their subordinate role in these temporary spokesperson roles.

Peterson suggests that *group maintenance skills* are valuable. While remaining in a subordinate position, advocates should lend their best efforts to integrating group action toward the goals at hand by maintaining communication among members of the task force or group and between the task force and its superiors (e.g., the chief and tribal council). If the task force is working with an outside body such as a governmental agency, the advocate should encourage communication links and harmony. Yet communication may break down; factionalism and personality disputes may come to the fore. Brokerage and communication are important. Rather than becoming too involved in the disputes under consideration, the anthropologist could provide some objective or detached insight to maintain the group and intergroup effort. Peterson gives such examples as advising members of the white bureaucracy that some of their behavior was objectionable to the Choctaw. It had been received as personally motivated and malicious rather than a product of culturally correct behavior in a white bureaucracy. Overall, anthropologists might have the insights to show how conflict was institutionally and culturally derived rather than fueled by personal animosities. This may lead to a cooling-off period and a return to useful intergroup cooperation.

Another set of skills that an advocate anthropologist brings is the capacity to *understand methods and techniques from a variety of subject disciplines*. In the scenarios Peterson examines, the anthropologist is usually a "jack of all trades," bringing together information relevant to the employer's advocacy positions. If anthropologists cannot always do that directly, then they should know what sorts of experts to consult. Experts might include people with specialized fields of knowledge such as public health, agronomy, education, or engineering, depending on the issue. If the client organization does not have the money to bring in such outside expertise, advocate anthropologists should know how to effectively research supporting evidence themselves. Anthropology is preadapted for this generalized role because of its own multidisciplinary and interdisciplinary attributes.

Two other related skills are mentioned by Peterson. These are the *ability to analyze situations from the clients' problem reference* and the anthropologist's skills as *a nonreactive translator of ideas.* It should be presumed that the members of communities are familiar with their own needs and priorities. As employees, the anthropologists should represent this familiarity in reports. Similarly, as nonreactive translators of ideas, the anthropologists should be open to the ideas of local people. As an example, Peterson alludes to a proposal for a new tribal education program. It was concluded that a Choctaw-designed preschool program was needed to prepare the children for other types of schooling. Most of the details and rationales for such a program were drawn up after a series of meetings among the Choctaw. These meetings detailed their practices and views on the nature of early childhood learning and the role of elders and nature in education. The proposal made very heavy use of Choctaw testimonies and insights. Later Peterson augmented these local testimonies with comparative materials about enculturation from the general social science literature.

Finally, he points out that, to work as advocates, anthropologists should have *organizational abilities.* Drawing upon skills as researchers and writers will not be enough. Significant clerical and administrative services must be maintained in order to carry out an advocacy cause for any group. Bookkeeping must be done; wages have to be paid; and tasks have to be allocated to particular people or subgroups.

While Peterson locates these qualities specifically within the context of advocacy practice, it should be noted that they also describe the basic circumstances for any practicing anthropologist working within an agency or company.

Case Study: Anthropology in Court

Traditional venues for advocacy have included the courts, and anthropologists have made some significant contributions there; for example, see Omar Stewart's (1983) frequent testimonies on behalf of the Native American Church (otherwise known as the Peyote Cult).

Another interesting case is Barbara Joans' (1984) expert testimony that defended six elderly Bannock and Shoshoni women. In 1978 these women were accused by the social services agency in Pocatello, Idaho, of withholding information that would have made them ineligible for supplementary security income (SSI). They were charged with fraud and ordered to make repayments of about $2,000 each. The women, with the assistance of the local legal aid office, contended that they could not afford the repayments and that they had been misinformed about the SSI regulations and did not know their responsibilities. The problem centered on small amounts of land from which they had been receiving small payments from white renters. The amounts, between $1,000 and $2,000, were received at the end of the year—in December—although the rental agreements began each January. When asked by social services about any incomes received, they had not reported these payments because they did not have them. Social services claimed that they should have reported them as if they had received them in January. Upon discovering the error, social services stopped all checks and demanded that the money already received be returned. The women were confused and felt that the government surely knew what it was doing when the money was sent.

Joans' task, as assigned by the legal aid lawyer, was to determine if the plaintiffs could understand what had been expected of them by social services. Joans chose capacity in language (i.e., English) as the index of their ability to understand the rules and regulations of the social service bureaucracy. If they could understand it well, the social service staff would be justified; if not, a case for misunderstanding the rules regarding SSI could be made. She construed three levels of possible English understanding for these Bannock and Shoshoni speakers. Level one was rudimentary and included everyday speech such as "How are you?" "I am fine," etc. Level two consisted of nuances, jokes, and puns related to discussions about town politics and social service bureaucracy. All of the women comprehended level one, but only one passed level two. That third person was tested with level three questions. In English, Joans queried the woman on Indian laws and regulations—the roles, regulations, and policies surrounding the administration and policing of the reservation. The woman understood and was able to describe them. Then she was asked to describe the functions and roles of the Pocatello town council as well as the town police. Could she describe them and compare them to reservation systems? She could not. In conclusion, Joans decided that there had to have been severe cultural misunderstandings in dealings with social services. To check on the validity of this hypothesis, she engaged in participant observation—keeping in touch with the women on the reserve, in their homes, and in town at her own and the lawyer's office for a period of three months. At the end of this period, she concluded that the social services personnel and the Indian women were operating at different levels of English and cultural understanding, and the women would not have been able to comprehend what was expected of them.

She used this testimony in court, explaining that the women, in their sixties and early seventies, normally spoke Bannock and Shoshoni in their everyday lives. There had been little opportunity for them to develop the kind of cultural understanding needed to comprehend the social service rules. In the court case, she was required to present a bibliography of cases of similar cultural misunderstanding and to provide a vita, documenting the experience and training that would make her a credible expert witness. Other evidence included notes that social services people always came to the reservation at busy times when other things were happening, that they spoke to many people at once and never provided individual attention, and that they always spoke English at level three, which the Indian women did not understand. Therefore, the women should not lose their SSI benefits or pay any money back. The judge agreed, and in his decision added that social services personnel would have to use an interpreter when they went to the reservation to explain programs and their requirements.

Case Study: The Bottle-Formula Controversy

Another type of advocacy role is one in which anthropologists provide research and expertise to support a public cause or protest movement. Such movements usually have identifiable protagonists, and they are normally conducted through the media, involve influencing the public and major policy-making bodies, and have to be sustained over a long time.

During the 1970s and into the 1980s a major consumer boycott and international protest was directed at the Nestlé Corporation, a large multinational food company. The corporation had been promoting the use of bottle-feeding and baby formulas in Africa, Latin America, and Southeast Asia at a time when its market share was diminishing in North America and Europe, because mothers were shifting back to breast-feeding, which was seen to have many health and psychological advantages.

From the point of view of Nestlé's opponents, the use of manufactured bottles and baby formulas could not be seen as beneficial, or even neutral, in Third World contexts. In fact, an argument could be made that they were detrimental to health and, sometimes, even life-threatening. First, the formulas required mixing with water, and most mothers living in dilapidated circumstances in urban slums found getting clean water to be extremely difficult. Boiling was not always possible or convenient, especially when scarce fuels were expensive. So contaminated water might be used to clean bottles after use. Diseases could then be passed on to babies who had not yet built up immunities. Furthermore, the use of bottles and formulas could be perceived as somewhat technologically advanced, because they required literacy for effective use. This made it difficult for most Third World mothers who were often illiterate and quite rushed in their daily chores. Infant mortality could be greatly increased through diarrhea, dehydration, and gastroenteritis. Moreover, because bottle-feeding mothers were not nursing, their chances of becoming pregnant were higher. Traditionally, women would not wean children until they were several years old. Bottle-feeding interfered with the birth-control cycle, therefore encouraging higher populations, contributing to poverty and overcrowding.

In addition, there are advantages to breast-feeding. Breast milk is a natural and replenishable resource. More important, impoverished families would not have to find the money to pay for it. Furthermore, mothers' milk is a healthy product; it passes on invaluable maternal immunities to young children who live in circumstances of dangerous and endemic microbial diseases. Nutritionally, it is sound, providing protein and calcium and other nutrients that are important for healthy growth. Mothers who breast-feed their young children are able to bypass infected water sources.

Yet Nestlé persisted in its promotion of formula-feeding in developing countries. The company was alleged to have used seductive advertising and promotional incentives to get local doctors and departments of health to support the widespread diffusion of its products. One of the more unfortunate dimensions of advertising through pamphlets and billboards was to associate this style of feeding with modernity and prosperity, thus inducing unsuspecting impoverished mothers to associate their families' betterment with the formula. During this period, international protests emerged; they began in 1977 and culminated, through the efforts of the World Health Organization and UNICEF, in a set of regulations ensuring the ethical promotion of such products. All countries signed the convention—except the United States, which supported deregulation in commerce. Yet during this time, there was also a build-up of a protest movement organized primarily by concerned Americans. The climax was a consumer boycott, which lasted until 1984 when Nestlé agreed to comply with the guidelines.

Engaged in the boycott and advocacy campaign against Nestlé were a range of parties and interests. Included were doctors, nurses, and research scientists with knowledge of the detrimental effects. This issue contained important political and economic implications;

many people were opposed to the overreaching approaches taken by the corporation and the U.S. government. This was also a woman's issue during the formative 1970s period for feminists. There were also more traditionally oriented women such as those in the LaLeche League, who emphasized "family values" but especially the importance of breast-feeding. After long and fierce resistance and in spite of sometimes very effective counteradvocacy, Nestlé bowed under the pressure of the negative publicity and agreed to the principles laid out in the United Nations agreement in 1984.

During this period, Penny Van Esterik, an anthropologist who did her dissertation fieldwork in Thailand, came to play an important role in the advocacy campaign through debates and providing arguments through research. She also provided highly perceptive analyses of the advocacy process and the anthropological roles in it (Van Esterik 1985, 1989). Advocacy, in its choice of an issue, is often highly charged and personal. In the preface to her book, Van Esterik describes how a local Thai doctor had recommended formulas during her own routine prenatal examination, and she noticed Nestlé promotional material in the waiting room. Given her knowledge of Thailand, families, poverty, and medical anthropology, she was quite familiar with the damaging effects of Nestlé's promotion of their products in the Third World. Upon her return to North America in the 1970s, she held a teaching job at a Midwestern university and became active in a group that discussed the issues and organized educational forums and the local boycotts. Three times—1979, 1980, and 1982—she participated in debates about the issue, the last time directly with officials from Nestlé. In the intervening years, she had become involved in a very large research project investigating the issue. She was in charge of a series of on-site ethnographic investigations in Indonesia, Thailand, Colombia, and Kenya to research the circumstances regarding mothers and their small children in conditions of urban poverty.

During the first two debates she acted as an impassioned private citizen, aware of the antiformula research literature and with some significant firsthand knowledge providing "punch" from her fieldwork. In the final debate, she was acting more as an expert—a research scientist, who had collated large amounts of data on the subject and become well versed in the medical and statistical data collected in the large-scale multidisciplinary research project. In retrospect, she outlines some pitfalls in taking the role of the expert researcher in advocacy cases.

Because of her awareness of the general literature, she realized how the same statistics could sometimes be used for different positions and how any study can be attacked for some methodological weaknesses. In preparing for the last debate, in which she was presented as an expert researcher, she also felt that she was cluttered with too many facts and did not know which were the best studies to cite.

At the debate itself, she was confronted by a male–female pair who represented the corporation, well versed in public relations, displaying a friendly, smooth demeanor with significant knowledge about research on the topic. As she put it, they were able "to take a lot of my thunder away." In a postmortem on the debate, she judged her performance this way: "I lost the simplicity and force of the advocate's voice, and spoke with the equivocal quaver of the academic" (Van Esterik 1989: 67). When she cited studies, the Nestlé officials replied with such objections as "that particular study was not based on a random sample." During the debate, the Nestlé officials made sincere and confident claims that their corporation was already following the ethical guidelines established by the World Health Organization. Yet

Van Esterik knew that it was not. In the debate, she did not have direct evidence at hand to precisely disprove that claim, so they were able to get away with it. They made other bold claims in their well-polished debating style: that there had been no significant reduction in breast-feeding in such countries; that there was already high infant mortality in the affected countries (presumably, therefore, not linked directly to the promotion or use of bottles); that there was no proven link between feeding decisions of mothers and advertising procedures. In addition, using their own reasoned, polite, and moderate debating styles, the hired advocates for Nestlé announced that they were not going to deal with "strident" lobby groups, thus appealing to American expectations of fair play and moderation.

In criticism of her own performance, Van Esterik judges that it was poor compared to that of the well-prepared Nestlé representatives. Nevertheless, eventually the boycott strategy did prevail, and her role was important.

Lessons from the Nestlé Boycott

The difficulties that Van Esterik confronted are informative because they form a series of warnings about the preparations needed for engagement in long-term advocacy. One of these is anticipation of *advocacy burnout*. A few dedicated and knowledgeable individuals cannot carry out all of the time-consuming activities needed to maintain advocacy campaigns. They have to build extensive networks and coalitions of volunteer supporters and allies. They also have to delegate many tasks to others. Corporations or governments that are the targets of advocacy protest movements are designed to perpetuate themselves over the long term. They may find the protests irritating and decry the negative publicity, but they are better able to muster financial and personnel resources for the long haul. Through efforts by paid experts in public relations, they can develop smooth, well-focused, and well-financed countercampaigns of advocacy. In contrast, citizen advocacy groups tend to be ephemeral. At some point, their cause will end; they may win, but there is a very good chance that they may lose or exhaust their resources. In that process, the morale of the principal advocates may be deflated: they may tire and lose the capacity to sustain the fight. It is essential to build up a solid awareness among the followers and to train other people to share in the important tasks.

The second set of observations centers around the style of *advocacy communication*. That form of discourse tends to be direct, emotional, and dramatic. It uses arresting slogans. Some slogans might include: "Nestlé kills babies" or a reference to infant formula as the "Kool-Aid of Jonestown." These effectively and emotionally focus attention on the key issues at hand. Slogans remain in the minds of members of the intended audience, the potential supporters from the public, who, in turn, might bring pressure on policy makers or the offending corporation. Accordingly, such rhetoric must be managed very carefully. Still, effective and emotion-raising communication is essential at some level for getting committed support for the cause.

Normal academic discourse is ill equipped for this. As Van Esterik (1985: 72) points out, scholarly communication tends to be the opposite of advocacy discourse. It is "indirect, detached, turgid and convoluted. It cannot easily generate slogans that can catch the imagination, and academics tend to equivocate, saying things like 'on the other hand.'" Advocates cannot do that.

Nonetheless, scientific knowledge, as provided by anthropologists and others, is valuable for these battles. A series of expert testimonies can be provided, sometimes for court cases, sometimes as part of public relations campaigns through the media or as preparation for public debates.

Scientists or other specialists will have to face opposition as they support an advocacy cause through testimony. If they are expert witnesses in a court case or in a debate, invariably they will be accused by lawyers or debating opponents of being biased and nonobjective. They may face personal discomfort in dealing with intense situations of cross-examination, media scrutiny, or debate. Worse yet, they may inadvertently make statements that might be used against them in the battle for public opinion. They might show evidence of emotional bias or uncertainty in their own position. Anthropologists and others voluntarily involved in advocacy are not usually trained for this sort of engagement, and advocacy groups do not have the mechanisms to provide such training. So anthropological and other scientifically based advocates may come across as very awkward and ineffective in such situations.

Van Esterik (1985) makes a valuable suggestion for such dilemmas of communication. Introducing the "native" perspective into the advocacy returns some of the needed emotionality and passion to the debate and provides authenticity for the advocate's case. Often that native experience has been buried within the debate. In the case of the breast-or-bottle controversy, the native perspective is that of Third World mothers who have to make some very difficult decisions regarding health and their children. Another example could be Indian elders who would argue passionately in a land-case hearing to redress past injustices to an indigenous people. Anthropologists can collect the testimonies of the people who cannot come to a debate at a cosmopolitan setting or facilitate bringing people with authentic voices to the public hearings.

A final concern that Van Esterik raises is that of *commitment*. This type of advocacy, though, requires no specific form of action; it is relatively passive. Capital "A" or active advocacy requires action and commitment by the advocate anthropologist, researching a group's case or position, testifying in court, or participating in large-scale public, media-directed protest campaigns on behalf of a cause.

To more academically inclined anthropologists, who do not participate in advocacy, it often seems capricious and based on sentiment or emotion. Advocacy is seen as something to be avoided, because it is unseemly and does not, in their view, reflect well on the discipline. Van Esterik (1985), responds that there are frequently very compelling reasons, on the face of the societal evidence, to participate in advocacy causes. The breast-or-bottle controversy that she dealt with had very much at stake—morbidity, mortality, factors of local empowerment, dimensions of social change, mother–child relations, continuing capacities to adapt, and the relationships of power among nation-states and large corporations. But any crystallization of commitment to big "A" (cause-related) advocacy is very difficult for many anthropologists, who might otherwise hear the "call."

It could be perilous for young academics just starting on a career to commit themselves to advocacy. They might have difficulty getting hired because of their opinions. They would have to devote a lot of their time to writing academic papers and books to ensure job security through tenure, promotion, and so forth. I might add that there might be serious obstacles for certain types of practicing anthropologists to becoming involved in capital "A" advocacy as well. Take the example of the public service—there are usually very explicit rules denying the civil servant the right to engage in political or advocacy activities. So the possibilities for advocacy are structurally limited for many young anthropologists, who, psychologically and physically, might actually be at their peak for advocacy. As they become more secure, they lose the "fire in their belly" or the intensive emotional involvement.

For a long time yet, capital "A" advocacy will probably be an activity for only a minority in the discipline. For those who will be so engaged, Van Esterik recommends learning certain skills. We need to broaden our communication styles—to be prepared to communicate differently for different audiences both through writing and speaking. Perhaps one effective way of doing this is to first write up the anthropological evidence according to the standards of academic anthropology and then translate it for the intended lay audience. As a strategic consideration, she also suggests that we not only need to gain an understanding of those being exploited and for whom we are engaged in advocacy, but we also need to know a lot more about the groups who are in power or who are benefiting from the undesirable circumstances. Also, she suggests that anthropologists working in advocacy become part of interdisciplinary teams and work for the long term with agencies that are focused on related causes. Advocacy anthropology (like many dimensions of applied anthropology) also needs shorter turnover periods in the production of information essential to the advocacy causes. She suggests that we seek other funding sources than the ones usually available for anthropology in order to maintain research components of advocacy. To develop longer-term commitment, it might also be a good idea to introduce advocacy issues much earlier into the anthropological curriculum—providing anthropological perspectives on issues like discrimination and underdevelopment. Sound scholarship should be associated with these issues at an earlier stage in the student's career. Over time, advocacy anthropology will become a more acceptable dimension of anthropological activity (Van Esterik 1985).

Advocacy for Individuals

There is one other way in which advocacy might enter the work of practicing anthropologists—in the day-to-day advocacy for the individual or family needs of clients. This advocacy is done in a manner similar to that of doctors, nurses, and social workers. Individuals may need counseling, direction, and referrals in trying to adjust to their life circumstances. Anthropologists in these contexts would speak, intercede, or write on behalf of their clients with officials from other agencies to meet specific needs. These advocacy needs could relate to income, specialized counseling, access to programs or instruction, health, finding sources of support and funding, and so forth. Although practicing anthropologists might more normally be seen as providing background research, evaluations, and program design that pertains to whole groups or categories of people, they also may call for attention to the best interests of individual clients. For instance, four of my department's former graduate students have held jobs at service agencies that help newly arrived government-sponsored immigrants (refugees) from many different countries. Their jobs have included administration, program design, and instruction. In all of these cases, while going through a lot of on-the-job training, their anthropological background has served them well, not the least of their assets being their cross-cultural sensitivities. Their jobs have called for direct counseling, and that requires seeing their clients in their contexts of culture, family, and community. This vision has helped them counsel clients at court appearances; consult with social workers; solve conflicts with neighbors, landlords, and bosses; consider health problems; and deal with problems or misunderstandings that may have arisen in school. This capacity to deal with the "hands-on" needs of individual clients and families is a skill worthy of cultivation in practicing anthropologists.

Summary

As we have seen, advocacy within anthropology can be a perilous and sometimes messy activity, yet it is essential for the viability of an applied and practicing anthropology and perhaps for the survival of anthropology as a whole. Although advocacy is not something new to anthropology, there may be greater urgency for it now because, with rapid social change and globalization, more and more vulnerable peoples are imperiled by development, profit-seeking, and the downsizing of government services. Concurrently, there is more societal awareness of past injustices that contribute to current harm, and these recognitions have generated social movements. Since the 1960s, these movements have persisted in their pressures for attention to environmentalism, human rights, and other issues. Related to these circumstances is the power of the media to define an issue and to see its course through to the end. That can be a mixed blessing; the media can intensify adversarial relations and high drama, and it can also ignore very worthy ones, thus trivializing them.

For all of these reasons, many anthropologists strongly feel the pull of conscience and social responsibility to engage in advocacy because they have information that is crucial to the debates. Ethnography and other anthropological perspectives can arm anthropologists with the strategic knowledge that can inform many advocacy causes.

Anthropologists are finding new niches to serve new needs. Tribal or First Nations governments, immigrant associations, urban consumer groups, environmentalists, ethnic minorities, and people with disabilities and other special interests have increased activities into such domains as law, conflict resolution, economic development, social services, health, and education. In the swirl of societal conflict and competition for resources, clients need assistance to confront the courts, bureaucracies, Congress, and state and provincial legislatures. Anthropologists can often be valuable in preparing the briefs that support their agendas.

There are other types of advocacy, including advocacy for applied anthropology itself. There is the ever-present need to publicize one's findings. One may be commissioned to prepare a report on a set of social needs or to evaluate a set of programs. Practicing anthropologists need to advocate effectively for the recognition of their findings and recommendations—such data frequently do not simply speak for themselves.

So anthropological advocacy contains a whole series of potential activities. All of them require convincing other people of the merits of a set of ideas through communication, argument, counterargument, persuasion, and the effective and convincing presentations of points of view, based on data, interpretation, and sometimes theory. Just because it is messy and many academic anthropologists do not like it does not mean that applied and practicing anthropologists should shun it. In its many varieties, advocacy is central to practice and application.

RECOMMENDED READINGS

Downing, Theodore E., and Gilbert Kushner (eds.)
1988   *Human Rights and Anthropology.* Cultural Survival Report 24. Cambridge, MA: Cultural Survival Inc.

Harries-Jones, Peter (ed.)
1991   *Making Knowledge Count: Advocacy and Social Science.* Montreal: McGill-Queens University Press.

Hastrup, Kirsten, and Peter Elass
1990   Anthropological Advocacy: A Contradiction in Terms. *Current Anthropology,* Vol. 31(3): 301–311.

Paine, Robert (ed.)
1985   *Anthropology and Advocacy.* St. John's: Memorial University, Institute of Social and Economic Research.

Peterson Jr., John
1974   Anthropologist as Advocate. *Human Organization,* Vol. 33(3): 311–318.

Schensul, Stephen L., and Jean J. Schensul
1978   Advocacy and Applied Anthropology. In *Social Scientists as Advocates.* George H. Weber and George I. McCall, eds. Pp. 121–166. Beverly Hills, CA: Sage.

11 Ethnography: Participant Observation and Key-Informant Interviewing

The next three chapters outline the primary research methods anthropologists use for practice. It is not my intention to provide a substitute for some fine books (see Agar 1996; Bernard 1995; Pelto and Pelto 1978; Spradley 1979, 1980) that are available on anthropological methodology. What I will do is relate how these techniques are used to practical ends. As has been underscored in the chapters on policy analysis, methodological virtuosity may be the most important skill to bring to practice. I discuss the applied dimensions of participant observation and key-informant interviewing in this chapter, group interviewing in the next, and some quantitative approaches using questionnaires and indicator analysis in Chapter 13.

Among the social sciences, anthropology has been a leader in the development of qualitative methodologies. Patton, a sociologist, outlines their major benefits for applied work:

> Qualitative data consists of *detailed descriptions* of situations, events, people, interactions, and observed behaviors; *direct quotations* from people about their experiences, attitudes, beliefs, and thoughts; and excerpts or entire passages from documents, correspondence, records, and case histories. The detailed descriptions, direct quotations, and case documentation of qualitative measurement are raw data from the empirical world. The data are collected as open-ended narrative *without* attempting to fit program activities or peoples' experiences into predetermined standardized categories such as the response choices that compromise typical questionnaires or tests. (Patton 1980: 22)

In applied situations, anthropologists' assets will continue to be their capacities for naturalistic, qualitative inquiry in local communities and organizations using participant observation and key-informant interviewing. The researcher can provide authenticity and empathy to social science "data" or information. Effective ethnographic portrayals are also very useful for correcting misrepresentations or misperceptions of a people's actions, motives, or needs. Accompanied by sensible recommendations, they can contribute to the design of more effective programming, services, and policies.

Ethnography and Participant Observation

An Omnibus Strategy

Ethnographic fieldwork or participant observation is really not a single method or set of precisely defined procedures. Instead, it is an omnibus strategy, an approach that contains a variety of information-gathering techniques that involve various forms of observation—from unobtrusive ones to full-scale participation by a researcher deeply and actively absorbed in local activities. Researchers record small snippets of informal daily conversation that yield valuable insights. They also perform lengthy open-ended key-informant interviews or administer structured interview schedules to representative samples of informants. Anthropologists also use formal data-gathering techniques such as mapping households and the local terrain, recording the use of natural resources, and collecting censuses. For long-term research, they collect genealogies and learn the language in order to comprehend important local cultural constructs and categories. Some research could even involve the administration of projective instruments like Thematic Apperception Tests, in which people are asked to describe or interpret the situations portrayed in a set of photographs or drawings. Toward the end of the fieldwork period, formal questionnaires may be administered.

Anthropological fieldwork, then, is not linear. It is sporadic and zigzags in numerous directions. Because it is flexible, it responds to the natural unfolding of events. A person might begin to follow one research lead or gain pieces of information relevant to some important subtopics, but new, often unanticipated, ones turn the researcher's attention and efforts elsewhere. Later, he returns to previous topics, augmenting or verifying previous bits of information through observation and interviews. Yet the process is not a random one. Derived from a formal research design, an inventory of relevant topics has been established and information is sought on each of them during fieldwork. But some topics may be discovered to be irrelevant to the situation, although immersion invariably reveals new and often more pertinent topics. Clearly, this flexibility has an advantage for the examination of issues and problems for practical solutions.

While doing community or organizational research, the ethnographer participates in networks of personal associations and friendships. He becomes involved with one cluster of people, engages in a number of activities and conversations, turns to another group, then may come back to one of the earlier networks. For instance, when doing fieldwork in Inuvik in the Northwest Territories, I would spend time with a number of circles of people—Inuit, Dene, and Métis—at different periods as the reasons for the interactions waxed and waned.

Anthropologists contend that information retrieved in these ways is equally or even more valid than those data that, on the surface, appear more rigorous, robust, or "scientific"—such as questionnaires and statistics from the more formalistic social sciences. There is also a certain amount of authenticity to participant observation, because the researcher was *actually there.* The variety of the interactions, waxing and waning in various completed and emerging episodes, allows for the possibility of cross-checking or validating previous assumptions or theories. Researchers may see hunches or leads negated, confirmed, or made indeterminate. Accordingly, a good fieldworker tends to develop a highly skeptical attitude about his or her own ideas or theories and checks them out through alternative techniques.

Time Spent in the Field

Typically, participant observation involves a reasonably long stay in the setting. Many recommend at least a year, so that researchers can experience the full seasonal cycle to account for any periodic anomalies that might occur in behavior. For instance, if people are seasonally dispersed for a portion of the year rather than living in nucleated settlements, they might exhibit temporary differences in social organization. That is true of many Native groups in the isolated communities of Alaska or northern Canada. If researchers restrict their time to one of the two periods, they may misunderstand the nature of overall social organization.

In applied venues, the time of stay may not always embrace the entire seasonal cycle. The anthropologist may already be familiar with the community, culture, or region from previous fieldwork. He or she may have a relatively defined focus instead of generating a holistic view of the community in the classical ethnographic style. The mandate usually requires that the investigation be done fairly quickly. Also, many applied anthropologists now work in their own countries and frequently with more mainstream populations and institutions. If they are already familiar with the more significant ways of doing things—the cultural rules—their "learning curves" may not be as steep. Finally, the applied anthropologist, as consultant, might also regularly visit the field site or sites, monitoring impact, reviewing the progress of programs, or supervising the work of co-researchers, who might be members of the local community. This would be a form of commuting, unlike the classical form of fieldwork but still involving participant observation.

Yet applied anthropologists may still fulfill normal expectations and spend a long time in the field even if they are already familiar with the people in question. For instance, a person might spend as much as two years doing a major social impact assessment, projecting and monitoring the results of a hydroelectric project that dislocates a community. Also, site visits in applied research may be spread out over several years, thus providing the equivalent of the more traditional year in the field.

Stages of Fieldwork

Ethnographic fieldwork or the participant observation process usually includes a number of stages. The first is entering the fieldwork setting. Typically, that could involve a number of things—gaining permission to be there, explaining one's presence, gaining some minimum or essential degree of trust, and attaining early familiarity with the setting. This stage can create anxious and unnerving moments for even the most seasoned fieldwork veterans. There are the possibilities of being refused admission, of unpleasant or even hostile encounters, a sense of personal vulnerability, all of which may threaten the researcher's self-esteem. It is rarely a smooth transition. Although the most serious difficulties of the initial stage usually disappear, they may resurface during fieldwork. Fieldwork can be marvelous and exhilarating, and many people get much enjoyment and satisfaction from it, yet most will readily admit that the period of entering the field can contain some anxious moments.

During this phase, a researcher has to establish clearance with the appropriate gatekeepers, officials such as district administrators, village and tribal councils, and executive directors of government and nongovernment organizations. It is usually appropriate to get the clearance at the highest levels first. Yet even line bureaucrats in the field, far away from head offices, can continue to be suspicious or exercise local autonomy by not providing the next level of clearances that a person needs to proceed or get information. Still, in applied work, you cannot be sure that even official endorsements or internal clearances, along with an explicit and pragmatic research design, will make it any easier to establish contacts and gain the trust of people.

Field researchers still have to explain why they are there to local people, who may decide not to comply. Sometimes, their attitude toward researchers may be more one of bemused tolerance rather than full acceptance. A number of years ago when we were setting up a field project in rural Saskatchewan, two graduate students were sent to scout the local communities we had chosen and to see if they could find us accommodation. They ran into a local farmer and became engaged in a friendly chat. When he asked why they were there, they painstakingly described our interests in investigating local farmers' ecological adaptations, marketing choices, shifts in strategies among choices of grains and livestock, and how these and other variables over time would collectively affect the shape and nature of local communities. "So then, you're fresh-air inspectors," he responded with a amused twinkle in his eye. He was expressing the local rural attitude that "surveys," as the locals labeled research, were not considered useful.

Because of experiences like this, I always prepare a one-page summary in lay language that explains the research project and includes a sketch of all subprojects. It indicates how people can get in touch with me as project director or with any other key participants among the research assistants. I state who has mandated the research and what its practical implications are. Once, while collecting life histories of Southeast Asian refugees, I had such a statement translated into Vietnamese by a native speaker, and then translated back into English by another Vietnamese to check the accuracy of the translation. The objective is to reduce misunderstanding about the project before inaccurate rumors spread. It is also a way of establishing informed consent in a more natural way than by administering release forms.

In the beginning, researchers may experience a phase of cultural shock (see Nolan, 1990, for a succinct overview of this phenomenon). Unfamiliarity with the culture, community, behavior, and values can promote anxieties, self-doubts, and negative feelings about the value of the work. These may be lessened if the applied anthropologist has a long-term familiarity with the situation. It may be relieved in urban situations in which the investigators commute daily to the setting of investigation and return to the comforts of their home situation. It may be further reduced if the study has been commissioned (possibly by the community as a whole or a respected agency within it) for obvious practical and socially relevant reasons. The stress for applied anthropologists might be eased in circumstances in which the project involves some forms of direct collaboration with local people as partners. Yet the possibility that they are dealing with policy issues revolving around scarce resources can add to the pressure on applied anthropologists. Some people will invariably feel threatened or resentful of the fact that the work is being done in the first place. The simple fact of the researcher's presence may be at issue as well.

Normally, though, this period of culture shock will subside, and over time the researcher's presence will start to seem more acceptable, and the researcher himself will feel more comfortable. Usually, investigators will overcome negativity by establishing rapport or trust in various ways. Researchers attempt to be on their best behavior. They show respect, courtesy, and attention to the wishes of the community members. Researchers accommodate as much as possible the needs and schedules of the local people, avoiding explicit favoritism or aligning with factions and keeping most opinions to themselves unless they are favorable to the group in question. During this period, the anthropologist will likely have made a number of reliable associations with people and established local friendships that serve for personal support and security as well as valuable sources of information. What is required is very diligent effort in building human relations, effective impression management, and persuasion, combined with amiability, integrity, and professionalism. Most anthropologists, in spite of residual difficulties and possibilities for anxiety and conflict, are successful in gaining entrée and fitting in. Most find that success, in itself, is quite exhilarating. Not to minimize the experience, but some broad parallels could be made with the sorts of challenges that children or adolescents face when they transfer schools and have to experience a trial period before being accepted and with their relief at eventually being accepted.

A stage of rapid learning and even euphoria often follows this normalization and building of trust. The euphoria is based on positive acceptance of the researcher and a rapid transfer of information during this period. The researcher might now make very strong and positive personal identifications with the people being studied. At this stage, the researcher may record impressions and "facts" rather inaccurately in an all-too-human and understandable desire to please local people. Information might be a bit one sided, even sugarcoated, or exaggerated. Because of this, policy makers, bureaucrats, and others may criticize anthropologists for a tendency to overidentify with community members and adopt their biased perceptions of the "facts" to the detriment of a more "balanced" and accurate view.

This is a controversial issue that applied anthropologists need to face. One justification of informant identification is that, given power imbalances, programs and services are often designed by experts and other outsiders who have aims and assumptions different from the local people. So, perhaps in a spirit of fair play, it is appropriate to nonjudgmentally understand the points of view of community members or "target populations," especially if there has been a legacy of abuse, misunderstanding or one-sided, policy formulation. Administrators and other power holders might continue to dominate through their power bases, and their biases might be supported by other policy scientists such as economists, who tend to share their criteria for judgment and making decisions. Taking a strong advocacy stance may be important for establishing the dialogue that could lead to beneficial change. Nevertheless, anthropologists do have a very strong responsibility to establish and maintain the credibility of their findings. So at this tempting stage of rapid learning, anthropologists should feel obliged to carefully record all their observations and emerging opinions, theories, and hypotheses. These should not be taken at face value but continuously scrutinized for accuracy and biases.

Bernard (1995: 162) suggests that the researcher should take a break at some point and leave the field setting. Then the research could be refocused to more accurately reflect recently discovered realities. New approaches could be designed to follow crucial but unexpected leads. Yet, given the nonlinear and often random aspects of participant observation and fieldwork, we can anticipate that more new directions are likely to emerge even after the return to the field. So, following Bernard's lead, there may be rationales for additional breaks and reassessments of the directions and findings for the research project. However, with the typical shorter terms of applied projects, there may not be time for such breaks. On the other hand, periodic commuting to the research site would also allow some time for assessment and redesign.

The final stages of a fieldwork project would include some form of cleaning-up or concentrated collection of crucial data, observations, and attempts to confirm or deny hypotheses. In applied research, that might involve the use of survey questionnaires to confirm or disconfirm some of the findings, hunches, and hypotheses that emerged during the course of the work. Some of these could have been derived serendipitously from casual conversations or observations in the course of participant observation, or they might have developed from more sustained and linear themes of investigation in the research.

A crucial dimension of applied research is the moral and logistic obligation to seek feedback from the people whose lives could be most affected by the research findings. At the very least, some key findings and possibly preliminary recommendations should be presented before leaving the field. After such a process, the anthropologist would then exit from the field setting to work on the detailed analyses and prepare the final report. Finally, in applied anthropology, it is typical for the researcher to return to the organization or community to discuss the report.

Observation and Recording

We have considered the broad stages of ethnography involving participant observation. What are some of the finer points of its operations? For one thing, the need for researchers to hone their observational powers cannot be overemphasized. As Spradley (1980: 33–38) points out, in the course of everyday life we normally block out many details of our experience; otherwise, there would be an unbearable sensory overload. We focus on those details germane to the action or experience and take for granted most other factors. We are on a sort of automatic "cruise control." But, for fieldworkers engaged in participant observation, many overlooked details may be highly crucial. However, the right balance for focusing detailed observations has to emerge through common sense and finding the significance of local behavior or attitudes. It may be pointless to enumerate all the items and colors of participants' daily clothing. On the other hand, it might be significant to note in observations of a meeting that some members of one negotiating party tended to keep their arms folded; some fidgeted; and many rolled their eyes when any members of the other party made points. These are ultimately judgment calls, but during ethnography, it is important to carefully determine what should be described and what can be ignored.

Related to improved powers of observation are good descriptive writing skills. Fieldnotes are an absolutely essential dimension of participant observation—researchers should not rely on memory. Notes should be written immediately or very shortly after the event before selective memory to distort accurate recall of the observed events. Times and dates should be noted. It might be valuable to record short versions of the events as well as long, more detailed ones. Wide margins can be used for significant keywords representing the topics that might have been part of the events being observed. Somewhere in the notes, the researcher might include hypotheses or impressions, bits of dialogue, and direct observations of actions, but they should be separated from each other and clearly noted as such. A separate daily journal has often been recommended for ethnographic fieldwork to record daily sequences of events and any difficulties, such as one's personal frustrations or anxieties that might have negatively colored perceptions of what happened.

Fieldnotes and journals become personalized: one knows what works best for oneself. The main objective, which is quite crucial, is to facilitate accurate, highly descriptive recording of information for effective retrieval in analysis.

The usual beginning procedure for analysis, as Bernard (1988: 196) has pointed out, consists of much "pawing and shuffling" through notes, searching for relevant information. Sometimes portions of long and highly detailed notes can be inserted directly into the final report. The same is true for verbatim quotes that add "punch" or impact to the points of view of participants or community members. The shorter version of notes helps to establish sequences of events or provides episodes from which generalizations will be drawn in the larger report. The keyword marginal headings allow investigators to locate and extract material relevant to particular topics easily, so that they can all be in place when needed. Of course, many computer programs allow for arranging materials automatically on the basis of key words.

As Spradley suggests (1980: 77), "grand"- and "mini"-tour descriptions of important recurrent settings relevant to the applied research are useful in field notes. For instance, programs being evaluated or needs being assessed might be located in an agency like a drop-in health clinic, a social service bureau, or an immigrant agency. Details of how such a facility appears to a new client could be valuable. How is a person received? What are the facilities like in terms of space, room, furniture, and other facilities? What is the staff doing? In other words, a grand tour accounts for relevant details about people, space, and facilities in the institutional setting. We can sense if the organization provides a welcoming but professional setting for clients or if it is intimidating and inaccessible. Next, a mini-tour could involve all the relevant ingredients as they might relate to more specific services or interactions conducted at the agency. As examples, descriptions of typical one-to-one or family counseling sessions would be valuable if permitted at a family service bureau. Other examples might include prenatal classes or checkups at a health clinic or, in the case of the immigrant agency, settings in which English or employment readiness training is done. I think that the reader probably can anticipate how some of these descriptions might contain information useful for evaluations as well as providing the necessary background for describing interactions and functions.

Experiences arising from participant observation should tell us something about the main actors and principal groups. When we study organizations, we should describe how their personnel interact with clients and community members. Another appropriate context for ethnographic study is a staff meeting or other kinds of meetings. Our observations should tell who is doing what, with whom, where, and when it is happening. The framework of interaction is provided, but then it is necessary to expand—filling in the rich details describing what is said and what is actually done. That is one of the major strengths of participant observation—the events are recorded as they occur. In terms of application, if done effectively, participant observation is potentially unbeatable in its contribution to policy solutions. Observations directly relevant to the significant actors within their settings, with participants voicing their opinions of the meanings, values, and levels of satisfaction along with their suggestions for change should carry a lot of weight. Conversely, statistics, questionnaires, the use of public records, and all of the other major research methods and sources of data cannot accurately convey what actually happens; they are only indirect measures or projections of that reality. Participant observation brings us much closer to "reality" in all of its nuances. Of course, validity can be undermined by researcher bias, and the presence of the investigator will influence the activities of those she is investigating, but these problems can be corrected by professionalism and experience in fieldwork.

Unobtrusive Observation to Full Participation

How much do fieldworkers actually participate? To what degree are they detached observers, and how intrusive are the observations? In some situations, anthropologists simply may not be able to enter directly into the social group or activities in question because they do not have the right qualifications to participate. Race, ethnicity, occupation, in-group affiliation, or definition of membership may preclude acceptance. For instance, an anthropologist would only get in the way of high-steel workers on the job setting. Age or gender could also present impediments in many situations. For their own reasons, the members of the group might resent or view the participation of the researchers as patronizing.

Unobtrusive observations are sometimes built in on the edges of normally inaccessible social scenes such as the galleries of operating rooms and waiting rooms of social or health agencies. Children are a special challenge. Sometimes unobtrusive observations of children in play groups can be done through one-way mirrors or on the edges of playgrounds as long as the necessary ethical precautions have been taken.

Sharing neutral or semi-neutral "offstage" contexts in which the anthropologist can be accepted could be another way of increasing participation and gathering information. The anthropologist might join steelworkers, surgeons, or off-duty policemen at their favorite bars or restaurants and participate in the general convivialities while hearing about recent exploits and listening in on the "shop talk." Much can be learned in these offstage contexts, so long as "tall tales" are kept in perspective and checked out through other approaches.

Another way to participate is by taking on an auxiliary participant role that is more or less improvised for the situation. Imagine an anthropologist studying the isolation and occupational hazards facing long-distance truckers. The anthropologist may not be allowed to actually drive an eighteen-wheeler, but he might accompany the trucker as a companion and share the experiences of the road. The trucker might find the companionship worthwhile and share his perceptions about the profession and the meanings of particular incidents. During the trip, the anthropologist might be able to directly observe some of the sources of risk and stress, but the level of participation would be limited to perhaps helping to change a tire or to load and unload.

There are opportunities for full-fledged or relatively complete participation. For instance, Patton (1890: 140–141) participated as a student in a Wilderness Training Program class. That participation was one phase of a program evaluation. Michael Agar (1973) in his research at an addiction research center, began as an employee—as a janitor—but later switched to being a full-fledged researcher after the patients became familiar with him.

In normal fieldwork situations, the opportunities to participate in the activities under review tend to wax and wane. In some cases, people might appreciate the anthropologist's assistance in such activities as haying, harvesting, house or barn building, hauling in nets, and looking after children, especially in local situations when labor is intensive and community members are normally expected to volunteer. In studies of agencies and their programs, researchers might relieve other staff by answering the phone or helping in office clean-ups. Although participating in these activities does not always yield research results, the camaraderie and appreciation for pitching in often lead to more open and trusting responses from the participants.

Another avenue for participant observation is at normal occasions of informal socializing. People value their leisure time, and many societies or groupings studied by anthropologists put a special emphasis on the importance of hospitality and visiting—often to a much greater extent than middle-class North Americans do. The informality of interactions can provide the potential for easier participation, and as a guest or fellow socializer, the anthropologist gains information and insight. Even in urban middle-class society, much business is really conducted through informal interaction.

Unlike some of the other techniques described in this book, it is impossible to teach participant observation by outlining precise steps. It has to be experienced directly and requires full immersion. Of course there are intermediate ways of giving a taste of the experience—through ethnographic field schools and applied internships. Neophytes immerse themselves in smaller doses and do not have full responsibilities for any failures of the research. Students about to do fieldwork can gain a certain amount of insight by reading the literature on fieldwork (some of which is listed at the end of the chapter). Particularly useful, from a morale viewpoint, are stories describing difficulties and stresses, ethical dilemmas, and general hardships experienced by veteran researchers. When novices later experience difficulties, they will realize that they are not unique and that the challenges are rarely the result of some personal or moral deficiency on the part of the researcher.

Key-Informant Interviews

A mainstay of anthropological work is the key-informant interview. It can be used within the general framework of participant observation or alone. For example, situations of more rapid research, as with needs assessment or program evaluation done over several weeks, might make heavy use of some well-placed key-informant interviews.

Informants

James Spradley (1979: 45–54) lists criteria for a good informant. First, the informant should have been thoroughly "enculturated' into the area of activity or knowledge being studied. Second, he or she should be currently involved with it. Third, the topics and cultural scenes being investigated should be basically unfamiliar to the investigator. Fourth, the informant should be able to devote enough time to the interviews to give satisfactory information. Fifth, the informant should be nonanalytical. Presumably, the job of analysis is meant to be done by the anthropologist, and any analytical comments provided by the informant would bias the analysis of the investigator.

These criteria are sensible in many respects for certain types of academic research, but I think they are a bit rigid for an applied anthropologist. First of all, consider direct and thorough enculturation in the domains under question. This implies that the informant should have experience of what he or she is talking about, but some informants may be keen observers rather than active participants. When I was doing fieldwork on issues of sociocultural change in the north, I interviewed people who had participated in the earlier trapping period and had lived a semi-nomadic life attached to the land. They were genuine participants and had been thoroughly enculturated into the life that they were talking about. On the other hand, I also interviewed several Catholic priests who had lived in the region for about three decades. They would accompany Dene people to trap lines, meet with them at their rendezvous, and deliver mass to them in the bush. As seasoned observers, they provided excellent commentaries on the seasonal cycles that augmented and corroborated details given by participants who had been directly enculturated into the domain.

Similarly, we might question the requirement that the informant must be currently engaged in the domain under investigation. As retired town-dwellers, the middle-aged and elderly Inuit and Dene people whom I interviewed were no longer occupied in the trapping and subsistence life-styles. Although their memories may have faded a bit, surely the value of such peoples' information should be incontestable.

Similarly, I do not think that we should avoid informants who give us analytical insights because, as key informants, their expertise might include the most astute commentaries about the topics in question. In other words, I do not think that it is the role of an informant to merely provide descriptive information on the topic. In my previously mentioned research, one of the Catholic priests provided an analysis of a topic that he was actually aware of as a result of reading anthropological literature. It had to do with the concept of reciprocity, normally associated with hunting and gathering peoples. In some previous ethnographic works, there had been descriptions of how moose hunters would butcher meat and give prize cuts to the needy, passing the hide on to a widow. They supposedly saved the least valuable cuts for themselves and their families. This was meant to display the value of sharing, a subversion of one's own desires and self-interest in order to fulfill the group's needs. There was an unstated expectation that one might be in a similar situation of misfortune in the future. The priest pointed out that although this was a culturally expected practice, most hunters would strategically provide the best cuts of meat to those considered the best hunters while still exercising generosity, at least on the surface level. This was done to ensure that such proficient hunters would, in turn, remember the givers when they had success. The priest's analytical observation was made in a detached manner and in no way judged the behavior.

Similarly, during that same research period, town-dwelling Inuit and Dene offered me analyses of some of the difficulties in their less-than-a-decade-long experience with semi-urbanized town life. They would make direct comparisons of their current lives with life-styles in the past and with life-styles of the dominant or temporary white middle-class residents. Among the more interesting analyses provided by one Dene informant was a comparison of child-rearing strategies. Both Inuit and Dene styles of child rearing were nondirective, and children had autonomy in their actions—staying up late under the midnight sun, wandering off, starting small fires, and so forth. As one person put it: the environment was the main disciplinarian for children, and they learned from such experiences. However, there were more dangers in the town, and such experiences did not fit with the realities of life there. More scheduling and adult supervision was the style of the white "southerners," and these expectations were imposed during school and work. I think that such observations were very useful and helped to draw out some significant contrast. It would have been very foolish to have ignored them. In fact, it is probably the case that most anthropologists owe much of their middle-range analyses to their informants. If it were not for the need to maintain informant anonymity for their own protection, it might be far more appropriate to list them as coauthors of many of our monographs.

Although Spradley's criteria for selecting informants may be a bit stringent, they probably can be explained by his main emphasis—that of uncovering the ingredients of unfamiliar cultural domains and the cognitive and linguistic logic underlying them. It does indeed make sense to locate those who are thoroughly enculturated and actively engaged in the topics under question. The criteria might be appropriate for segments of many applied projects, such as coming to understand local knowledge of resource use and conservation practices. Yet, for many applied projects, more flexibility in selecting informants makes sense.

How do we find key informants? Some of them might obviously be prominent local figures or gatekeepers in the community who are familiar with organizations and topics under investigation. These could include officials such as chiefs, tribal councilors, directors of government bureaus or nonprofit agencies, religious or healing leaders. They could also be outsiders who have had long-term, sympathetic liaisons with the peoples in question. Other informants are experts in the areas of health, education, conflict resolution, agriculture, and so forth. Interviewing front-line workers who deliver services under investigation makes good sense. Such people can be interviewed for their particular areas of expertise or knowledge and can provide opinions and information on broader areas of concern. Their responses should always be considered with some understanding of the biases and agendas coming from any vested interests. The nature of the research project will dictate how much we should rely on their opinions. If the study is very broad and covers all aspects of the community, it makes sense to have them participate in interviews. Given their knowledge and possible insight, they may be able to direct us to other leads and subdomains of study not previously considered. Also, if the study deals with the interactions and difficulties of service providers and clients in programming, part of the equation would be to interview those providing the services as well as those receiving them.

For most applied anthropological studies, there is no substitute for directly collecting information and opinions at the grass-roots level. In studies focusing on the needs of street children or to reshape local health facilities so that they are more rooted in the community, it makes much more sense to go quickly and directly to those whose opinions matter the most. Relying too heavily on prominent citizens or gatekeepers as key informants will distort the data that a researcher eventually needs.

Although categories of informants may be relatively easy to identify, how are specific ones identified? They may emerge more or less automatically as the result of knowledge gained during participant observation. They frequently emerge as a result of a "snowballing" effect, whereby informants identify other likely informants. They can sometimes be selected on the basis of random sampling although that tends to be unusual.

The Interview

In the actual process of interviewing, one of the key things to remember is that, although it might resemble a natural dialogue, the interview should be largely a one-way conversation, in which the informant does most of the talking. As Bernard (1995: 212) notes: "The rule is: Get an informant onto a topic of interest and get out of the way. Let the informant provide information that he or she thinks is important." Similarly, it is essential to record the responses in the local idiom as much as possible. This will provide clues to significant local categories and meanings that are valuable for themselves but also useful for later stages such as phrasings in the design of questionnaires. Taperecorders are highly desirable but optional, depending on the feelings of either the informant or even the researcher. Yet note-taking is mandatory. I feel that it is a good idea to show the list of questions in advance to put the person at ease and also to mentally prepare him or her for the questions. I also stress to informants that it is not helpful to merely answer questions in ways that might be presumed as pleasing to me. I tell them that truth and accuracy are more important. To overcome possible diffidence or reluctance to be interviewed, I spend some time reminding the interviewees that they are authentic experts in the topics that I am investigating. Otherwise, I would not be interviewing them.

Questions

It is a good idea to initiate the interview with questions that are immediate, focus on present circumstances, and not too controversial. *Present-tense questions* are meant to warm the interviewee up to the topic, because recall is better about things that happened recently. For example, " Please tell me about what has happened so far in your day, in coping with life as a visually impaired person?" The interviewer might want to ask what Spradley (1979: 86–88) has called *"grand-tour" questions*—those that cover the scope of the domain in question. For example, "Tell me about a typical day in the life of a blind person." In most cases, the investigator should have a set of questions from which to draw upon in the course of the interview—ask alternative questions if one line of questioning is not working out well. For a successful interview, the interviewee should have confidence in the abilities and purposes of the interviewer.

A number of years ago, I took a patient-interviewing course from a psychiatrist, when we were sent around a hospital to interview patients on some very sensitive topics. His point of view was that people will readily answer almost any question if they sense that you have a good reason for asking it, especially if it is clearly formulated, understandable, and you ask it with confidence. I am not entirely sure this always holds true in nonclinical or field situations. We must not forget that in this case the context was a teaching hospital in which patients were more inclined to cooperate because they believed that the interviewing might relate to their eventual treatment. In more natural settings, the informant might not be so willing to comply with the researcher. Yet, if the project is applied and the researcher has gained all the legitimate clearances and established trust, the informant could see value in answering most questions. So, a professional questioning style is an important ingredient.

However, in many cultural situations, direct questioning and sometimes even the key-informant interview are not appropriate. For example, among Native or Indian people, in many situations direct questioning is considered impolite. A researcher is better off seeking what is needed through fragments of conversations or through indirect questioning. Or, if the investigator is lucky and people have decided that he is trustworthy, they will *tell* him what they think is important to know. It is essential that the interviewer *really listen* at that point.

Some suggest that there should not be a list of preestablished questions in key-informant interviews, because the object is to find out how the informants perceive everything that is relevant to them, especially when we start out in a barely understood domain. I believe that an interviewer should, in most cases, come well prepared with a set of a few good questions. If only one of them serves to keep the interview going, so much the better. If the informant has something completely new to talk about, obviously the interviewer should improvise on that opportunity. But to come unprepared to an interview is unprofessional and sacrifices credibility. Clearly though, the effective interviewer is flexible, alert to nuances, and ready to shift directions.

Returning to the actual questioning, we should remember that, although resembling natural conversations, interviews should essentially be one way. The stage is given to the informant. The interviewer does have to interact in ways beyond the mere asking of questions. What should happen when there is a long pause in the narrative? There is a big temptation, especially for those with middle-class backgrounds, to fill the silence with comments of their own. But informants may be collecting their own thoughts. It is important not to interfere with that process. After awhile, though, the appropriate response might be to show affirmation for what the person has been saying by reiterating some points already mentioned. Then the appropriate thing is to ask if the informant would like to say anything else about the topic. If not, then it would be appropriate to move on to another question. On the other hand, this may be the appropriate time for a *probe*—a further elaboration on a new topic or subtopic raised by the informant during the interview. An example from a study evaluating an English-as a Second-Language Class for immigrants is: "You said that you learned from your instructor and the class a lot more than just about speaking English and North American customs. Can you tell me more about what you meant by that?" The capacity to probe further is a very essential part of the interviewer's skills. Much more will be discussed in the course of an interview than what was anticipated. It is also important to give some *feedback* during the interview. It would be very disconcerting to face a blank or even smiling face that does not respond by giving *affirmation*. The affirmation, incidentally, does not mean direct agreement. It means indicating that you respect the person's opinions and knowledge and that you understand him although it is not generally appropriate to give your own opinions on the subjects.

Patton (1980: 207–211) suggests a number of types of question areas that could be covered. First, there are *experience questions* that ask about what a person does or has done. Second, there are questions that try to elicit *cognitive and interpretive processes*—or *opinion/value questions*. Third, *feeling questions* are designed to comprehend the emotional responses of people to their experiences and thoughts. Patton suggests that feelings and opinions are different. A person might express the feeling, "that is all that can be done" (in reference to some action meant to ameliorate a situation), but in reality that would be an opinion. Instead, the actual feelings about the incapacity to do much about something might range among emotions—sadness, anger, despair, and so forth. Fourth, *knowledge questions* are asked to find out what the informant knows about the facts involved in the situation—such as who is eligible for particular programs, the characteristics of their fellow clients, and so forth. Fifth, *sensory questions* try to tap into what is potentially touched, tasted, smelled but above all seen or heard. In eliciting ex-convicts' impressions of their jail terms, an interviewer could ask, "If I entered your cell, what would I see and what would I hear." Sixth, *background* or *demographic questions* are always useful, in fact they may be essential to the whole of the study. What are the ages, genders, education, residence, and other pertinent characteristics of people participating in the study. Instead of asking such questions directly during an interview, I usually give the participant a profile form, which I ask him or her to fill out. Alternatively, we might fill it out together, if the interviewee has difficulty with reading or writing.

Patton points out that questions can be asked within *time frames*—present, past, and future. Queries could be made about peoples' actions in the past and present and about what they might be doing in the future (work, residential moves, and so on). Regarding the sequencing of queries, Patton encourages beginning with questions that are not too controversial as well as those which can locate the informant in the present. Both types encourage the person to speak descriptively. After a good basis of experience and activities has been established, the interview could move on to interpretations, opinions, and feelings. Doing this is easier, because, in effect, the informant will have mentally and verbally relived the experience, establishing a context, and the chances of accuracy increase. Similarly, questions about skills and knowledge are best asked after contexts have been established. Rapport or trust has to be confirmed before asking opinion and knowledge questions that can be seen as threatening. Inquiries about the future would best be asked after the contexts for the present and the past have been established, because questions involving future speculations tend to generate less reliable answers.

The actual phrasing of questions is highly important. Some general tips are relatively standard. They include:

- Avoid dichotomous questions that can be answered by a simple yes or no.

    Example: "Are you satisfied with the trappers' income supplement program?" You would want the respondent to provide some depth of response, giving details about experiences, opinions, feelings, and so forth.

- Make sure that questions are truly open ended, because you should be interested in the elicitation of the categories, opinions, feelings, etc., from the respondent rather than measuring them along some preconceived continuum.

    Example: Instead of asking "How satisfied are you with the trappers' income supplement program?" it would be better to ask: "What do you think of the trappers' income supplement program?" or "Tell me about your experiences with the trappers' income program" (assuming that it has been established that the informant has had some experience with it).

- Avoid questions that combine too many ideas, leading to confusions as to which parts to answer.

    Example: "Tell me what you think of the government's programs for health, education, and employment training." It would be more appropriate to ask questions that examine each area separately and even better to focus on aspects of each.

Summary

Qualitative research, as exemplified by ethnographic fieldwork, constitutes the best set of skills that anthropologists can bring to applied research. Participant observation is important because it is authoritative. It means that the researcher has "been there" and has had the opportunity to divest him or herself of possible preconceived biases that often naively govern many other types of research. Categories, behavior, and important ingredients can be studied within their own contexts of meaning. The researcher can observe what actually happens. Especially if done over a reasonable length of time, the method entails checks and balances ensuring validity and the accuracy of information. Most frequently during participant observation, the researcher will have made contact with informants who can provide detailed insider's information and opinions about the topics. The use of key-informant interviewing is essential because the researcher cannot observe everything and does not know what the issues or circumstances under question feel like to the persons involved.

RECOMMENDED READINGS

Agar, Michael
1996   *The Professional Stranger,* Second Edition. New York: Academic Press.
1986   *Speaking of Ethnography.* Beverly Hills, CA: Sage.
1982   Toward an Ethnographic Language. *American Anthropologist,* Vol. 84: 779–795.

Bernard, H. Russell
1995   *Research Methods in Anthropology: Qualitative and Quantitative Approaches,* Second Edition. Walnut Creek, CA: Altamira.

Edgerton, R., and L. L. Langness
1974   *Methods and Styles in the Study of Culture.* San Francisco: Chandlar and Sharp.

Fetterman, David M.
1989   *Ethnography, Step by Step.* Newbury Park, CA: Sage.

Nolan, Riall W.
1990   Culture Shock and Cross-Cultural Adaptation. Or, I Was O.K. until I Got Here. *Practicing Anthropology,* Vol. 12(4): 2, 20.

Patton, Michael Quinn
1980   *Qualitative Evaluation Methods.* Beverly Hills, CA: Sage.

Pelto, Pertti, and Gretchen Pelto
1978   *Anthropological Research: The Structure of Enquiry.* New York: Cambridge University Press.

Spradley, James P.
1979   *The Ethnographic Interview.* New York: Holt, Rinehart and Winston.
1980   *Participant Observation.* New York: Holt, Rinehart and Winston.

Wolcott, Harry F.
1995   *The Art of Fieldwork.* Walnut Creek, CA: Altamira.

12 Focus Groups and Other Group-Interviewing Techniques

Focus Groups

Short of full-scale ethnography, if I were limited to one method because of time or finances, I would likely choose the focus group. It is flexible and produces a great amount of information.

A focus group consists of a number of people, usually six to twelve, who are of roughly equal status and have some identifiable common interests, characteristics, and shared knowledge. Under the guidance of an interviewer or moderator, they discuss specific questions, or areas of experience. Participants are experts because of their experience or knowledge about the topic to be discussed. A focus group can be a natural group such as workmates or a group of people, previously unknown to each other, who are called together to discuss common issues. An example of the latter group might be parents of autistic children.

A focus group resembles a lively and informal discussion among friends at a kitchen table. Participants freely share opinions and feelings about a topic for a predetermined time. So, in some ways then, it can be seen as a natural social experience just as key-informant interviews have similarities to conversations. The major difference is that both have interviewers or moderators who keep their own participation to a minimum while recording the interaction. Respondents may find rigorously structured questionnaires administered by social scientists tedious or awkward. Focus-group participants, on the other hand, tend to find the exercise enjoyable, especially because they have considerable control over the discussion, and they may even renew enthusiasm or inspiration about the subject. For the researcher, the experience is more one of discovery than an opportunity to confirm a hypothesis.

Recently, there has been a lot of attention paid to the methodology of focus groups (see Kreuger 1988; Merton et al. 1990), but in fact, they have been around for quite a long time. For instance, my late thesis supervisor, Demitri Shimkin, used to tell us about his group discussions with African Americans when he was engaged in a community health project in Holmes County, Mississippi, during the mid-1960s. Holmes County then had the highest rates of infectious disease in the United States, and many of these diseases resulted in infant mortality and early childhood deaths. Physicians and public health officials gave highest priorities to those issues. However, Shimkin's group discussions led to an unexpected discovery. The residents of the county wanted priority health care to be given to their seniors, who they felt had sacrificed and suffered during the most vicious periods of discrimination against black people. Because the project was meant to be controlled by the community, priority was shifted to match local people's expectations. Shimkin discovered that the policy expectations of the experts and those of community members can be greatly at odds. Similarly, the findings from the methodology preferred by medical scientists—epidemiological indicators—were in clear conflict with local perception of needs. And for any kind of community development, there will be no real success unless the felt needs of the participants are met.

A personal discovery about the value of focus groups or group discussions came in the 1970s. With the aid of several students, I was conducting a study of changes in community structure and farming procedures in my region of the Great Plains. I went with a student, whose task was a description of the pioneering era, to a local senior citizens' home to interview people on a one-to-one basis about the details of the typical seasonal cycle in the early 1900s as associated with longer-maturing crops and the use of horses. The administrator of the home suggested that we should organize a seniors' club meeting that afternoon. There we asked our questions and were met by enthusiasm and nostalgia when the seniors remembered that period of their lives. But they also vigorously corrected each other when they thought somebody was in error, and they worked toward consensus on such details as when planting of particular crops occurred. Much more useful information and valuable corroboration of the details were achieved than if they had each been interviewed separately.

I have continued to use focus-group techniques to great profit. For instance, several years ago, I investigated chronic illness and disability for a larger community needs assessment (see Chapter 6). I held a focus group with a blind and visually impaired group in which I learned that group members objected to being labeled with chronic illness. Instead, they stressed independence and self-reliance in their lives. Getting participants' views of themselves and how they wish to be viewed by others helps to overcome preconceptions or stereotypes and establish a sensitivity toward the research population. This can be very important when the research goes beyond the initial focus groups, and good rapport (or the establishment of trust) is essential for other situations. At the same time, it is also important to discover something about internal disagreements and intracultural variation. If they handle them with sensitivity, researchers can make some of those discoveries through focus groups.

A final example of discovery came from a project involving immigrants. The mandate of that research was to identify and prioritize indicators of successful adaptation and integration. Preliminary discussions with service providers had suggested that language and jobs would rank very highly, as they eventually did. However, immigrants from six focus groups raised the issues of health, family harmony, and the safety and well-being of their children, all of which had been overlooked by the service providers. The high rankings of these indicators were later confirmed through a Likert-scaled questionnaire (see the next chapter) and a priority-setting exercise.

The focus-group approach is an adaptable tool that can be used in almost any kind of social science research, applied or not. In applied, community-based research, it is useful for needs assessments, program evaluations, and social impact assessments. In fact, I would say that group discussions are essential, with growing pressures for participatory action (see Chapter 15) and community development styles of research. Focus groups establish rapport, build confidence, maintain continuity, and provide a sense of participation and ownership of the information among community members. Expression of opinions within focus groups is often liberating for the participants. People may even develop a sense of group identity and feel a growing strength from participation. Moreover, the information shared at a focus group may be useful to the participants beyond any of the research goals.

Using focus groups may be a good way to get started on some research projects. Researchers can pretest questions to be used in other methods through a focus group. Researchers can establish local sensitivities regarding certain topics and terminology and get some direct reactions to their questions.

It is relatively easy to train members of any research team in the focus-group approach. A person can conduct one or two focus groups a day, thus collecting a large amount of information in a short time. In contrast, interviewing and recording information from twelve to twenty people separately would take several weeks. Focus groups can be particularly valuable in rapid assessments, when there is very little time for questionnaires and key-informant interviews. Most important, they are a good way of establishing the contexts for research and setting the stage for developing interpretations that remain true to the way members of the community think. By involving knowledgeable community members, we may discover important categories, peoples, and needs that very easily could be overlooked by an outside researcher.

Focus groups are useful in establishing "face validity" (verifying whether the researcher and the subjects are talking about the same thing) and internal triangulation or corroboration (verifying common perceptions). We can sample degrees of consensus and uncover differing opinions by hearing a number of people. A focus group allows opportunities for checking out the meaning of concepts that are important for the research and for the development of future lines of questioning. Also, the flexible nature of its format allows the moderator to rephrase questions that are misunderstood and to probe further to verify truthfulness or degree of consensus in responses. People have a face-to-face opportunity to correct one another, which cannot be done in key-informant interviews or surveys.

Because focus groups tend to be lively and rich in content, they often provide pithy or profound quotes that help to communicate the community's needs, problems, and aspirations. These realities can be transmitted in realistic and forceful ways to decision makers rather than by "dry" or impersonal graphs, tables, or survey summaries.

What are the disadvantages of focus groups? For those who closely follow the canons of precise, probability-oriented social science, seeking to reproduce the strengths of natural sciences, there may be a few problems. For instance, it may be next to impossible to select a random sample of participants. However, if the researcher has become familiar with the community, judgment or convenience sampling (see the next chapter) could draw together roughly proportionate numbers of people who represent the community. Also, it must be acknowledged that the shy, the nonvocal, or the hostile members may not be adequately represented in focus groups. Although these groups have advantages for rapid research, there may also be delays in identifying significant groups and categories of people as well as difficulties in getting them together at scheduled times. There can be problems or delays in the training of research assistants and recorders and in the transcription, analysis, and write-up of results.

Another disadvantage is associated with reliability. Reliability is an important expectation in scientific methodology. It demands the same results from the same method even with different researchers. But each focus group is unique and takes on a shape of its own. To some extent, we also have to recognize that each moderator can influence differently the tone and direction of the group discussion. However, with careful analysis and questioning, results can be compared. When the issues are pressing and shared, they will tend to come up in discussions anyway.

The inappropriate raising of expectations among participants can be a weakness, especially in applied projects. People may think that just because there is a focus group, there must be a commitment to follow through on their hopes and recommendations. Unfortunately, the researcher may not be in a position to deliver on these expectations. People become cynical when they have been consulted before with no followthrough on their suggestions or the research. Also, focus groups occasionally "raise more heat than light." Conflict and bitterness may arise. Sensitive issues that are normally avoided may be raised unwittingly, or members may be condemned for revealing community secrets to outsiders. If we are working with a small community, a perceived offender might be subject to gossip and other sanctions.

A graduate student working with me on a study of immigrant adaptation used a focus group with a job-finding club at a settlement agency and ran into a minor version of such a problem. Two Latin American men expressed some bitterness about the difficulties of getting jobs and complained that employers discriminated against immigrants. A Vietnamese participant, perhaps adopting his culture's communication style, minimized the problems and expressed gratitude for being in the host community. During the focus group, he was bitterly denounced by the other two and then afterwards expressed his distress to the moderator. Sometimes these conflicts are unavoidable and will be temporary, but the researcher has to be aware that they may arise.

Logistics, Principles, and Techniques
for Conducting Focus Groups

The obvious starting point is the selection of the number and types of focus groups as well as the actual participants. This step has to be well planned and can be time consuming. The researcher will need the assistance of well-placed key informants in the community, or he must already have a good familiarity with the community through ethnography. Yet, perhaps a beginning focus group, selected from some knowledgeable community members, will help to map the range of people, categories, and groups needed to be taken into account. Such a group could serve in a continuing consultative role throughout the project.

The number of focus groups held will depend on available time and the other types of methods being used. If intensive knowledge is required about a particular subject with a particular subpopulation (say, the health problems of single mothers), then two or three might be appropriate. A general rule of thumb applies in such cases: providing that there is sufficient time, continue focus groups until no new information is gained. If, on the other hand, the project is of a wider scope (say, a community needs assessment focused on health), then one group in each important category or subgrouping should suffice. In a broad study, though, it may be necessary to probe deeper into certain areas that contain more compelling issues, disabled elderly in rural areas, for example.

How many people should be selected for each focus group? Most experts advise having eight to twelve people, a good range to ensure a lively discussion but still allowing everybody an opportunity to talk. But it is possible to retrieve valuable information if only three or four people actually show up. Incidentally, contacting people, explaining the project, scheduling, and inviting them to participate can be very time consuming and sometimes frustrating. Improvisations like "overbooking" (inviting slightly more than the optimum number) might be used to ensure good attendance if locals tend to be rather relaxed about schedules and meeting appointments.

Most sources (Kreuger 1988; Merton et al. 1990, for example) pay a great deal of attention to the formulation of questions to be used in the focus groups. Here are some suggestions from my experience and the literature.

- Make sure that the question has been phrased so that the participants know what kinds of information are actually being sought.

    Sometimes the researchers are unsure of what they are studying or, if they are overly inductive, want all the information to gradually arise out of its natural situation. Or researchers may be so ideologically committed to participatory-action research that they want the participants to have "complete ownership" over both the questions and the information. In such cases, researchers may be too passive in questioning and may ask some unclear questions such as "What do you think about what is going on in the community?" I know of a very expensive research project that more or less "crashed" and produced vague and inconclusive data because it followed such an approach.

- Nonetheless, it is important to phrase questions in such a way that they are open ended enough so that the respondents can provide their own structure and style of response.

    In most cases, a major purpose is to get rich, detailed responses in the local idiom and get new information and nuances.

- As with key-informant interviews, do not combine more than one idea in each question. Avoid questions that can be answered with a simple "yes" or "no" answer, and avoid leading questions.

- It may be necessary to have probes ready for certain areas crucial to the project's research design that have not been covered by the participants.

    For example, ask, "How does the local health-care system affect members of your community?" Also, invariably, it will be necessary to improvise probes during the focus group to elaborate on new ideas or information that have been revealed.

- As an "icebreaker," it may be important to ask "grand-tour questions" that put things in concrete perspective, allowing the participants to establish context before going on to more specific questions.

    For example, in a study focused on the needs of mobility-impaired people, you might ask, "Please describe a typical day in the life of a person using a wheelchair."

- Try not to have too many questions. One to five may suffice. Otherwise the participants may feel bombarded and unable to establish their own natural flow of the choice of topics and content.

    For instance, in several focus groups with blind and visually impaired people, I asked one question, "What are the informational needs that are most important to blind and visually impaired people?" Probes were available to cover areas like education, employment, and purchasing if they were not raised by the participants. Yet for the most part, the whole ninety-minute discussion easily flowed from the single question.

■ In some rare circumstances it might be necessary to have more questions, even as many as twenty or so.

> This would be the case if the project required detailed information on behavior and attitudes in particular domains. Scrimshaw and Hurtado (1987) give such an example of numerous questions on immunization practices for a manual devoted to the study of health-care delivery in developing countries.

How does one maintain the focus and the flow of focus groups? It is important to clearly explain at the beginning what is being done and why. I think that it is a good idea to write a one-page (or less) summary of what the research is intended to accomplish and who is sponsoring it. Researchers should also identify and explain the concepts that are important for the discussion. The participants must have confidence in the process and understand that they have significant opinions or knowledge about the issue that will be taken into account through the research process.

A moderator should be attentive and supportive but should not appear to favor one position. He or she should be careful to not show biases toward particular members, should not appear to be an authority on the topic, and should be aware of nonverbal responses and try to speak in a neutral tone of voice. He or she should not worry about silences or try to immediately fill gaps in the conversation. After several minutes of silence, the moderator could ask if anything else needs to be said and, if not, move on to the next topic. The moderator should be flexible and alert to the possibility of unanticipated new and significant topics that may emerge during the discussion.

In the course of the focus group itself, the moderator should politely enter into the dialogue when it seems that a topic has been exhausted or the participants have strayed from it by stating the major conclusions about the topic and then asking if there are other points to be made. He or she then leads the participants into the next topic or subtopic. At some point, midway or three quarters of the way, it is usually appropriate to directly solicit the opinions of those who have been silent or have not been very vocal up to that point. The researcher should not say very much.

It is essential to have someone assist the moderator by recording the proceedings, ideally through the use of tape recorders and flip charts. Sometimes it is appropriate to have two tape recorders operating in case one breaks down. It is mandatory to ask permission of the group regarding the use of a tape recorder. If permission is refused, then the assistant will have to write very detailed notes. Sometimes, if the focus group is going to run a long time, it is a good idea to call for a break at the midpoint and to get together with your colleagues about advisable changes in the approach.

If the first group does not go as well as planned, or the information is "flat" and inadequate, try again. One should consider it a form of pretest; the next groups will be likely to get better. New topics and lines of questioning might have been revealed that should be explored for subsequent focus groups.

Finally, there is the analysis and write-up. Transcribing tapes is extremely time consuming. I have found that it usually takes about three or four times the length of the actual focus-group meeting to transcribe the proceedings. It is useful to make three- or four-page summaries identifying the number and ranges of participant characteristics, the topics covered, and some principal findings. These summaries are useful in comparing information with data from other methods used in the project as well as making comparisons across focus groups. A caution should be made about the analysis of focus groups. The interpreters or moderators run the risk of emphasizing what they want to hear, being subconsciously influenced by their biases. It is a good idea to have several people (time permitting) analyze the tapes or transcriptions for corroboration in analysis.

Nominal Groups

A nominal group is a more structured form of focus group. It follows many of the same principles and is about the same size. But the interaction is much more controlled, and specific priorities and consensus are sought.

Focus groups are good for "airing out" issues, but they can rarely be used for directly setting policy and long-range planning. Nominal groups are useful for getting specific and prioritized results, because the moderator is much more directive. Nominal groups are also useful because they overcome some of the deficiencies of focus groups, such as the interpersonal politics that can occur in small-group interactions. Some people may come to dominate; others defer. Or, perhaps, in an atmosphere of conformity, everybody will defer to each other and express agreement with most ideas in a spirit of mutual encouragement. Another relative advantage of nominal groups is that they establish a sense of relative measurement or quantitative value placed on an item.

I used a modified nominal group procedure in the research project with a blind and visually impaired organization previously mentioned. After formulating a list of informational needs through focus groups and informant interviews, twenty-two of the members of the organization voted on priorities among the needs, using braille, tape recorders, and large print as their medium of expression. I have also used nominal groups for class evaluations, in which I ask the students to rank the "techniques that are most useful for encouraging learning in the classroom situation."

It is sometimes useful to combine focus groups with nominal groups to eventually establish policy and priorities. For instance, a researcher working with local people through focus groups on the issues relevant to the health of their community may identify widespread meanings of "health." At first, there has to be much exploration and airing of concerns in order to identify differences and conflicts as well as consensus or virtual agreement. This would be done with as many representative groups in the community as possible. Focus groups might meet several times or more. Eventually, after appropriate discussions, there might be a clear set of priorities regarding issues, policies, and needs. The nominal group procedure could then be used with the same focus groups to rank such priorities. The specifics of a nominal group are as follows:

- A moderator calls a group together for from ninety minutes to four hours.
- He provides the central question, and explains the nature and purpose of the exercise as well as the rules.
- Participants (usually the same number as in focus groups) are asked to make a list in response to the questions. In a needs assessment, for instance, "What are the significant immigrant needs for successful integration?"

- The moderator asks each participant in turn to state one item. It is recorded by an assistant on flip charts or on the blackboard. Each participant provides his or her list in "round-robin fashion" until all the items (needs, problems, solutions, etc.) are exhausted and recorded.
- The moderator asks each person to take two minutes or less to explain what he or she means by each item with some examples.
- The moderator negotiates the collapsing or combination of some of the items into single entities. For instance, in the immigrant-integration case, one person might state "being able to financially support myself and my family." Another might state "financial independence." The researcher might negotiate the statement of a single need, "financial independence for immigrants and their families." In the end, a shortened list is reached.
- The participants are then asked to take some time to reflect on the total list and consider their prioritization or ranking in terms of the top five or ten or whatever seems appropriate.
- The participants are then asked to list each of their top five (if, for instance, that was the number chosen) on a separate three-by-five-inch file card. They are to indicate, on each card, if the rank was first, second, third, fourth, or fifth. No ties are allowed. They could, if desired, provide the score for each item. For instance, first place receives five points; second place receives four; third receives three; fourth receives two; and fifth receives one. This scoring is done anonymously, which is very crucial to the nominal group technique.
- The moderator and his assistants collect all the cards. They sort the cards in piles that indicate a particular item. The total number of votes relevant to each item is totaled. Then the aggregate raw score for each item is determined along with the range of particular scores for each item.
- The results are presented back to the participants. The rankings of priorities are established by the raw scores, the aggregate of each weighted vote for items.
- The participants discuss the results over a period of fifteen to twenty minutes to deal with any surprising results and possible misunderstandings. Participants also have an opportunity to make the argument for higher or lower rankings of particular items.
- A second round of secret voting is done, and the results are tabulated and presented in the same manner as the first round. Another discussion may follow, providing clarification or debate as a reflection on these results. Results may have stayed basically the same. If so, the exercise is terminated. If results are more varied than before, a decision will have to be made with regard to a third vote. Some would feel that the results should eventually approach a consensus, yet that may not be possible.

When the nominal group has been completed, it will have produced tangible results. It has identified a list of priority needs, suggesting policy directions for the group. For example, in the case of the blind and visually impaired group that I worked with (see Chapter 15), its participants established high priorities on getting direct access to employment information and on the availability of published material through alternate media, such as tapes, braille, and large print. As a result, there has been lobbying directed at agencies (e.g., libraries, government employment offices) responsible for the distribution of such information.

Nominal groups are most effective with people who are comfortable with working in a structured fashion and who do not necessarily feel the need to express themselves in a relatively free form. Participants must be willing to follow the instructions of the moderator. They may have previously experienced focus groups as warm-up to the nominal group exercise or may already have a widely discussed deep knowledge of the topic.

Delphi Groups or Conferences

A Delphi group is a nominal group executed through the mail. It is anonymous but interactive. In Delphi conferences, up to thirty participants are identified because of their expertise and capacity to comment informatively on an issue. Delphi conferences are used when the participants are too busy or too far apart to meet at the same time for focus or nominal groups. There is also usually some good rationale for taking extended time to make decisions, rather than having them done at a single meeting. People participating in a Delphi conference have to be comfortable and effective in written communications and able to keep to schedules. Certainly Delphi conferences are very time-consuming for the researchers, but they are very rewarding ways of getting information and as direct ways of making decisions about priorities. They are best used in combination with other methods for community research. They are also quite useful within organizations. They can achieve a certain degree of consensus among the participants although they may not reflect the widest range of opinion in the community.

I have used Delphi conferences three times in recent research projects. The first was a set of twenty-eight executive directors of agencies funded by the local United Way. I asked them to rank and comment on priority needs for the city's health and social services. The second was held with nineteen service providers who worked with immigrant-serving agencies in four different communities in my region, asking them to rank and comment on indicators of immigrant adaptation and integration (partial results are provided in the appendix to this chapter). The third example was a partial Delphi. A panel of thirty immigrants ranked and commented on the indicators generated through the service providers' Delphi and augmented by a set of further indicators revealed through six focus groups held with fifty-three immigrants. In all of these cases, the procedures took about ninety days and involved sixteen different steps, including letters, reminder letters, and phone calls.

I will now outline some details of the procedure.

- The participants are selected and contacted. Step one involves sending a letter to them explaining the purpose, scope, and procedures of the project.
- A single question is posed to them. For example, "What are the most important indications of successful immigrant adaptation in Saskatchewan?" They are asked to list their responses (without comment) on a single sheet of paper. That sheet of paper is divided into ten to fifteen equally spaced boxes depending on the number requested. They are asked to mail back their results in self-addressed and stamped envelopes within a specified time (e.g., two weeks).
- After photocopying the responses, the researchers cut out all of the boxes and sort the items.
- A common phrasing is selected for similar items, and a master list is developed.

- In the second round of the Delphi conference, the participants are asked to choose and rank a specified number of items (e.g., twelve or fifteen) from the total list and insert them in boxes on a preprinted form according to priority. Room is provided in the boxes for supporting comments, and the participants are strongly encouraged to provide commentaries of several sentences or a paragraph on each choice.
- Again, they are asked to return the results by self-addressed envelopes within a specified time (each usually two weeks). Reminder letters are usually sent out half-way, and phone calls are usually necessary for stragglers.
- The researchers compile the results in a manner similar to that of a nominal-group procedure. If fifteen items were to be voted on, first-place votes receive fifteen points down to the fifteenth-ranked items, which receive one point each.
- Rank order is established by the total raw scores for each item. The number of votes for each is provided, along with the full ranges of individual scores for each item (see the chapter appendix for an example). The comments provided are summarized or reproduced verbatim after each item; this is an important way that the participants communicate with each other.
- The results of this second stage are then sent back to the participants. In this third stage, they are asked if they wish to reconsider their votes in light of the current rankings and comments. A set of forms identical to that provided in the second stage is sent out again. Participants might indicate whether they want simply to keep their votes the same or whether they want to change them. It might not be necessary to provide comments. As usual, they are asked to return the results within two weeks, and reminder letters and phone calls are often necessary.
- Again, the researchers analyze the results according to raw scores and rank order.
- The results, now usually final, are mailed back to the participants along with a thank-you letter containing some commentary on the significance of the results of the Delphi.
- In some rare cases the researchers and the participants may wish to proceed with one or two further steps in voting if close consensus is desired.

Delphi results are often more satisfactory than nominal group results because they give more time for reflection and the supporting commentaries are richer in detail. Sometimes, they are more satisfactory than focus groups because there are definite rankings and senses of measurement. However, as indicated, a great deal of time-consuming effort is required of the researcher, and the participants may not be as representative of the grassroots community as desired. Also, quantified results may sometimes provide a false sense of concrete priority. And, of course, it would be extremely unlikely to reproduce precisely the same results with another Delphi panel.

Summary

I have found all three of these group methods of qualitative research very effective in applied research. Two of them—nominal groups and Delphi groups—have been especially useful for establishing priorities. Focus groups provide rich contextual information laden with the local or insiders' meanings. They can be processes of important discovery, and they allow for the possibility for at least partial "ownership" and involvement in research by the participants.

However, they all can and should be used with other research methods whenever possible. For instance, Agar and MacDonald (1995: 85) make the reasonable claim that the most effective interpretation of focus-group results comes from a well-established knowledge of the group's culture, derived from previous fieldwork. When the researcher, on the basis of ethnicity, education, or other factors, has a background similar to members of an organization or community, a focus group may be an entirely appropriate and time-saving way to launch a project.

Remember that there are sometimes problems with the use of focus groups. The opinions expressed or confidences divulged could be disruptive to relations in small communities or organizations. Alternatives, like participant observation or confidential key-informant interviews should be kept in reserve. Some groups' cultural styles might not lend themselves to focus groups. The technique may be perceived as too frank and focused, thus incompatible with local styles of communication. It is also important to check whether the opinions raised in group interviews match observable behavior and general conditions. Furthermore, it is sometimes possible for a false consensus to be imposed on a focus group. Specialized nominal and Delphi groups may be too structured and constraining for some people in the community.

So, a considerable amount of improvisation is called for in the choice of these techniques. All such caveats aside, group-interviewing techniques constitute a very flexible and potentially powerful set of methodological tools that applied anthropologists can draw upon. They are certainly culturally compatible in many mainstream North American contexts.

RECOMMENDED READINGS

Agar, Michael, and James MacDonald
1995   Focus Groups and Ethnography. *Human Organization,* Vol. 54(1): 78–87.

Bryant, Carol A., and D. Bailey
1991   The Use of Focus Group Research in Program Development. In *Soundings: Rapid and Reliable Research Methods for Practicing Anthropologists.* Edited by J. van Willigen and T. Finan. NAPA Bulletin 10. Washington, DC: National Association for the Practice of Anthropology.

Delbecq, Andre L., Andrew H. van den Ven, and David H. Gustafson
1975   *Group Techniques for Program Planning.* Glenview, IL: Scott, Foresman.

Kreuger, R. A.
1988   *Focus Groups: A Practical Guide for Applied Research.* Newbury Park, CA: Sage.

Merton, Robert K., Marjorie Fiske, and Patricia L. Kendall
1990   *The Focused Interview: A Manual of Problems and Procedures.* Second Edition. New York: Free Press.

Morgan, David L.
1988   *Focus Groups as Qualitative Research.* Newbury Park, CA: Sage.

Scrimshaw, Susan, and Elena Hurtado
1987   *Rapid Assessment Procedures for Nutrition and Primary Health Care: Anthropological Approaches to Improving Programme Effectiveness.* Los Angeles: U.C.L.A. Latin American Center Publications.

Sample Results from a Delphi Conference Held with Service Providers to Immigrants in Saskatchewan

Background:

From each of four immigrant-serving agencies in four communities, five participants were selected to participate. Nineteen of the twenty complied. These were all front-line workers who did hands-on work in resettlement assistance and counseling. Seven, or 40 percent of them, were immigrants themselves. (Later a modified one-stage Delphi conference was held with another thirty immigrants for purposes of comparison.) The service providers were asked a single question in the first round: *What are the significant indicators of successful immigrant adaptation and integration?* In the subsequent two rounds, they were asked to rank fifteen indicators. These selections were drawn from a substantial list of almost 100 items generated from the first round. The final results showing the first five indicators are listed below. By adding up all of the scores, the *raw score* determined the rank of each item. The *number of votes* shows how widespread was the recognition for the need or indicator. The *range of scores* indicates the prevalence and strength of the weighting placed on each item. It could indicate a near consensus or possibly a dichotomy of opinion if there were both high and low scores. Verbatim comments are provided as a composite when the participants gave justifications for their choices. These comments are very useful for providing context and meaning to each item as well as providing a more comprehensive background to immigrant needs in the host society (Ervin 1994b).

The Results:

1. The ability to speak and listen in English and to be able to understand the subtleties of ordinary English and slang.
   Raw Score—181
   Number of Votes—13
   Range of Scores—13, 13, 14, 15, 15, 15, 13, 14, 14, 13, 15, 13, 14
   Comments: Communication (including nonverbal communication) is the most important skill needed in all areas of adaptation and integration. People who can communicate in the mainstream language are better equipped to handle all the other areas of their lives in a new culture. An important factor in learning a language is

the ability to listen. Listening will teach the learner many aspects/nuances of the new language—regardless of the personal ability to learn languages. To be able to communicate by listening and speaking, to be able to understand the ordinary person in an ordinary situation is imperative. To be at ease with the common person and interact socially creates a bonding and acceptance in human relationships. This does not happen overnight, especially for someone with no English whatsoever. Nevertheless, this need must be met with priority. Failure to give quality language training to new residents promotes isolation and, eventually, friction. In Saskatchewan, this must come before other adaptation and integration processes can be met. Once this barrier is surpassed, life in general becomes easier, and employment is then viewed as more of a possibility.

2. Maintaining or establishing a functional, harmonious family life.

   Raw Score—135
   Number of Votes—14
   Range of Scores—11, 3, 12, 12, 2, 12, 12, 7, 10, 9, 6, 13, 12, 14
   Comments: This is an inclusive or general statement, which may include such things as finding suitable day care, harmonious roles, and good communication within the home (and with schools, etc.). Maintaining or establishing a functional family life is probably the best support system for anyone. For the majority of people, their family is the first and, at times, only supportive feature and center point of their lives. This provides a base of security and well-being, which permits a person to go forward in other areas outside the family (education, vocation, social). A functional, harmonious home is an indication of adjustment and general happiness of all family members. However, the stresses of the process of migration itself often cause such strain and discord that the family may even break apart. If there is no happiness or harmony in one's family, then the purpose of coming to a new country will fail. There is a general need for counseling, support, and stress management skills for families and singles who have been dislocated from their families as a result of the migration process. This does not mean, however, that we should be assisting singles to form families.

3. A sense of well-being and optimism (good mental health) as well as a general sense of physical well-being.

   Raw Score—129
   Number of Votes—11
   Range of Scores—12, 4, 13, 11, 15, 13, 15, 11, 13, 12, 10
   Comments: Mental and physical health are often measures or indicators of stress involved with adaptation. Physical and mental problems may accompany immigrants to the host country but are apt to be exaggerated when coupled with the new culture, new climate, new language, new mores, and different educational, financial, and legal systems. A sense of general physical and mental health is necessary to cope with adjustments and pressures that confront the immigrant during the integration process. This is an area that affects all aspects of one's life. A sense of well-being is the ultimate achievement because it indicates an absence of negative stress

and possibly a satisfaction with general, current situations. Not everyone is able to have this kind of mental attitude, though. Ensuring that good support systems exist would be very helpful to settlement in Canada.

4. Settlement in a safe, permanent home or apartment and acquiring satisfactory household goods.

    Raw Score—121
    Number of Votes—10
    Range of Scores—11, 14, 10, 13, 8, 11, 15, 10, 15, 14
    Comments: This is a very stabilizing factor. The privacy and security of having one's own home (or apartment) play an important role in settlement. A lot of people have not had a permanent, safe home and have had few possessions. Basic needs (i.e., food, shelter, etc.) must be met before moving forward to adaptation, and a home can provide a safe, nurturing environment in which to foster individual and familial social needs. The emphasis on "satisfactory goods" is somewhat less important than housing. As well, this indicator is linked with health and financial indicators. Some feel it is important to settle near one's own ethnic area. However, cautions arise regarding turning hotels and reception houses into "mini refugee camps" prior to satisfactory settlement. Both satisfactory housing and household goods are available in Saskatchewan.

5. The willingness to accept available as well as suitable employment.

    Raw Score—104
    Number of Votes—8
    Range of Scores—14, 12, 11, 13, 12, 14, 14, 14
    Comments: This is key. We cannot even guarantee every current resident of Canada a job in the field that most interests him or her. Immigrants must not be led to expect an employment opportunity that is not really available. It is important for the newcomers to realize and understand that their skills, education, or occupation may not necessarily be absorbed immediately into the workforce. The ability to accept available as well as suitable employment will encourage or help the newcomer to adapt to the new country, to meet and socialize with Canadians when the opportunity presents itself, and finally, to hear about other possibly better employment, using improved or new skills learned on the job. That is, realistic expectations and a plan of action will enable the immigrant to integrate into the Canadian fabric in a timely process. Unrealistic goals and inflexibility can increase the stress levels of the newcomers. This may, in turn, have an effect on the mental health of the immigrant as well as the family unit.

13 Quantification through Social Indicators and Questionnaires

Measurement is a standard expectation for applied social scientists. To ensure validity of findings and acceptable levels of probability, applied research is normally bolstered by statistics and evidence drawn from formal methods. Decision makers want findings and recommendations that *quantitatively* and *directly* reflect the issues addressed. They want the money devoted to research and programming to produce commensurately accountable results. They have an almost instinctive (sometimes obsessive) concern for the bottom line—How much is it going to cost and what kinds of results can be predicted if certain amounts of money are spent?

Much of the training of such policy scientists as economists, social psychologists, sociologists, and epidemiologists has involved intensive drilling in statistics, questionnaire design, and the skills needed to present vast amounts of information through graphs and tables. Such emphasis on quantification was relatively infrequent in anthropology until the 1970s. Bennett and Thaiss (1970) give a number of reasons for anthropology's neglect of statistically oriented surveys. The principal reason was a holism in which "the movements of the investigator are adjusted to the rhythms of everyday life and not to the demands of a structured instrument" (317). The emphasis of anthropological investigation—a deep understanding of cultural context—required more of the kinds of methodologies described in the preceding two chapters.

Some earlier uses of enumeration strengthened descriptions of context—typically with community censuses of age, sex, occupation, household, religion, and other relevant categories. Quantification also became essential to any analysis calling for measurements of economic or ecological performance. A good example of this is Roy Rappaport's (1968) intricate analysis of carrying capacity for pigs and humans in a small territory as linked to warfare and ritual cycles in the New Guinea highlands.

Survey research, the most common type of quantifiable method in social science, uses a "standardized stimulus," a questionnaire administered to a selected sample to probe more deeply into opinions, attitudes, and preferences within a larger population. By the 1970s, the few surveys done by anthropologists included studies of stratification in a small American town, examinations of distinctions within the folk urban continuum of an Indian village, studies of African urbanization, and other topics. Applied examples included Scotch's (1960) excellent use of survey questionnaires and large random samples in the linking of Zulu urbanization, social change, and stress to increased rates of hypertension. Bennett and Thaiss remind us that anthropologists rarely administered questionnaires early in their research—there first needed to be a well-established understanding of the local culture and ways of communicating based on the findings of ethnography. That remains true today.

Triangulation

A methodological principle, *triangulation,* reinforces the rationale for the combination of quantitative and qualitative methods. Triangulation is derived from the common approach to surveying locations on a landscape. Using readings from two points and knowing the distance between them, the surveyor can calculate distances and elevations relevant to a third point by using angles and distances already known. Applied to the social sciences, the concept refers to hypotheses and findings that can survive tests of validity after several separate methodologies have confirmed them.

How does triangulation translate into a tool for social sciences? We can say that when several unrelated approaches point to the same conclusions, the probability of their validity is increased. Fielding and Fielding (1986) point to potential means of triangulation: several researchers or theoretical orientations can be used to examine the same phenomena. Most frequently, however, triangulation refers to a combination of methods or means of collecting information. Although it is possible to approach triangulation through the combination of exclusively qualitative methods (e.g., the simultaneous use of participant observation, focus groups, and public records) or solely by quantitative sources (e.g., censuses, questionnaire surveys, tests of performance, etc.), it is more common and more fruitful to combine a few qualitative and quantitative methods (e.g., participant observation, questionnaires, focus groups, and census materials). Extra benefits result from the fact that measurement is bolstered by contextual and cultural knowledge.

In the best of triangulated research designs, no one method predominates or is an appendage of a more favored one. The several methods mutually reinforce each other, and their benefits are greater than their individual strengths as methods. For that very reason (beyond the desirability of measurement per se) there is ever-increasing use of quantitative methods in applied anthropology, combined with our traditional strengths in qualitative research.

The first broad area to be looked at is that of social indicators. It is concerned with the analysis of trends generated from statistics that are regularly collected in contemporary societies. The second area, the use of survey questionnaires, is familiar to readers and is often indispensable as a tool for applied anthropologists, especially in North American settings.

Social Indicators

Analyzing statistics relevant to communities or larger jurisdictions such as states, provinces, or countries is a familiar activity in policy planning. Economists, sociologists, city planners, and epidemiologists frequently use them. Yet, some critics note an over-reliance on statistics for policy planning, claiming that what is measured can represent the biases and presumptions of cause and effect held by middle-class experts. Furthermore, reliance on such statistics can lead to the exclusion of what people being studied or represented say are *their realities* and what they think needs to be measured as a reflection of their circumstances. So, some consider statistics shallow, or culture bound. Although she does not reject indicators, Nancy Scheper-Hughes provides an interesting anthropological commentary on the topic as illustrated through her frustrating attempt to get accurate statistics on birth and child death rates in northeastern Brazil.

> Public records, whether official censuses, birth or baptismal certificates, are obviously not "neutral" documents. They are not in any sense "pure" sources of data. Censuses and other public records count only certain things, not others. They count some things better than others, as in this instance they count infant and child deaths better than births. They reveal a society's particular system of classification. So they are not as much mirrors of reality as they are filters, or "collective representations," as Emile Durkheim might have put it. (1992: 292)

Nonetheless, statistical indicators do attract a great deal of attention, and they do frequently have significant merit for planning. Indicators are aggregated numbers chosen to represent trends and assumed to be measurements of a country or region's well-being. Significant shifts in the numbers indicate changes in circumstance. We are most familiar with economic indicators—the rising and lowering of the gross national product (the total of goods and services produced in a year), fluctuating employment rates, new business or construction starts, and so forth.

Health is another field that is very frequently targeted by indicator analyses. Changing epidemiological statistics of all sorts measure prevalencies of particular health problems. Such numbers can be presented for the population as a whole or for segments relevant to women, infants, the elderly, and other age groups. Ratios that involve hospital beds, doctors, and other health personnel per thousand of the designated population are measures on the overall availability of health care.

Housing is a domain that can be subjected to indicator analysis. Averages and ranges regarding the ages of dwellings, sizes of dwellings in square feet, average number of square feet per person, numbers of rooms, whether the units are homes or apartments, along with amenities such as indoor plumbing, have been used as indicators of the quality of housing.

Purely demographic data are often valuable on their own, or they can be combined with other indicator information to get a significant view of a region's well-being or changes in it. Total populations, population densities, composition of particular sectors, such as age and sex categories, or particular social groupings, and birth and growth rates are considered important. Growth in indigenous or immigrant populations might alert planners to the need to formulate more culturally relevant programs in health, education, or social services.

Social and socioeconomic indicators are probably the most significant for our purposes as applied anthropologists. They include measurement of household and family composition, marriage and divorce rates, education levels, ethnic and racial compositions, ranges of income, poverty indices, age distributions, adult and juvenile crime rates, occupations, residential mobility, and many other things.

A few hypothetical scenarios suggest how indicator analysis might be used for social planning at a community level.

Consider an area of a city with low property values, consisting of substandard apartment dwellings with high government-subsidized rents. Demographically, there are high proportions of immigrant and minority groups. The zone has the highest rates of unemployment, lowest incomes, highest uses of welfare, and other revealing statistics, such as the number of children taken from the custody of their parents. It has high rates of sexually transmitted diseases and victims of violent crime. It has the highest concentrations of psychiatric outpatients in low-rent or group housing. Households are disproportionately headed by single mothers. General statistics like these suggest an urban area in need of many social, health, and public-safety services. For social planning, such an area may need more subsidized day-care facilities for single mothers seeking jobs or undergoing job training. There could be a need for youth centers devoted to recreation and counseling. There is probably very good justification for drop-in clinics and more public health nurses devoted to home visits, especially for single mothers and their children.

Another scenario might see a county's permanent population supplemented by large seasonal influxes of Latin American migrant workers and their families. They might have very little education, lack trade skills, and have more health problems than the permanent population. The politics of convenience may allow county and state officials to excuse themselves from serving these temporary populations because they see them as not really being under their jurisdiction as voters or taxpayers. Yet after discovering the relevant social indicators and needs through their own research efforts, an interchurch group takes action and provides English-as-a-second-language training for adults, schooling for children, and regular health clinics to deal with some of the special health problems of this population.

Consider yet another scenario. Trends through indicators reveal that a large farming community (population, 4,000–5,000) is in the process of becoming a retirement community, with a higher-than-normal percentage over sixty-five (say, 30 percent, as is the case of many small towns on the Great Plains). Retirement incomes are moderate on the average but still have a rather wide range, suggesting pockets of poverty for some elderly. Adding to the difficulties, the settlement patterns of the community are quite dispersed. Some of these indicators could lead to planning for programs like home care, Meals on Wheels, chronic care outpatient services, special-needs housing, and other considerations of needs of rural seniors.

It behooves practitioners to be aware of the meanings of such indicators and realize that planning and programming cannot be done simply through the collection of qualitative data. To estimate the amounts for budgeting and determining types and amounts of services, carefully match resources to the local situation. As an obvious example, there would be no point in developing extensive and expensive home care services, chronic health care facilities, and other activities that are relevant to a standardized proportion of the elderly if the actual community consists primarily of transient young adults.

Social indicators have been around for a while and have primarily been derived from national censuses that are usually taken every ten years in developed countries. Van Dusen and Parke (1976) discuss their significance in the social sciences. Overall, they are a form of social bookkeeping meant to assist social forecasting by predicting trends and advising for social policy. Indicator research has become an interdisciplinary field with participation from sociology, economics, demography, political science, epidemiology, geography, and social psychology. Research involves the original formulation of statistical categories and establishment, verification, or critiques of their supposed association with well-being and social change. For instance, Kue Young (1989) points out that although health care expenditures for Canadian Native people have been at a par with Canadians, their health status remains much below that of the general population. Obviously, in this case, the data should generate skepticism about the value of per-capita expenditures as indicators of improved health. We must look for answers about Native health within much broader political, economic, social, and environmental frameworks.

The need for indicators arose during the 1960s when governments in developed countries became concerned with the dislocations and social consequences of very rapid change. Such statistics would monitor trends in public safety, poverty, health, family structure, income, and employment that seemed to be most affected by these disruptions. Most of the data has been collected through government departments like the Bureau of the Census and the Centers for Disease Control in the United States and Statistics on Health Canada as well as their state and provincial counterparts. They are tracked annually or at five-year or ten-year intervals, to identify trends. For example, steadily escalating divorce rates might be associated with other changing indicators such as unemployment and rising costs of living.

Anthropologists have tended to avoid participation in social-indicator research, partly because, given the division of labor in the social sciences, such quantitative analysis has not been their mandate. Yet there are also possible niches for anthropologists in the field of social-indicator research and policy-making.

Generally, anthropologists can combine qualitative methodologies with standardized indicator research and seek more contextual meaning in the numbers (see Ervin 1996b). Wikan (1985) shows further opportunities for anthropological contribution. She constructively critiques the twelve standardized United Nations indicator areas of "level of living," including health, housing, nutrition, recreation, clothing, and others. As enumerated by economists over a twenty-year period, they inaccurately suggest, according to Wikan, a stagnation in level of living among the poor in Cairo, Egypt. Yet according to the local standards of seventeen households studied ethnographically, Wikan counters that the residents saw their level of living as significantly improved. They pointed to better clothing, recreation, employment, appliances, and other things. These were all leading to more household stability, gains in mutual respect between spouses, and increased hopes for the future. Wikan largely attributes these improvements to the culturally based (Islamic) initiatives and planning of the women and advocates anthropologists' collaboration with economists and others to establish more meaningful indicators.

Case Study: Anthropological Improvisation Using Indicators

An example of anthropological ingenuity can be seen in research by Joseph Jorgenson and colleagues (1985). Using standard social and economic indicators, they improvised and added some indicators more culturally and socially appropriate to Inupiat and Aleut peoples in Alaska. The study also uses complex multivariate analysis and indicators to show how, in spite of large public and private expenditures to "develop" or benefit regions of Native Alaska, the opposite has actually occurred. Native people, relying more and more on wage labor and transfer payments, are worse off than they were before. Essentially, they have lost self-sufficiency because of the decline of their subsistence base.

Standardized indicators such as population growth, household size, income, residence patterns, housing amenities, sources of income, and so forth were all collected locally by the research teams for eight villages and two regions. Others were tailored to local realities. Some of these were directly quantifiable, such as the value of subsistence sources (as opposed to wages), and the expense of harvesting wild foods as a percentage of total income.

Others were categories of contrast that were established after periods of rapid field-work in each of the eight villages. Some of these indicators examined religion and values, classifying them as traditional, mixed, or modernized. Examples of questions to determine these categories included queries about Native healers; questions determined whether the ethos was traditional, mixed, or primarily Christian or whether ethical responsibilities were primarily toward the self or others.

Other qualitatively constructed indicators looked at specific circumstances of contemporary village life. Was the school curriculum perceived as being adequate by the local people? Were there high turnovers of staff in social and educational services, possibly suggesting job and social stress? Were there political disputes, and did they involve Natives and/or non-Natives? To what extent did the residents make use of formal family, social, health, and financial services?

Together, indicators provided excellent profiles of the villages and, with reference to some indicators, changes through time. Selection of appropriate nonstandard and improvised categories came through the long-time familiarity that Jorgenson, his colleagues, and their Native consultants had with Alaskan village life. Their work shows the anthropological potential for indicator-styled research.

Survey Questionnaires

The use of survey questionnaires has become very common among applied anthropologists over the past twenty years. This has happened because of increased work in complex societies, the need to test hypotheses with much larger samples, the tendency to work in interdisciplinary teams, and the expectation of funders and policy makers for more quantitative measurements. Just about any issue of *Human Organization,* the bellwether of applied anthropology, will usually include at least one, if not more examples of survey questionnaire research. For instance, John Young (1982) surveyed 221 small-scale farmers in five Western states about income, values, goals, and other factors affecting their livelihood. He concluded that more institutional supports were needed to increase the financial rewards of this productive sector rather than encouraging small farmers to undergo the uncertain risks of expanding their operations. John Gatewood and Bonnie McCay (1990) used a survey with several hundred New Jersey fishermen of six different types (scallopers, long-liners, and others) to assess various aspects of their working conditions and job satisfaction. Among their policy conclusions was a suggestion that it would be inappropriate to establish blanket fishing regulations for the different operations because of some very fundamental differences among them. Many more examples could illustrate the increase in questionnaire use in applied anthropology.

Elements of Questionnaire Design and Administration

Preliminary Design

The first step is to establish the purpose of the survey and whether it is advisable or feasible. Although that may seem obvious, it is important because launching a questionnaire can be very expensive and time-consuming. Questionnaire design and implementation require meticulous attention to detail. Alternate approaches, such as the examination of existing studies, might prove to be more effective and economical. Can a questionnaire actually collect the information sought? Are the main topics researchable? Can the population be properly sampled? Would respondents be likely to answer the questions? Would the answers be reliable?

Next, there should be a clear outline of all the questions that the survey is intended to ask—a broad outline that anticipates logical subtopics that connect to the study's primary goals. Its objectives have to be clear to both the researchers and the respondents from the beginning. Because of the need for precision and the possibilities of major methodological flaws, the researchers have to carefully calculate all of the necessary details of budgeting, sampling, staff, time, training, ethics, and informed consent as well as the precise research goals. Sampling is just one area for careful calculation—how many people are to be selected and on what basis? After an examination of all of these preliminary factors and their interrelationships, a final set of decisions is made regarding the scale of the survey and the essential information to be collected. That plan may have to be adjusted in response to changes and compromises in some of the factors just mentioned.

Preparing the Questions

Designing and writing the actual questions are the next steps. The main aims of the survey, briefly stated, along with a list of the types of relevant information, must guide the design of questions. In the beginning, there should be a section for the retrieval of standard information about the respondents—age, sex, occupation, education. Careful attention should be paid to noting or enumerating important information that is directly relevant to the people or topic being studied. For instance, if one is researching a disabled population, factors connected to their particular impairments will be needed to make effective correlations later or to explain the variations among answers. Next, subsections should be logically delineated although there may have to be some degree of improvisation here. Some sensitive information surrounding, for instance, criminal activity, substance abuse, or sexual preference, although perhaps germane to the research, may have to be asked much later in the questionnaire, thus allowing the respondents time to become comfortable with the interviewing process.

Then, within each section, lists of potential questions are written. Each question needs to be examined in the light of the specific aims of the study. Nonessential sections and questions should be removed. It is important that a questionnaire be tidy in content and format. The designers should make sure that the questions are very clear and unambiguous, simple, short, and reasonable and that the respondents have the experience and knowledge to be capable of answering them. They must decide whether the questions are to be closed or open. Early on, the researchers have to anticipate whether the interview instrument takes too long to complete, which might alienate the respondents.

Closed, Open, and Filter Questions

Closed questions facilitate tidiness and ease of analysis, but *open-ended questions* allow respondents to add new information that could be very important in the ultimate analysis. Closed questions offer the respondent a limited set of possible responses (i.e., listing an exhaustive set of options that cover the full range of possibility for the subtopic under consideration). They can be constructed as *two choices* (mutually exclusive, like yes or no), *multiple choice* among options provided, or by *ranking, rating,* or the use of *scales,* such as *Likert* ones. A *rating scale,* for instance, might ask about the importance of certain actions that could be taken. The scale provided consists of ten numbers, and the respondent has to place his choice precisely within the confines of the numbered choice to prevent ambiguities in analysis. For example,

How important do you think it is for the health board to develop a needle exchange program?

Check One

Not at all important									Extremely important
1	2	3	4	5	6	7	8	9	10
( )	( )	( )	( )	( )	( )	( )	( )	( )	( )

Likert-scaled questions ask respondents to register the strength of their agreement or disagreement with particular statements. Normally, there are five choices, although seven are possible. In one study, analyzing six focus groups, I collected over fifty statements of immigrant opinion regarding resettlement policies relevant to English-language learning, education, employment training, adjustment to Canadian society, and so forth. These statements, in terms of levels of agreement, were then administered to a larger sample of immigrants. Here are a few examples of such Likert-scaled questions.

There is a need for programs that are integrated with regard to learning English, employment readiness, and life-skills.

Strongly Disagree	Disagree	Neutral	Agree	Strongly Agree
1	2	3	4	5

Job-finding clubs, such as those found at settlement agencies, adequately prepare immigrants for the job market.

Strongly Disagree	Disagree	Neutral	Agree	Strongly Agree
1	2	3	4	5

Limited-range or *exhaustive questions* are often important for establishing comparisons or associations later.

Please check the range that best describes your household income from all sources in the past 12 months.

$ 0–10,000	O	50,000–60,000	O
10,000–20,000	O	60,000–70,000	O
20,000–30,000	O	70,000–80,000	O
30,000–40,000	O	80,000–90,000	O
40,000–50,000	O	90,000+	O

Open-ended questions allow respondents to reply in their own terms and reduce the risk of their being overly influenced by the alternatives provided. Answers can provide unexpected insights and amplification, but they require more time on the part of the interviewer and respondent, more articulate and motivated respondents, and are more difficult to analyze. Most questionnaires require a combination of both open and closed questions, with closed predominating. When open-ended options are provided, they tend to be only several lines long to somewhat limit the length of responses. That is markedly in contrast to the more open-ended procedures that we discussed in other chapters.

The use of *filter questions* is another standard device for questionnaires. If a set of questions is not pertinent to some respondents because it does not have the significant characteristics for a subtopic (e.g., child care for single or childless people), so they should skip to the next set of questions in which the subtopic changes or their experiences become relevant again.

Layout and Format

Tidiness, clarity, ease of transition from section to section, and effective explanation are all indispensable. They benefit interviewers, respondents, and the people who analyze the responses, which could involve three separate groups in addition to those who designed the questionnaire in the first place.

An effective format follows a standard sequence. The interviewer introduces herself or himself, explains the purposes of the questionnaire, and points out that information is confidential and that the interview will take a specified time. At the beginning of each section, the interviewer, in a sentence or two, informs the respondent of a change in focus and gives the reasons for asking the next set of questions. Within each section, questions are asked in a logical order, usually the easier and less sensitive ones first. The interview ends with statements that again express the importance of the study and the confidentiality of the responses. Careful consideration of the physical layout is very important to make it user-friendly, to reinforce reliability, to make sure that the interviewers and respondents can easily follow instructions, to ease coding and analysis, and to promote the answering of all questions.

Pretesting Questionnaires and Training the Interviewers

It is mandatory to pretest the questionnaire with a panel of people who have similar characteristics to the research sample in order to discover any flaws in wording, layout, length, and other unexpected factors. It also tests the feasibility of using certain concepts in the study. The pretest can lead to the elimination, rephrasing, or addition of some questions. Observation and discussions with the pretest respondents are part of the process. Researchers need specific details about what is wrong with the questions—what terms and phrasings are ambiguous, not understood, or lead to inappropriate answers. Sometimes pretesting can be done in focus groups, or through separate practice interviews with about fifteen to thirty-five people. The process can involve taperecording or even videotaping the interviews so that any glitches can be discovered and properly analyzed over several hearings. It might include very careful cognitive exercises in which the respondents are asked to speak their reactions aloud as they hear the questions (Fowler Jr. 1997).

After the questionnaire takes its final form, interviewers have to be hired and trained because sample sizes are usually too large to be covered by a single investigator. When there are large budgets and urban settings, the researchers may be able to hire college graduates with social science backgrounds who are already familiar with survey questionnaires. However, if the budget is limited, it might be necessary to train staff already on payroll, for example, at a clinic, to administer the questionnaire, providing that issues of confidentiality and informed consent can be solved. Anthropologists are often faced with the challenge of administering questionnaires in an ethnic setting in which respondents are not used to questionnaires. It might be appropriate to train members of the community, perhaps using some with a high school education (providing that the ethical challenges can be met). In such situations, learning curves for these novice interviewers can be quite steep. They need to understand the reason for the questionnaires, know how to convey instructions, ensure informed consent, know how to ask and record the questions in reliable ways, use reminder probes, and not ask leading questions, all the while maintaining friendly neutrality in response to the answers. They should go through practice runs in front of the principal investigators.

Sampling

Sampling often provides challenges for questionnaire use. Only a few problems can be discussed here. *Probability samples* improve validity and lend themselves to tests of statistical significance. Validity of the results from a questionnaire and generalization of those results are enhanced by the nonbiased selection of the study population.

In probability sampling, each unit in a population has an equal chance of being selected for the study. For that, the sample has to be drawn through some random process that is free from human judgment and other biases that might affect the independence of each selection. Probability sampling involves a lottery-like procedure whereby all the members or units (e.g., households) of the population to be sampled have been identified and assigned numbers that can be drawn in such a way that they are not influenced by the selection of any other person or unit. In probability sampling, there must be a listing of a known population (Henry 1997b). Perhaps, if households or neighborhoods are to be surveyed in a community, Zip or postal codes and addresses or telephone numbers might be drawn randomly. Telephone numbers are much more reliable than they once were because the overwhelming number of households now have telephones. Yet people with unlisted numbers may present some problems. Addresses or names may be assigned numbers on the basis of random-numbers tables and then drawn according to the criteria needed. In more isolated regions, researchers may first have to complete their own census as a part of ongoing fieldwork. Another dimension to probability sampling is *random stratified sampling,* to make sure that appropriate proportions of significant subpopulations are drawn and accounted for, based on factors like gender, ethnicity, and occupation.

Nonprobabilty sampling takes various forms. *Convenience sampling* relies on the simple availability of participants. Alternatively, various types of more systematic *judgment sampling* can be constructed as follows:

- *typical cases*—selecting cases that are known to be broadly representative and not extreme;
- *most similar and most dissimilar cases*—selecting those that are known to have very similar characteristics or experience very different conditions, perhaps using both in the same sample;
- *snowball cases*—those contacted identify others that can be included;
- *quota sampling*—whereby people or units are chosen on the basis of known proportions in the population (the analogy of random stratified sampling);
- *critical cases* involves selecting cases that are key and quite essential to the objectives and credibility of the study. (Henry 1997b: 105)

Certain obstacles may require researchers to rely on nonprobablity samples. A common one is that the total population is not known because records or censuses have not or cannot be kept. Another related impediment may be that there is no adequate listing of the population's members. For instance, who knows how many intravenous drug users at risk of contacting HIV/AIDS live in any North American city? Who are they, and where precisely can they be found? Convenience sampling may have to be used to get such people to participate in a questionnaire evaluating the services of a needle-exchange program. Similarly, the staff at a human service agency may be too busy delivering services to keep accurate statistics about their clients. Yet they know the rough proportions, so various types of judgment criteria can be developed to draw up a sample. However, in any such situation, every effort must be made to minimize biases. In the last scenario, the obvious one could be the degree to which the agency staff influenced (at least subconsciously) the selection of client/respondents known to be satisfied with services.

Many other decisions and variables in sampling cannot be considered in a cursory overview. Among other questions are: How large should the sample be? What are the potential sources of sampling bias? How can they be minimized? (See Bernard 1995: 71–102; Henry 1997b).

Administering and Analyzing the Questionnaire

One of the earliest decisions during the planning stages is whether the questionnaire will be administered in person by a trained interviewer or the respondents will reply on their own (perhaps through a mailed survey or at a certain location such as an agency office), or if the questions will be asked over the phone. There are comparative advantages to any of these formats—cost, accuracy, response rates, and more complex information. *Face-to-face interviews* are the most expensive but can deal with the most complex information and have potentially the highest accuracy and response rate. *Telephone interviews* tend to be less effective in all of these variables, but they take the least time, because twenty minutes is about the maximum time most people will spend on the phone. Telephone interviews have significant advantages in that the interviewer does not have to travel to the location, which might be dangerous or create misunderstandings in the neighborhood. Trained interviewers can conduct many telephone interviews daily, thus potentially increasing the sample size. However, *mailed* or *self-administered questionnaires* are the cheapest and allow even larger samples to be reached, but their format must be the most lucid; the complexity of information gathered will be the lowest, and, because there is no supervision, they will have the lowest accuracy of the three. Furthermore, their response rates will likely be the lowest because there is no one interviewer present to encourage the respondents. Yet as Dilman (1978) has shown, there are ways to maximize return rates to a level of over 80 percent through careful formatting, reminder letters, and phone calls. These self-administered questionnaires can be less time-consuming than face-to-face interviews and more time-consuming than telephone interviews. In some circumstances, response rates can be raised by having the respondents fill out the questionnaires at a set location such as a school or agency office. For instance, in the evaluation of immigrant services I mentioned earlier, clients completed the questionnaire when they came to the agency for other purposes.

Arrangements should be made to codify the data for easy and manageable retrieval by hand or by computer. Data need to be entered into a centralized format such as a computer data bank and then analyzed descriptively in terms of frequencies, means, medians, standard deviations as well as correlations, multivariate analyses, tests of significance, and so forth. Thorough analysis is completed, and then the findings are prepared and presented in digestible forms to appropriate stakeholders.

Another general area that merits some examination is the construction of graphs and tables summarizing quantitative data (see Henry 1997a; Zeisel 1968)—a whole realm of statistics with intricate and standardized rules for presenting numerical data in digestible form. This is quite important for practitioners in the preparation of reports and for oral presentations using overheads with tables and graphs. The area of statistics is vitally important, but, with the exception of Thomas (1986), anthropologists will have to rely mainly on nonanthropological courses and books (see Hopkins et al. 1996) for their statistical training, at least in the short term.

Case Study: Attitudes on Needle Transfer among Injecting Drug Users in Ohio

Anthropologists have been doing policy-relevant research on drug use and the spread of HIV/AIDS and other sexually transmitted diseases (Feldman 1994; Gorman et al. 1997; Singer et al. 1991; Whitehead 1997). Ethnographic research complements large-scale epidemiological and questionnaire surveys and sometimes provides triangulated insight by pointing out the reasons for variations in drug use or the transmission of HIV/AIDS. We have already learned that public health planning has to allow for more variation among cities.

One such project, supported by the National Institute on Drug Abuse, is located in Dayton and Columbus, Ohio. Ethnographic work done there by Robert Carlson has been essential in primary research and organizing risk reduction trials. He studied crack use (smoked rather than injected) accompanied by high-risk sexual behaviors associated with HIV/AIDS (Carlson and Siegal 1991). However, most of the work has been concentrated on intravenous drug users (IDUs) because they run even higher risks of HIV/AIDS by using contaminated needles. In addition to doing ethnography, five outreach workers distribute risk-reduction kits among IDUs and their sex partners and then monitor the results. These kits include condoms, bottles of bleach and water for cleaning needles, and succinct information on safe sex and needle use.

There are estimated to be 5,000 to 7,000 active IDUs in the metropolitan areas of Dayton and Columbus. Carlson recorded the activities of IDUs in their "copping areas" and "shooting galleries," and he explored many other attributes of the drug culture through observations and interviews over two years (Carlson et al. 1994b).

The project involved a number of directions and requirements. It had to recruit at least 35 new participants a month into risk-reduction trials. Samples should consist of 70 percent IDUs and 30 percent crack users, be sensitive to ethnic distribution, and would be at least 25 percent female. As we shall see shortly, some ethnographic discoveries and hypotheses were tested through questionnaires with much larger samples.

Given that the total population was unknown and that its activities were illegal, researchers had to come up with a solution that best approximated random, stratified sampling. The approach that they developed is referred to as "targeted sampling," a product of several triangulated methods. Fundamentally, the procedure allowed outreach workers to proportionately draw volunteers for the risk trials and questionnaires from particular geographic districts within Montgomery County, Ohio.

This was done by using Zip code areas within the county. Various indices were then developed to estimate the number of IDUs or crack users in the thirty-two code areas as well as the presence and intensity of drug facilities—crack houses, crack-copping areas, shooting galleries, dope houses, IDU-copping areas, and IDU residences. There were estimated to be 239 facilities within the county; again ethnographical research was essential for their identification and enumeration. Another indicator source was the addresses of about 650 people who variously had entered treatment programs for cocaine and opiate problems, were victims of drug overdose deaths, and represented syphilis cases (as inferential of high-risk sexual behavior often correlated with crack use). Residences of 390 previous participants in the National AIDS Demonstration Project formed yet another data source. Out of these various pools of information, four measures of relative drug intensity were calculated for all thirty-two Zip code areas in the county. For instance, in one test, the lowest Zip code area would have the measurement of 0.0000, whereas the highest had a rating of 0.6455, meaning that it contained over 64 percent of that activity or measurement. The various indices were compared with each other through statistical tests, and the correlations of significance were quite high. The Zip code areas were then classified into low, medium, and high zones. As expected, the four highest were in the inner city, followed by five medium zones adjacent to it. However, evidence of drug use was found in most of the remaining twenty-three areas, including the outlying suburbs.

As the project advanced, outreach workers were instructed to draw participants from these zones according to representative proportions rather than simply following convenience or snowballing procedures as had been done in similar studies elsewhere. In the risk-reduction work with IDUs, thirty-eight people were to be recruited in each quarter of the year—twenty-five from the high-density zones, seven from the medium zones, and six from the low-density zones. This would also be done in accordance with the ethnic and gender requirements (Carlson et al. 1994a). Furthermore, the study made use of the targeted sampling approach for administering a questionnaire.

Among Carlson's ethnographic findings was the initially surprising discovery that IDUs did not value the sharing of needles. A kind of mythology had developed with the earliest public health research on the transmission of AIDS through intravenous drug use that needle "sharing" was a strongly felt normative bond in the drug culture of American cities. The interpretation was that needle sharing served as a ritual to create or reinforce friendships and as a symbol of group identity. Consequently, many public health officials thought that one of the most effective ways to deal with the risks of HIV/AIDS transmission was to change the values associated with needle sharing. This preconception occurred early in Carlson's fieldwork and was reinforced through sixty-five taped interviews with African American and white needle users. They overwhelmingly indicated that they do not value "shooting up" with used needles and do not regard it as a form of social bonding. The term sharing needed to be replaced with needle "transfers." Generally, transfers occur because no new needles are available, or because in many jurisdictions it is virtually impossible to purchase new needles without prescriptions. People can be arrested for the mere possession of needles.

Informants offered a number of reasons why they do not want previously used needles: dulled and barbed needles make it difficult to puncture veins; it is excruciating for an addict to wait until another person is finished; it indicates a subordinate status to wait for another person to finish injecting; and using another's needle is often perceived as an unwanted intimacy, like using another's toothbrush.

It is significant here that two questionnaires were used to test some of these findings (a form of triangulation with ethnography) through a larger sample (276) drawn from the target-sampling procedure discussed earlier. Some of the questions regarding needle transfer (measured on a seven-point scale of very strongly agree to very strongly disagree) included:

> When shooting up with other people, I feel like I have to use the same outfit everyone else uses.

> If a friend wanted me to shoot up with a needle he/she just used, I would find it hard to say no.

Some of the statements regarding perceptions about needle access, drug paraphernalia, laws, and AIDS risk included:

> I don't carry outfits with me, because I'm afraid I'll get busted.

> It is difficult for me to get new/sterile needles.

Questions of a sociodemographic nature were also asked as well as the number of times used needles were given or loaned to others, the number of times interviewees injected with used needles, and the number of times they injected with used needles without cleaning with bleach and water. The findings were analyzed descriptively and subjected to statistical tests of significance. They matched very well with ethnographic findings. Yet it was discovered that white IDUs were more likely to inject with previously used needles than were African Americans. Crack users were more likely to employ used needles when they injected, and the same was true for people who were married or living together.

In this research, ethnographic findings were operationalized and tested through a questionnaire. While confirming the central hypothesis, it also revealed some significant variations within the Dayton-Columbus sample that had not been confirmed through the ethnography. The study helped to confirm a hunch that researchers were beginning to realize nationally: that participants in drug "cultures" do not, on the whole, favor needle sharing. Therefore, other prevention strategies for HIV/AIDS transmission have to be considered. (Carlson et al. 1996).

Case Study: Programs for Inmates

Criminal justice, involving the courts, prisons, police, and the sociocultural context of crime, is yet another domain that begs for anthropological attention. In the United States, there have been staggering increases in the incarceration of criminals—134 percent from 1980 to 1990. Research needs to be done on the damage to victims, costs to society, and the effects of imprisonment upon inmates and their families. The small amount of available anthropological research mainly investigates the perspectives of inmates who face various programs of discipline and rehabilitation (see Glasser and Sutro 1992). Ultimately, one of the most serious concerns is how to reduce rates of recidivism. For applied anthropologists, the evaluation of programs, especially as directed to different ethnic groups, may be the main research task.

Although lower, Canada's incarceration rates have paralleled those of the United States. Higher proportions of inmates, as compared to their proportion in society, are Indians, Inuit, and Métis. James Waldram has been doing anthropological research at the Regional Psychiatric Center (RPC) in Saskatoon, Saskatchewan, a forensic hospital that assesses the needs and potentials for program and counseling needs of violent offenders. Approximately one third of the patients are Aboriginal, and most have experienced disruptive family backgrounds, child abuse, and severe drug and alcohol problems. With its large staff of therapists, the center provides various programs directed to those suffering psychiatric illnesses, substance abuse, sexual deviancy, and personality disorders. Individual counseling, alcohol and substance abuse programs (such as Alcoholics Anonymous), small-group therapy sessions, and various types of religious counseling and services are some of the treatments offered.

Access to Native spiritual elders has been an important option available for Native inmates. These can include one-on-one sessions, as well as one- to four-day workshops on Aboriginal spirituality with rituals and demonstrations about the practices and meanings of sacred pipes, tobacco, sweetgrass, sweat lodges, and medicine wheels. Sessions include discussions about culture, values, and Native experiences. For some, it can be the most intensive introduction to their own culture. Using ethnography and open-ended interviewing, Waldram (1993) evaluated the program and found that the prisoners placed great value on this healing approach. It helped them to sort out difficulties surrounding identity and gave renewed and positive meaning to their shattered lives as well as fostering solidarity and cooperation among fellow Natives. Renewed spirituality allowed them to better cope with alcohol and other substance abuse.

Waldram and a psychologist (see Waldram and Wong 1994) analyzed the effectiveness of mixed Native and non-Native group therapy sessions. Because the standards and expectations surrounding communication were largely defined by non-Native prisoners, guards, and counselors, the program did not work very well and was a source of anxiety for many Native inmates. Yet those Natives who fared better were the ones who had more experience with Euro-Canadian society.

Waldram was aware that Native people were not homogeneous. However, that is the way that they had frequently been perceived by other researchers and prison officials. There was a tendency to lump Natives together in comparisons to non-Natives for the analysis of psychological testing, determining rehabilitation efforts, and in evaluating programs. While a Native overlay of identity was valid, it ignored sources of differentiation based on individual experience and cultural and linguistic categories such as Cree, Assiniboine, Chipewyan, and Inuit. In his research, he began to uncover three distinct orientations—"traditional," "Euro-Canadian," and "bicultural."

Waldram (1996) was commissioned by the Federal Correctional Service of Canada to develop a scaled instrument to describe and measure variables influencing the cultural orientations of Aboriginal offenders. For that purpose, he used a sample of 249 men from RPC and three other federal penitentiaries. As a form of triangulated research, thirty-one men also participated in open-ended interviews that more deeply explored context and meaning. The questionnaire asked about languages spoken, cultural background, age, education (before any upgrading in prison), length of sentence, amount of sentence already served, places of residence before prison, whether they were raised by their parents or in foster homes, and amount of time spent in residential schools.

A large battery of questions was then asked that provided clues of orientation among traditional, white-oriented, and bicultural life-styles and identity.

Questions were asked about language; for example:

B.22 "Which language do you think you speak the best?"

Name: _____ _____

0. An Aboriginal language
1. Speak both equally as well
2. English or French
3. N/A

Questions were asked about religion; for example:

C.2 "When you were growing up, as a child, what was your religion?"

0. Aboriginal spirituality/Indian religion
1. Both Aboriginal and Christian (name Christian: _____)
2. A Christian denomination (name) _____
3. Other (name) _____
4. None
5. N/A

Questions were asked about the communities where the inmates were brought up; for example:

D.3   "Were there more Native people than white people or more white people than Native people in this community?"

0. More Natives than whites *[GO TO D.4]*
1. More whites than Natives *[GO TO D.15]*
2. Equal Natives and whites *[GO TO D.4]*
3. Not Applicable
4. N/A

Other questions related to friendships, identity, spirituality, and attitudes. Most questions could not have been formulated without previous ethnographic familiarity. Various statistical tests and specialized forms of analyses (e.g., cluster and factor analyses) identified important factors in predicting "traditional" orientations—childhood residence (e.g., isolated northern communities and reserves, diet, and exposure to native spirituality).

The emerging picture of "traditional" men was one in which an Aboriginal language was primary, and they were raised in remote communities with little direct exposure to Euro-Canadian society. These men were likely to experience the most cultural problems within the prison system and to have their behavior misinterpreted. Those of "Euro-Canadian" orientation had often been raised in urban settings without enculturation into an Aboriginal culture and did not speak an Aboriginal language. These men are likely to have identity problems. The "bicultural" types, although raised in predominantly Aboriginal environments and speaking Aboriginal languages, came from areas that had relatively large numbers of Euro-Canadians. They speak English well and are familiar with Euro-Canadian ways. Given their variability, it would seem that more care is needed in selecting treatment modalities for them.

Summary

In spite of the desirability of using quantitative research, Phillipe Bourgois reminds us of the power of the ethnographic approach and its utility for anthropology. Participant observation techniques

> are better suited than exclusively quantitative methodologies for documenting the lives of people who live on the margins of a society that is hostile to them. Only by establishing long-term relationships based on trust can one begin to ask provocative personal questions, and expect thoughtful, serious answers. Ethnographers usually live in communities they study, and they establish long-term, organic relationships with the people they write about. In other words, to collect "accurate data," ethnographers violate the canons of positivistic research; we become intimately involved with the people we study. (1996: 13)

As anthropologists, it is indeed important to remind ourselves of our intellectual roots, social responsibilities, and our fundamental niche within the social sciences. Yet, regarding application, the older debates over the superiority of either quantified or qualitative approaches remind me of the old beer commercial in which two factions of ex-professional athletes argue vehemently over whether a particular brand of beer "tastes great" or is "less filling." Both were meant to be correct in the concept of the commercial myth makers. Similarly, modern applied anthropology benefits from both dimensions of the quantitative and the qualitative.

Almost all applied anthropologists wish that they had more quantitative training as undergraduate and graduate students. Current students are advised to go deeply and extensively in their reading and training.

RECOMMENDED READINGS

Bernard, H. Russell
1995   *Research Methods in Anthropology: Qualitative and Quantitative Approaches,* Second Edition. Walnut Creek, CA: Altamira.

Fowler Jr., Floyd J.
1997   Design and Evaluation of Survey Questions. In *Handbook of Applied Social Research Methods.* Leonard Bickman and Debra J. Rog, eds. Pp. 343–375. Thousand Oaks, CA: Sage.

Henry, Gary T.
1997a Graphing Data. In *Handbook of Applied Social Research Methods.* Leonard Bickman and Debra J. Rog, eds. Pp. 527–557. Thousand Oaks, CA: Sage.
1997b Practical Sampling. In *Handbook of Applied Social Research Methods.* Leonard Bickman and Debra J. Rog, eds. Pp. 101–127. Thousand Oaks, CA: Sage.

Hopkins, Kenneth D., B. R. Hopkins, Gene V. Glass
1996   *Basic Statistics for the Behavioral Sciences.* Third Edition. Boston: Allyn and Bacon.

Jorgenson, Joseph G., Richard McCleary, and Steven McNabb
1985   Social Indicators in Native Village Alaska. *Human Organization,* Vol. 44: 2–18.

Oppenheim, A. N.
1992   *Questionnaire Design, Interviewing and Attitude Measurement.* London and New York: Pinter Publishers.

Organization for Economic Co-Operation and Development (OCED)
1976   *Measuring Social Well-Being: A Progress Report on the Development of Social Indicators.* Paris: OCED.

Pelto, Pertti J., and Gertel H. Pelto
1978   *Anthropological Research: The Structure of Inquiry.* Second Edition. London: Cambridge University Press.

Rossi, Robert J., and Kevin J. Gilmartin
1980   *The Handbook of Social Indicators: Sources, Characteristics and Analysis.* New York: Garland STPM Press.

Thomas, David Hurst
1986   *Refiguring Anthropology: First Principles of Probability and Statistics.* Prospect Heights, IL: Waveland Press.

van Dusen, Roxann A., and Robert Parke
1976   Social Indicators: A Focus for the Social Sciences. In *Anthropology and the Public Interest: Fieldwork and Theory.* Peggy R. Sanday, ed. Pp. 333–345. London: Academic Press.

CHAPTER

14   Rapid Assessment Procedures (RAPs)

This chapter examines some recent attempts to make applied anthropological research more timely, focused, comparative, and policy relevant. The emphasis is on streamlined methods and much shorter periods of data collection. This chapter deviates slightly from previous ones in that it draws more heavily from the work of anthropologists working in Third World settings because rapid assessment procedures have been most used there. Rapid research styles could also be used in North American settings when appropriate.

The Problem: Policy Makers in a Hurry, Anthropologists Taking Their Time

Anthropologists have much to offer in assessing needs, evaluating programs, and forecasting impacts of policies and projects. They can make such contributions in developing countries, with ethnic minorities in modern urban society, and within mainstream society itself. However, academic anthropology is still poorly prepared for these opportunities.

A major difficulty is that it often takes far too long for an anthropologist to collect information to inform policy. Because of bureaucratic, legal, or political constraints, decisions often have to be made quickly about how a project should proceed. Such urgency is sometimes artificially constructed, but the detailed information needed for the design of a specific program must meet deadlines and exclude all that is extraneous.

Given the tradition of holism, anthropologists may feel that it is important to record in almost encyclopedic detail the customs and behavior of a people or community. Inculcated in many, then, is the idea that such information is useful for its own sake. Adding to the impasse may be the assumption that framing our findings within anthropological theory can somehow promote flashes of insight or enlightenment previously absent with policy makers. This still may be possible if presented in small doses in well-thought-out and accessible language. Appealing to common sense and empathy tends to be the best way of presenting theoretical generalizations. Too often, theories that are not easily understood can reinforce the esoteric image that anthropology may have with policy makers.

Anthropologists often shy away from making specific recommendations in part because they realize that their predictions cannot be guaranteed. Similarly, out of ethical concern, anthropologists sometimes worry about being presumptuous in recommending courses of action that manipulate the lives of others. Indeed, practicing applied anthropology can be a very formidable responsibility.

Another problem is that ethnography is usually done in particular communities or in segments of a community. A skeptic could ask a number of questions. First, regarding replicability, how can one know that the same conclusions would be still reached if the research were done by another investigator? Second, how does the reader know that the information collected is valid or a "true" reflection of circumstances in this particular community? Third, do the personal biases of the investigators or the randomness of unorganized and never-repeated incidents of participant observation lead to inaccurate generalizations about the community? Fourth, and more serious, whatever the replicability or validity of the information, could the reader be certain that the information has any relevance beyond the specific community or people studied? Given fiscal responsibilities and other restraints, policy makers normally have to design policies suitable for more communities than just the one described by the ethnographer. What if the programs in question are related to crucial but expensive choices such as water improvement, sanitation, nutrition, agricultural change, or education for many impoverished and underdeveloped communities in a region? To be confident about recommendations, the policy maker needs larger samples of communities and information than the "one-shot," detailed ethnography can provide.

To be fair to anthropologists, I should mention the other sides of these predicaments. Often policy makers are in too much of a hurry. They might naively assume that there are "quick fixes" available in the social realm, analogous to building bridges or marketing a product. They might have other agendas than helping to solve human problems or performing a public service. They may be self-serving: the more they seem to get done, the more achievements they can cite in annual reports to higher authorities. They might be ambitious for personal advancement in elected politics or promotion through the bureaucratic system. The decision-making may even be a raw exercise in power. Or, in trying to establish programs and policies, policy makers may be attending to the interests of particular interests rather than intended local beneficiaries.

Anthropologists might say that the decision makers have a responsibility to slow down and inform themselves of the very complicated circumstances and cultures of people designated as "targets" for new programs or policies. Also, anthropologists find it difficult to convince others that cultural or social "facts" and even solutions can only be properly understood through deep immersion into context. Perhaps the policy makers need to develop longer-range views and take more care in collecting information used for making decisions that affect whole communities. Perhaps they need to learn more about the social sciences and anthropology, in particular, to better understand the basis and importance of method and theory as well as findings. They may have an obligation to understand more clearly what anthropologists can do for them.

In their rush, policy makers have too frequently relied on the advice of "instant" consultants who have only a superficial knowledge of local societies and their cultures. Such consultants may rely too much on their own preconceived and culture-bound assumptions. They may go to the field site for two or three weeks, then provide conclusions and recommendations to fit the biases of their employers or their own previous experiences and assumptions, and collect lucrative consultants' fees after "quick and dirty" studies. Most anthropologists feel that it is better not to be involved at all than to do shoddy and possibly harmful work. Certainly policy makers should be encouraged to rely on more long-term, in-depth studies based on the strengths of traditional ethnography.

But, as you may have already anticipated, it often just does not work out that way. Those ideals may or may not develop with time, but, meanwhile, applied anthropologists have to be engaged with policy and decision makers. To be effective, the reality is that anthropologists have to make more accommodations if they want to influence more benign changes. In many cases, there is just not enough money to support large-scale ethnographic research to inform policy issues.

There has been some progress over the past few decades in dealing with these dilemmas. One method that has met some of the problems outlined here is rapid assessment procedures (or RAPs, as it is sometimes known).

What Is Meant by Rapid Assessment?

A few anthropologists (see Beebe 1995; van Willigen and Finan 1991; Harris et al. 1997) have attempted to define and explore the parameters of rapid research. So far, most of this work has been done in Third World contexts where development problems are so massive (relevant to hundreds of thousands of villages) and so profound (e.g., virulent outbreaks of infectious disease) that anthropologists can agree to the urgency for rapid collections of information directly relevant to policy solutions. RAPs are normally collaborative, involving multidisciplinary teams of development researchers and service providers, and they usually include villagers as stakeholders and research participants. What makes RAPs interesting for anthropologists is that they rely primarily on qualitative techniques and contain many dimensions similar and compatible to ethnographic fieldwork. Even more significant, they pay close attention to local values and perceptions of reality.

Rapid assessment procedures work best when there is already a clear understanding of the central problem. In the realm of health, examples could include HIV/AIDS epidemics or high rates of infant mortality due to dysentery. In agriculture, drought and soil erosion could be contributing to precariously low agricultural production. There may be a need to collaborate in the promotion of a crop that meets local criteria for subsistence preference as well as needed cash so that villagers can meet their other goals. Yet in such cases, policy makers and researchers are also aware that the ultimate solutions cannot merely be technical. Surrounding each issue will always be a significant number of social, behavioral, and cultural variables that are not yet known. Such variables, constituting the "human dimension," must be understood and included in any technical solution. Thus, there is frequently a need to get as much information on factors essential to the successes of any proposed implementations as quickly as possible. Rapid assessments are also potentially very helpful for evaluating programs recently started, so that they can be improved while there is still time. Generally, when RAPs are conducted in community settings, they are done over periods of from one to six weeks.

The Field Manual Approach to RAP:
An Example from the Health Field

A superb example of rapid assessment is found in a manual titled *Rapid Assessment Procedures for Nutrition and Primary Health Care: Anthropological Approaches to Improving Programme Effectiveness* by Susan Scrimshaw and Elena Hurtado (1987). It was published on behalf of the United Nations to assist in the understanding of health resources, problems, and potentials in Third World developing communities. It focuses on the health of women and children as related to immunization, nutrition, growth and development, pregnancy, and pre- and postnatal care.

The purpose of Scrimshaw and Hurtado's approach to RAP is to collect replicable and comparable data from many villages in a very short period by collaborating with local people. Anthropologically trained people or public health nurses and trained lay people could collect the data. Some recommended procedures entail direct observations of the health-related behavior in question. As examples, the observers are instructed to record how women handle oral rehydration solutions for dealing with infant diarrhea and to determine whether they use the recommended amounts of salt. Another recurrent feature of each study is the collection of local epidemiological data. The remainder of the approaches are qualitative, oriented to ethnographic interviews within selected households. Here, the emphasis is on culture and the beliefs associated with health and illness. Researchers are advised to return frequently to households and to key informants for reiterations and confirmations of information. The manual outlines recurrent topics and lines of questioning that foster replicability and a readiness to improvise in circumstances that are unique to the community or to the culture. Most importantly, it shows the necessity of framing questions that are sensitive to local styles of communication.

Scrimshaw and Hurtado's manual deals with three broad categories—community, household, and primary health-care givers—from which replicable and comparable information should be collected. These sources of information are still conceived ethnographically and holistically but in more specified ways because they specifically focus on information related to health. In considering community information, there is a provision for descriptions of local geography, demography, and epidemiology. Investigators are asked to look for information on standard health-related factors such as live births per thousand, number of children under five years of age, and the climate and the quality of water sources as well as the prevalence of diseases. The RAP would contain some broad descriptions of subsistence and socioeconomics. It would describe such political dimensions as authority. Who are the local decision makers, and how well coordinated are they with national institutions? Questions would be asked to determine the broad range of attitudes toward the national government and such services as health clinics. There is a description of all the basic health facilities and health personnel, including traditional healers. Investigators describe the facilities related to health care and are alert to important factors such as their accessibility to potential users.

The next, perhaps more crucial area of investigation is the household. As many households as possible might be surveyed, or the investigators might use random or judgment samples. Factors related to the composition (including a kinship chart) and socioeconomic status of each household are recorded. Its facilities and amenities are noted, including water resources, waste disposal, aspects of food storage, diet, sources of food, and the basic household economy. Questioning on health and illness is largely open-ended. Some of the questions related to health practice and beliefs include:

How do you know when a child is healthy?

How do you know when a child is ill?

How does one keep a child healthy?

What are the most common illnesses of children? (The investigator is to get more details, including symptoms and methods of treatment about each one mentioned if possible.)

What foods are eaten by mothers and children?

Are there special diets for weaning? Diets for sick children? Diets for specific conditions?

Investigators collect morbidity histories from each household, paying special attention to the illnesses of children five years and under. They usually make an inventory of household remedies, finding out what they are used for and where they come from. They try to collect the details on the most recent pregnancy, taking note of what foods a pregnant woman is allowed to eat. Questions are asked about the health resources that people use when family members are sick. These could include relatives, neighbors, folk healers, homeopaths, and cosmopolitan (Western) health officials such as doctors and public health nurses. Inquiries are made about their general experiences and attitudes toward cosmopolitan health resources provided by the national government or other agencies. When do they visit such facilities and for what reasons? They also try to reconstruct the details of vaccination histories for all the children of the household.

The final category of assessment is the local institutions of primary health care based on the cosmopolitan or Western models and provided by the national government. Interviews are held with the directors of such agencies and, in the process, investigators develop an inventory of equipment, personnel, and services offered. Note whether the staff is drawn from the local community. Do employees speak the local language? What are the staffs' perceptions of problems or obstacles in delivering services? The researcher observes the clinical setting and describes the physical aspects of the facilities and its health resources. Then, a great deal of attention is to be paid to observations of interaction between staff and patients, to consultations, what types of explanations and instructions are given to patients, and to activities such as the dispensing of food and drugs and the collection of growth and weight measurements of children.

Next, the researchers provide summary descriptions of the typical users of the clinics, describing their personal characteristics and the complaints that they have brought to the primary health-care facilities. They hold exit interviews with these patients and elicit their perceptions of what just transpired as well as try to measure and describe their levels of satisfaction with the visits. They are asked why they came there, what could be done to make the visits better, and what needs were then left unmet. They should also try to visit some homes to see what has happened since the clinic visits and what has been the degree of compliance regarding prescriptions and other remedies. Because most emphasis is placed on the health of children, details about preparations for oral rehydration, follow-ups for booster shots, and so forth are necessary to gauge the linkages from the clinic to the home.

This broad plan for doing a rapid ethnographic study is straightforward and very effective in covering health behavior and attitudes that might have an impact on the design of health-care delivery. In addition to needs assessment, the approach could be used in program evaluation and social impact assessment.

Scrimshaw and Hurtado's approach reminds practitioners to frame research in policy-relevant ways. It does not load potential researchers with a whole series of extraneous academic categories, theories, and perspectives. It also means that researchers other than anthropologists can do this very crucial type of research. Some issues in the Third and Fourth Worlds are extremely vital, but there are just not enough anthropologists to investigate them all. Drawing from local resources makes sense. Another valuable dimension is that categories of information from one village to another can be compared, and then assessments can be made as to whether it is desirable to design uniform health promotion strategies or tailor them to particular local problems.

One community needs to revitalize its horticulture so as to provide nutritious and less costly food for young children. Another has been slow to participate in immunization programs. Yet another village shows very little use of the local health clinic because residents are suspicious and resentful of the national power elites. Representatives of the latter are doctors and nurses at the local clinics, so local people use traditional healers more frequently. Each of these scenarios calls for a different campaign in health promotion.

Other RAPs in the health field include research into malaria (Manderson et al. 1996), sexually transmitted diseases (Helitzer-Allen et al. 1996), diarrhea (Bentley and Herman 1996), women's health (Gittlesohn and Bentley 1996), and epilepsy (Long et al. 1988).

Rapid Assessment in Agricultural Development

RAPs are frequently used in agricultural development (see Beebe 1995; Perez 1997). They are often done through partnerships of government agencies, agricultural research stations, governmental aid organizations, and international agencies such as the World Bank. They are also routinely done by regional development centers such as the International Potato Center in Peru. Whatever agencies and organizations are involved, agricultural RAPs always rely on the cooperation of small farmers at the village level.

There is a long list of development issues in agriculture. It includes conservation, soil regeneration, reforestation, and improvement of agricultural production through the use of new tools, irrigation, crop rotations and diversification, and pesticide and fertilizer use. There may be a search for alternative crops more suitable to the local environment that will provide higher or more reliable yields while matching local subsistence tastes and serving as cash crops.

Since the major failures of top-down planning in the 1950s and 1960s, an effort has been made to create development programs and services to fit local circumstances and to include local farmers in decision-making. Attention has been paid to local values, knowledge, and social organization for agricultural programming although that ideal is still far from universal. New research approaches have been variously labeled as farming systems research and agroecosystems analysis (see Shaner et al. 1982; Conway and Barbier 1990). There is an understanding that farming requires holistic analysis. This needs to be done by interpreting local environmental constraints and opportunities; cultural and historical factors in the choice of crops, livestock, and farming procedures; and the effects of markets and national agricultural policies on local farms. Essential to these systems are the roles of community, family, and domestic cycles in agricultural decision-making. Religion and ritual cycles as well as political economy might also be significant in the analyses. The goal of farming systems research is to first define and account for the local system, its subsystems, and variables. It then becomes a matter of carefully matching highly variable technical solutions (including the decision not to intervene) to a regional agroecosystem.

Longer-term ethnographic and survey-styled research can still have a significant place in these assessments as well as in monitoring or evaluating long-term results. But such projects can be very expensive, take too long, not cover enough territory or village situations, and may end up representing unbalanced disciplinary biases (e.g., agronomy, engineering, etc.) in separate reports. On the other hand, an informal style of speedy research, disdainfully labeled "development tourism," a form of brief investigation of communities on well-travelled roads, aimed at influential men not disenfranchised farmers, and administered only during good weather, does not solve the research needs either.

As a response, various forms of rapid research have emerged with more focused and disciplined attention to defining local farming systems and seeking knowledge of farmers' preferences. Some of these rapid approaches have been formalized—Rapid Rural Appraisal (RRA), Rapid Assessment (RA), Participatory Rural Appraisal (PRA)—and handbooks have been developed for their standard use (see Beebe 1995). The approaches share important elements. They last from six days to six weeks, almost always consist of multidisciplinary teams of both technical experts and social scientists, frequently involve local people as co-researchers (especially in the case of PRAs), and do much of the research on farm sites. Although quantitative methods such as census materials and soil and production figures are used, the methods are largely qualitative. In many cases, informal conversations are used along with observations of behavior although focus groups, village meetings, and key-informant interviews are also frequently used. Some other methods may be included— transects or walking tours of representative areas of the farming territory, the collection of seasonal cycle calendars, and exercises with groups or individuals that seek to establish how local people make decisions and determine priorities. Judgment rather than random sampling is generally used. Efforts are made to interview and observe poor as well as more affluent farmers, both men and women, a good range of operational types. The purposes vary—from gaining information on specific crops or technical solutions to defining the ingredients of the agroecosystem before proceeding any further.

One of the more well-known rapid approaches is the *sondeo,* which was created for agricultural development research in Latin America (see Hildebrand 1982). A *sondeo,* Spanish for *reconnaissance survey,* takes place over six to ten days and is meant to orient the work of a team to develop effective technical solutions for farming in a defined region. The background research is intended to establish the first year's work in plant selections and field trials. The survey outlines the current cropping systems, the socioeconomic circumstances of the farmers, and the restrictions of their operations. The team is composed of specialists such as plant breeders, general agronomists, plant pathologists, agricultural engineers, anthropologists, sociologists, and economists, drawn equally from the technical and socioeconomic subgroups and with about ten members. They generally examine homogeneous cropping systems to make sure that the farmers will face broadly similar adjustments and restrictions.

Only informal interviews and observations are used, not questionnaires, so that farmers do not become alienated with the process. On the first day the group stays together, traveling the area, talking to farmers, and interpreting their preliminary observations on the local cropping systems. The next two days are spent in half-day segments, with pairs of investigators roaming, observing, and interviewing farmers. The pairs are composed of one member each from the technical and socioeconomic groups. Pairs shift at the end of each interview period. Also, at the end of each interview period, the group gets together to share findings and begin to define the variables that need further research. On the fourth day, each team member is assigned a section of the report to write. Normally each author consults individually with other members of the team to check insights already derived. On the fifth day, while still devoting a half-day to writing a report, team members also return to farm sites to collect answers on data gaps. The sixth day is spent in final report writing with group discussions on every aspect. Conclusions and specific recommendations are closely scrutinized by everybody.

The final report is multidisciplinary, and all members are expected to understand all of its findings and recommendations, even those outside their own disciplines. Some of the standard sections of the report consist of outlining the purposes, providing descriptions of the research area, existing technologies, land tenure and labor systems, potential sources of capital investments, then descriptions of the most important components of crop systems, such as corn, beans, livestock, and vegetables, along with conclusions and recommendations. Most of the team will then be returning (or commuting) to the field to try to bring about improvements over the next year.

Some Cautions and Criteria for Effective RAPs

Researchers should be on guard against uncritical seduction by the logic of rapidity and focused research. As with any methodological approach, they have to be aware of potential shortcomings and make special efforts to compensate for them. A review by Harris et al. (1997) succinctly reminds us of four relevant criteria. They are accuracy, utility, feasibility, and propriety.

Accuracy in assessment requires as full a description of the problem, context, local circumstances, and relevant programs and services as possible, which is a very tall order. In attempts to examine replicable categories of information, consideration of some important topics such as political, economic, or even religious factors might not be properly anticipated and thus sloughed off in the service of brevity. Somehow, the normal anthropological anticipation of factors on the "margin" as being potentially very important has to be maintained.

Also relevant to accuracy, a consideration of validity is needed. Do the observations accurately measure reality as it is understood by all the participants—the researchers and the researched? Establishing this can be a major problem when the research is done cross-culturally and where meanings do not easily translate. Does the researcher understand the local meanings of concepts, categories, and behavior? Participants need to know that they are talking about the same thing in order to construct any measurements, observations, or statements that accurately reflect local realities.

The authors use an example from infant diarrhea studies. Although in some Third World regions various types of diarrhea are attributed to "hot" and "cold" imbalances of particular foods, other types are categorized with different etiologies such as the presence of parasites. Researchers need to be aware of such differences in definition, otherwise they may inappropriately lump or alternatively split categories in ignorance of local meaning. This may be crucial in seeking solutions to differently perceived kinds of diarrhea that threaten the lives of small children. With full-fledged ethnographic studies, researchers would be present in the field long enough to recognize and sort out such distinctions. But in a RAP, they could miss them entirely. As a precaution, the authors recommend that researchers use several, or even many, methods. For instance, they could use observation and focus groups to study the same issues, thus triangulating or confirming findings as well as their range of information.

Another dimension to accuracy is the question of whether the findings can be generalized beyond the specific community. The validity of any conclusions could (or perhaps should) be tested through limited key-informant interviews with nearby cultural groups or villages to determine if conclusions are valid for these groups as well. Reliability in the results can be thrown off by observer bias and in the selection of participants. Observer bias might be reduced by using multidisciplinary teams and carefully training field workers from the community. Here, the different perspectives would provide checks and balances against a single biased perspective. Also, there should be attempts to randomly select interview participants and communities as much as possible.

The second significant criterion is *utility:* the findings and recommendations should be useful to all those who have a stake in them. But, given the short time of study, key-informant interviews might not be held with all or even a significant representation of the relevant stakeholders—be they community members or program deliverers. The final results may not then be useful to all potential stakeholders. Furthermore, it is important that the findings be timely, well constructed, and informative to the issues at hand. For these expectations, make sure that the research team is composed of a well-thought-out variety of community representatives. This helps to establish the credibility of the project. Then the chances are higher that results will move toward gaining credibility among local people and be framed for eventual usefulness.

Providing the right mix of quantitative and qualitative results may be another important decision. Community members may prefer statements of a verbal or qualitative nature; decision makers may want "facts" bolstered by numbers. Also, as the authors suggest, perhaps RAPs are more effective when they are administered as part of ongoing change projects than if they are used simply as "fishing expeditions" to figure out what should be done in the first place. If something is already going on, then there would likely be some commitment to finding out what makes the program work or fail. Although I am sure that there are occasions when RAPs will be useful as background studies.

Feasibility refers to the principles that guide the decision to use RAPs: "Are they appropriate, affordable, politically viable, and easy to implement?" (Harris et al. 1997: 377). Among other things the procedures for RAPs are used when resources and opportunities call for them. If they are cheap, time is short, and people are willing to answer the questions, then they are feasible. Generally, that is when other methods, principally participant observation or complex surveys, are not possible because of limits on time, human resources, and money. When more ambitious projects are feasible, it might be important to slow down and use them instead.

Propriety is the final criterion to be considered in the choice of RAPs. Are the procedures ethical and fair to those involved? Can confidentiality be assured and can the rights of human subjects be ensured through formal and informal consent procedures? The criterion of propriety is, of course, essential in any project, rapid or not.

While paying attention to utility, feasibility, and propriety, the principal challenge for RAPs is to achieve accuracy and reliability of findings. There are significant challenges when there is so little time. Harris et al. (1997) suggest that these problems can be eased when the projects use multiple data-collection techniques, involve some team members who are indigenous to the culture, and use teams that are multidisciplinary in composition.

Improvisation on the Field Manual Approach

As seen, most examples of RAPs come from anthropologists working in international development settings. Common sense tells us that anthropologists operating in many domestic applied domains could redesign rapid research strategies on a variety of subjects. Whatever the topic, researchers would need to provide background on the communities under question, drawing upon existing statistical data, and an inventory of relevant institutions and services. Then they could focus on smaller units of study like households and generate statistics and descriptions of how the problem or behavioral phenomenon is expressed through the smaller units. Improvised rapid procedures and manuals could be developed for topics such as disabilities, child welfare, conflict mediation, community development in fisheries, forestry, agriculture, housing, education, political development, cultural heritage, and quite a few other issues.

Summary

Important focused and multisited investigations, like those described in this chapter, are rarely commissioned in either academic and applied anthropology. Common research problems and lines of questioning have largely been abandoned, and nowadays each scholar or practitioner has largely been on his or her own, pursuing minor and particular questions that are of interest only to himself, his thesis advisor, or a small cadre of colleagues. Rapid researchers like Beebe or Scrimshaw and Hurtado remind us of the desirability of following through consistently with common questions, using replicable methods, and dealing with urgent policy questions. Furthermore, we can expect that improvements in RAPs will be very influential in applied anthropology. Any aspiring applied anthropologist would benefit from following their development.

RECOMMEND READINGS

Beebe, James
1995   Basic Concepts and Techniques of Rapid Appraisal. *Human Organization,* Vol. 54: 42–51.

Chambers, Robert
1997   *Whose Reality Really Counts?: Putting the First Last.* London: Intermediate Technology Publications.

Harris, Kari Jo, Norge Jerome, and Stephen B. Fawcett
1997   Rapid Assessment Procedures: A Review and Critique. *Human Organization,* Vol. 56: 375–379.

Manderson, Lenore (ed.)
1996   Handbook and Manuals in Applied Research. Special Issue. *Practicing Anthropology,* Vol. 18(3): 3–40.

Scrimshaw, Susan, and Elena Hurtado
1987   *Rapid Assessment Procedures for Nutrition and Primary Health Care: Anthropological Approaches to Improving Programme Effectiveness.* Los Angeles: U.C.L.A. Latin American Center Publications.

van Willigen, John, and Timothy L. Finan (eds.)
1991   *Soundings: Rapid and Reliable Research Methods for Practicing Anthropologists.* NAPA Bulletin 10. Washington, DC: National Association for the Practice of Anthropology.

15 Participatory Action Research

This chapter explores a recent trend among some researchers to turn more of the actual process and ownership of research over to citizens' groups and local communities. They believe policy should be democratically shaped, based on local knowledge (see Grenier 1998).

There has been ever-increasing pressure on community-based, citizens' groups to plan policies. The situation can force those groups newly entering highly developed and competitive policy arenas to be more explicitly conscious of what they are trying to accomplish. Their purposes could include negotiating with governments, influencing public opinion, and improving their own activities, programs, and services. Such activity usually calls for some kind of research or information gathering.

Many types of people do not have much power or organizational capacity to improve their circumstances and have been largely excluded from policy-making. These include impoverished villagers in developing countries, slum dwellers, and countless other vulnerable groups and categories. In North America, marginalized ethnic groups, many women, impoverished youth, the elderly, the disabled, and those suffering from domestic violence or substance abuse have had little influence over programs intended to aid them. In recent years, however, self-help and advocacy groups have appeared with potentials for social and personal transformation. Others are on the verge of development. All of them seek to make their conditions better understood and addressed through public awareness and government action. They usually want more resources, especially through a revitalization of local culture and community so that they can engage much more directly in their own development.

Also, powerless or marginalized peoples frequently become angry when others define what their problems are. Even the research of sympathetic social scientists and people in the helping professions can be galling. Try as we might to avoid it, there is the very real possibility that social scientists can patronize or unconsciously cast their findings according to middle-class sensitivities or biases. Unfortunately then, conventional social science may be seen as part of the problem. Still, relatively powerless and impoverished groups often find it difficult to formulate their own goals and then get on with the job. For the disadvantaged, this requires a significant level of consciousness. The group needs a realistic hope that something can be accomplished, a hope that may be rarely experienced. Yet for some, the sheer experience of organizing action can be rewarding, no matter the outcome.

Such concerns contribute to a wave of interest in a style of enquiry known as participatory action research (PAR). Interest is growing in it, especially among people involved in more bottom-up policy-making, such as in community development, social work, public health, nursing, health promotion, education, feminist research, and with some practicing anthropologists. Such people also feel that the requirements of normal social science frequently fail the goals of social justice. They argue that "objectified" standards make it virtually impossible to accurately reflect the actual needs, desires, and aspirations of real people. Proponents of participatory research believe that the people most affected have the most say in how their own realities are analyzed and in the courses of action taken to improve their conditions. In fact, they advocate that the marginalized, impoverished, and exploited should be encouraged to do their own research and formulate their own policy. That means that participants should determine the actual questions for research, choose the methods and the sources of data, and ultimately have ownership over the information and how it is to be used. In the process itself, they will gain self-knowledge about their lives and relationships and discover strengths. This is essential for people who have been marginalized by society or within their own communities. In participatory action, people have an opportunity to "re-search" (or look into again) their lives to investigate the meanings of their own experiences and situations.

Furthermore, they typically engage in this investigation in groups of peers. They shed their isolation and marginality by getting to know what is shared with their fellows. The research process may provide a unique opportunity to form a solidarity, a collective identity, and even "community" with one another. While researching their conditions, they may spend long periods discussing and debating the courses of action that they should take. They should then be more capable of controlling their collective destiny. Research is frequently done with the assistance of professionally trained researchers as equals in consultancy or co-investigator roles. The aim, though, is to eventually dispense with such facilitators, so that the participants can continue on their own. Generally, the researchers have a very strong commitment to social justice and are more than willing to relinquish their influence.

One of the most important things to be remembered about participatory action is that it is a process that goes beyond a research agenda. For that reason, things may not always go as smoothly as expected by linearly focused researchers. The participants may make major mistakes, or they may not finish the project. They may go back and start all over again with a new set of objectives. They may not precisely fulfill expectations of validity, probability, and reliability. We need to remember that they are pursuing their own goals, which are more important than the research per se. They are entitled to learn from their mistakes as are the researchers involved in the enterprise.

From a number of sources, we can isolate some salient points of participatory research (Tandon 1988; Ryan and Robinson 1990, 1996). The community defines the problem and then analyzes and solves it. The people themselves own the information, analyze the results, and come to conclusions from the research. A radical transformation in the lives of the people involved is possible when there is a full and active participation. It is a process creating a greater awareness of community members' own resources. It is a scientific method of research that also represents a democratization of research. Outside researchers (or consultants) can also experience a set of changes within themselves. Finally, participatory action research is usually associated with advocacy—the results demand improvements in the conditions of the group and require communication to other levels and sources of power within the society).

Challenges of Participatory Action Research

Although participatory action research can be very fulfilling and interesting for potential researchers, they should be aware of the pitfalls and difficulties. For instance, a colleague worked for several years on a participatory action project with a group of Native women. The study focused on domestic abuse, an important but highly sensitive topic in their communities because it also touched on delicate topics like gender relations, the family, substance abuse, personal histories and pain, relationships with the larger society, anger, grief, and hopelessness. My colleague had an enormous amount of patience and very well-honed sensitivities regarding cross-cultural matters, was totally dedicated to social justice, and was nondirective in her approaches, all of this bolstered by many years of community development. In the process, she had been encouraged to use the work as thesis material for a doctorate. However, she was asked by the women to leave the project after two years, before she had finished her dissertation work. To her credit, she chose to interpret this setback as a sign of their independence, indicating that they no longer needed someone from the dominant society to help them. Fortunately, she was able to find a replacement topic, working in the same style and again with women on a health issue, and completed her doctorate.

Participatory action requires many qualities not as essential in other types of research. Patience is obviously the first virtue—patience to allow the group to determine its own direction and pace whether or not they are compatible with the researchers' timetable. It may be hard for the group to define itself, determine its directions, and then gain the confidence to proceed after deciding the important questions and procedures. Uncertainty may arise about a project getting started or ever finishing. There may be anxiety that the project might be terminated for reasons out of the researchers' control like funding cutbacks, or there may be problems of conflict or low morale among the participants.

The researchers themselves may have difficulty in gaining acceptance and properly defining their roles while trying to help and, at the same time, conscientiously avoiding being directive. A significant issue is always—how do the researchers and the community groups contact each other in the first place? Do the researchers make the offers, or do the community groups approach them? Do intermediaries make the suggestion, or does the partnership emerge out of an ongoing relationship or context? Then there are the technical aspects of any research. Does the group attempt to collect information that has the appearance of being "hard" or measurable, like statistics or its own census materials, and does it attempt random sampling? To what extent does it rely on standard social science methods in both qualitative and quantitative realms? To what extent should it improvise methods? How will it present the information? Will it attempt to duplicate some of the criteria for technical reports in the policy sciences? Will it use the media? Will it attempt hearings with politicians and other policy makers? Will it try styles of writing or communicating that retain its members' voices? These and many other types of considerations might make it quite challenging for social scientists, who usually like to have some control over the research process.

The main methodological choice in participatory action research is group discussion, including focus groups. Meetings should be less focused at the beginning so that people can find their bearings and explore the most significant questions rather than predetermining questions and launching into them right away. A group dynamic edging toward solidarity and consensus has to be shaped. Later in the research, it might even be feasible to use structured procedures like nominal groups. One of the most effective approaches is the key-informant interview. Here the participants could ask other members of their group for the information or opinions they need. It is possible, but probably unusual, for a group to use a questionnaire or even to collect its own census materials (see Flora et al. 1997). Such formal methods could be introduced but would depend on the will of the participants. They may be fundamentally suspicious of expert-driven, conventional methods. Ultimately, most people are likely to be comfortable with open-ended and relatively unfocused discussions. If social scientists are involved, they must be flexible, prepared to improvise, and not too quick to suggest the approaches. The researchers have to remember that it is the participants' project, and they are there only to give advice when asked.

Much of the interest in the field of participatory action research has stemmed from the inspiring work of the late Paulo Friere (1970, 1981), a Brazilian who worked for many years in adult education among Latin American peasants. Using group discussions and other means, unschooled, poor people came to discover and understand the historical and political roots of their current circumstances. They decided upon action to overcome their marginality and exploitation.

In anthropology itself, an even older tradition stems from the pioneering work of Sol Tax and his long-term action anthropology beginning with the Fox or Moquawkie Indians of Iowa in the 1940s. He and his graduate students worked with tribal members in defining their important issues and problems and seeking active ways to redress them (Tax 1958; Gearing 1960). Furthermore, these traditions within anthropology can be seen as extended through the work of contemporary anthropologists such as Barger and Reza (1989), Light and Kleiber (1981), O'Neil et al. (1993), Perez (1997), Ryan and Robinson (1990), Stull and Schensul (1987), and Warry (1990). General sociological works (Tandon and Fernandes 1984; Tandon 1988; Whyte 1991; Park et al. 1993), international development (Chambers 1997), and feminist approaches (Maguire 1987) should be consulted as well. Two case studies can illustrate some of the dynamics of this research style.

Case Study: Language and Heritage Research in the Northwest Territories

Joan Ryan and her colleague Michael Robinson at the Arctic Institute of North America (AINA) in Calgary, Alberta, have been working on a number of pioneering participatory projects (Ryan and Robinson 1996). The earliest was the Gwich'in Language and Cultural Project, located at Fort McPherson in the Northwest Territories. It began in the early 1980s when some community members tried to develop a language and cultural heritage project using oral history. A number of people referred AINA's staff to the Fort McPherson project.

Because community members and the local chief were interested in nurturing it, AINA arranged the legal and financial agreements for it in 1987. Its objectives were "to provide Native people with skills which allow them to recover local control of education to start on the road to full self-government" (Ryan and Robinson 1990: 61).

Two phases were established. The first, related to training, focused on local oral history collection by interviewing, videotaping, mapping, and collecting genealogies and stories about local heroes and heroines. These materials were intended for community archives. The second phase involved the preparation of the findings into units suitable for local schools. In keeping with the emphasis on education, literacy training in Gwich'in (a Dene language) and English was to be provided throughout the project.

Ryan, as the field researcher, shaped her contributions through commitments to principles of cultural relativism, the group dynamic approach to community development, and her feminist perspective. The sharing of power was acquired through consensus rather than by majority votes. In those processes, she and the other members of the project eventually developed a collective identity.

Only Ryan's feminist approach to dealing with conflict was new. Ryan sees the commitment to cultural relativity and democracy as directly compatible with Native, specifically Dene, ways of doing things. In the past, Dene groups have tended to avoid public discussions of conflict even when gossip recognized it. Shared access to power and the notion of equality have not been dimensions of recent Dene gender relations. These aspects of Ryan's approach were the most difficult to accomplish, along with one other—that of being able to make the Dene (both the researchers and the general community) comfortable with the notion that they were experts on their own culture. Unfortunately, Euro-Canadian domination had caused a collective sense of denigration. Ryan felt that the project achieved considerable progress on all these difficult fronts.

After funding was established and all of the major logistic arrangements made, a local advisory committee hired five people out of fourteen applicants. They were selected on the basis of reliability, commitment, and capacity to speak, read, and write Gwich'in. Later, several others were added to the staff from other funding. Most of the participant/trainees were women, widows with traditional skills whose children were grown. One man also had significant experiences of traditional land-based life-styles. One part of the early training was a ten-day trip in February to an isolated area as a refresher in bush life and survival skills. As with many mature people entering or reentering the workforce, there was an exhilaration about having jobs but also some anxieties about whether they would be able to complete the assigned tasks.

Based on their memories of authority from their school days, the staff initially expected that Ryan would direct them on what to do. Ryan refused to do this, requiring them to quickly become genuine partners. Similarly, it was also important for the participants to learn to approach each other for help if they were having difficulties with their own tasks. Conflict and differences, for example, gender tensions (two men out of eight), were resolved and dealt with in different ways, including the use of joking relationships. During the training period, there were attempts to make the project visible in the community through the use of a local radio program to periodically update the project's activities. They also suspended training when some important community event was going on—such as the visiting of dignitaries and speeches by chiefs. These events were photographed and videotaped by project members. The use of Gwich'in became more widespread as the training period advanced.

In keeping with the emphasis placed on consensus in the project, all decisions affecting the group were jointly taken—including the setting of pay, benefits, holidays, and participation in community events. One measure of success was that there was no absenteeism and no attrition of participants—a rarity for training projects.

After a year of training, including developing skills in interviewing, recording, photographing, videotaping, and working on English and Gwich'in literacy, the project members started to concentrate on the main tasks. Among other things, they started to transcribe and standardize the formats for stories already taperecorded during the previous project. They also did a pilot study for another regional organization, the Déné Cultural Institute, on the traditional use of plants and animals for healing. Its purpose was to develop methodologies culturally appropriate for use in other Déné communities. Traditional elders were approached to see if they would participate—all did—and an elders' committee was formed. A payment schedule was developed, and then the participants proceeded to interview the elders using an open-ended check-list approach. Up to three interviews were held with each individual. Elders started to meet as a group at the project offices, thus reducing their sense of isolation and working on consensus about their knowledge of plant and animal healing properties.

After the information was collated, it was tested at an elders' conference for the whole Mackenzie Delta region, thus confirming the knowledge base and the methodology. The year ended with another elders' workshop in the community itself. Elders discussed traditional ways of preparing hides and working with fish and meats, told stories, and a traditional feast was held.

The second full year of activity was directed toward arranging the materials into curriculum units for the schools. For this, literacy training was important. Ryan further trained the group in English literacy, and one of the participants did the same with written Gwich'in. Among other things, the literacy program involved determining ways of standardizing materials and preparing booklets on birds, fish, and animals. They also worked on a series of "how to" booklets on topics that had been developed at the various elders' workshops. Notably, they worked on a book commemorating an elder who had died that year. Incorporated in the book were six of his stories in Gwich'in and four in English. A Gwich'in alphabet and dictionary were constructed, and, in addition to the book, several other old-time stories were transcribed. Teaching guides were developed for all of these materials. In turn, with the cooperation of the teachers in grades two through six, they were all tested through the local school. As a complement to the stories, an art program was developed in which the children were asked to illustrate the final versions. Because the trainees were not teachers, it was hard for them to know which materials would be useful for classroom use, especially as complementing other projects like art or creative writing. In the future, closer liaisons with teachers or other curriculum designers would be recommended right from the start.

At the end of the three-year period, the project was externally judged to be successful. The local institution was then declared a regional learning and language center with a mandate to further develop such materials. All of the project participants went on to other types of education, related work, or continued with the same programs.

Ryan attributes the project's success to a number of factors. The following factors are worth reiterating as generalizations for the success of participatory projects.

1. The project was initiated and defined by the community, but it needed some external help in getting funds and some training to fulfill its intentions;
2. The community continued to support the project because it had defined its purposes and directions in the first place and continued to have control over it;
3. The group dynamics and feminist approach, Ryan claims, led to sharing of power and, overall, was compatible with Gwich'in cultural ways of doing things;
4. The project reinforced some traditional institutions such as the position of elders in the community as decision makers and enhanced local people's pride in their identity and culture;
5. Tribal and government levels of jurisdiction also supported the project.

Case Study: Work with a Blind and Visually Impaired Group on the Topic of Informational Needs

In 1991, members of a self-help and advocacy group approached me about advising them on a possible research project. The Visually Impaired People's Action Council (VIPAC) consisted of around thirty members devoted to improving the lives of people with impaired vision and blindness. Their primary goal was to enhance their independence in the community. They felt it essential that their abilities, rather than their handicaps, be recognized and that they obtain jobs, improve social standing, and many other normal things commensurate with their abilities. They also felt that all the established organizations that had taken on the role of representing their needs to society were too passive, paternalistic, or ineffectual.

Blind and visually impaired people frequently need translation services from printed to braille or to taped versions. For example, those attending university need to have practically all of their reading materials, term assignments, and examinations translated. They have to go through many bureaucratic stages—reminding the professor several weeks in advance, making sure that assignments are delivered to the office of the organization (found in a remote suburb) and finding sighted volunteers in their classes to taperecord important reading assignment materials. This can be very tedious and, sometimes, humiliating. Other visually impaired people need materials for skill upgrading or counseling in how to deal with visual problems. They also want to be informed about community events, employment opportunities, and training programs.

VIPAC members complained that the services of the principal organization ostensibly representing them were fundamentally inadequate or too slow to be of use. They thought that the organization's agenda was to create a dependence on its services, thus perpetuating itself. To them, it was a basic form of paternalism that actually perpetuated their dependency and marginality. Therefore, a significant part of their motivation was frustration with their lack of autonomy.

More general dissatisfactions were expressed by VIPAC. Realizing that they live in an "information age," they were extremely frustrated that they could gain so little access to the knowledge available in newspapers, magazines, books, and the Internet. Advanced technology using voice-assisted translation programs might encourage participation in jobs that were emerging in the postmodern information revolution. But to date, they had many complaints that libraries, newspapers, and other outlets to printed materials were operating at a snail's pace in providing them access to these sources of information. They believed society should eventually legally require that all commercial sources of information (e.g., book publishers, magazines, and newspapers) provide all items in alternative format and at equal cost.

In our research project, we constructed a profile of the participants. They tended to be younger visually impaired people who had been educated in integrated settings with "sighted" people. An overwhelming majority had completed high school, and almost half had gone to university, with one quarter having received degrees. About one third were totally blind, and the remainder claimed some degree of partial sightedness. For their information needs, most relied on spouses, relatives, friends, and the radio. Besides word of mouth, reading and writing were their important means of getting information. They mentioned several sources—large and regular print and audiocassettes were especially important. A surprising number made use of computers. Braille use was not as widespread as one might have thought.

About half indicated that they were usually unemployed, and only about one third had full-time employment. Some of the occupations included telephone operator, hospital lab technician, occupational counselor, university professor, music and piano teacher, and social worker. More than half reported earnings of less than $20,000 ($14,000 U.S.) which placed them in the Canadian low-income category. In contrast to their poverty, their education levels were quite high—probably higher than that of the general population.

A very high rate of unemployment and poverty suggests a large waste of talent and capabilities, a reality the participants felt very poignantly. They believed that the larger society underestimated their abilities and did not provide them with equal access to information needed to improve their situation. Working with these participants, I was, indeed, struck by the high levels of intelligence and motivation among them and could understand why they were frustrated and sometimes angry that both mainstream institutions and institutions for the visually impaired are unresponsive to their needs and abilities. Their poverty, dependence, and marginality were fundamentally defined by a lack of information—the essence of vision problems.

Their dilemma was that there were so many fronts to work on at once: schools, stores, hospitals, newspapers, transportation, and communications. What were their priorities and where should they start? Activists within VIPAC decided that they needed to consult with its members and people in similar situations to democratically establish the priorities in dealing with issues.

Several of the most active members of the organization met with me to discuss options of methodology for their project and to see if I would continue to act in an advisory capacity. They had recently received a small grant from a federal department that supported citizen initiatives for self-study and improvement. We discussed a number of research methods, and they decided that first there should be a community forum for their members and as many other blind and visually impaired people in the city as they could locate to discuss the project. About forty people attended. People discussed and often humorously described their information problems. The research agenda and methods were also approved at the meeting.

Focus groups and key-informant interviews were used to retrieve as full an inventory of felt needs as possible. A technique similar to Delphi or nominal groups was used to establish priorities. We discussed the questions that would be asked in interviews and focus groups. I favored a set of very general and open-ended questions that would allow all informants or focus-group participants to express themselves in their own ways and to initiate topics. The five VIPAC researchers instead wanted a more formal questionnaire that would elicit opinions on areas that they thought were the most important to the visually impaired. I felt we had to minimize the possibilities of researcher bias, and, by having visually impaired researchers predetermine the questions, we might be doing just that. After the debate, the research team decided on a relatively open format, one that would use probing questions to remind people of specific topics—community affairs, education, employment, health—that needed some explicit and direct opinions. We designed a participant profile, covering standard variables such as age, sex, level of education, employment, and income, but we also included data that are specific to the visually impaired. These included the degree and type of their impairment, what sorts of media they relied on to read or write, the timing of their impairment, whether they had received special education at a school for the blind, and so forth. These questions could only have been designed with the expert or "native" knowledge of the visually impaired research team.

On consecutive weeks, two focus groups were held. I asked general questions framed in our deliberations as well as the probes that the core group wanted me to use. Then we pretested the questions for the key-informant interviews. I interviewed each member of the research team, looking for any glitches or needs for clarification. My interviews also demonstrated interviewing procedures to the researchers. Because the researchers were blind and members of VIPAC, their opinions about needs were considered part of the final results. After all, they were looking into the nature of their own needs and advocacy goals. Forty-five people were interviewed.

Researchers then sifted though all of the materials that had been taperecorded and transcribed. Altogether, they extracted sixty-eight distinct informational needs, as well as twelve other needs, out of a total of over 500 mentioned during interviews and focus groups. They divided the informational needs into fourteen categories such as employment, education, health, and current events. The researchers did this all without my assistance. It was no easy task, because only a couple of them had even partial sight. They operated with the aid of very large print materials and tape recordings.

All of the participants were invited to engage in a priority-setting exercise to rank needs. I had explained to the research team the basics of nominal and Delphi groups for setting priorities, and the researchers came up with their own improvisations. Approximately twenty-five participants showed up for a meeting. The items from each of the fourteen categories were slowly read aloud; tapes recording their listings were made available; and they were transcribed in braille and large print. Within each category, the number of needs was quite manageable—about three to six. In each category, the participants were asked to vote for their top two needs, and the results for each category were determined, keeping the ultimate top two for everybody. Altogether, a total of thirty-two needs were retained, because there were a few ties in some categories. Another meeting was held a little later with most of the same participants, and at that meeting they voted on their top five priorities out of the remaining list. They were:

First: Integrated information about available employment through listings such as newspapers, Employment Canada, and workplace bulletin boards as well as more accessible job applications

tied with

First: Informational support services in the community to help visually impaired persons learn about their conditions, deal with daily barriers, meet others who have the same disability, and adjust to sight loss

Second: Information about barriers to various kinds of employment and ways of getting around those barriers in order to get those types of jobs.

Third: Access to all published material in mainstream and alternative media (current, noncondensed, and at the same price). This would include magazines, newspapers, and media listings as well as books

Fourth: Adequate, integrated counseling services for blind persons, their families, and friends

Fifth: Affordable access to technology

The two most active members of the research team wrote up the results in a report titled "Naming Our Information Needs." It was very succinctly written, consisting of an executive summary and thirty-four pages of text. It indicated the rationale for the study, the general position of visually impaired people in society, the role of VIPAC and its goals, and discussed all of the needs emerging from the study. I provided two appendices, one describing the methodology and the other summarizing the characteristics of the participants. Presumably my contributions, especially the explanations of the methodology, were meant to lend it some authority as a social science document.

Summary

Participatory action research is not likely to be a passing fad. Citizens and sectors of the public at various levels of organization will increasingly demand to participate in the policy decisions that directly affect them. On the optimistic side, there may be easier and more public access to information that people need for their own research, advocacy, and action through the "information highway." For instance, disability and patient-support groups are already organized through the Internet, and, through the same media, people can gain access to medical information that local doctors have not provided. Grassroots, self-help, and advocacy groups are emerging. In some cases, older organizations, including government bureaucracies and human service nongovernment organizations, can become more accountable to the clients they serve. They will feel more pressure to allow clients more say or more access to information in policy. Grassroots organizations will have to become more focused in their research for effective lobbying if their voices are to be heard in the media and public forums. This trend is a reaction to the ever-growing organizational powers of multinational corporations and international forms of government (common markets, etc.) as well as the significant powers of the state. Citizens will continue to feel the need to band together against the power of such corporatist entities.

Parallel changes are occurring in the relationships between researchers and the researched. We live in a world of increasing literacy and access to electronic media. As a result, researched populations are much more able to access what has been written about them. In the anthropological context, for instance, this has stimulated changes in relationships with North American Native peoples, who may often question our motives and findings in research. It has been quite some time since anthropologists have been able to do old-fashioned "lone-wolf" academic ethnography, unencumbered by obligations, criticisms, and possible hostile rejections of the people being studied. There are very strong pressures to be accountable to the communities being researched, to return something of value, and to allow research products to be scrutinized. There are more demands for collaboration with community interests in research. From the anthropological perspective, the logical extension is toward participatory action research in the comprehensive sense of the term.

As the case studies and the earlier discussions should have revealed, anthropologists have many assets to bring to this field. But, as a whole, the profession is going to have to make some adjustments. So far, those who have chosen this kind of work are rare. They may be motivated through personality and personal preference and by their capacities to develop effective relations with normally suspicious groups and their long-term adherence to certain ideologies of empowerment (such as feminism). So, although in many respects participatory action is a logical and natural extension of the anthropological perspective, not many anthropologists are doing it yet. There are also controversies about and objections to this style of research that are parallel to those discussed in the chapter on advocacy. We need to pay more attention to the lessons accumulated with experience in fine-tuning methodologies.

Participatory action research should become a fundamental part of any anthropology graduate student's education through seminars and practicum experience. We should allow participatory action research to qualify as a thesis project. The styles needed for participatory research sometimes run counter to much of the practice and "canons" of thesis work, which produce tidy and coherent problem statements, extensive and exhaustive literature reviews, elegant theoretical perspectives, and sophisticated methodologies. Such theses are expected to be presented in academic writing styles, avoiding empathy and first-person reflection. All evidence presented should anticipate harsh peer reviews according to the critical standards found in refereed journals. Finally, the author should take responsibility for all conclusions in preparing a thesis defense.

Such academic standards do not take into account what actually happens in participatory action research. Some compromise or accommodation is needed, or we are in danger of not being able to make meaningful contributions. Fields like health promotion, community development, social psychology, nursing, and so forth, could well supersede us in a domain that should naturally be ours. It is an area that provides for meaningful reciprocity in the relationships between anthropologists and communities and small groups. There is no obvious reason why anthropologists cannot contribute to their subject through the findings of participatory research.

The amount of work (paid or otherwise) for anthropologists participating in this kind of action research is unlimited. It can be used in so many different types of groups in both domestic and international contexts. People are being pressured, through some sort of orga-nizational format, to develop the equivalent of mission statements with long-term goals and objectives, identify priorities, and focus on the effectiveness of their own activities. Small, semi-organized self-help and advocacy groups are sometimes willingly, but more frequently, reluctantly forced into these activities for many reasons—not the least of which is funding. But they have to do all of this without the advantages of the full-time planning departments or experts found in municipal, provincial, state, and federal agencies or even in well-developed NGOs in the private sectors of human services. Anthropologists can be of major assistance to these less powerful and less well-organized groups. Beyond their direct hands-on collaborative roles in research, anthropologists might consider developing manuals out-lining procedures and methods for other people to use without direct assistance. Given our wide-ranging set of methods, we can indicate some of the flexibility and improvisations that people can use. Partnerships of participatory action are logical matches for anthropologists.

RECOMMENDED READINGS

Chambers, Robert
1997   *Whose Reality Really Counts?: Putting the First Last.* London: Intermediate Technology Publications.

Freire, Paulo
1970   *Pedagogy of the Oppressed.* New York: Seabury Press.
1981   *Education for Critical Consciousness.* New York: Continuum.

Grenier, Louise
1998   *Working with Indigenous Knowledge.* Ottawa: International Development Research Center.

Maguire, Patricia
1987   *Doing Participatory Research: A Feminist Approach.* Amherst, MA: The Center for International Education: University of Massachusetts.

Park, Peter, Mary Brydon-Miller, Budd Hall, and Ted Jackson (eds.)
1993   *Voices of Change: Participatory Research in the United States and Canada.* Toronto: Ontario Institute for Studies in Education Press.

Perez, Carlos
1997   *The Colors of Participation.* Special Issue of *Practicing Anthropology,* Vol. 19(3).

Ryan, Joan, and Michael Robinson
1990   Implementing Participatory Research in the Canadian North: A Case Study of the Gwich'in Language and Culture Project. *Culture,* Vol. 10: 57–73.
1996   Community Participatory Research: Two Views from Arctic Institute Practitioners. *Practicing Anthropology,* Vol. 18: 7–12.

Tandon, Rajesh
1988   Social Transformation and Participatory Research. *Convergence,* Vol. 21(2–3): 5–18.

Tandon, Rajesh, and Walter Fernandes
1984   *Participatory Evaluation: Theory and Practice.* New Delhi: Institute for Social Research.

Whyte, William F. (ed.)
1991   *Participatory Action Research.* Newbury Park, CA: Sage.

CHAPTER

16 Some Principles for More Effective Practice

This chapter and the next are interrelated: they examine the skills and principles of practice that applied anthropologists use to get jobs and to promote the use of their work. Yet, anybody who is familiar with the topics knows that there can be no "recipe" approach. This is partly because the issues and topics of practice are as wide or wider than anthropology itself. Furthermore, the settings are infinitely diverse—cross-cultural, urban, rural, developed, and underdeveloped—and constantly changing. Jobs can variously require one to be a consultant, researcher, evaluator, administrator, advocate, part-time academic, subordinate employee, freelancer, expert witness, trainer, community developer, program planner, or something else. Working conditions depend on whether one works with an unorganized category of people or within a formal organization, with all sorts of possibilities within those categories.

In fact, one criticism of applied anthropologists was that they were buried in hundreds of particular reports and made little attempt to generalize from the experiences. Enough time, studies, and experiences have accumulated to extract some principles for more effective practice (see Higgins and Parades 1999; Stull and Schensul 1987; van Willigen et al. 1989; Wulff and Fiske 1987a). A list of principles could include keeping a policy focus, consulting with stakeholders, maintaining flexible and effective communication, engaging in advocacy, constantly upgrading skills, exhibiting ethical practice, emphasizing team and multidisciplinary work, establishing networks, and submerging one's ego.

Keeping a Policy Focus

Reports commissioned by governments and other third parties that seek advice from anthropologists on human and social problems are frequently indistinguishable from academic monographs in format and content. After the identification of the policy problem or practical reason that initiated the study, the author launches into a standard holistic ethnography, telling everything that he or she thinks is relevant about the community. This could involve detailed descriptions of social organization and culture—ritual cycles, belief systems, descriptions of kinship networks, and countless other topics—without considering their direct and specific relationship to the policy questions being asked. This approach often blurs the basic intent of the research and loses readers who are looking for practical advice on particular topics.

For example, the original policy question may have been one of social impact assessment. What might be the effect of building a paved road for tourists and commercial uses through an Alaskan village that had previously only been accessible by bush plane once a week? Anthropologists may feel that it is important to tell all about the cultural history of the people, to provide exhaustive treatments of the basic institutional structure of the society, and describe recent trends in social and cultural change.

Instead what is needed is the identification of direct and measurable impacts upon specific domains of the people's lives. A road will probably noticeably affect the villagers' own mobility, inducing them to travel to outside centers for jobs, to visit relatives, and to purchase supplies. It would likely have impacts on local employment and subsistence. Many more outsiders are likely to come through the village and have direct effects on employment, public safety, housing, sociability, and many other areas.

In cases like this, there should be a clear outline of all the possible impact areas right at the beginning. Even when they have not been made explicit, the researcher should find out what the policy makers are interested in knowing. The policy framework of constraints and opportunities should be anticipated long in advance. Although subject to revision, research and recommendations flow from such steps, and the researcher must not be drawn into irrelevant academic sidetracks. Familiarity, through a preresearch study that gets to know the policy context, is essential because it is so important to isolate the policy context in advance so that findings and recommendations can be framed to match utilization needs. That brings us to the vital question of collaboration and consultation.

Consulting with Stakeholders

In any kind of application or practice, it is essential to identify all those individuals, categories of people, institutions, decision makers, and others who might have some stake in the recommendations, program designs, or services. As recommended elsewhere in this book, it is wise to do a kind of preliminary ethnography. At a minimum, that involves charting the players and social organizations in the project. What government or nongovernment agencies share responsibility for the domain in question? Within each of these, which branches and individuals are most directly responsible for shaping policy? Which ones are most responsible for delivering programs, and which serve as liaisons with outside agencies and politicians? Which people will be directly responsible for delivery of services or are in most intensive contact with the people affected? Within any of these organizations, there will be formal chains of command, but anthropologists can also identify important unofficial mechanisms for making decisions. Accordingly, they might be able to identify other individuals who know what is going on or can influence outcomes in subtle but essential ways. For example, anybody who really knows the way that university departments operate knows the crucial role played by the departmental secretary!

For example, in the immigrant resettlement field that I am most familiar with in Canada, various local or line offices of the Federal Department of Employment and Immigration, along with officials of Multiculturalism Canada, and provincial departments are responsible for social services pertinent to immigrant resettlement. Then there are all the NGOs associated with the field—local settlement agencies, various ethnic associations, immigrant women's groups, and multicultural associations at the local and provincial levels. I need to understand how all of these institutions operate locally, what their mandates are, what services and programs they offer, and where their responsibilities and interests overlap or compete. What sorts of opposition and jealousies might they have regarding each other? Are there any issues or events from the past that may make it difficult for agencies or individuals to cooperate? On the other hand, what sorts of things would make interaction more fluid and effective?

Whatever the issue or domain, a population is affected by any decision. Usually that population is not formally organized or has only remote affiliations to the interests of the stakeholders within formal organizations. Because of the way that power and decision-making structures have been set up, these populations may often have the least say in planning of outcomes that affect them the most. In the immigrant example, these may be newly arrived people from varied places such as Bosnia, Somalia, Vietnam, and Kampuchea. The agencies and bureaucracies may well have their own implicit agendas and biases as they try to serve their clients. Practitioners need a balanced perspective on both organizations and clients.

The anthropologist may also need to identify other individual stakeholders. They might be people who have been socially active in the field, whose opinions cannot be ignored, or whose influence or knowledge of the community and affected populations is enormous.

All these stakeholders should be involved in as many stages of the policy research and recommendation processes as feasible. As Schensul and Stull remind us, "any anthropologist seriously interested in influencing social change must work with nonresearch collaborators" (1987: 2). Social problems always need the intervention of nonresearchers directly involved in politics or policy-making, who can bring about policy changes, new legislation, or the reallocation of scarce resources.

As much as possible, the stakeholders should be involved in planning the research. They can assist or advise in framing research questions, the selection of methods and logistics, the discussions of preliminary findings, the framing of recommendations, the design of new policies and programs, and sometimes even the collection of data. On one level, it is obviously important that certain stakeholders, beyond the decision makers or power brokers or certain stakeholders, be consulted because project findings could affect their lives in very significant ways. To encourage potential use of the findings, the stakeholders should feel a sense of ownership of them. If people have committed their time and energy to collaborations or consultations, they will not want their effort to be wasted. They will be motivated to advocate the findings. Applied work requires allies and advocates. The scientific merits of the findings simply do not speak for themselves or inevitably lead to their acceptance.

So the key considerations are to determine which stakeholders should be included and at what levels and types of involvement. One way to manage this is to create a stakeholders' advisory committee (see Patton 1982). Its members could be consulted frequently and kept informed at all stages of the research process and policy planning. They should be made aware of preliminary results and recommendations. It would be logical to invite all the institutions concerned to make appointments to the advisory committee. The choices ought to be well balanced among the key decision makers and the front-line workers in the activities (e.g., health care) under question. In putting together such a committee, it may be necessary to make tough choices among some key stakeholders to avoid crippling conflict.

Finally, there are the unorganized publics, the people who may be affected the most by recommendations brought about through applied research—for example, immigrant youth in job-training programs, or people on an Indian reservation who are going to be affected by major shifts in responsibility for health care. How do they come to be represented on any such committees? Can they appoint themselves? Can we rely on front-line workers to make recommendations? Can we ask for volunteers? What if more volunteer than can be accommodated? It is a difficult matter of representation that may not always be resolved satisfactorily. Nonetheless, without some input from the intended beneficiaries, there will be an institutional or organizational bias to any results or recommendations.

Communicating Effectively

Communication is vital to effective practice. A great deal of flexibility in communication through different modalities is needed because the audiences and formats can vary so much. Although there are benefits to what we learn through our training in academic anthropology, some of it has to be unlearned.

Consider the average doctoral or master's thesis. In the standard format, the first section is a problem statement, frequently phrased in jargon or concepts inaccessible to the layperson. Usually a very extensive literature review follows to prove the author has a solid and authoritative grip on any literature that can be linked to the research problem at hand. The writer usually makes reference to all of the theoretical and field studies that are related to the writer's topic. Many of these citations are merely "courtesy" references, acknowledgements that work has been done in a related area, and are made simply because it is customary to do so. Actual descriptions of any of the cited work may consist of no more than a fragment of a sentence. Findings or generalizations from some other pieces of work might take several pages, especially if the author finds the work significant or a basis for argument. By the time we have finished reading this literature review, several scores of references may have been cited in what would appear to the uninitiated reader as a hodgepodge of fragmented and disconnected ideas.

The next stage identifies the research population. That involves historical backgrounds, descriptions of the setting, and many other characteristics relevant to the researched population. We then reach the rough midpoint, the body of the thesis that contains exhaustive treatment of any ethnographic, textual, or statistical information considered crucial to the thesis. This section usually runs several hundred pages. One only has to think of Malinowski's (1922) description of the Trobrianders' Kula Ring or Evans-Pritchard's (1940) discussions of Nuer lineage structure to recall thoroughness in academic standards of evidence. Despite their scientific value and use for further studies, it is often a struggle for the reader to see the relevance of such data. Then, the standard conclusions require careful reiteration of all previous points with suggestions for future research. Such academic styles of writing do have merits for instilling rigor, thoroughness, and other standards, yet they communicate poorly to nonanthropologists.

Applied writing for nonanthropological audiences must be approached differently. First, authors should provide their main conclusions at the beginning of the report. This has commonly been called an *executive summary*—a two- to four-page abstract of the purposes, principal findings, and recommended policy actions of the study. A well-crafted executive summary may be the most important section of any applied report. Its clarity and brevity constitute the "hook" that will convince the busy and skeptical policy maker that the report has something worthwhile to communicate about his or her area of responsibility. And it may even be the only part of the report that is read. Following this, there is usually a larger discussion of all the recommendations. It is possible, and perhaps logical, to consider making the recommendations a concluding chapter as long as there are very good connecting links throughout all parts of the report. But stating the recommendations first is effective because that is equivalent to the "bottom-line" in financial transactions. When stating the recommendations, it is effective to make them stand out typographically, so they will be noticed by the people who tend to scan reports rather than to read them in detail. You can use indents, boldface, and "bullets." A bullet consists of an asterisk or some similar symbol before an indented phrase or a succinct statement. The bullet or other attention-getting device may be followed by a short paragraph justifying or providing context for the statement or recommendation. Here is an example from one of my research projects.

■ **A need for government employment agencies to provide direct and accessible employment counseling to blind and visually impaired people.**

> Until recently, blind and visually impaired people have had to rely on the employment counseling services of organizations that specialize in services to the blind. Those organizations tend to advise visually impaired people to take very narrow occupational tracks, such as piano tuners or dark-room technicians, which have sometimes been set aside for them. Such organizations often receive any information about other jobs when it is too late to be useful for clients. Instead, visually impaired people who have many skills need direct and equal access to job information and counseling. They feel that current practices of ghettoizing employment services are counterproductive for them and society. Such an approach only contributes to their isolation, dependence, and poverty.

Either as the second or first chapter (depending on the recommendations placement), there should be a discussion of what the study is all about. Why was it commissioned in the first place and by whom? It might be a good idea to list all of the objectives in "bullet" form to draw the reader's eye. Also, it should be made clear precisely what the policy context is, so that it can be focused and maintained through succinct reiteration throughout the whole report. The reader needs to keep hold of the thread.

Somewhere (probably in an appendix), there should be a very brief account of the research process itself. Who were the researchers and what were their qualifications? When and where did they do their work? Explain what methods were used (but not in great detail) at this time. Perhaps it is useful to give a statement of the problem in anthropological or social science terms, but such a statement must be accessible to the layman. Avoid an expanded and footnoted discussion of anthropological theory or previous works unless it is directly pertinent to the topic. Keep discussions of methodology to a minimum. Put any extended discussions about the participants in the project in an appendix. Overall, any introductory chapter should be limited to a succinct ten pages or less.

The various parts of the research that can justify the conclusions and recommendations would then follow and might broadly resemble the middle parts of an academic report, thesis, or book although much shorter. An effective summary of the conditions and characteristics of the community as related directly to the research question is important. Statistical tables and graphs (and sometimes photographs) may be useful for this background as are historical profiles and a summary of relevant trends. Next, chapters that elaborate on the ethnographic dimensions and findings of the research are suitable as are detailed descriptions of the basic problems and issues under consideration.

For instance, the policy question might be how to manage an outbreak of tuberculosis in a Native community. A discussion of the disease in its cultural and historical context and in association with current social, economic, and health practices would be pertinent. Logically, a discussion on why existing services and programs do not provide effective solutions to recent outbreaks would come next. In constructing the evidence, a number of verbatim statements from the people most involved will be effective. This is usually the most salient contribution of the anthropologist. In addition to citing statements of opinion and fact by the people being researched, the writer would describe the behavioral components of the findings (e.g., use of water resources, diet, and public interaction). Any social, economic, and cultural constraints would be noted as well as opportunities for solutions. In any of these chapters, the central problems being researched should be consistently highlighted.

You should usually discuss the services and facilities of the policy-based institutions or organizations charged with dealing with the problems. In the example of resurgent tuberculosis in northern Native communities, you would discuss the existing health services, such as nursing stations, regional hospitals, medical evacuation services, inoculation programs, and so forth. A miniature ethnography of these settings might be useful in elaborating on any constraints or opportunities for dealing with the problem.

After the principal findings are documented, a set of conclusions are in order. Again, they must be directly related to the policy issues. These could be followed by a reiteration of the recommendations or an amplified discussion of them. Recommended courses of action should be specific, concrete, and within the realistic frameworks of policy mandates and fiscal possibilities. There should be as much detail as possible on specific courses of action—including the identification of substages and methods of evaluating the successes of each stage. Most reports should be 100 pages or less and organized for the reader's benefit and not for the author's or that of any presumed anthropological audience. Of course, the precise format will vary with the commissioned task at hand.

Other types of communication are employed in anthropological practice. Oral presentations are the most significant. Peggy Martin McGuire (1996) tells us of being faced with very different settings and audiences when giving short speeches to explain very complicated and controversial policy initiatives that related to First Nations (tribal) treaty entitlements in Saskatchewan. She spoke to tribal councils, at community meetings on reserves, to service clubs, and at emotionally charged public meetings in small Saskatchewan towns in which citizens felt threatened by possible losses of land and tax bases to Indian reserves. In each situation, she had to maintain a sense of humor, make the presentation understandable and interesting, and deal with projected anger while carefully not saying things that are unsupported by official policy and adroitly answering delicate questions.

Practicing anthropologists are often expected to provide oral presentations of proposed research, preliminary findings, results, and recommendations at various venues and at frequent intervals to stakeholders. In fact, most of the important decisions are made as a result of these meetings rather than because of written reports. The practitioner should be able to develop entertaining yet informative and nonpedantic oral presentations. These can make good use of graphs, slides, cartoons, and humorous anecdotes. One-on-one meetings with influential people are also often crucial in getting recommendations and findings accepted and put into policy practice.

Another critical communication skill (overlapping with advocacy) is the ability to deal with newspaper, radio, and television journalists to effectively reach the public (see McCracken 1988; Jordan et al. 1992; Hess Jr. 1992). You must master the fifteen-second clip for television interviews and be able to understand the needs of the working press. Practicing anthropologists would be well advised to develop good personal contacts with members of the media who can help the practitioner to get a compelling message about the research out to the public. This may be particularly important if there is reluctance or "foot-dragging" on the part of the policy makers.

Finally, with regard to communication, competence (or even a high level of expertise) in one or several foreign languages may be essential to the domain of practice, depending upon the linguistic or ethnic groups being worked with.

Advocacy

The earlier chapter on advocacy described the many different meanings and settings for anthropological advocacy. For example, anthropologists working through human services agencies can advocate for their individual clients by finding solutions and referrals to improve their lives. They can advocate in a more direct form through the courts as an expert witness in a land-claims case. They can advocate in support of a cause through the media and op-ed columns of newspapers. Advocacy has spin-off benefits because the act itself displays the unique values of anthropological knowledge and perspective. Furthermore, engagement in advocacy helps us to hone our capacities to communicate to publics other than fellow anthropologists.

It is important for the anthropologist to be able to persuade the right people and right groupings to accept the findings or recommendations. Putting forward the right arguments in a mode tailored to each audience is critical. The vital information must be distributed through all the important channels and points of decision-making. Are the rationales for support financial (i.e., the program would not cost too much or mean a new outlay of money)? Could the argument be normative (the agency or policy makers would gain in public good will, and it is the right thing to do to because of past injustices)? Could the proposal be supported because there is a widespread public support for the proposals and therefore is not a source of controversy? These are examples of some of the types of advocacy or persuasion that can be mustered to fit pressure points and the issues at hand.

Maintaining a Wide Range of Skills and Upgrading Them

The core skills for practicing anthropologists have been discussed in this book, but it behooves the practitioner to keep in touch with any new ones that arise. The art of proposal writing will be exceptionally important, because grant proposals are not just for research but also for financial support from governments and foundations to develop or maintain programs. Another vital skill is the capacity to retrieve large amounts of information. For this reason, keeping up with computer software and the Internet will continue to be valuable assets. One of our former students, who works full-time with a research commission on health utilization, has been able to turn her knack for quickly understanding new computer programs into a major asset.

It is likely that practitioners will have to change jobs or tasks many times in their careers. The more skills they accumulate, the better. Bookkeeping, conflict mediation, group facilitation, workshop training, cross-cultural sensitivity, knowledge of personnel relations, budgeting, long-range planning, the capacity to develop mission statements, community development, and a host of other practical skills will make the practitioner more employable. Because many organizations are too small to hire a number of specialists, the practitioner who can do several or many things will be all the more valuable. Tied to this is a growing recognition of the desirability of generalists who can make connections by drawing upon a wide range of skills. There seems to be a trend away from over-reliance on specialists. Also, practitioners in consulting businesses are themselves more marketable if they possess a wide range of skills.

Maintaining Professionalism and a Sense of Social Responsibility in Ethical Practice

Practicing anthropology and its academic applications still do not have high visibility or recognition in society. Establishing places for practicing anthropologists requires persistent effort. Fortunately, especially in the United States, people are carving out niches for anthropological practice in different settings. In many cases they have to temporarily submerge their anthropological identities in the tasks at hand. As time goes on, policy makers and the consumers of their research and practice gradually become more aware of the special contributions of anthropology to their fields.

Beyond its intrinsic value, consistent ethical practice reinforces our collective stake in the nonacademic practice of anthropology. We need to use all of our methodological skills and conceptual tools effectively and competently in the service of clients in both public and private sectors. We owe them the very best of our scientific and writing skills. Tied to this is the absolute necessity of understanding the societal and policy contexts of our research, advocacy, program design, and practice. We cannot engage in it through the perspectives of academia, simply because such viewpoints are not shared by people that we must work with. We are socially obligated to make our findings accessible when we are engaged in practice. So we need the combination of professionalism in practice as engaged in a context of social responsibility.

We must pay attention to a series of standard ethical considerations. Should we take the job in the first place? Should we work for military intelligence? Should we work as market researchers for corporations selling things that people really do not need or that might actually be harmful for them? Should we market something that might even seem benign or useful such as a health promotion strategy or extended schooling if it is incompatible with local ideas? People can give powerful reasons against these situations, but the decision is always an individual matter.

Once the practicing anthropologist has agreed to do the work, then he or she should fulfill all obligations to the clients. It is important to write clear contracts that cover all ethical contingencies. There are questions of informed consent, accountability, and choice of research procedures. The anthropologist should carefully consider the priorities in his or her responsibilities. Applied anthropologists need to maintain a sharp focus of professionalism in all aspects of practice devoted to the clients and communities that they work for.

Emphases on Team and Multidisciplinary Work, Establishing Networks, and Submerging Egos

As in any setting in life, practitioners may occasionally end up in contentious situations, competing for contracts, entering into personality and factional conflicts, and so forth. Yet, practicing anthropologists have an added responsibility to submerge their egos and become congenial team players. Collaboration in all aspects of research, program design, and administration are much more characteristic of applied than academic anthropology. Reports will normally have multiple authors or be anonymous and attributed to the unit or consulting company as a whole. Although acknowledgments may mention who did particular tasks, responsibilities and credits for decisions tend to be jointly taken. Submerging the ego means openness to the possibilities of collaboration and participation. Invariably, it also means willingness to take on tasks that have been defined by others rather than chosen by the practitioner because they appeal to him.

Practicing anthropologists need a talent for building networks. Although they tend to be jacks-of-all-trades in their research and implementation skills, they cannot do everything. But they should know who to consult after having built good working relationships with other specialists. Besides collaborating with coworkers and stakeholders from the client community or organization, practicing anthropologists frequently work with technical experts. Engineers, biologists, agronomists, foresters, health professionals, economic developers, community developers, technicians, and a whole variety of others may be involved. Being on good terms with skilled or influential people helps when an expert is needed on a short-term basis. An anthropologist who has been working for a long time in a particular field acquires allies and potential collaborators. All sorts of agencies in the public and nongovernment sectors compete for scarce resources, and it is necessary to build alliances to get what is needed or to come to some collaborative solution or compromise regarding cost-sharing, research, or program development. Networks, found locally, regionally, and nationally, can bear unexpected fruit over a long period of time.

Summary

Our major aim should be, as Linda Whiteford (1987) suggests, to "stay out of the bottom drawer," to make sure that our findings and recommendations are actually used. To achieve this, she suggests paying attention to six concepts. *Relevance* refers to the formulation of research issues that correspond to the user's concerns. This includes translating the content and styles of research into forms that can be understood. *Credibility* requires the researcher to adopt units of measurements and standards of validity and reliability acceptable to all parties. Early sharing of opinions on categories and means of measurement is essential to collaboration. This would discourage the researcher from examining populations and issues that are not directly relevant to the implementation needs of the commissioning group. *Process* involves seeking ways to make sure that the results are communicated in ways appropriate to all parties. *Accessibility* means ensuring a clear understanding of who the results are intended for, which people are important to reach, and what the best channels for that are. A *recognition of constraints* is always necessary, so that recommendations fit realistic possibilities for implementation according to the mandate and resources of the commissioning organization. Some changes can be made, some cannot. *Perspective* alerts the applied researcher to consider information, dimensions, and causal influences that may go beyond the immediate short-term planning of a commissioned project. It involves specifying other things that might have to be dealt with eventually and that are beyond short-run constraints. For instance, consider human service realms, such as substance abuse, child welfare, and spousal abuse. There may be ways of improving programs and services, but there may also be a need to deal with larger issues like unemployment, poverty, and racism that may underlie the undesirable behaviors and conditions. Yet, inattention to specific, short-term constraints and opportunities will reduce the value of anthropological insight in applied contexts.

RECOMMENDED READINGS

Higgins, Patricia J., and J. Anthony Parades (eds.)
1999   *Classics of Practicing Anthropology: 1978–1998.* Oklahoma City: Society for Applied Anthropology.

Scheinfeld, Daniel R. (ed.)
1987   *Utilizing Applied Research.* Special Issue, *Practicing Anthropology,* Vol. 9(1): 4–14.

Stull, Donald D., and Jean J. Schensul
1987   *Collaborative Research and Social Change: Applied Anthropology in Action.* Boulder, CO: Westview.

Van Willigen, John, Barbara Ryklo-Bauer, and Ann McElroy
1989   *Making Our Research Useful: Case Studies in the Utilization of Anthropological Knowledge.* Boulder, CO: Westview.

Wulff, Robert M., and Shirley J. Fiske
1987   *Anthropological Praxis: Translating Knowledge into Action.* Boulder, CO: Westview.

CHAPTER
17

Becoming a Professional

This chapter surveys skills and aptitudes required for practice as well as some ways that people might equip themselves for employment. The following list might seem intimidating, because no one person can muster them all. Yet, anthropology students will find that they already have some of these skills, and most of the rest can be mastered through persistence, training, and work experience. Similarly, most jobs now demand that we regularly upgrade our skills and sometimes even our attitudes.

Skills and Aptitudes for Practice

Flexibility, Adaptability, and Coping Skills for the Workplace

A practicing anthropologist has to be flexible and adaptable. Traditionally, anthropologists have lived in settings in which local values and customs differ from those at home. To be rigid or unchangeable would be counterproductive for any anthropologist. He or she often meets unfamiliar expectations when working with clients, coworkers, hosts, or bosses. These may include gender expectations, ways of making decisions, ways of sharing or excluding influence, ways of taking credit for solutions, and many other things. Clearly, the only way to thrive is through tolerance, flexibility, and adaptability as well as maintaining perspective on difficulties, issues, and circumstances.

Anthropology students are attracted to the subject because they already have some of these qualities. The exceptionally wide scope of anthropology's subject matter and its flexibility of theory and methods also attract students because anthropology can be applied to gain a significant understanding of just about any problem or issue that faces human beings. As students progress through the study of anthropology, they usually extend that flexibility and adaptability. A fieldwork setting fosters these qualities. Those who end up in the practicing field tend to have their adaptability stretched even further through their variable work experience.

Practitioners may sometimes have to work in isolated situations far from normal amenities and their families or to commute long distances. They may have to be discrete around stressful situations of conflict and factionalism among colleagues in their workplaces. A good sense of humor, stamina, and patience are assets. In practicing situations, anthropologists may be ethnically or racially different from their workmates or bosses as well as the population being served or studied. If, by background, they represent a dominant, perhaps even colonialist, society, they may find themselves under suspicion and only reluc-tantly accepted. Patience and a "thick skin" are important, because people may have reasons (at least in the short run) to resent their presence. The tensions may be based on a long his-tory of oppression by dominant societies or on past memories of financial gains made by "instant" researchers or consultants. There may be a phase of "testing," a kind of rite of pas-sage. But after the period of discomfort passes, it is usually followed by many compensating factors of adventure, memorable human contacts, and the potential to become involved in something worth doing.

Social Skills, Resourcefulness, and Knowing One's Biases

In the applied fields, it is important to exercise good social skills, balanced with initiative and resourcefulness. The practitioner needs to be well organized and demonstrate assertiveness when appropriate. However, excessive aggressiveness and the appearance of presumption will be counterproductive. Fellow workers may not always appreciate these behavioral styles. Sensitivity and analytical abilities are required to sense the right time to contribute ideas or to act upon them and to learn the appropriate ways of doing things.

Accordingly, it is essential to understand how our own preferences and values have been socially constructed through family and other experiences. We need to stretch our flex-ibility and adaptability; they are checks on the all-too-frequent tendency to project policy solutions to match our own values or expectations. For instance, people with middle-class backgrounds may have unrealistic expectations of planning or time allocation that might be inappropriate in other people's lives.

The Capacity for "Lateral" or Innovative Thinking

Practicing anthropologists, like their academic colleagues, need an aptitude for lateral or "loose thinking" at least initially. Cognitively, that refers to the capacity to see unexpected connections—to disassemble various assumptions and ways of doing things and to recon-nect them to provide unexpected understandings or solutions. Anthropologists look for connections among seemingly diverse areas like religion, economic exchange, family, sub-sistence, art, politics, and other aspects that other people have not been able to notice. This capacity to disassemble yet maintain multiple associations may lead to innovative solutions in policies and programs. For example, because of the anthropologists' knowledge of the family unit and values, they might find a way of linking some desirable agricultural practice or marketing objective to aspirations of the farmer or to dimensions of the family farm's developmental cycle.

Focus on Social Justice and a Commitment to Public Service

At least in theory, anthropologists are devoted to social justice and the liberation of people through self-determination. For those who do applied anthropology, commitment to better-ing peoples' lives seems to be an essential prerequisite. Intellectual curiosity or a detached orientation to serving the market as a "hired gun" does not suffice. More has to be behind the quest. The intensity of the commitment to social justice, nonetheless, could cover a variety of political opinions.

Similarly, practicing or applied anthropologists must be committed to public service, which will involve some degree of self-sacrifice from time to time. Many of them, at the beginning, might be working for struggling human service nonprofit organizations with no core funding, small salaries, few or no fringe benefits, and little opportunity for professional development. They may have to put up with some uncertainty and changing career tracks a number of times, but the personal rewards of working with people, being in helping professions, and sometimes working in exotic settings may far outweigh any initial material benefits. And as with many professions these days, it takes longer to become established than in the past. Yet tenacity can lead to rewarding careers. The practitioners I know really like the work that they do and find sufficient financial rewards eventually. Besides, the earlier difficult front-line work experiences are usually carried out with the enthusiasm of youth, and they often serve as valuable experiences to draw from in later administrative positions. Senior practitioners often look back with nostalgia to these formative experiences.

Anthropology students usually have humanistic values and wish to contribute to the betterment of society. Undergraduates, who are not sure whether they are really interested in public service, may explore volunteer work in a human service organization in their community. They could choose to work with organizations like Big Brothers or Big Sisters, organizations for the disabled, or an immigrant resettlement agency. They can acquire skills and experiences in the process and develop some meaningful items for résumés. In some cases, the volunteer work may actually lead to a permanent job. Similarly, public service through organizations like the Peace Corps has also brought many people to anthropology.

Communication, Interpretation, Mediation, and Being a Broker

As elaborated in the last chapter, communication is an essential skill. Communication leads to another dimension of the potential role of interpreter or cultural broker among positions and interests that are in potential conflict. Consider a typical situation in both the United States and Canada involving Indian or Inuit people, government bureaucrats, lawyers, developers, and environmentalists in disputes over land use and occupancy. Deep-seated conflicts are often based on lack of cultural understanding. Other peoples' positions in negotiations may be misunderstood, and their opinions may come from hidden and poorly understood culturally held values or sentiments.

Contractually, and through other moral considerations, anthropologists will be expected to work for the interests of the client. But this does not preclude analyzing the values and assumptions of those in opposition and explaining them to clients. It is always better to understand the assumptions of both adversaries and allies. Because anthropologists are sometimes members of the larger, more dominant society, they can explain some assumptions of their own clients to the more powerful parties. A former student, now permanently working for a tribal government, has traveled to Ottawa to explain, in a precise and linear style, the positions of his Native employers to federal bureaucrats. Of course, when anthropologists play such roles, they have to be careful not to be too presumptuous or too independent in speaking about the positions of others. They should be very familiar with the hopes and desires of the client population and have any explanations preapproved. Spokespersons from such groups can often communicate quite well, or better, about their own positions. As Chambers (1985: 26–33) outlines the role, it can take on several facets—representing positions, facilitating exchanges of information, acting as informants or analysts about a situation, and actually mediating a solution.

Knowledge of Organizations and Influence in Complex Societies

Applied anthropologists should know how modern organizations work (see Britan and Cohen 1980; Jordan 1994; Sachs 1989; Schwartzman 1993; Wolfe 1977). In fact, they should consider taking courses in sociology or psychology on organizational theory as well as examining the growing literature in anthropology. Similarly, they should have a good understanding of how complex societies operate. Although anthropology is rapidly changing, the public has tended to see it as the study of quirky, arcane, and archaic subjects among simple non-European societies. There are no simple societies anywhere, anymore.

Beyond this, an understanding of social networks and different links to power and influence is important, in itself, for explaining a current impasse in promoting changes, but it is also important to know who needs to be influenced. Knowing organizations, their values, cultures, and mandates is as important as knowing individuals within organizations and their responsibilities, influence, and roles in making decisions. Ethnographic savvy would be helpful here; each organizational circumstance will differ formally and informally.

Firm and Varied Foundation in Methodological Skills

A practicing anthropologist needs a very firm foundation in and continuous upgrading of methodological skills. These would be skills traditional to anthropology like participant observation and key-informant interviewing as well as supplementary ones such as archival and textual analysis. Newer qualitative interviewing techniques such as focus, nominal, and Delphi groups are of great benefit to anthropologists, who definitely should become well versed in the new styles of collaborative and participatory-action research. An understanding of rapid assessment techniques is becoming more and more important. Knowledge of policy analysis is a must, as is a basic grounding in needs and social impact assessment and program evaluation. Anthropologists have participated effectively in all three of these areas. Courses in political science or public administration can ground the student in policy research.

It is clearly important to pay attention to quantitative skills. Basic statistical, demographic, and social indicator analyses give the users of the research confidence that the findings are well measured, reliable, and valid. Elementary, intermediate, and advanced statistics should be considered by students of anthropology.

Broad Theoretical Foundations in the Social Sciences

There has been a tendency in academic anthropology to emphasize theory, and some interesting and perceptive theories have been developed. From an applied perspective, some are more useful than others. Theoretical orientations chosen for application will depend on the topic: substantive economics or political economic perspectives match development issues; theories from psychological anthropology related to enculturation can elucidate inquiries about education; formulations about ethnomedical systems might highlight practical research into health-seeking behavior.

Any kind of applied enterprise ultimately rests on some kind of theory even if only implicitly. Even the choice of methods in a project needs some sort of theoretical justification. Any data and recommendations are presented with some underlying assumptions in their choice. It would be better to be more explicit in shaping these theories, at least for ourselves and colleagues if not necessarily always for clients. We need to know what works beyond the specific case. For those reasons more theory is needed in applied anthropology, and being a student of academic theory does help to hone that theoretical capacity.

To some extent, and to varying degrees, the relation between theory and practice is still not very direct. Anthropological theories sometimes provide perceptive background explanations for peoples' motivations, aptitudes, and behavior. More often than not, they help us to understand why people will not participate in a program rather than why they might. Yet much more needs to be done in the practical development of workable theories in applied anthropology. We may be entering a new phase of anthropology that will pay more attention to issues of practicality at the very beginning of the development of any new theories or the reformulation of older ones.

After getting a solid foundation in anthropological theory, students should become exposed to theories from other social sciences such as sociology, public health, social psychology, and so forth. Theories that can aid practice are especially important; social marketing, for instance, assists in designing social programs to meet beneficiaries' needs and perceptions (see Andreason 1995; Brown 1997). Flexibility and eclecticism in the choice and synthesis of theoretical orientations are highly recommended because explanations should closely match pragmatic needs. The effective analogy is the carpenter's tool box: methods and theories are chosen to fit the task at hand.

Specialization in Regions or Cultural Areas

Like many academic anthropologists, practicing anthropologists are likely to specialize in a culture area or a particular ethnic group. Many applied anthropologists in the United States and Canada work in practical and policy research and consulting with Native peoples such as Inuit or Indians in regions such as the Southwest, Plains, Northwest, and so forth. Some in the multicultural and immigration fields may specialize in knowledge and public policy associated with immigrants originating from particular areas of the world. More Native North Americans and members of other ethnic groups are becoming anthropologists themselves, thus contributing to a generic "native" anthropology. "Native" anthropologist or not, the regional specialist becomes knowledgeable about the prehistory, history, languages, customs, values, conflicts, aspirations, needs, and public policy issues that are important for their area or group of people.

Anthropologists are frequently called upon to provide some information about customs among a cultural group. A typical situation regarding North American Indian peoples is for an anthropologist to be called to court to testify on traditional justice, customary land uses and occupancy, or how the group defines its own membership. Many anthropologists often start their applied careers this way as graduate students working on their theses or established academics who are called upon to provide expert testimony about people whom they have researched.

Developing Technical Knowledge in a Second Domain

A potential practicing anthropologist needs some relatively intensive knowledge about a second domain. This could be in some cognate field like the social science of medicine or public health, agronomy, agricultural economics, architecture, housing, forestry, fisheries, commerce, communications, technology, social work, developmental psychology, gerontology, or whatever domain will support a person's specialty. Many people combine their anthropological expertise with knowledge from the other field to create a new and demonstrably useful niche (e.g., the cultural dimensions of marketing). Through their methods and perspectives, anthropologists usually bring fresh insights, especially cultural ones, on the behaviors and topics in question. The success of medical and business anthropologies is a good example. Some people take second degrees in fields such as public health, nursing, commerce, and business administration. A surprising number of people from commerce, nursing, community development, teaching, or medicine are returning to college for degrees in anthropology because they know that anthropology provides a set of perspectives that is indispensable to their field.

The knowledge of the other field may be gained through intensive reading, but the prospective student should consider course work in the second field. One can also take an ethnographic approach. The anthropologist comes to know the other field (such as health or education) through participant observation, by collaboratively working with people, by attending seminars, writing for the other profession's journals, and being involved in public policy discussions. Overall, it is important to understand the language, culture, and approaches taken in sister applied fields.

Although expertise in one domain is a good idea, it is possible to branch out into second or third domains later. The skills, perspectives, and methods of applied anthropology are transferrable to business, development, health, and so forth. As argued elsewhere (Ervin 1996a), it may even be possible to play "rover-like" generalist roles, helping to link one policy domain to others (e.g., health, economy, and community development).

Becoming a Generalized Applied Social Scientist with a Focus on Policy

In many respects, practicing anthropologists or university-based applied anthropologists should consider themselves general applied policy scientists. A colleague with whom I first worked almost thirty years ago in the north came out of the discipline of human geography but has spent most of his time doing consulting and advocacy research on resource-based issues on behalf of tribal governments. He tells me that he no longer sees himself as a human geographer but as a "generic" social scientist. He blends anthropological, sociological, economic, historical, and demographic perspectives in his work. We must remember that in the work situation most people will not care whether a person is an anthropologist. It is what she can *do* that is at issue. For this reason, it behooves the aspiring practicing anthropologist to gain a broad training in the social sciences, especially in practical methodological skills, perspectives on public policy, and some theories or developed domains of analysis derived from other social science disciplines. It is what a person can accomplish, more than the profession that he or she identifies with, that is the most relevant.

Creating New Niches

Practicing anthropologists have to be adaptable and flexible in their areas of knowledge and culture. Broadly speaking, they know anthropology, the rapidly advancing field of applied anthropology, general social science, and quantitative and qualitative policy-related methodology. They know some other field of analysis connected with human service delivery and know the details and scope of the field of action itself in terms of bureaucracies, stakeholders, and their assumptions. They know a great deal about the people who may be subjects of the practice and policy domain. For all of this intricate and flexible knowledge, there is usually no established road map. Most practitioners have the responsibility of developing it on their own. They need to learn a lot about these other groupings and societies, but the other parties have no obligation to learn about anthropology or the assumptions of anthropologists. This can be very frustrating in the setting of practice. However, this is often where the real advantage for the anthropologist lies, in that she or he can develop strategic knowledge that, given at least intuitive anthropological analysis, can lead to interpreting and mediating knowledge among the other various stakeholders. It leads to special niches that anthropologists can form for themselves.

Some Basic Steps Toward Getting a Job

After a broad undergraduate exposure, you will probably want to choose your specialties and interests within anthropology. For example, these interests could include economic and social development, business, conflict resolution, education, the environment, health, and urban issues. It might also be appropriate to fine tune these interests into more specific areas of research and practice that have potentially long-lasting practical appeal beyond anthropology. Some current examples include drug use, sexually transmitted diseases, housing, environmental preservation, aging, women's health, multiculturalism, and immigration. For these choices, diligent background research, through what John van Willigen (1993: 13–14) has called "pathfinders," is advisable. Among other things, pathfinders involve researching the main issues and dimensions of the area, interviewing people who have direct experience with the practice, and searching out the main journals, books, and professional associations dealing with it.

The pathfinder should lead to some conclusions about the need for further training and skill upgrading. For instance, someone who wishes to work in the international development field might first serve a stint in the Peace Corps or Canadian University Students Overseas (CUSO) or work with nongovernment organizations in which the pay is low but the experience is highly valuable. There are probably local opportunities for such experiences in practice; check with your university's student advising facilities. In these early decisions, it makes sense to seek out mentors, such as academic advisors familiar with applied anthropology and the options available and people already practicing in the chosen field who can serve as sounding boards or give specific advice.

For those who have chosen applied anthropology as a career, a graduate degree is probably essential. A very good argument can be made for master's-level training as the basis for practitioners' credentials: the master's is a flexible degree for seeking employment, and you can gain more experience and qualification through research and formal training. A number of master's programs are explicitly designed for people who plan to become practitioners rather than academic anthropologists. More specialized training in applied anthropology, as outlined in this book, could be achieved along with some strategic training in a secondary field (e.g., public health, urban planning). A thesis project of studying local practices and beliefs surrounding intravenous drug use would demonstrate to future employers your qualifications in that domain and your capacity to do socially relevant research that generates policy recommendations.

An internship experience or its equivalent is essential to any applied master's-level training. Internships involve a collaborative arrangement with an institution, such as a human service delivery agency, to do practical work for them using social science skills. This service is almost mandatory because it provides an exposure to nonacademic practice that cannot be provided through reading and classroom experience (see Kushner and Wolfe 1993; Wolfe et al. 1981). Internships involve direct exposure to real policy contexts of administration, planning, delivery, and implementation of programs and services. They normally involve a contract and joint supervision from an academic advisor and a representative of the organization. They frequently (although not always) involve some form of remuneration. In many cases, internships incorporate agency reports as well as a master's thesis.

The student can choose a master's program based on an expertise in a chosen area (e.g., medical, business, or urban anthropology, the anthropology of development) or a specialization in applied anthropology and its practitioners' training program (see Hyland and Kirkpatrick 1989; Trotter 1988, the Applied Anthropology Computer Network (ANTHAP), http://www.acs.oakland.edu/~dow/anthap.htm, or the American Anthropological Association's *A Guide to Programs,* published annually). Ideally, a prospective student will visit the campus, consult with faculty and current and past students, and ask about the job placement success for graduates. It is possible, as Eric Chambers (1997) points out, to construct an applied master's program in a nonapplied department by the careful selection of a thesis topic and the arrangement of practicum and internship experiences.

Although a master's is a practical degree (see Quirk and Jenakovich 1997), some students may seek a Ph.D. in applied anthropology. Again, there are various programs, either in this department or within more academically oriented programs that contain plenty of room for applied topics. Doctoral degrees are valuable in international or public health work; they may be most effective for people wishing to set up their own consulting companies or to work in large institutions such as government departments. Similarly, large NGOs may value the credibility that Ph.D.'s can bring to applied social research. A person may have a personal preference for a Ph.D. because of a commitment to the subject and as a fulfillment of a goal.

Furthermore, there will be some additional opportunities for employment in academic departments to teach applied anthropology as well as adjunct or full-time opportunities in schools of business, urban planning, medicine, nursing, business, medicine, and education.

A job search comes after a graduate degree. Practitioner Theresa Trainor (1997) calls this a liminal phase between the status of graduate student and that of full-fledged practicing anthropologist. Accordingly, she found some interesting analogies to rituals of passage when she analyzed her own experiences leading to a job with the U.S. Environmental Protection Agency. One of the best sets of practical advice for the job quest can be found in a volume edited by Koons et al. (1989), *Stalking Employment in the Nation's Capital: A Guide for Anthropologists.* Although focusing on employment in Washington's governmental departments and agencies, advocacy and lobby groups, international, nongovernment, and private voluntary aid organizations, professional associations, and so forth, it contains a number of effective job hunting tips that can easily be generalized to fit other settings.

In the job search, it is important to recognize that few jobs will specifically call for a degree in anthropology but rather for generic social science, communication, and analytical skills, many of which are outlined in this book. Some jobs may call for specific research, administrative, program planning, and delivery skills. The aspiring practicing anthropologist has to apply his or her skills first in identifying possible jobs, researching them, and communicating particular skills and aptitudes to potential employers.

Some suggestions for an effective job search include:

- Develop a résumé that highlights skills, aptitudes, and experiences that are understandable to the nonanthropologist. For example, change some of the traditional phrasings, such as "holistic ethnographic analysis" to "knowledge of a wide range of qualitative applied research methods" and specify what they are (see Omohundra 1998). Emphasize research, writing, and other communication skills. Have both a short and longer version of the résumé. Tailor the résumé and application letter to match each job you apply for.
- Seek out a mentor, preferably one already in the practicing field, who can provide advice and perspective during the initial, and possibly prolonged, job search.
- Form extensive networks of people who know of your search for a job as well as your qualifications. Jobs come more often through networking and good timing than through direct applications. The deeper and wider your personal network, the more likely a job will eventually emerge to match your qualifications and expectations.
- Come to know the agencies and organizations in which you might like to work. Ask for interviews and show an interest in and knowledge of their activities. Consider that process as an ethnographic experience, one that will better prepare you to eventually do the job.
- Be prepared to take on short-term jobs at short notice. Sometimes organizations have brief contracts and the people designated for the jobs are not available, so replacements have to be quickly chosen. Taking such jobs enhances the résumé, and you become known as a willing and effective worker.
- Seek out voluntary activities with service agencies in your field. For instance, a number of our students working in the immigrant field volunteered their services for the

immigrant-serving agency in our city. One later became its executive director, and others have done short-term contracts in service provision or research.

The most useful of these recommendations is the suggestion that you use networks, both in your initial job search and in your later work. Networking is a way to continuously tap into new work opportunities. It is also an actual tool of practice because applied anthropologists' work is highly collaborative, depending on skills, referrals, and alliances with many people.

Summary

Employment surveys show that from 29 percent to 54 percent of graduating American Ph.D.'s in anthropology are working in nonacademic practicing settings. In addition, there are a thousand or so master's-degree and as many as eight thousand bachelor's-degree annual graduates from anthropology programs in the United States and Canada (American Anthropological Association 1997: 308–321). Most of them end up in some form of nonacademic practice. There are no indications that any trends toward application will abate or dramatically reverse themselves. The applied field will probably grow as universities reduce their faculty and restructure to provide distance learning.

Fortunately, there have been significant and positive transformations in training for nonacademic practice. Since the establishment of the first specialized program in the nonacademic practice at the University of South Florida in 1974, about thirty revamped practitioners' programs have been established. A growing body of literature supports the field of applied and practicing anthropology, perhaps even as a fifth subdiscipline. There are now thousands of highly competent graduates coming from the specialized programs, and people have discovered, through their own diligent efforts on the job, how to best improve the practice of anthropology. They represent the field through international aid agencies, schools of business, medicine, public administration, architecture, charitable organizations, state, federal, provincial, and municipal agencies, unions, policy research institutes, private consulting companies, and advocacy and consumer protection agencies. Many other venues have yet to be heard from, and more will undoubtedly open up in the future. We are benefiting greatly from the experiences of pioneering practitioners in these areas just as we are learning from university-based applied anthropology, which is becoming more sensitive to the direct needs of policy-framed analysis and recommendation.

This book has been written to summarize the skills, perspectives, and work of applied and practicing anthropologists. Space considerations have prevented writing in detail about some subfields of practice such as business anthropology (Baba 1986; Ferraro 1998; Sherry 1995), educational anthropology (Fetterman 1984, 1986), developmental anthropology (Green 1986), medical anthropology (McElroy and Townsend 1996), gerontology (Rodin and Iris 1998), agriculture (Bartlett 1980; Durrenburger and Thu 1996), cultural resource management (Treitler and Stoffle 1994; Stapp 1998), fisheries (Anderson 1978; Durrenberger 1996), housing (Esber Jr. 1987), tourism (Smith 1992), and many other domains of emerging practice. However, most of the principles, methods, and perspectives of this book apply to them, whether they are used in the United States and Canada or overseas.

Anthropology's most lasting contribution should be a result of the efforts of its thousands of practitioners working beyond academia. The subject of anthropology will thrive if its practitioners are responsive to their communities, are humanistically motivated, professionally focused, and use their skills in practical policy relevant ways. I hope that this book has shown that there are almost limitless opportunities to do so.

RECOMMENDED READINGS

Davis, Nancy Yaw, Roger P. McConochie, and David R. Stevenson (eds.)
1987   *Research and Consulting as a Business.* NAPA Bulletin No. 4. Washington, DC: National Association for the Practice of Anthropology.

Giovannini, Maureen J., and Lynne M. H. Rosansky
1990   *Anthropology and Management Consulting: Forging a New Alliance.* NAPA Bulletin No. 9. Washington, DC: National Association for the Practice of Anthropology.

Koon, Adam, Beatrice Hackett, and John P. Mason (eds.)
1989   *Stalking Employment in the Nation's Capital: A Guide for Anthropologists.* Washington, DC: The Washington Association of Professional Anthropologists.

National Association for the Practice of Anthropology
1993   *Anthropologists at Work: Careers Making a Difference.* Video. Washington, DC: NAPA.

Omohundra, John T.
1998   *Careers in Anthropology.* Mountain View, CA: Mayfield.

Quirk, Kathleen M., and Marsha Jenakovich (eds.)
1997   *Mastering Anthropology: Anthropologists Practicing with Masters' Degrees.* Special Issue of *Practicing Anthropology,* Vol. 19(2): 2–36.

van Willigen, John
1987   *Becoming a Practicing Anthropologist: A Guide to Careers and Training Programs in Applied Anthropology.* NAPA Bulletin No. 3. Washington, DC: The National Association of Professional Anthropologists.

BIBLIOGRAPHY

Acury, Thomas H., and Barbara Rose Johnston (eds.)
1995 *Anthropological Contributions to Environmental Education.* Special Issue of *Practicing Anthropology,* Vol. 17(4): 3–36.

Agar, Michael
1996 *The Professional Stranger.* Second Edition. New York: Academic Press.
1986 *Speaking of Ethnography.* Beverly Hills, CA: Sage.
1982 Toward an Ethnographic Language. *American Anthropologist,* Vol. 84: 779–795.
1973 *Ripping and Running.* New York: Academic Press.

Agar, Michael, and James MacDonald
1995 Focus Groups and Ethnography. *Human Organization,* Vol. 54(1): 78–87.

American Anthropological Association
1997 *Guide to Programs and Directory of Members.* Washington, DC: American Anthropological Association.

Anderson, Raoul
1978 The Need for Human Science Research in Atlantic Coast Fisheries. *Journal of the Fisheries Research Board of Canada,* Vol. 35: 1031–1049.

Andreason, Alan
1995 *Marketing Social Change: Changing Behavior to Promote Health, Social Development, and the Environment.* San Francisco: Jossey-Bass.

Angrosino, Michael V.
1976 The Evolution of the New Applied Anthropology. In *Do Applied Anthropologists Apply Anthropology?* Edited by Michael V. Angrosino. Pp. 1–10. Athens, GA: University of Georgia Press.

Asad, Talal (ed.)
1973 *Anthropology and the Colonial Encounter.* New York: Humanities Press.

Baba, Marietta L.
1994 The Fifth Subdiscipline: Anthropological Practice and the Future of Anthropology. *Human Organization,* Vol. 53(2): 174–186.
1986 *Business and Industrial Anthropology, An Overview.* NAPA Bulletin No. 2. Washington, DC: National Association for the Practice of Anthropology.

Barger, W. K., and Ernesto Reza
1989 *Policy and Community-Action Research.* In *Making Our Research Useful: Case Studies in the Utilization of Anthropological Knowledge.* Edited by

John van Willigen, Barbara Rylko-Bauer, and Ann McElroy. Pp. 257–283. Boulder, CO: Westview Press.

Barnett, Homer G.
1956 *Anthropology in Administration.* New York: Harper and Row.

Bartlett, Peggy F. (ed.)
1980 *Agricultural Decision Making: Anthropological Contributions to Rural Development.* New York: Academic Press.

Bee, Robert L.
1974 *Patterns and Processes: An Introduction to Anthropological Strategies for the Study of Sociocultural Change.* New York: The Free Press.

Beebe, James
1995 Basic Concepts and Techniques of Rapid Appraisal. *Human Organization,* Vol. 54: 42–51.

Bell, E.
1942 *Culture of a Contemporary Rural Community, Sublette, Kansas.* Washington, DC: U.S. Department of Agriculture, Bureau of Agricultural Economics Rural Studies No. 2.

Benedict, Ruth
1946 *The Chrysanthemum and the Sword, Patterns of Japanese Culture.* Boston, MA: Houghton Mifflin.

Bennett, John W., and Gustav Thaiss
1970 Survey Research in Anthropological Field Work. In *A Handbook of Method in Cultural Anthropology.* Edited by Raoul Naroll and Ronald Cohen. Pp. 316–338. New York: Columbia University Press.

Bentley, Margaret E., and Elizabeth Herman
1996 To Improve Household Management of Diarrhea. *Practicing Anthropology,* Vol. 18(3): 15–20.

Bernard, H. Russell
1995 *Research Methods in Anthropology: Qualitative and Quantitative Approaches.* Second Edition. Walnut Creek, CA: Altamira.
1988 *Research Methods in Cultural Anthropology.* Newbury Park, CA: Sage.
1974 Scientists and Policy Makers: An Ethnography of Communication. *Human Organization,* Vol. 33(3): 261–276.

Berreman, Gerald D.
1968 Is Anthropology Alive? Social Responsibility in Social Anthropology. *Current Anthropology,* Vol. 9: 391–397.

Bodley, John H.
1998   *Victims of Progress.* Fourth Edition. Mountain View, CA: Mayfield.
1995   *Anthropology and Contemporary Human Problems.* Third Edition. Mountain View, CA: Mayfield.

Bolton, Patricia A., Edward B. Liebow, and Jon L. Olson
1993   Community Context and Uncertainty Following a Damaging Earthquake: Low-Income Latinos in Los Angeles, California. *The Environmental Professional,* Vol. 15: 240–247.

Bourgois, Phillipe
1996   *In Search of Respect: Selling Crack in El Barrio.* New York: Cambridge University Press.

Bowles, Roy T.
1981   *Social Impact Assessment in Small Communities: An Integrated View of Selected Literature.* Scarborough, Ontario: Butterworth.

Bradshaw, Jonathan
1972   The Concept of Social Need. *New Society,* Vol. 30: 640–643.

Britan, Gerald
1981   *Bureaucracy and Innovation: An Ethnography of Policy Change.* Beverly Hills, CA: Sage.

Britan, G., and R. Cohen (eds.)
1980   *Hierarchy and Society: Anthropological Perspectives on Bureaucracy.* Philadelphia: ISHI Press.

Brown, Christopher
1997   Anthropology and Social Marketing. *Practicing Anthropology,* Vol. 19(4): 27–30.

Bryant, Carol A., and D. Bailey
1991   The Use of Focus Group Research in Program Development. In *Soundings: Rapid and Reliable Research Methods for Practicing Anthropologists.* NAPA Bulletin no. 10. Edited by J. van Willigen and T. Finan. Pp. 24–40. Washington, DC: National Association for the Practice of Anthropology.

Buchignani, Norman
1982   *Anthropological Approaches to the Study of Ethnicity.* Toronto: The Multicultural Historical Society of Ontario.

Camino, Linda A.
1997   What Can Anthropologists Offer Ethnographic Evaluation? In *Practicing Anthropology in a Postmodern World: Lessons and Insights from Federal Contract Research.* NAPA Bulletin no. 17. Edited by Michael C. Reed. Pp. 41–57. Washington: National Association for the Practice of Anthropology.

Carlson, Robert G., and Harvey A. Siegal
1991   The Crack Life: An Ethnographic Overview of Crack Use and Sexual Behavior among African-Americans in a Midwest Metropolitan City. *Journal of Psychoactive Drugs,* Vol. 23(1): 11–21.

Carlson, Robert G., Jichuan Wang, Harvey Siegal, Russell S. Falck, and Jie Guo
1994a   An Ethnographic Approach to Targeted Sampling: Problems and Solutions in AIDS Prevention Research among Injection Drug and Crack-Cocaine Users. *Human Organization,* Vol 53(3): 279–287.

Carlson, Robert G., Harvey A. Siegal, and Russell Falck
1994b   Ethnography, Epidemiology, and Public Policy: Needle-Use Practices and HIV-1 Risk Reduction among Injecting Drug Users in the Midwest. In *Global AIDS Policy.* Edited by Douglas A. Feldman. Pp. 185–215. Westport, CT: Bergin and Garvey.

Carlson, Robert G., Harvey A. Siegal, Jichuan Wang, and Russell S. Falck
1996   Attitudes toward Needle "Sharing" among Injection Drug Users: Combining Qualitative and Quantitative Research Methods. *Human Organization,* Vol. 55(3): 361–370.

Cassell, Joan
1980   Ethical Principles for Conducting Fieldwork. *American Anthropologist,* Vol. 82: 29–42.

Chambers, Eric Karl
1997   Masters of (Our) Education: Applied Anthropology in the Non-Applied Program. *Practicing Anthropology,* Vol. 19(2): 13–17.

Chambers, Erve
1987   Applied Anthropology in the Post-Vietnam Era: Anticipations and Ironies. *Annual Review of Anthropology,* 16: 309–337.
1985   *Applied Anthropology: A Practical Guide.* Englewood Cliffs, NJ: Prentice Hall.
1977a   Policy Research at the Local Level. *Human Organization,* Vol. 36: 418–421.
1977b   Working for the Man: The Anthropologist in Policy Relevant Research. *Human Organization,* Vol. 36(3): 258–267.

Chambers, Robert
1997   *Whose Reality Really Counts?: Putting the First Last.* London: Intermediate Technology Publications.

Chelimsky, Eleanor, and William R. Sadish (eds.)
1997   *Evaluation for the 21st Century, A Handbook.* Thousand Oaks, CA: Sage.

Clay, Jason W.
1994   Resource Wars: Nation and State Conflicts of the Twentieth Century. In *Who Pays the Price? The Sociocultural Context of Environmental Crisis.* Edited by Barbara Rose Johnston. Pp. 19–31. Washington, DC: Island Press.

Clemmer, Richard O.
1974 Truth, Duty, and the Revitalization of Anthropologists: A New Perspective on Cultural Change and Resistance. In *Reinventing Anthropology*. Edited by Dell Hymes. Pp. 213–225. New York: Vintage Books.
1969 The Fed-up Hopi: Resistance of the American Indian and the Silence of the Good Anthropologists. *Journal of the Steward Anthropological Society,* Vol. 1(1): 18–41.

Clifton, James A. (ed.)
1970 *Readings in the Uses of the Sciences of Man.* New York: Houghton Mifflin.

Cochrane, Glynne
1980 Policy Studies and Anthropology. *Current Anthropology,* Vol. 21(4): 445–459.

Conway, Gordon R., and Edward B. Barbier
1990 *After the Green Revolution: Sustainable Agriculture for Development.* London: Earthscan Publications.

Davis, Anthony
1989 Between a Rock and a Hard Place: Applied Social Science Policy in the Atlantic Canadian Fisheries. *Newsletter, Society of Applied Anthropology in Canada,* Vol. 8(1): 3–7.

Davis, Nancy Yaw, Roger P. McConochie, and David R. Stevenson (eds.)
1987 *Research and Consulting as a Business.* NAPA Bulletin no. 4. Washington: National Association for the Practice of Anthropology.

Dawson, Susan E.
1992 Navajo Uranium Workers and the Effects of Occupational Illnesses: A Case Study. *Human Organization,* Vol. 51(4): 389–396.

Delbecq, Andre L., Andrew H. van den Ven, and David H. Gustafson
1975 *Group Techniques for Program Planning.* Glenview, IL.: Scott, Foresman.

Derman, William, and Scott Whiteford (eds.)
1985 *Social Impact Analysis and Development Planning in the Third World.* Boulder, CO: Westview.

Dilman, D. A.
1978 *Mail and Telephone Surveys: The Total Design Method.* New York: Wiley.

Dixon, Mim
1978 *What Happened to Fairbanks? The Effects of the Trans-Alaska Oil Pipeline on the Community of Fairbanks, Alaska.* Boulder, CO: Westview.

Donahue, John M., and Barbara Rose Johnston (eds.)
1998 *Water, Culture and Power: Local Struggles in a Global Context.* Washington, DC: Island Press.

Downing, Theodore E., and Gilbert Kushner (eds.)
1988 *Human Rights and Anthropology.* Cultural Survival Report 24. Cambridge, MA: Cultural Survival Inc.

Durrenburger, E. Paul
1996 *Gulf Coast Soundings: People and Policy in the Mississippi Shrimp Industry.* Lawrence, KA: University of Kansas Press.

Durrenburger, E. Paul, and Kendall M. Thu
1996 The Expansion of Large Scale Hog Farming in Iowa: The Applicability of Goldschmidt's Findings Fifty Years Later. *Human Organization,* Vol. 55: 409–416.

Eddy, Elizabeth, and William L. Partridge (eds.)
1986 *Applied Anthropology in America.* Second Edition. New York: Columbia University Press.

Edgerton, R., and L. L. Langness
1974 *Methods and Styles in the Study of Culture.* San Francisco: Chandlar and Sharp.

Erasmus, Charles J.
1961 *Man Takes Control: Cultural Development and American Aid.* Indianapolis: Bobbs-Merrill.

Erickson, Paul A.
1994 The Social Environment. In *A Practical Guide to Environmental Impact.* Pp. 147–201. San Diego: Academic Press.

Ervin, Alexander M.
1997a Anthropological Practice in Anglophone Canada: Multiculturalism, Indigenous Rights and Mainstream Policy Potentials. In *The Global Practice of Anthropology.* Edited by Marietta Baba and Carole E. Hill, Pp. 47–81. Williamsburg, VA: College of William and Mary.
1997b Trying the Impossible: Relatively Rapid Methods in a City-Wide Needs Assessment. *Human Organization,* Vol. 56(4): 379–388.
1996a Collaborative and Participatory Research in Urban Social Planning and Restructuring: Anthropological Experiences from a Medium-Sized Canadian City. *Human Organization,* Vol. 55(3): 324–334.
1996b Social Planning Councils, Social Indicators, and Child Well-Being. *Practicing Anthropology,* Vol. 18(4): 21–25.
1994a *Immigrant Integration and Adaptation Project, Phase VI: Final Analysis and Recommendations.* Presented to the Saskatchewan Association of Immigrant Settlement and Integration Agencies: Saskatoon: Department of Anthropology and Archaeology and Prairie Region Health Promotion Research Centre.
1994b Service Providers' Perceptions of Immigrant Well-Being and Implications for Heath Promotion and

Delivery. In *Racial Minorities: Medicine and Health.* Edited by B. Singh Bolaria and Rosemary Bolaria. Pp. 225–247. Halifax, NS: Fernwood Publishing.

1991 Some Reflections on Anthropological Advocacy. *Proactive,* Vol. 9(2): 24–28.

1985 Culture and Agriculture in the North American Context. *Culture,* Vol. 5(2): 35–51.

1969 Conflicting Styles of Life in Northern Canadian Town. *Arctic,* Vol. 22: 90–106.

1968 *New Northern Townsmen in Inuvik.* Mackenzie Delta Research Project, No. 5. Ottawa: Department of Indian Affairs and Northern Development.

Ervin, Alexander M., Antonet T. Kaye, Giselle Marcotte, and Randy D. Belon

1991a *Community Needs, Saskatoon—the 1990s: The Saskatoon Needs Assessment Project.* Saskatoon: The United Way of Saskatoon and the University of Saskatchewan.

1991b *Community Needs, Saskatoon—The 1990s: The Saskatoon Needs Assessment Project. Summary of Findings.* Saskatoon: The United Way and the University of Saskatchewan.

Esber Jr., George S.

1987 *Designing Apache Homes with Apaches.* In *Anthropological Praxis: Translating Knowledge into Action.* Edited by Robert M. Wulff and Shirley J. Fiske. Pp. 187–197. Boulder, CO: Westview.

Evans-Pritchard, E. E.

1940 *The Nuer: A Description of the Modes of Livelihood and Political Institutions of Nilotic People.* Oxford: Oxford University Press.

Feldman, Douglas A. (Ed.)

1994 *Global AIDS Policy.* Westport, CT: Bergin and Garvey.

Ferraro, Gary P.

1998 *The Cultural Dimension of International Business.* Third Edition. Upper Saddle River, NJ: Prentice Hall.

Fetterman, David M.

1989 *Ethnography Step by Step.* Newbury Park, CA: Sage.

Fetterman, David M. (ed.)

1984 *Ethnography in Educational Evaluation.* Beverly Hills, CA: Sage.

1986 *Educational Evaluation.* Beverly Hills, CA: Sage.

Fielding, Nigel G., and Jane L. Fielding

1986 *Linking Data.* Qualitative Research Methods Series, No. 4. Beverly Hills, CA: Sage.

Fink, Arlene, and Jacqueline Kosecoff

1978 *An Evaluation Primer.* Beverly Hills, CA: Sage.

Finsterbusch, Kurt, L. G. Llewellen, and C. P. Wolf (eds.)

1983 *Social Impact Assessment Methods.* Beverly Hills, CA: Sage.

Firth, Raymond

1981 Engagement and Detachment: Reflections on Applying Social Anthropology to Social Affairs. *Human Organization,* Vol. 40(3): 193–202.

1936 *We, the Tikopia: A Sociological Study of Kinship in Primitive Polynesia.* London: Allan and Unwin.

Fiske, Shirley J., and Erve Chambers

1997 Status and Trends: Practice and Anthropology in the United States. In *The Global Practice of Anthropology.* Edited by Marietta Baba and Carole E. Hill. Pp. 283–311, Williamsburg, VA: College of William and Mary.

1995 The Inventions of Practice. *Human Organization,* Vol. 55(1): 1–12.

Fischer, J. L.

1979 Government Anthropologists in the Trust Territory of Micronesia. In *The Uses of Anthropology.* Edited by Walter Goldschmidt. Pp. 238–253. Washington: American Anthropological Association.

Fitchen, Janet

1988 Anthropology and Ground Water Problems in the U.S.A. *Practicing Anthropology,* Vol. 10(3–4): 5, 18, 19, 20.

Flora, Cornelia Butler, Fernando Larrea, Charles Ehrhart, Marta Ordóñez, Sara Báez, Fernando Guerrero, Sandra Chancay, and Jan L. Flora

1997 Negotiating Participatory Action Research in an Ecuadorian Sustainable Agriculture and Natural Resource Management Program. *Practicing Anthropology,* Vol. 19(3): 20–26.

Fluehr-Lobban, Carolyn

1996 Reply to Wax and Herrera. *Human Organization,* Vol. 55: 240–241.

1994 Informed Consent in Anthropological Research: We Are not Exempt. *Human Organization,* Vol. 53: 1–11.

Fluehr-Lobban, Carolyn (ed.)

1991 *Ethics and the Profession of Anthropology: Dialogue for a New Era.* Philadelphia: University of Pennsylvania Press.

Foster, George M.

1969 *Applied Anthropology.* Boston, MA: Little, Brown.

1962 *Traditional Cultures and the Impact of Cultural Change.* New York: Harper and Row.

Foster, George M., and Barbara Gallatin Anderson

1978 *Medical Anthropology.* New York: Wiley.

Fowler Jr., Floyd J.

1997 Design and Evaluation of Survey Questions. In *Handbook of Applied Social Research Methods.*

Edited by Leonard Bickman and Debra J. Rog. Pp. 343–375. Thousand Oaks, CA: Sage.

Frankel, Barbara, and M. G. Trend
1991   Principles, Pressures, and Paychecks: The Anthropologist as Employee. In *Ethics and the Profession of Anthropology: Dialogue for a New Era*. Edited by Carolyn Fluehr-Lobban. Pp. 175–198. Philadelphia: University of Pennsylvania Press.

Freeman, Milton (ed.)
1976   *Inuit Land Use and Occupancy Project: A Report*. 3 Volumes. Ottawa: Department of Supply and Services.

Freire, Paulo
1970   *Pedagogy of the Oppressed*. New York: Seabury Press.
1981   *Education for Critical Consciousness*. New York: Continuum.

Gardner, Burleigh B.
1945   *Human Relations in Industry*. Chicago: Richard D. Irwin

Gatewood, John B., and Bonnie J. McCay
1990   Comparison of Job Satisfactions in Six New Jersey Fisheries. *Human Organization*, Vol. 49(1): 14–26.

Gearing, Fred
1960   The Strategy of the Fox Project. In *Documentary History of the Fox Project: 1949–1959*. Edited by Fred Gearing, R. McC. Netting, and L. R. Peattie. Pp. 294–300. Chicago: Department of Anthropology, University of Chicago.

Geilhufe, Nancy L.
1979   Anthropology and Policy Analysis. *Current Anthropology*, Vol. 20(3): 577–579.

Gilad, Lisa
1990   *The Northern Route: An Ethnography of Refugee Experiences*. Institute of Social and Economic Research. Social and Economic Studies No. 39. St. John's: Memorial University of Newfoundland.

Gilbert, M. Jean, Nathaniel Tashima, and Claudia Fishman
1991   Ethics and Practicing Anthropologists' Dialogue with the Larger World: Considerations in the Formulation of Ethical Guidelines for Practicing Anthropologists. In *Ethics and the Profession of Anthropology: Dialogue for a New Era*. Edited by Carolyn Fluehr-Lobban. Pp. 198–211. Philadelphia: University of Pennsylvania Press.

Giovannini, Maureen J., and Lynne M. H. Rosansky (eds.)
1990   *Anthropology and Management Consulting: Forging a New Alliance*. NAPA Bulletin No. 9. Washington: National Association for the Practice of Anthropology.

Gittlesohn, Joel, and Margaret Bentley
1996   Development and Use of the Women's Health Protocol. *Practicing Anthropology*, Vol. 18(3): 7–10.

Gjessing, Gutorm
1968   The Social Responsibility of the Social Scientist. *Current Anthropology*, Vol. 9: 397–403.

Glasser, Irene, and Livingston D. Sutro (eds.)
1992   *Addressing Issues in Criminal Justice*. Special Issue of *Practicing Anthropology*, Vol. 14(3): 3–36.

Gmelch, George
1983   Who Returns and Why: Return Migration Behavior in Two North Atlantic Societies. *Human Organization*, Vol. 42(1): 46–55.

Goldschmidt, Walter
1947   *As You Sow*. Glencoe, IL: The Free Press.

Goldschmidt, Walter (ed.)
1979   *The Uses of Anthropology*. Washington, DC: American Anthropological Association.
1986   *Anthropology and Public Policy: A Dialogue*. Washington, DC: American Anthropological Association.

Goodenough, Ward H.
1963   *Cooperation in Change: An Anthropological Approach to Community Development*. New York: Russell Sage Foundation.

Gorman, E. Michael, Ben David Barr, Anthony Hansen, Bruce Robertson, and Caleb Green
1997   Speed, Sex, Gay Men and HIV: Ecological and Community Perspectives. *Medical Anthropology Quarterly*, Vol. 11(4): 505–516.

Gough, Kathleen
1968   New Proposals for Anthropologists. *Current Anthropology*, Vol. 9: 403–407.

Green, Edward C. (ed.)
1986   *Practicing Development Anthropology*. Boulder, CO: Westview.

Greenberg, James B., and Thomas K. Park
1994   Political Ecology. *Journal of Political Ecology*, Vol. 1(1): 1–13.

Grenier, Louise
1998   *Working with Indigenous Knowledge*. Ottawa: International Development Research Center.

Guyette, Susan
1996   *Planning for Balanced Development: A Guide for Native American and Rural Communities*. Santa Fe: Clearlight Publications.

Hall, Edward T.
1959   *The Silent Language*. Greenwich, CT: Premier Books.

Hansen, Art, and Anthony Oliver-Smith (eds.)

1982 *Involuntary Migration and Resettlement: The Problems and Responses of Dislocated Peoples.* Boulder, CO: Westview.

Harries-Jones, Peter (ed.)

1991 *Making Knowledge Count: Advocacy and Social Science.* Montreal: McGill-Queens University Press.

Harris, Kari Jo, Norge Jerome, and Stephen B. Fawcett

1997 Rapid Assessment Procedures: A Review and Critique. *Human Organization,* Vol. 56: 375–379.

Harris, Marvin

1968 *The Rise of Anthropological Theory.* New York: Crowell.

Hastrup, Kirsten, and Peter Elass

1990 Anthropological Advocacy: A Contradiction in Terms. *Current Anthropology,* Vol. 31(3): 301–311.

Hawthorn, Harry (ed.)

1955 *The Doukabhors of British Columbia.* Vancouver: The University of British Columbia and Dent.

Hawthorn, Harry, Cyril S. Belshaw, and S. M. Jamieson

1958 *The Indians of British Columbia.* Toronto and Vancouver: The University of British Columbia and University of Toronto Press.

Hawthorn, H., M.-A. Tremblay, A. C. Cairn, F. G. Vallee, S. M. Jamieson, J. Ryan, and K. Lysyk

1967 *A Survey of the Contemporary Indians of Canada: Economic, Political and Educational Needs and Policies, Parts I and II.* Ottawa: Queens Printer.

Hedley, Max

1976 Independent Commodity Production and the Dynamics of Tradition. The *Canadian Review of Sociology and Anthropology,* Vol. 13: 413–422.

Helitzer-Allen, Deborah, Hubert Allen, Mary Lyn Field, and Gina Dallabetta

1996 Targeted Intervention Research on Sexually Transmitted Illnesses. *Practicing Anthropology,* Vol. 18(3): 20–24.

Henderson, Neil J.

1997 Dementia in Cultural Context: Development and Decline of a Caregiver Support Group in a Latin Population. In *The Cultural Context of Aging: Worldwide Perspectives.* Second Edition. Edited by Jay Sokolovsky. Pp. 424–443. Westport, CT: Bergin and Garvey.

Henderson, Neil J., Marcella Gutierrez-Mayka, Juanita Garcia, and Sara Boyd

1993 A Model for Alzheimer's Disease Support Group Development in African-American and Hispanic Populations. *The Gerontologist,* Vol. 33(3): 409–415.

Henry, Gary T.

1997a Graphing Data. In *Handbook of Applied Social Research Methods.* Leonard Bickman and Debra J. Rog, eds. Pp. 527–557. Thousand Oaks, CA: Sage.

1997b Practical Sampling. In *Handbook of Applied Social Research Methods.* Leonard Bickman and Debra J. Rog, eds. Pp. 101–127. Thousand Oaks, CA: Sage.

Henry, Jules

1965 *Culture Against Man.* New York: Vintage.

Herrera, C. D.

1996 Informed Consent and Ethical Exemptions. *Human Organization,* Vol. 55: 235–238.

Hess Jr., G. Alfred

1992 Popular Coverage of Policy Relevant Research. *Practicing Anthropology,* Vol. 14(4): 27–32.

Higgins, Patricia J., and J. Anthony Parades (eds.)

1999 *Classics of Practicing Anthropology: 1978–1998.* Oklahoma City: Society for Applied Anthropology.

Hildebrand, Peter

1982 Summary of the Sondeo Methodology Used by ICTA. In *Farming Systems Research and Development: Guidelines for Developing Countries.* Edited by W. W. Shaner, P. F. Philip, and W. R. Schmehl. Pp. 289–293. Boulder, CO: Westview Press.

Hill, Carole E., and Marietta Baba

1997 The International Practice of Anthropology: An Overview. In *The Global Practice of Anthropology.* Edited by Marietta Baba and Carole E. Hill. Pp. 1–25. Williamsburg, VA: College of William and Mary.

Hinshaw, Robert E.

1980 Anthropology, Administration, and Public Policy. *Annual Review of Anthropology,* Vol. 9: 497–522.

Hinsley Jr., Curtis M.

1979 Anthropology as Science and Politics: The Dilemmas of the Bureau of American Ethnology, 1879 to 1904. In *The Uses of Anthropology.* Edited by Walter Goldschmidt. Pp. 15–33. Washington: American Anthropological Association.

Holmberg, Allan R.

1958 The Research and Development Approach to the Study of Change. *Human Organization,* Vol. 17: 12–16.

Hopkins, Kenneth D., B. R. Hopkins, Gene V. Glass

1996 *Basic Statistics for the Behavioral Sciences.* Third Edition. Boston: Allyn and Bacon.

Hughes, Charles C., M.-A. Tremblay, R. N. Rappaport, and A. H. Leighton

1960 *The People of Cove and Woodlot.* New York: Basic Books.

Hyland, Stanley, and Sean Kirkpatrick
1989 *Guide to Training Programs in the Application of Anthropology.* Third Edition. Memphis, TN: Society for Applied Anthropology.

Hymes, Dell (ed.)
1974 *Reinventing Anthropology.* New York: Vintage Books.

Jacobs, Sue-Ellen
1977 *Social Impact Assessment: Experiences in Evaluation Research.* Mississippi State University Occasional Papers in Anthropology.

Jacobs, Sue-Ellen, and Joan Cassell (eds.)
1987 *Handbook of Ethical Issues in Anthropology.* Washington, DC: American Anthropological Association.

Joans, Barbara
1984 Problems in Pocatello: A Study in Linguistic Misunderstanding. *Practicing Anthropology,* Vol. 6(3–4): 6, 8.

Johnston, Barbara Rose
1994 Introduction, Concluding Remarks. In *Who Pays the Price? The Sociocultural Context of Environmental Crisis.* Edited by Barbara Rose Johnston. Pp. 1–3, 233–237. Washington, DC: Island Press.

Johnston, Barbara Rose (ed.)
1994 *Who Pays the Price? The Sociocultural Context of Environmental Crisis.* Washington, DC: Island Press.
1997 *Life and Death Matters: Human Rights and the Environment at the End of the Millennium.* Walnut Creek, CA: Altamira.

Johnston, Barbara Rose, and Susan Dawson
1994 Resource Use and Abuse on Native American Land: Uranium Mining in the American Southwest. In *Who Pays the Price? The Sociocultural Context of Environmental Crisis.* Edited by Barbara Rose Johnston. Pp. 142–155. Washington, DC: Island Press.

Jones, Charles O.
1977 *An Introduction to the Study of Public Policy.* Second Edition. North Scituate, MA: Duxbury Press.

Jordan, Ann (ed.)
1994 *Practicing Anthropology in Corporate America: Consulting in Organizational Culture.* NAPA Bulletin No. 14. Washington, DC: National Association for the Practice of Anthropology.

Jordan, Ann, Lorna McDougal, Karen Curtis, Linda Lenz, Joanna Brown, and Valerie Denney
1992 Commentary: Making Use of the Media. *Practicing Anthropology,* Vol. 14(4): 2, 3–38.

Jorgenson, Joseph G., Richard McCleary, and Steven McNabb
1985 Social Indicators in Native Village Alaska. *Human Organization,* Vol. 44: 2–18.

Kimball, Solon T.
1979 Land Use Management: The Navajo Reservation. In *The Uses of Anthropology.* Edited by Walter Goldschmidt. Pp. 61–79. Washington: American Anthropological Association.

Kollmorgen, W. M.
1942 *Culture of a Contemporary Rural Community, The Old Order Amish of Lancaster, Pennsylvania.* Washington: U.S. Department of Agriculture, Bureau of Agricultural Economics, Rural Studies No. 4.

Koons, Adam, Beatrice Hackett, and John P. Mason (eds.)
1989 *Stalking Employment in the Nation's Capital: A Guide for Anthropologists.* Washington: The Washington Association of Professional Anthropologists.

Kormondy, Edward J., and Daniel E. Brown
1998 *Fundamentals of Human Ecology.* Upper Saddle River, NJ: Prentice Hall.

Kreuger, R. A.
1988 *Focus Groups: A Practical Guide for Applied Research.* Newbury Park, CA: Sage.

Kushner, Gilbert
1994 Training Programs for the Practice of Applied Anthropology. *Human Organization,* Vol. 53: 186–192.

Kushner, Gilbert, and Alvin Wolfe (eds.)
1993 *Internship and Practice in Applied Anthropology.* Special Issue of *Practicing Anthropology,* Vol. 15(1): 3–33.

Lane, Theodore
1987 *Developing America's Northern Frontier.* Lanham, MD: University Press of America.

Leighton, Alexander H.
1959 *My Name Is Legion: Foundations for a Theory of Man in Relation to Culture.* New York: Basic Books.
1945 *The Governing of Men: General Principles and Recommendations Based on Experience at a Japanese Relocation Camp.* Princeton, NJ: Princeton University Press.

Levis-Pilz, Gladys
1997 "If a Dog Has Teeth, It Bites": The Impact of Multiple Stakeholder Perspectives in Contract Research. In *Practicing Anthropology in a Postmodern World: Lessons and Insights from Federal Contract Research.* NAPA Bulletin no. 17. Edited by Michael C. Reed. Pp. 58–69. Washington: National Association for the Practice of Anthropology.

Liebow, Edward B.
1988 Permanent Storage for Nuclear Power Wastes: Comparing Risk Judgements and Their Social Effects. *Practicing Anthropology,* Vol. 10(3–4): 10–12.

Liebow, Edward B., and Amy K. Wolfe (eds.)
1993 Communities at Risk: Communication and Choice of Environmental Hazards. Special Issue of *The Environmental Professional,* Vol. 15(3): 237–316.

Liebow, Elliot
1967 *Tally's Corner: A Study of Streetcorner Men.* Boston: Little, Brown.

Light, Linda, and N. Kleiber
1981 Interactive Research in a Feminist Setting: The Vancouver Women's Health Collective. In *Anthropologists at Home in North America.* Edited by D. Messerschmidt. Pp. 159–168. Cambridge: Cambridge University Press.

Long, A., S. Scrimshaw, and E. Hurtado
1988 *Epilepsy Rapid Assessment Procedures (ERAP): Rapid Assessment Procedures for the Evaluation of Epilepsy Specific Beliefs, Attitudes, and Behaviors.* Landover, MD: Epilepsy Foundation of America.

Lowie, Robert H.
1935 *The Crow Indians.* New York: Farrar and Rinehart.

Lurie, Nancy O.
1955 Anthropology and Indian Land Claims Litigation: Problems, Opportunities, and Recommendations. *Ethnohistory,* Vol. 2: 357–375.

McCracken, Grant
1988 Promoting Anthropology: Idle Thoughts from a Talking Head. *Culture,* Vol. 8(2): 75–81.

McElroy, Ann, and Patricia K. Townsend
1996 *Medical Anthropology: An Ecological Perspective.* Third Edition. Boulder, CO: Westview.

McGuire, Peggy Martin
1996 Doing Treaty Land Entitlement Research in Saskatchewan. *Practicing Anthropology,* Vol. 18(4): 29–33.

McKillip, Jack
1998 Needs Analysis: Forces and Techniques. *In Handbook of Applied Research Methods.* Edited by Leonard Bickman and Debra J. Rog. Pp. 261–285. Thousand Oaks, CA: Sage.

1987 *Needs Analysis: Tools for the Human Services and Education.* Newbury Park, CA: Sage.

MacLeish, K., and K. Young
1942 *Culture of a Contemporary Rural Community, Landoff, New Hampshire.* Washington: U.S. Department of Agriculture, Bureau of Agricultural Economics, Rural Studies No. 3.

McNickle, D'Arcy
1979 Anthropology and the Indian Reorganization Act. In *The Uses of Anthropology.* Edited by Walter Goldschmidt. Pp. 51–61. Washington: American Anthropological Association.

Maday, Bela C. (ed.)
1975 *Anthropology and Society.* Washington, DC: The Anthropological Society of Washington.

Magistro, John
1996 An Emerging Role for Applied Anthropology: Conflict Management and Dispute Resolution. *Practicing Anthropology,* Vol. 19(1): 5–10.

Maguire, Patricia
1987 *Doing Participatory Research: A Feminist Approach.* Amherst, MA: The Center for International Education: University of Massachusetts.

Mair, Lucy P.
1957 *Studies in Applied Anthropology.* London School of Economics, Monographs on Social Anthropology, No. 16. London: University of London, Athlone.

Malinowski, Bronislaw
1929 Practical Anthropology. *Africa,* Vol. 2: 23–39.

1922 *Argonauts of the Western Pacific.* New York: Dutton.

Manderson, Lenore (ed.)
1996 Handbook and Manuals in Applied Research. Special Issue, *Practicing Anthropology,* Vol. 18(3): 3–40.

Manderson, Lenore, Irene Agyepong, Bertha Aryee, and Helen Dzikuna.
1996 Anthropological Methods for Malarial Interventions. *Practicing Anthropology,* Vol. 18(3): 32–37.

Mathiesen, Per
1990 Comments. On Hastrup, Kirsten and Peter Elass' Anthropological Advocacy: A Contradiction in Terms. *Current Anthropology,* Vol. 31(3): 308, 309.

Mead, Margaret
1979 Anthropological Contributions to National Policies during and Immediately after World War II. In *The Uses of Anthropology.* Edited by Walter Goldschmidt. Pp. 145–158. Washington: American Anthropological Association.

1956 *New Lives for Old.* New York: Mentor.

1955 *Cultural Patterns and Technological Change.* New York: Mentor.

1944 The Yank in Britain. Current Affairs. (Army Bureau of Current Affairs Pamphlet Series No. 64). March 11, 1944.

1932 *The Changing Life of an Indian Tribe.* New York: Columbia University Press.

Mead, Margaret, and Rhoda Métraux (eds.)
1953   *The Study of Culture at a Distance.* Chicago: University of Chicago Press.

Merton, Robert K., Marjorie Fiske, and Patricia L. Kendall
1990   *The Focused Interview: A Manual of Problems and Procedures.* Second Edition. New York: Free Press.

Miner, Horace
1949   *Culture and Agriculture: Study of a Corn Belt County.* Ann Arbor: Occasional Contributions from the Museum of Anthropology of the University of Michigan.

Moe, E. O., and C. G. Taylor
1942   *Culture of a Contemporary Rural Community, Irwin, Iowa.* Washington: U.S. Department of Agriculture, Bureau of Agricultural Economics, Rural Studies No. 5.

Mooney, James
1896   *The Ghost Dance Religion and the Sioux Outbreak of 1890.* Fourteenth Annual Report. Washington, DC: Bureau of American Ethnology.

Moran, Emilio F.
1982   *Human Adaptability: An Introduction to Ecological Anthropology.* Boulder, CO: Westview.

Moran, Emilio (ed.)
1990   *The Ecosystem Approach in Anthropology: From Concept to Practice.* Ann Arbor: University of Michigan Press.

Morgan, David L.
1988   *Focus Groups as Qualitative Research.* Newbury Park, CA: Sage.

Nader, Laura
1980   The Vertical Slice: Hierarchies and Children. In *Hierarchy and Society: Anthropological Perspectives on Bureaucracy.* Edited by M. Britan and R. Cohen. Pp. 31–45. Philadelphia: Institute for the Study of Human Issues.
1972   Up the Anthropologist—Perspectives Gained from Studying Up. In *Reinventing Anthropology.* Edited by Dell Hymes. Pp. 284–312. New York: Vintage Books.

Nash, Philleo
1989   Anthropologist in the White House. In *Applied Anthropologist and Public Servant: The Life and Work of Philleo Nash.* NAPA Bulletin no. 7. Edited by Ruth H. Landman and Katherine Spencer Halpern. Pp. 3–7. Washington: National Association for the Practice of Anthropology.

National Association for the Practice of Anthropology
1993   *Anthropologists at Work: Careers Making A Difference.* Video. Washington, DC: NAPA.
1988   *Ethical Guidelines for Practitioners.* Ms.

Neuber, Keith A.
1980   *Needs Assessment: A Model for Community Planning.* Beverly Hills, CA: Sage.

Nolan, Riall W.
1990   Culture Shock and Cross-Cultural Adaptation. Or I Was O.K. until I Got Here. *Practicing Anthropology,* Vol. 12(4): 2, 20.

Officer, James E.
1989   Philleo Nash: Anthropologist as Administrator. In *Applied Anthropologist and Public Servant: The Life and Work of Philleo Nash.* NAPA Bulletin no. 7. Edited by Ruth H. Landman and Katherine Spencer Halpern. Pp. 11–16. Washington: National Association for the Practice of Anthropology.

Olen, L., and C. Loomis
1941   *Culture of a Contemporary Rural Community, El Cerrito, New Mexico.* Washington: U.S. Department of Agriculture, Bureau of Agricultural Economics, Rural Studies No. 1.

Oliver-Smith, Anthony
1996   Anthropological Research on Hazards and Disasters. *Annual Review of Anthropology,* Vol. 25: 308–328.

Omohundra, John T.
1998   *Careers in Anthropology.* Mountain View, CA: Mayfield.

O'Neil, J., J. Kaufert, P. Kaufert, and W. Koolage
1993   Political Considerations in Health Related Participatory Research in Northern Canada. In *Anthropology, Public Policy, and Native Peoples in Canada.* Edited by N. Dyck and J. Waldram. Pp. 215–233. Montreal: McGill-Queens Press.

Oppenheim, A. N.
1992   *Questionnaire Design, Interviewing and Attitude Measurement.* London and New York: Pinter Publishers.

Organization for Economic Co-Operation and Development (OCED)
1976   *Measuring Social Well-Being: A Progress Report on the Development of Social Indicators.* Paris: OCED.

Paine, Robert (ed.)
1985   *Anthropology and Advocacy.* St. John's: Memorial University, Institute of Social and Economic Research.

Park, Peter, Mary Brydon-Miller, Budd Hall, and Ted Jackson (eds.)
1993   *Voices of Change: Participatory Research in the United States and Canada.* Toronto: Ontario Institute for Studies in Education Press.

Partridge, William L., and Elizabeth M. Eddy
1986   The Development of Applied Anthropology in America. In *Applied Anthropology in America.* Sec-

ond Edition. Edited by Elizabeth M. Eddy and William L. Partridge. Pp. 3–56. New York: Columbia University Press.

Patton, Michael Q.
1990   *Qualitative Evaluation and Research Methods.* Newbury Park, CA: Sage.
1982   *Practical Evaluation.* Beverly Hills, CA: Sage.
1980   *Qualitative Evaluation Techniques.* Beverly Hills, CA: Sage.

Peattie, Lisa R.
1960   The Failure of the Means-Ends Scheme. In *Documentary History of the Fox Project: 1949–1959.* Edited by Fred Gearing, R. McC. Netting, and L. R. Peattie. Pp. 300–304. Chicago: Department of Anthropology, University of Chicago.

Pelto, Pertti J., and Gertel H. Pelto
1978   *Anthropological Research: The Structure of Inquiry.* Second Edition. London: Cambridge University Press.

Pelto, Pertti J., and Jean J. Schensul
1986   Toward a Framework for Policy Research in Anthropology. In *Applied Anthropology in America.* Second Edition. Edited by Elizabeth Eddy and William L. Partridge. Pp. 505–528. New York: Columbia University Press.

Perez, Carlos
1997   *The Colors of Participation.* Special Issue, *Practicing Anthropology,* Vol. 19(3).

Peters, Thomas J., and Robert H. Waterman Jr.
1982   *In Search of Excellence: Lessons from America's Best Run Companies.* New York: Harper and Row.

Peterson Jr., John
1974   Anthropologist as Advocate. *Human Organization,* Vol. 33(3): 311–318.

Piddington, Ralph
1960   Action Anthropology. In *Documentary History of the Fox Project: 1949–1959.* Edited by Fred Gearing, R. McC. Netting, and L. R. Peattie. Pp. 199–213. Chicago: Department of Anthropology, University of Chicago.

Preister, Kevin
1987   Issue Centered Social Impact Assessment. In *Anthropological Praxis: Translating Knowledge into Action.* Edited by Robert M. Wulff and Shirley J. Fiske. Pp. 39–56. Boulder, CO: Westview Press.

Quirk, Kathleen M., and Marsha Jenakovich (eds.)
1997   *Mastering Anthropology: Anthropologists Practicing with Masters' Degrees.* Special Issue, *Practicing Anthropology,* Vol. 19(2): 2–36.

Rappaport, Roy
1968   *Pigs for the Ancestors.* New Haven, CT: Yale University Press.

Redfield, Robert, Ralph Linton, and Melvin J. Herskovits
1936   Memorandum for the Study of Acculturation. *American Anthropologist* Vol. 38: 149–152.

Reed, Michael C. (ed.)
1997   *Practicing Anthropology in a Postmodern World: Lessons and Insights from Federal Contract Research.* Washington: National Association for the Practice of Anthropology, Bulletin Number 17.

Reining, Conrad C.
1962   A Lost Period of Applied Anthropology. *American Anthropologist,* Vol. 64: 593–600.

Richardson, F. L. W.
1979   Social Interaction and Industrial Productivity. In *The Uses of Anthropology.* Edited by Walter Goldschmidt. Pp. 79–100. Washington: American Anthropological Association.
1955   Anthropology and Human Relations in Business and Industry. In *Yearbook of Anthropology.* Edited by William L. Thomas Jr. Pp. 397–419. New York: Wenner Gren Foundation for Anthropological Research.

Rodin, Miriam, and Madelyn Iris
1998   *Anthropology and Applied Gerontology.* Special Issue, *Practicing Anthropology,* Vol. 20(2): 2–26.

Roper, Roy
1983   Ethnography. In *Social Impact Assessment Methods.* Edited by Kurt Finsterbusch, Lynn G. Llewellyn, and C. P. Wolf. Pp. 95–111. Beverly Hills, CA: Sage.

Rossi, Robert J., and Kevin J. Gilmartin
1980   *The Handbook of Social Indicators: Sources, Characteristics and Analysis.* New York: Garland STPM Press.

Rouse, Michael J.
1993   Folk Technology in a High Tech. Industry: Cultural Objects in a British Columbia Coal Mine. *Proactive,* Vol. 12(2): 46–58.

Rutman, Leonard
1980   *Planning Useful Evaluations.* Beverly Hills, CA: Sage.

Ryan, Joan
1985   Decolonializing Anthropology. In *Anthropology and Advocacy.* Edited by Robert Paine. Pp. 208–215. St. John's: Memorial University, Institute of Social and Economic Research.

Ryan, Joan, and Michael Robinson
1990   Implementing Participatory Research in the Canadian North: A Case Study of the Gwich'in Language and Culture Project. *Culture,* 10: 57–73.
1996   Community Participatory Research: Two Views from Arctic Institute Practitioners. *Practicing Anthropology,* Vol. 18(4): 7–12.

Sachs, P. (ed.)
1989   *Anthropological Approaches to Organizational Culture.* Special issue, *Anthropology of Work Review.* Washington, DC: Society for the Anthropology of Work.

Salisbury, Richard F.
1986   *Homeland for the Cree.* Montreal: McGill-Queens University Press.

Sanday, Peggy Reeves (ed.)
1976   *Anthropology and the Public Interest: Fieldwork and Theory.* New York: Academic Press.

Scaglion, Richard
1987   Customary Law Development in Papua New Guinea. In *Anthropological Praxis: Translating Knowledge into Action.* Edited by Robert M. Wulff and Shirley J. Fiske. Pp. 98–109. Boulder, CO: Westview.

Schapera, I.
1947   *Migrant Labour in Tribal Life.* Oxford: Oxford University Press.

Schensul, Stephen L.
1974   Skills Needed in Action Research: Lessons from El Centro de La Causa. *Human Organization,* Vol. 33: 203–209.

Schensul, Stephen L., and Jean J. Schensul
1978   Advocacy and Applied Anthropology. In *Social Scientists as Advocates.* Edited by George H. Weber and George I. McCall. Beverly Hills, CA: Sage.

Schensul, Jean J., and Donald D. Stull
1987   Introduction. In Collaborative *Research and Social Change: Applied Anthropology in Action.* Edited by Donald D. Stull and Jean J. Schensul. Pp. 1–9. Boulder, CO: Westview.

Scheper-Hughes, Nancy
1992   *Death without Weeping: The Violence of Everyday Life in Brazil.* Berkeley: University of California Press.

Scheinfeld, Daniel R. (ed.)
1987   *Utilizing Applied Research.* Special Issue, *Practicing Anthropology,* Vol. 9(1): 4–14.

Schoolcraft, Henry R.
1852–   *Information Respecting the History, Condition and*
1857   *Prospects of the Indian Tribes of the United States.* Philadelphia: Lippincott.

Schwartzman, Helen B.
1993   *Ethnography in Organizations.* Newbury Park, CA: Sage.

Scotch, Norman A.
1960   A Preliminary Report on the Relations of Socio-Cultural Factors to Hypertension among the Zulu.

Annals of the New York Academy of Sciences, Vol. 84(17): 1000–1009.

Scrimshaw, Susan, and Elena Hurtado
1987   *Rapid Assessment Procedures for Nutrition and Primary Health Care: Anthropological Approaches to Improving Programme Effectiveness.* Los Angeles: U.C.L.A. Latin American Center Publications.

Shaner, W. W., P. F. Philip, and W. R. Schmehl (eds.)
1982   *Farming Systems Research and Development: Guidelines for Developing Countries.* Boulder, CO: Westview Press.

Sherry Jr., John F. (ed.)
1995   *Contemporary Marketing and Consumer Behavior: An Anthropological Sourcebook.* Thousand Oaks, CA: Sage Publications.

Shore, Chris, and Susan Wright
1997   Colonial Gaze to Critique of Policy: British Anthropology in Policy and Practice. In *The Global Practice of Anthropology.* Edited by Marietta Baba and Carole E. Hill. Pp. 139–155. Williamsburg, VA: College of William and Mary.

Singer, Merrill
1994   Community-Centered Praxis: Toward an Alternative Non-Dominative Applied Anthropology. *Human Organization,* Vol. 53(4): 336–345.

Singer, Merrill, Ray Irizarry, and Jean Schensul
1991   Needle Access as an AIDS Prevention Strategy for IV Drug Users: A Research Perspective. *Human Organization,* Vol. 50: 142–153.

Smith, Valene L. (ed.)
1992   *Anthropology and Tourism: A Career Passport.* Special Issue, *Practicing Anthropology,* Vol. 14(2): 3–36.

Social Science Research Council
1954   Acculturation: An Exploratory Formulation. *American Anthropologist,* Vol. 56: 973–1002.

Society for Applied Anthropology, Ethics Committee
1983   *Professional and Ethical Responsibilities,* Revised Ms. (Reprinted in each issue of *Human Organization*).

Society of Applied Anthropology in Canada, Ethics Committee
1983   *Ethical Guidelines.* Ms.

Spicer, Edward H.
1979   Anthropologists and the War Relocation Authority. In *The Uses of Anthropology.* Edited by Walter Goldschmidt. Pp. 217–238. Washington: American Anthropological Association.
1976   Beyond Analysis and Explanation?: Notes on the Life and Times of the Society for Applied Anthropology. *Human Organization,* Vol. 35(4): 335–344.

Spicer, Edward H. (ed.)

1961 *Perspectives in American Indian Culture Change.* Chicago: University of Chicago Press.

1952 *Human Problems in Technological Change: A Casebook.* New York: Sage.

Spradley, James P.

1980 *Participant Observation.* New York: Holt.

1979 *The Ethnographic Interview.* New York: Holt.

1970 *You Owe Yourself a Drunk: An Ethnography of Urban Nomads.* Boston: Little, Brown.

Stack, Carol

1974 *All Our Kin.* New York: Harper and Row.

Stapp, Darby (ed.)

1998 *Changing Paradigms in Cultural Resource Management.* Special Issue, *Practicing Anthropology,* Vol. 20(3): 2–33.

Steadham, Stephen

1980 Learning to Select a Needs Assessment Strategy. *Training and Development Journal.* Vol. 34(1): 56–62.

Steward, Julian

1969 The Limitations of Applied Anthropology. *Journal of the Steward Anthropological Society,* Vol. 1(1): 1–18.

1955 *Theory of Culture Change.* Urbana: University of Illinois Press.

Stewart, Omar

1983 Historical Notes about Applied Anthropology in the United States. *Human Organization,* Vol. 42(3): 189–195.

Stocking Jr., George W.

1979 Anthropology as Kuturkampf: Science and Politics in the Career of Franz Boas. In *The Uses of Anthropology.* Edited by Walter Goldschmidt. Pp. 33–51. Washington: American Anthropological Association.

Stull, Donald D., and Jean J. Schensul (eds.)

1987 *Collaborative Research and Social Change: Applied Anthropology in Action.* Boulder, CO: Westview.

Tandon, Rajesh

1988 Social Transformation and Participatory Research. *Convergence,* Vol. 21(2–3): 5–18.

Tandon, Rajesh, and Walter Fernandes

1984 *Participatory Evaluation: Theory and Practice.* New Delhi: Institute for Social Research.

Tax, Sol

1958 The Fox Project. *Human Organization,* Vol. 17: 17–19.

Tester, Frank J., and W. Mykes (eds.)

1981 *Social Impact Assessment: Theory, Method, and Practice.* Calgary, Alberta: Detselig Enterprises.

Thomas, David Hurst

1986 *Refiguring Anthropology: First Principles of Probability and Statistics.* Second Edition. Prospect Heights, IL: Waveland Press.

Topper, Martin D.

1995 Managerial Anthropology and Public Policy. *Practicing Anthropology,* Vol. 17(3): 26–28.

Trainor, Theresa

1997 Formulating a Practitioner Identity. *Practicing Anthropology,* Vol. 19(2): 7–10.

Treitler, Inga, and Richard Stoffle (eds.)

1994 *Federal Law, Native Americans, and Natural Resources.* Special Issue, *Practicing Anthropology,* Vol. 16(3): 3–34.

Tremblay, Marc-Adélard

1990 *Les Fondements historiques et theoriques de la pratique professionelle en anthropologie.* Quebec Cité: Laval Université, Laboratoire d'anthropologie.

Trotter, Robert T.

1988 *Anthropology for Tomorrow: Creating Practitioner-Oriented Applied Anthropology Programs.* Washington, DC: American Anthropological Association.

Valentine, Charles A.

1968 *Culture and Poverty: Critique and Counter-Proposals.* Chicago: University of Chicago Press.

Vallee, Frank G.

1962 *Kabloona and Eskimo in the Central Canadian Arctic.* NCRC-62–2. Ottawa: Department of Northern Affairs and Natural Resources.

van Dusen, Roxann A., and Robert Parke

1976 Social Indicators: A Focus for the Social Sciences. In *Anthropology and the Public Interest: Fieldwork and Theory.* Edited by Peggy R. Sanday. Pp. 333–345. London: Academic Press.

Van Esterik, Penny

1989 *Beyond the Breast-Bottle Controversy.* New Brunswick, NJ: Rutgers.

1985 Confronting Advocacy Confronting Anthropology. In *Anthropology and Advocacy.* Edited by Robert Paine. Pp. 59–78. St. John's: Institute of Social and Economic Research, Memorial University of Newfoundland.

van Stone, James W.

1963 *The Snowdrift Chipewyan.* NCRC-63–4. Ottawa: Department of Northern Affairs and Natural Resources.

van Willigen, John

1993 *Applied Anthropology: An Introduction.* Second Edition. Westport, CT: Bergin and Garvey.

1991 *Anthropology in Use: A Sourcebook on Anthropological Practice.* Boulder, CO: Westview.

1987 *Becoming a Practicing Anthropologist: A Guide to Careers and Training Programs in Applied Anthropology.* NAPA Bulletin No. 3. Washington: The National Association for the Practice of Anthropology.
1986 *Applied Anthropology: An Introduction.* Westport, CT: Bergin and Garvey.

van Willigen, John, and Timothy L. Finan, eds.
1991 *Soundings: Rapid and Reliable Research Methods for Practicing Anthropologists.* NAPA Bulletin 10. Washington: National Association for the Practice of Anthropology.

van Willigen, John, Barbara Rylko-Bauer, and Ann McElroy
1989 *Making Our Research Useful: Case Studies in the Utilization of Anthropological Knowledge.* Boulder, CO: Westview Press.

Voget, Frederick W.
1975 *A History of Ethnology.* New York: Holt.

Waldram, James B.
1993 Aboriginal Spirituality: Symbolic Healing in Canadian Prisons. *Culture, Medicine, and Psychiatry,* Vol 17: 345–362.
1996 *Cultural Orientation and Aboriginal Offenders. Final Report. Saskatoon:* Federal Correction Services, Canada, MS.

Waldram, James B., and Stephen Wong
1994 Group Therapy of Aboriginal Offenders in a Canadian Forensic Psychiatric Facility. *American Indian and Alaskan Native Mental Health Research,* Vol. 6(2): 34–56.

Wallace, Anthony F. C.
1956 Revitalization Movements. *American Anthropologist,* Vol. 58: 63–74.

Warner, W. Lloyd (ed.)
1941– *Yankee City Series.* New Haven: Yale University
1947 Press.

Warry, Wayne
1992 The Eleventh Thesis: Applied Anthropology as Praxis. *Human Organization,* Vol. 51(2):155–164.
1990 Doing unto Others: Applied Anthropology, Collaborative Research, and Native Self-Determination. *Culture,* Vol. 10: 61–73.

Wax, Murray L.
1995 Informed Consent in Applied Research: A Commentary. *Human Organization,* Vol. 54: 330–331.
1996 Reply to Herrera. *Human Organization,* Vol. 55: 238–240.

Weaver, Sally
1981 *Making Canadian Indian Policy: The Hidden Agenda.* Toronto: University of Toronto Press.

Weaver, Thomas
1985a Anthropology as a Policy Science: Part I, A Critique. *Human Organization,* Vol. 44(2): 97–106.
1985b Anthropology as a Policy Science: Part II, Development and Training. *Human Organization,* Vol. 44(3): 197–206.

Weaver, Thomas (ed.)
1973 *To See Ourselves: Anthropology and Modern Social Issues.* Glenview, IL: Scott, Foresman.

Weber, George H., and George J. McCall (eds.)
1978 *Social Scientists as Advocates.* Beverly Hills, CA: Sage.

Weiss, Carol H.
1972 *Evaluation Research: Methods of Assessing Program Effectiveness.* Englewood Cliffs, NJ: Prentice Hall.

Weatherford, J. McIver
1985 *Tribes on the Hill.* South Hadley, MA: Bergin and Garvey.

Wells, Miriam J.
1981 Success in Whose Terms? Evaluations of a Cooperative Farm. *Human Organization,* Vol. 40(3): 239–247.

Whiteford, Linda M.
1987 Staying out of the Bottom Drawer. *Practicing Anthropology,* Vol. 9(1): 9–12.

Whitehead, Tony L.
1997 Urban Low-Income African American Men, HIV/AIDS, and Gender Identity. *Medical Anthropology Quarterly,* Vol. 11(4): 411–448.

Whyte, William F.
1948 *Human Relations in the Restaurant Industry.* New York: McGraw-Hill.

Whyte, William F. (ed.)
1991 *Participatory Action Research.* Newbury Park, CA: Sage.

Wiedman, Dennis
1998 Effective Strategic Planning Roles for Anthropologists. *Practicing Anthropology,* Vol. 20(1): 36–40.
1992 Effects on Academic Culture of Shifts from Oral to Written Traditions: The Case of University Accreditation. *Human Organization,* Vol. 51(4): 398–407.

Wikan, Unni
1985 Living Conditions Among Cairo's Poor—A View from Below. *The Middle East Journal,* Vol. 39(1): 7–27.

Willis Jr., William S.
1974 Skeletons in the Anthropological Closet. In *Reinventing Anthropology.* Edited by Dell Hymes. Pp. 284–312. New York: Vintage Books.

Wilson, Geoffrey
1940 Anthropology as a Public Service. *Africa,* Vol. 13: 43–61.

Witkin, R. B.
1994 Needs Assessment since 1981: The State of the Practice. *Evaluation Practice,* Vol. 15: 17–27.

Wolcott, Harry F.
1995 *The Art of Fieldwork.* Walnut Creek, CA: Altamira.

Wolf, C. P.
1983 A Methodological Overview. In *Social Impact Assessment Methods.* Edited by Kurt Finsterbusch, Lynn G. Llewellyn, and C. P. Wolf. Pp. 15–35. Beverly Hills, CA: Sage.

Wolf, Eric
1982 *Europe and the People without History.* Berkeley: University of California Press.

Wolfe, Amy K. (ed.)
1988a Anthropology in Environmental Risk Studies. *Practicing Anthropology,* Vol. 10(3–4): 4–22.

Wolfe, Amy K.
1988b Environmental Risk and Anthropology. *Practicing Anthropology,* Vol. 10(3–4): 4.

Wolfe, Alvin W.
1977 The Supranational Organization of Production: An Evolutionary Perspective. *Current Anthropology,* Vol. 18(4): 615–636.

Wolfe, Alvin W., Erve Chambers, and J. Jerome Smith
1981 *Internship Training in Applied Anthropology: A Five Year Review.* Tampa: Human Resources Institute, University of South Florida.

Wood, Merry
1996 Facilitating Program Evaluation at Greater Vancouver Mental Health Service. *Practicing Anthropology,* Vol. 18(4): 16–21.

Wulff, Robert M., and Shirley J. Fiske (eds.)
1987a *Anthropological Praxis: Translating Knowledge into Action.* Boulder, CO: Westview Press.

Wulff, Robert M., and Shirley J. Fiske
1987b Introduction. In *Anthropological Praxis: Translating Knowledge into Action.* Edited by Robert M. Wulff and Shirley J. Fiske. Pp. 1–15. Boulder, CO: Westview.

Wynne, W.
1943 *Culture of a Contemporary Rural Community, Harmony, Georgia.* Washington: U.S. Department of Agriculture, Bureau of Agricultural Economics, Rural Studies No. 6.

Yans-McLaughlin, Virginia
1980 Science, Democracy, and Ethics. *In Malinowski, Rivers, Benedict, and Others: Essays on Culture and Personality.* Edited by George Stocking. Pp. 184–218. Madison: University of Wisconsin Press.

Young, John A.
1982 Productive Efficiency and the Adaptation of Small-Scale Farmers. *Human Organization,* Vol. 41(3): 208–216.

Young, Kue
1989 *Health Care and Cultural Change: The Indian Experience in the Central Subarctic.* Toronto: University of Toronto Press.

Zeisel, Hans
1968 *Saying It with Figures.* New York: Harper.

NAME INDEX

SUBJECT INDEX

propriety, 197
utility, 196
farming systems, 193
field manuals, 191
health care, 191
households, 191
improvisation, 197
meaning, 190
primary health care, 191
rationale, 188–190
sondeos, 194
utility, 196
Rapid Rural Assessment, 194
Refugees, 80–81
Reliability, 158
Report writing, 214–216
Risk assessment, 113–117
Royal Anthropological Society of Great Britain and
Ireland, 14

Sampling, 179–181
convenience, 180
judgment, 180
nonprobability, 180
probability, 179
stratified, 180
targeted, 182
Social indicators, 172, 175
Alaska Natives, 174, 175
critique, 172
growth of, 174
purposes, 174
Social Impact Assessment, 98–112
baseline, 105
challenges, 109
community variables, 105
controversies, 109
development, 98, 99

ecological perspective, 107
ethnography, 107–109
stages
alternative formulation, 104
assessment, 106
evaluation, 106
management, 107
mitigation, 106
monitoring, 107
problem identification, 103
profiling, 104, 105
projection, 106
scoping, 106
Society for Applied Anthropology, 18, 30, 118
Society of Applied Anthropology in
Canada, 30
Self help/advocacy, 199
Sondeos, 194
Stakeholders, 88, 89
Stirling County Study, 23
Structural-functionalism, 15
Systems evaluation (*see* Evaluation)

Tables, 181
Transects, 194
Triangulation, 171

Uranium mining, 120, 121

Vicos Project, 21
Visual impairment, 205–208
informational needs, 205–208

War Relocation Authority, 20
Wheeler-Howard Act, 16
World War II, 18–20

"Yankee" City, 18